What Color Is
Your Parachute?

Other Books by Richard N. Bolles

The What Color Is Your Parachute? Workbook

How to Find Your Mission in Life

The Three Boxes of Life,
*   and How to Get Out of Them*

Books by Richard Bolles with Co-authors

Job-Hunting on the Internet
*   (Mark E. Bolles as co-author)*

The Career Counselor's Handbook
*   (Howard Figler as co-author)*

Job-Hunting for the So-Called Handicapped
*   (Dale Brown as co-author)*

What Color Is Your Parachute? For Teens
*   (Carol Christen, with Jean M. Blomquist,*
*   as co-authors)*

What Color Is Your Parachute? For Retirement
*   (John E. Nelson as co-author)*

The
2008
What Color Is Your Parachute?

A Practical Manual for Job-Hunters and Career-Changers

by
Richard Nelson Bolles

TEN SPEED PRESS
Berkeley | Toronto

This is an annual. That is to say, it is revised each year, often substantially, with the new edition appearing in the early Fall. Counselors and others wishing to submit additions, corrections, or suggestions for the 2009 edition must *submit them prior to February 1, 2008, using the form provided in the back of this book, or by e-mail (RNB25@aol.com). Forms reaching us after that date will, unfortunately, have to wait for the 2010 edition.*

PUBLISHER'S NOTE

This publication is designed to provide accurate and authoritative information in regard to the subject matter covered. It is sold with the understanding that the publisher is not engaged in rendering professional career services. If expert assistance is required, the service of the appropriate professional should be sought.

The drawings on pages vi, vii, 254, 330, and 331 are by Steven M. Johnson, author of *What the World Needs Now.*

Copyright © 2008, 2007, 2006, 2005, 2004, 2003, 2002, 2001, 2000, 1999, 1998, 1997, 1996, 1995, 1994, 1993, 1992, 1991, 1990, 1989, 1988, 1987, 1986, 1985, 1984, 1983, 1982, 1981, 1980, 1979, 1978, 1977, 1976, 1975, 1972, 1970 by Richard Nelson Bolles.

Distributed in Australia by Simon and Schuster Australia, in Canada by Ten Speed Press Canada, in New Zealand by Southern Publishers Group, in South Africa by Real Books, and in the United Kingdom and Europe by Publishers Group UK.

All rights reserved. Without limiting the rights under copyright reserved above, no part of this publication may be reproduced, stored in or introduced into a retrieval system, or transmitted, in any form or by any means (electronic, mechanical, photocopying, recording, or otherwise), without the prior written permission of both the copyright owner and the publisher of this book, except for brief reviews.

Library of Congress Catalog Card Information on file with the publisher.
ISBN-13 : 978-1-58008-867-1 (paper)
ISBN-10 : 1-58008-867-8 (paper)
ISBN-13 : 978-1-58008-868-8 (cloth)
ISBN-10 : 1-58008-868-6 (cloth)

Published by Ten Speed Press
PO Box 7123, Berkeley, California 94707
www.tenspeed.com

Typesetting by Star Type, Berkeley
Cover design by Betsy Stromberg

Printed in Canada

First printing this edition, 2007
1 2 3 4 5 6 7 8 9 10 — 11 10 09 08 07

The wonderful actress
Anne Bancroft (1931–2005) was once
loosely quoted as saying
about her husband, Mel Brooks,
My heart flutters whenever I hear his key
Turning in the door, and I think to myself,
Oh goody, the party is about to begin.

That is exactly how I feel
about my wife,
Marci Garcia Mendoza Bolles,
God's angel from the Philippines,
whom I fell deeply in love with, and married
on August 22, 2004.

What a gift, such a marriage is!

"Run, Spot, run."

The 2008 Table of Contents

Your Next Step: vi
The Many Paths You Can Take (Map)

Preface   viii

Grammar and Language Note   xvi

Part I

The Things School Never Taught Us About the Job-Hunt

Introduction: The Three Essential Life Skills   3

1. The Five Best Ways to Hunt for a Job   7
    (and the Five Worst)

2. The Nature of the Job-Market   21
    There Are Always Many More Vacancies Out There
    Than You Think, and Here's Why

3. How to Deal with Handicaps   39
    Informational Interviewing: Enthusiasm or Passion
    A Word to the Shy: Daniel Porot's PIE System

4. How Much Help Is the Internet?   51
    The Good, the Bad, and the Ugly

5. Resumes & Contacts: How to Get in
    to See an Employer   59
    Alternatives to Resumes: Cover Letters, Portfolios
    Who or What Is a Contact?
    The Person Who Has the Power to Hire You

6. Interviews: The Employer's Fears   83
    Secrets for Conducting a Successful Interview
    The Only Five Questions That Matter

7. Salary Negotiation: Getting Paid What You're Worth   115
    The Six Secrets to Successful Negotiation

Part II

When The Unexpected Happens: How to Deal with Change

8. *On This Restless, Unpredictable, Ever-Changing Earth:*
   How to Pick a New Place to Live   139
   What to Do When Disaster Strikes: Katrina, et al.

9. *In This Restless, Unpredictable, Ever-Changing Job-Market:*
   How to Choose a New Career   161
   How Much Help Are Vocational Tests?
   Developing a Picture of What You Want
   Developing "A Career-Choice Vocabulary"
   How Women Can Earn More

10. *In the Restless, Unpredictable, Ever-Changing Worklife of Yours:*
    How to Start Your Own Business   185
    The Secret: A minus B equals C
    The Most Helpful Websites
    Part-Time, Contract, and Temp Work
    Operating on a Shoe-String: Finding Help Overseas

11. *In This Restless, Unpredictable, Ever-Changing Long Life of Ours:*   215
    Entering the World of 50+

12. *In This Restless, Unpredictable, Ever-Changing Brain of Ours:*
    How to Get "Unstuck"   225

Part III

Resuming the Search to Find Your Dream

Introduction: The Reawakening 238

13. The Three Secrets to Finding That 239
    Dream Job of Yours

    What Did You Come into the World to Do? 239
    What the World Most Needs from You 240
    Why People Fail to Find Their Dream Job 241
    Exercise: Who Am I? 242
    Brain Scientists' Findings 244
    The Flower Exercise 246–247
    Example of Completed Flower 249
    What Are Competencies? 250
    Summary: How Do You Identify Your Dream Job? 251

    Step One: WHAT Skills Do You Most Enjoy Using? 254
        A Crash Course on Transferable Skills 255
        Example of a Story: The Stationwagon 261

        Exercise: My Life Stories 264
        Analyzing Your Story: Three Sets of Skill Keys 265

        Exercise: The Prioritizing Grid 273
        The Building Blocks Pyramid 276

        Exercise: Your Strongest Traits 277
        Clinic: The Five Most Common Problems 280

    Step Two: WHERE Do You Want to Use Your Skills? 283

        Your Petal #1: Your "Fields of Fascination" 283
        The Intuitional Way to Approach This 285
        The Step-by-Step Way to Approach This 288

        Exercise: Fields That Use Your Mental Skills 289
        The "Subjects Chart" 292

        Exercise: Fields Dealing with People's Needs 293
        "The People List" of Needs 294

Exercise: Fields Dealing with Things   298
"The Things Phone Book"   300

Your Petal #2: Your Favorite Places to Live   301
Chart: "My Geographical Preferences"   304–305

Your Petal #3: Your Favorite People   308
"The Party" Exercise: John Holland's System   310
Helpful Websites   311

Your Petal #4: Your Favorite Values   312
Exercise: Your Testimonial Dinner   313

Your Petal #5: Your Favorite Working Conditions   316
Exercise: Distasteful Working Conditions   317

Your Petal #6: Level & Salary   318
Exercise: Estimated Monthly Expenses   319
Ideal Salary: Maximum and Minimum   321
Other Rewards   322

Step Three: HOW Do You Put It All Together?   325
When a Light Bulb Goes On   326
When You Haven't a Clue   327
Exercise: The Five Friends   327
Chart: The Job Families   329
Giving Your Flower a Name   333
Cutting Down the Territory   336
Expanding the Territory   337
Informational Interviewing Explained (Again)   341
The Chart: Guide to Relations in Job-Hunting   342
How to Research Places Before You Go There   347
Identifying the Person Who Has the Power to Hire   348

Always Send a Thank-You Note   350

14. How to Find Your Mission in Life   355

Appendix: A Guide to Choosing a Career Coach   379

A Sampler   394

Index   417

Preface

The Diary of a Grateful Man

April 24, 2007

People often say to me, "Oh yes, I've read your book." When I'm in a playful mood, I tend to respond, "When?"

If the most recent edition you've read was 2005, or earlier, you haven't really read my book. This book comes out in annual editions, you know, and those editions are not mere polishing up last year's edition, so as to sell new copies. My thinking, lately, has been altering quite a bit. Each new edition represents an attempt to convey my latest thinking. I've worked particularly hard on the three most recent editions—2008, 2007, and 2006—and I think *(immodestly)* they are the best I've ever done. Well, why not? As I get older, I get more experienced; and I get a little bit wiser. Hopefully.

It's fun for me to see what new developments have occurred in Job-Hunting Land each year, to keep up with the latest technologies each year, and to observe the twists and turns in how job-hunting gets better in this country and elsewhere (and also, alas!, those respects in which it gets worse!)

I try to keep up with *everything*. The economy, outsourcing, new technologies, Twitter, Twittervision, Jaiku, Blogger, Podcasts, IM, hip-hop, Workblast (video resumes), etc. It's hardly surprising that I've changed the book radically these last three years.

In fact, I do not think of this any longer as *a book*. It's much more like *a living organism*, evolving, changing, growing. It takes on a life of its own, year by year. In some ways, rewriting this book each year is like getting on a bucking bronco. It's thrilling and exciting, and you never know what's going to happen next.

I have learned that job-hunters and career-changers need two things above all else: we need tools for discovering our truest vision for our own life. And then we need practical tools for finding that vision, that work, and that mission.

This edition has both kinds of tools: in the first section, the practical tools for job-hunting or career-changing. In the third section, the vision tools for uncovering your ideal work. Oh, and in the second section *(there are three, as you can see in the table of contents)*, how to deal with unexpected changes.

Beyond job-hunting there is the issue of our character. Our character springs from our mind and our heart. What are we thinking about? What are we concerned about, in life? Global warming, Darfur, the Iraq war, poverty in the world? Under the heading of *Values*, in the third section of this book, I newly deal with *that*.

The wildly popular video and publishing phenomenon this year, *The Secret*, follows in the footsteps of Norman Vincent Peale *(The Power of Positive Thinking, 1953)*, and—for that matter—the Bible *("For as a man thinketh in his heart, so is he."*[1]) in emphasizing the power of thought over our day-to-day happiness, and the growth of character in each of us. For me that means many things, but in this introduction to my book it means above all, thinking about gratitude. I didn't get here, alone. I do not stay here, alone. I am not inspired, alone. I am not able to write, alone.

So, I thank God[2] that I am still in splendid vigorous health, that I still have all my marbles and wits about me, that I love to write more than ever—and that I am enchanted by every moment

---

1. Proverbs 23:7
2. Hardly surprising, given my background (I was an ordained Episcopal minister for over fifty years).

of my life with such a wondrous woman as my wife, Marci, from the Philippines. Not to mention her two children, Janice and Adlai, and my four and a half children, and their families: Stephen, Mark, Gary, Sharon, and my stepdaughter, Dr. Serena Brewer.

And so: I want to express my gratitude this year, especially to Daniel Porot of Geneva, Switzerland; Joel Garfinkle; Tom O'Neil from New Zealand; Howard Figler; Richard Leider; Warren Farrell; Marty Nemko; BJ Chobju of Korea; Debra Angel MacDougall of Scotland; Brian McIvor of Ireland; Pete Hawkins of Liverpool, England; Jim Kell; Dick Gaither; Rich Feller; Madeleine Leitner of Germany; the folks over at Ten Speed Press (Phil Wood, Lorena Jones, Kristine, George Young, Linda Davis, Debra Matsumoto, Michelle Crim, Zak Nelson, Brie Mazurek, Lisa Westmoreland, Aaron Wehner, and Betsy Stromberg); and all my readers—all nine million of you—for buying my books, trusting my counsel, and following your dream. Many of you write me; you are wonderful people! I am so thankful for you.

In closing, I must not fail to mention my profound thanks to The Great Lord God, Father of our Lord Jesus Christ, Who all my life has been as real to me as breathing, and Who has been my Rock through every trial, tragedy, and misfortune in my life, including the assassination of my only brother, Don Bolles. I thank God for giving me strength, and carrying me through—everything. I am grateful beyond measure for such a life, and such a mission as "He" has given me: to help people find meaning for their lives. He is the source of whatever grace, wisdom, or compassion I have ever found, or shared with others.

I am a grateful man.

Dick Bolles
RNB25@aol.com
www.jobhuntersbible.com

Grammar and Language Note

I want to explain four points of grammar, in this book of mine: pronouns, commas, italics, and spelling. My unorthodox use of them invariably offends unemployed English teachers so much that they write me to apply for a job as my editor.

To save us unnecessary correspondence, let me explain. Throughout this book, I often use the apparently plural pronouns "they," "them," and "their" after *singular* antecedents— such as, "You must approach *someone* for a job and tell *them* what you can do." This sounds strange and even *wrong* to those who know English well. To be sure, we all know there is another pronoun—"you"—that may be either singular or plural, but few of us realize that the pronouns "they," "them," and "their" were also once treated as both plural and singular in the English language. This changed, at a time in English history when agreement in *number* became more important than agreement as to sexual *gender*. Today, however, our priorities have shifted once again. Now, the distinguishing of sexual *gender* is considered by many to be more important than agreement in *number*.

The common artifices used for this new priority, such as "s/he," or "he and she," are—to my mind—tortured and inelegant. Casey Miller and Kate Swift, in their classic, *The Handbook of Nonsexist Writing*, agree, and argue that it is time to bring back the earlier usage of "they," "them," and "their" as both singular and plural—just as "you" is/are. They further argue that this return to the earlier historical usage has already become quite common *out on the street*—witness a typical sign by the ocean that reads, "*Anyone* using this beach after 5 P.M. does so at *their* own risk." I have followed Casey and Kate's wise recommendations in all of this.

As for my commas, they are deliberately used according to my own rules—rather than according to the rules of historic grammar (which I did learn—I hastily add, to reassure my old Harvard professors, who despaired of me weekly, during English class). In spite of those rules, I follow my own, which are: to write conversationally, and put in a comma wherever I would normally stop for a breath, were I *speaking* the same line.

The same conversational rule applies to my use of *italics*. I use *italics* wherever, were I speaking the sentence, I would put *emphasis* on that word or phrase. I also use italics where there is a digression of thought, and I want to maintain the main thought and flow of the sentence. All in all, I write as I speak. Hence the dashes (—) to indicate a break in thought.

Finally, some of my spelling (and capitalization) is *weird*. (Well, some might say "weird"; I prefer just "playful.") I happen to like writing it "e-mail," for example, instead of "email." Fortunately, since this is my own book, I get to play in my own way; I'm so grateful that nine million readers have *gone along*. Nothing delights a child (at heart) more, than being allowed to play.

P.S. Speaking of "playful," over the last thirty-five years a few critics (very few) have claimed that *Parachute* is not serious enough (they object to the cartoons, which poke fun at almost *everything*). A few have claimed that the book is *too* serious, and too complicated in its vocabulary and grammar for anyone except a college graduate. Two readers, however, have written me with a different view.

The first one, from England, said there is an index that analyzes a book to tell you what grade in school you must have finished, in order to be able to understand it. My book's index, he said, turned out to be 6.1, which means you need only have finished sixth grade in a U.S. school in order to understand it.

Here in the U.S., a college instructor came up with a similar finding. He phoned me to tell me that my book was rejected by the authorities as a proposed text for his college course, because the book's language/grammar was not up to college level. "What level was it?" I asked. "Well," he replied, "when they analyzed it, it turned out to be written on an eighth grade level."

Sixth or eighth grade—that seems just about right to me. Why make job-hunting complicated, when it can be expressed so simply even a child could understand it?

R.N.B.

The Things School Never
Taught Us About

The
Job-Hunt

*"What do you mean 'don't expect miracles'?
Why shouldn't I expect miracles?"*

The Three
Essential Life Skills

When you get out of school,
or when you've been out of school for some time,
And then are looking back,
You realize there are three things a good education
should have given you . . .
But in your case, did not.

1. High school or college should have taught you
How to choose and find **a job**.
A job that matches your gifts, skills, and experience.
A job that not only puts bread on the table,
Clothes on your back,
And a shelter over your head,
But also makes you happy,
And gives you a sense of purpose in life.

2. High school or college should have taught you
How to choose and find an appropriate **partner**,
Or husband, or wife.
Principles for the heart; principles for the mind,
That make relationships more likely to happen,
More likely to endure.
How to find and how to value friends

3. And last, but not least, high school or college
Should have taught you
How to **think**, and how to make good decisions.
The principles for making good decisions,
And for avoiding the bad. Included here,
School should have taught us the way in which
Work, *money*, **sex**, *and* **religion** *become playpens*
Throughout our lives, wherein each of us acts out and spells out
Who we really are.

We might call these three
The Three Basic Life Skills.
After "the elementary stuff"—readin', writin' and 'rithmetic[1]—these
Are the three things we would most hope
School would help us with.[2] Instead,
We are left to flounder for ourselves, after graduation.
Hence the high unemployment rate
In our country, and the even higher percentage
Of people who are unhappy in their work.
Hence the high divorce rate
In our country, and the even higher percentage
Of people who are unhappy in their relationships.
Hence the high percentage of people who
Make really bad decisions in their life,
And are taken in by all kinds of scams,
And "get-rich-quick" schemes.

Yes, our schools teach us nothing,
About these three essential things. Or, worse,
They teach us something
But it is wrong. So, we are left with not only things to lea
But also things to *un*learn,
After we get out of school.
Take job-hunting, for example. Our schools teach us
That the way to job-hunt is
To prepare a good resume,
And learn to conduct a good interview.

Job-hunting: Resumes and interviews.
And they are done.
Oh, My Lord! We needed school
To tell us so much more
About how the job-hunt works.
No wonder it takes, on average,
In America today, eighteen weeks
To find a job.

Oh well, you know, it's never too late.
So let's get started.
Let's look at
The things that school forgot to teach us,
About choosing and finding a job.
And I think we will find
As we go,
That all three skills: jobs, relationships,
And how to use our brains,
Are related and intertwined.
So that, to master even one of them,
Is simultaneously
To master all three.
Hence, the job-hunt is the doorway.
The job-hunt is the key.

---

1. Or, applied mathematics.
2. Employers and educators, of course, have a far broader agenda for education reform. They want education to be multidisciplinary, they want it to not be so governed by tests, they want high school to end with eleventh grade, not twelfth. See the report of the National Center on Education and the Economy, *Tough Choices or Tough Times: The Report of the New Commission on the Skills of the American Workforce*, released December 14, 2006, published by Jossey-Bass.

He or she who gets hired is not necessarily the one who can do that job best; but, the one who knows the most about how to get hired.

Richard Lathrop
in his classic *Who's Hiring Who?*

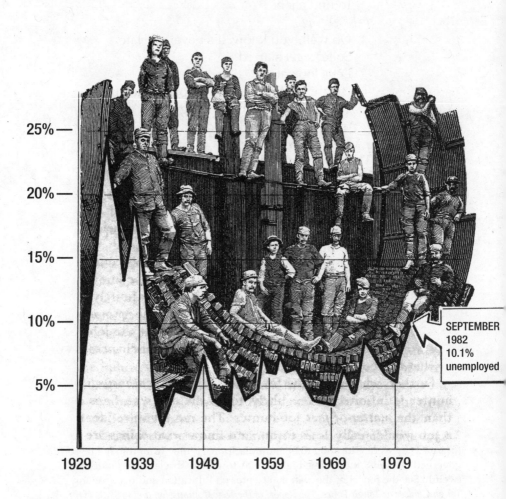

When Things Were at Their Worst

The Things
School Never Taught Us
About the Job-Hunt:

The Five Best Ways
to Hunt for a Job
(and the Five Worst)

In the sandboxes of my life, over the years I have spelled out who I am: chemical engineer, physicist, counselor, writer, poet, lover, mystic, and man. But I gradually came to realize that, above all else, I was at heart an investigative reporter, like my brother[1]: I loved to research, investigate, indulge my curiosity, find out what is true, and expose falsehoods.

I investigated many things. And studied things that other investigators had turned up. And somewhere along the way, I discovered, with some astonishment, that one of the most thoroughly studied subjects in all of human activity, was and is the job-hunt. Who would have thought it! *Who knew?*

School never tells us this. But we know many, many things about the whole process of job-hunting. Let me give you an example: how many different ways do you suppose there are, to go looking for a job? Well, it turns out the answer is: 16.

We call these "16 different job-hunting *methods*." In a nutshell, they are:

1. Mailing out resumes.

2. Answering local "want-ads" (in newspapers).

---

1. Don Bolles, a famous investigative reporter, who was assassinated in Phoenix, AZ, in June of 1976.

3. Going to the state/federal unemployment service.

4. Going to private employment agencies.

5. Using the Internet, either to post your resume or to look for employers' "job-postings," on the employer's own website or elsewhere (*Monster, Career Builder, Yahoo/Hot Jobs, etc., etc.*).

6. Asking friends, family, or people in the community for job-leads.

7. Asking a former professor or teacher for job-leads, or career/alumni services at schools that you attended (*high school, trade schools, online schools, community college, college, or university*).

8. Knocking on doors: of any employer, factory, or office that interests you, whether they are known to have a vacancy or not.

9. Using the phone book's yellow pages, to identify subjects, fields, or interests that you have—that are located in the city or town where you are, or want to be.

10. Joining or forming "a job club."

11. Doing a thorough self-inventory of the *transferable* skills and interests that you *most enjoy*, so that you can define *in stunning detail* exactly the job(s) you would most like to have.

12. Going to places where employers pick up workers: well-known street corners in your town, or union halls, etc.

13. Taking a civil service exam.

14. Looking at professional journals in your profession or field, and answering ads there.

15. Going to temp agencies (agencies that get you short-term temporary work in places that need your skills, short-term) and letting them place you, again and again, until some place says, "Could you stay on, permanently?"

16. Volunteering to work for free, short-term, at a place that interests you, whether or not they have a known vacancy.

Researchers discovered, some years ago, that while a typical job-hunt lasted around fifteen to nineteen weeks, depending on the economy, one-third to one-half of all job-hunters simply *give up* by the second month of their job-hunt. They stop job-hunting. (*Of course, they have to resume, somewhere further down the road, when and if things get really desperate.*) But why do they initially *give up so soon*?

It turns out, *that* was related to how many job-hunting methods a job-hunter was using. In a study of 100 job-hunters who were using only one method to hunt for a job, typically 51 abandoned their search by the second month. That's more than one-half of them. On the other hand, of 100 job-hunters who were using several different ways of hunting for a job, typically only 31 abandoned their search by the second month. That's less than one-third of them.

You might conclude from this, that the more job-hunting methods you use in looking for a job, the more successful you will be. But, you would be wrong.

Further research found out that your chances of uncovering a job, does indeed increase with each additional method that you use—but only up to four, in number. If you use more than four methods of job-hunting, your likelihood of success begins to decrease, and continues to decrease with each additional method that you add to your job-search, beyond four. *Naturally, I have my theories about why these things are so; but for now I just want to give illustrations of my central thesis: that the job-hunt has been researched in exquisite detail, but school never tells us any of this stuff. That's pretty sad, considering that knowing these research findings can go a long way toward taking you out of the ranks of the unemployed.*

Want more examples of things school never taught us?

Okay. It's been discovered that in a job-interview, you are most likely to get hired if you talk half the time, and the interviewer talks half the time. On the other hand, if you talk 90 percent of the time, or the interviewer talks 90 percent of the time, things are not likely to go well for you there.

Further, it's been discovered that when you are answering questions during a job-interview, you are more likely to get hired if each answer you give is at least twenty seconds in length, but not more than two minutes. *And if your answer just can't fit within the two-minute limit, it's okay if you conclude your two-minute answer with: "I can go into more detail, if you ever want it." Then, if they **beg** you to go on, go no more than two additional minutes, with the rest of your answer. And then, let it be, let it be!*

Another research finding: it's been discovered that you are much more likely to get hired, if right after the interview you send two thank-you notes, one e-mailed and one hand-written by "snail-mail," as techies now call the U.S. Postal Service. E-mailed for promptness, hand-written for the personal touch. And if your handwriting absolutely sucks, then at least keyboard it, and on nice paper (30 lb paper, or heavier). U.S. Postal costs for first class mail: 41 cents for the first ounce, but 17 cents for each additional ounce; while e-mail costs nothing, but is subject to the dictum: *"Message sent" does not necessarily equal "message received."*

Research Plus

I could go on and on, with examples. But I have made my point: no school has educated us about the job-hunt if all it teaches us is *how to write resumes* and *conduct interviews*. There is so much more we *need* to know, and *can* know, because the job-hunt is one of the most researched of all human activities.

To be sure, the research isn't always *pure*. What is? Many times it is *a mashup*, as it were, of scientific studies *and* experts' hunches, based on long-range observations by those whose business it is, to study and observe these things.

Now, hunches are not to be sneezed at, because if experts work in a field long enough, and keep their eyes wide open, they get a definite sense of what is true and what is not. Their contributions are often highly dependable, and accurate. It's like *Wikipedia*, the online encyclopedia/dictionary/etc. where anyone can add to, or correct an entry; and yet, for all of that, Wikipedia has proved as reliable as the *Encyclopedia Britannica*—sometimes more so.

A mashup of research and hunches. This is how we arrive at a list of the relative effectiveness of various job-hunting methods, a list of vital importance to every job-hunter or career-changer. We would hope, at this point, that experts would be able to come up with a compelling list, backed by studies and statistics, to guide us as to which job-search methods are most likely to repay our investment of time, and which ones aren't. But, experts don't always have accurate statistics or anything other than anecdotal stories, to guide us. Studies—if there are any—are often of questionable value, because they were either done too long ago, or with too small a sample, or before new technological developments arrived, or whatever.

But first, a word about that list.

You will notice that some job-hunting methods are more *inef*-fective than others; sometimes much more *in*effective.

You will further notice that some of your favorite job-hunting strategies, since time immemorial, are on the list of *least effective*. Whoops! Guess school should have told us *that*.

Here then are the percentages: they tell us what percentage of job-hunters who use *each method* **succeed** thereby in finding a job.

The Five Worst Ways to Look for a Job

4 to 10%

1. **Using the Internet.** The evidence that job-hunting on the Internet actually works, can be found in countless anecdotes from one job-hunter after another who have successfully conducted their job-hunt online. The media are filled with such stories.

One job-seeker, a systems administrator in Taos, New Mexico, who wanted to move to San Francisco posted his resume at 10 p.m. on a Monday night, on a San Francisco online bulletin board (*Craigslist.org*). By Wednesday morning he had over seventy responses from employers.

Again, a marketing professional developed her resume following guidance she found on the Internet, posted it to two advertised positions she found there, and within seventy-two hours of posting her electronic resume, both firms contacted her, and she is now working for one of them.

It is not just the media that are filled with such stories. So is my mail. Here's a letter that I received: "In May I was very unexpectedly laid off from a company I was with for five years. I was given a copy of your book by a ministry in our church that helps people without jobs. I read the book, and it was a great source of encouragement for me. The day I was laid off I committed my job search to the Lord. He blessed us, provided for us, and gave me peace of mind throughout my job-hunt. The Internet was my lifeline in finding the right job. I did 100 percent of my job search and research via the Internet. I found all my leads online, sent all my resumes via e-mail, and had about a 25 percent response rate that actually lead to a phone interview or a face-to-face interview. It was a software company that laid me off, and I am [now] going to work for a publishing company, a position I found online."

And another: "Thanks to the Internet, I found what I believe to be the ideal job in [just] eight weeks—a great job with a great company and great opportunities. . . ."

And so, we see the Internet can do a marvelous job of making it possible for an employer and a job-hunter to get together, in a way that was rarely possible even a decade or so ago. Internet sites currently devoted to job-hunting—some experts say 1,000; some say 5,000; some, 10,000; some 40,000; and some, 100,000 or more—make it possible to get together *faster* than ever before in history.

Of course, it doesn't always work. Aye, and there's the rub! It actually doesn't work for a huge percentage of those who try it. Research has turned up the fact that out of every 100 job-hunters who use the Internet as their search method for finding jobs, 4 of them will get lucky and find a job thereby, while 96 job-hunters out of the 100 will not—if they use only the Internet to search for a job.

Exception: if you are seeking a technical or computer-related job, an IT job, or a job in engineering, finances, or healthcare, the success rate rises, to somewhere around 10 percent. But for the other 20,000 job titles that are out there in the job-market, the success rate remains at 4 percent only.

Did they teach you this in school? Of course not! So you may suppose that the Internet is working for everyone. Except, of course, you. And if you think *that*, and if you fail to find a job on the Internet, you can end up with lowered self-esteem, or even a mammoth depression.

7%

2. **Mailing out resumes to employers at random.** This job-search method is reported to have about a 7 percent success rate. That is, out of every 100 job-hunters who use only this search method, 7 will get lucky, and find a job thereby. Ninety-

three job-hunters out of 100 will not—if they use only resumes to search for a job.

I'm being generous here with my percentages for success. One study suggested that outside the Internet only 1 out of 1,470 resumes actually resulted in a job. Another study put the figure even higher: one job offer for every 1,700 resumes floating around out there. We do not know what the odds are if you post your resume on the Internet. We do know that there are reportedly at least 40,000,000 resumes floating around out there on the Internet, like lost ships on the Sargasso Sea.[2] No one's bothered to try to count how many of these actually found a job for the job-hunter.

7%

3. **Answering ads in professional or trade journals, appropriate to your field.** This search method, like the one above, has just a 7 percent success rate. That is, out of every 100 job-hunters who use only this search method, 7 will get lucky and find a job thereby. Ninety-three job-hunters out of 100 will not—if they use only this method to search for them.

5 to 24%

4. **Answering local newspaper ads.** This search method has a 5 to 24 percent success rate. That is, out of every 100 job-hunters who use only this search method, between 5 and 24 will get lucky and find a job thereby. Seventy-six to 95 job-hunters out of 100 will not—if they use only this method to search for them.

(The fluctuation between 5 percent and 24 percent is due to the level of salary that is being sought; the higher the salary being sought, the fewer job-hunters who are able to find a job—using only this search method.)

5 to 28%

5. **Going to private employment agencies or search firms for help.** This method has a 5 to 28 percent success rate, again depending on the level of salary that is being sought. Which is to say, out of every 100 job-hunters who use only this

---

2. Some put the estimate way higher.

method, between 5 and 28 will get lucky and find a job thereby. Seventy-two to 95 job-hunters out of 100 will not—if they use only this method to search for them.

(The range is for the same reason as noted in #4. It is of interest that the success rate of this method has risen slightly in recent years, in the case of women but not of men: in a comparatively recent study, 27.8 percent of female job-hunters found a job within two months, by going to private employment agencies.)

Other Job-Hunting Methods in the Least Effective *category:* For the sake of completeness we should note that there are at least four other methods for trying to find jobs, that technically fall into this category of Worst Ways. Those four are:

Going to places where employers pick out workers, such as union halls. This has an 8 percent success rate.

(Less than 15 percent of U.S. workers are union members anyway, but it is claimed that those among them who do have access to a union hiring hall, have a 22 percent success rate. What is not stated, however, is how long it takes to get a job at the hall, and how temporary and short-lived such a job may be; in the trades it's often just a few days.)

Taking a civil service examination. This has a 12 percent success rate.

Asking a former teacher or professor for job-leads. This also has a 12 percent success rate.

Going to the state/federal employment service office. This has a 14 percent success rate.

The Five Best Ways to Hunt for a Job

Okay, so much for the Worst Ways to hunt for a job; if you have only limited time and energy to give to your job-hunt, you'll probably be wise to give the previous methods only the time they merit.

But now, let's look at the other side of the coin. What are the job-hunting methods that will pay off better, for the time and energy you have to invest in your job-hunt?

I call these the "best ways"; now, what on earth does that mean? Well, one useful way to think about this is in terms of *your personal energy*. During your job-hunt, your energies are limited (especially if the job-hunt stretches on for weeks or even months); so, it's important to know which are the best strategies *that you should start with*, in case your energy runs out before you've finished working your way down through all the alternatives.

33%

1. **Asking for job-leads from: family members, friends, people in the community, staff at career centers— especially at your local community college or the high school or college where you graduated.** You ask them one simple question: do you know of any jobs at the place where you work—or elsewhere? This search method has a 33 percent success rate. That is, out of every 100 people who use this search method, 33 will get lucky, and find a job thereby. Sixty-seven job-hunters will not—if they use only this method to search for work.

What! This is one of the five best ways to look for a job? Well, yes; but it's all relative. "The fifth best" out of all those job-hunting methods that are out there, isn't necessarily saying much. Sixty-seven job-hunters out of 100 will still not find the jobs that are out there—if they use this so-called "one-of-the-best methods." But to put things in perspective, do note that this method's success rate is almost five times higher than the success rate for resumes. *In other words, by asking for job leads from your family and friends, you have an almost five times better chance of finding a job, than if you had just sent out your resume.*

47%

2. **Knocking on the door of any employer, factory, or office that interests you, whether they are known to have a vacancy or not.** This search method has anywhere up to a 47 percent success rate. That is, out of every 100 people who use only this search method, 47 will get lucky, and find a job thereby; 53 job-hunters out of 100 will not—if they use only this one method to search for work. But, again for perspective, note that *by going face-to-face* you have an almost seven times better chance of finding a job, than if you had just sent out your resume.

69%

3. By yourself, using the phone book's yellow pages to identify subjects or fields of interest to you in the town or city where you want to work, and then calling up the employers listed in that field, to ask if they are hiring for the type of position you can do, and do well. This method has a 69 percent success rate. That is, out of every 100 job-hunters or career-changers who use only this search method, 69 will get lucky and find a job thereby. Thirty-one job-hunters out of 100 will not—if they use only this one method to search for them. For perspective, however, note that by doing *targeted phone calls by yourself*, you have an almost ten times better chance of finding a job, than if you had just sent out your resume.

84%

4. In a group with other job-hunters, a kind of "job-club," using the phone book's yellow pages to identify subjects or fields of interest to you in the town or city where you are, and then calling up the employers listed in that field, to ask if they are hiring for the type of position you can do, and do well. This method has an 84 percent success rate. That is, out of every 100 people who use only this method, 84 will get lucky and find a job thereby. This is one of the five best ways to look for a job, but even so . . . 16 job-hunters out of 100 will not find a job—if they use only this one method to search for them. Still, that's a success rate that is over 11 times higher than if you just sent out resumes.

86%

5. Doing a Life-Changing Job-Hunt. This method, invented by the late John Crystal and myself, depends upon your doing extensive homework on *yourself* before you go out there pounding the pavements. This homework revolves around three simple words: What, Where, How.

1. WHAT. This has to do with your skills. You need to inventory and identify what skills you have *that you most enjoy using.* I didn't say: *that you are best at.* No, these are the ones you *enjoy* using the most. They are called your transferable skills, because they are transferable to any field/career that you choose, regardless of where you first picked them up.

2. WHERE. This has to do with job environments. Think of yourself as a flower. You know that a flower that blooms in the desert will not do well at 10,000 feet up—and vice versa. Every flower has an environment where it does best. So with you. You are like a flower. You need to decide where you want to use your skills, where you would thrive, and where you do your most effective work.

3. HOW. You need to decide how to get where you want to go. This has to do with finding out the names of the jobs you would be most interested in, **and** the names of organizations (in your preferred geographical area) that have such jobs to offer, **and** the names of the people or person there who actually has the power to hire you. And, how can you best approach that person to show him or her how your skills can help them with their problems. How, if you were hired there, you would not be part of the problem, but part of the solution.

This method has an 86 percent success rate. That is, out of every 100 job-hunters or career-changers who use only this job-search method, 86 will find a job or new career thereby.

Such an effectiveness-rate—86 percent—is astronomically higher than most traditional job-hunting methods. That's why when nothing else is working for you, this is the method that you will thank your lucky stars for.

As usual, it does not work for everyone—specifically, 14 job-hunters out of 100 will still not find the jobs that are out there—if they use only this one method to search for them. But—perspective again—this is 12 times more effective than resumes. **In other words, by putting in the hard time that this method requires, you have a 1,200 percent better chance of finding a job than if you just send out resumes!**

Well, there's your list. Its end message: there are 16 alternative ways of looking for a job; but not all these alternatives were created equal. It would pay you to know which ones are better, which ones are less draining of your energy. Even if school never taught you *that*.

What If You Use More Than One
of These Alternatives?

Well, why not? Not matter what the experts say, you're probably going to be sending out your resume, all over the place, anyway. Force of habit. Human nature. And you'll almost certainly want to try the Internet as well. From the perspective of fifteen years ago, it's relatively new; and everyone *wants* to believe in it. (Until proven otherwise.) That's two methods; and you can try two more, remember? (Each additional job-hunting method up to four in number, increases your chances of finding a job.)

Alternatives keep you from "job-hunting insanity." And what, pray tell, is *that*? It's when something doesn't work, and your response is to just try more of it. It's the type of thinking that says: *500 resumes didn't work? Let's try 1,000.* The only cure for this kind of desperation is alternatives.

And, in Conclusion: Tack This on Your Mirror
So Long as You're Unemployed

1. *Job-hunting is an activity that repeats itself over and over again, in most people's lives.* Lucky you, if that is not the case; but the odds are overwhelming that it will be. According to experts, the average worker, under 35 years of age, will go job-hunting every one to three years. And the average worker over 35 will go job-hunting every five to eight years! And, in this process, so the experts say, we will each of us probably change *careers* three to five times, as we go.

2. *Job-hunting is not a science; it is an art.* Some job-hunters know instinctively how to do it; in some cases, they were born knowing how to do it. Others of us sometimes have a harder time with it, but fortunately for us in the U.S. and elsewhere in the world, there is help, coaching, counseling, and advice—online and off.

3. *Job-hunting is always mysterious.* Sometimes *mind-bogglingly mysterious.* You may *never* understand why things sometimes do work, and sometimes do not.

4. *There is no **always wrong** way to hunt for a job or to change careers.* Anything *may* work under certain circumstances, or at certain times, or with certain employers. There are only *degrees of likelihood* of certain job-hunting techniques working or not working. But it is crucial to know that likelihood, as we have just seen.

5. *There is no **always right** way to hunt for a job or to change careers.* Anything *may* fail to work under certain circumstances, or at certain times, or with certain employers. There are only *degrees of likelihood* of certain job-hunting techniques working or not working. But it is crucial to know that likelihood, as we just saw.

6. *Mastering the job-hunt this time, and for the rest of your life, done right, is a lot of **hard work** and takes some **hard thinking**.* The more work, the more thinking, you put into pursuing your job-hunt, and doing the homework on yourself, the more successful your job-hunt is likely to be. *Caution: Are you lazy, day by day? Uh, oh! Most people do their job-hunt or career-change the same way they do Life.*

7. *Job-hunting always depends on some amount of **luck**.* Luck, pure luck. Mastering the job-hunt doesn't mean absolutely, positively, you will always be able to find a job. It does mean that you can get good at reducing the amount that depends on luck, to as small a proportion as possible.

Wise job-hunters know from the beginning that they are hunting *secondly* for a job but *first* of all for Hope. Alternatives keep **Hope** alive. And to someone out of work, that is everything.

So, if you answer ads in the newspapers, or if you answer job-postings on the Internet, or send out your resume everywhere, or sign up with agencies, and so far it has turned out to be all in vain, don't just do more of whatever you've been doing. Change your tactics. Try a new strategy.

CHAPTER 2

The Things
School Never Taught Us
About the Job-Hunt:

The Nature
of the
Job-Market

There Are Always Many More Vacancies
Out There Than You Think,
and Here's Why

The Nature of the Job-Market:
1. Unemployment Statistics

In the U.S., on the first Friday of every month, the government reports how many new jobs were created in the previous month. Often, it's depressing news. On May 4, 2007, for example, the government announced that only 88,000 new jobs were created during all of April. That's depressing. Because there were 6,800,000 unemployed that month who had searched for work in the previous four weeks, not to mention the additional 1,400,000 who wanted and were available for work, but had not searched for work in the last four weeks. The spectacle of 8,200,000 souls competing for 88,000 spaces is a real downer for any job-hunter or career-changer.

But, wait a minute. The report said 88,000 *new* jobs. That means a *net gain* over the previous month's figures. But what about the *old* jobs, the 145,800,000 people who were already employed in that previous month? How many of *their* old jobs turned over, and were quietly, quickly filled—thus maintaining the total employment figure at the same base level?

Good question!

And, for years we didn't know the answer. It remained for Ben Bernanke, Alan Greenspan's brilliant successor, to finally find the answer for us. He was curious, back a while, and so he researched it. On March 30, 2004, he published his findings: "about 30,000,000 jobs are lost each year in the United States" and—he added—*this has been true for the past ten years.* Some were short-term, some were not, but all had to be refilled, replaced.

That breaks down to an average of 1,250,000 to 2,500,000 vacancies in the U.S. each month. Plus the *new* jobs that month, of course—the ones that the government reports on, the first Friday of each month.

Vacancies.

Open to people within their respective organizations.

Open, also, to job-hunters and career-changers. That is why the U.S. is known as "the greatest job-making machine" in the history of the world.

The vacancies exist. But, ah! finding them—that's what makes us sweat. The methods we use to do this are often deeply flawed, as we saw in the previous chapter. And, that is why—in the phrase "your job hunt"—the emphasis is on the word "hunt."

The Nature of the Job-Market:
2. Churning

Some 30,000,000 jobs turning over each year may be very good news for job-hunters. But it sure does produce a lot of turmoil or what experts call "churning" in the job-market, out there.

The job-market is anything but a well-organized system. It sometimes careens wildly out of control. (Hence the word "career," which is related to the word "careen," both derived from the Old French word *carrière*, meaning "racecourse.") Images of horses running wildly down the track. *Feels like that, sometimes, doesn't it?*

The natural churning is aided and abetted by constantly unfolding developments in technology, plus the changing demand for old products or services, here, there, or everywhere. Also the creation of new products, services, and demand.

The result of all this churning in the job-market is as follows (*see how many of these have affected you*):

1. Whole new industries have risen, for example the cell-phone industry, or MP3 devices such as the iPod, in a moment, in the twinkling of an eye. And whole old industries or companies have died or are dying, such as CD stores, and small retailers.

2. Waves of unannounced and unexpected layoffs, as companies, organizations, corporations, the armed forces, government programs, and other employers downsize.

3. The fleeing of jobs overseas, to India, China, and elsewhere.

4. The increasing disappearance of well-paying jobs.

5. The increase in the number of hours that full-time employees have to work, inasmuch as employers prefer to use present employees who are already paid benefits, rather than hire new workers to whom such benefits would have to be given.

6. More and more of the unemployed forced to take part-time jobs, or work as "temporaries" or "contract workers."

7. More and more of the unemployed forced to accept jobs where their paychecks are smaller, sometimes much smaller, than they were formerly accustomed to—forcing an attendant drop in their standard of living.

The Nature of the Job Market

The Nature of the Job-Market:
3. There's Always a Bogeyman[1]

Every decade creates its own "bogeyman" to scare job-hunters, and make them fear for their jobs. One decade it may be *illegal immigrants.*[2] In another, *"Made in Japan."* In another decade it turns out to be *the taking over of manufacturing by robots.* And in yet another decade it turns out to be China. Each and every one of them—so the fear goes—is going to rob us of our jobs.

In this decade, our bogeyman is *outsourcing* in general, and China in particular.

If you haven't been living in a cave the last five years, you probably know what *outsourcing* is, or—more particularly— offshore outsourcing. With the death of *distance-as-obstacle*, employers can increasingly send jobs overseas, jobs which once would have been *ours*, and give those jobs to cheaper labor elsewhere in the world, including not only China, but also India, Mexico, and Eastern European countries.[3] The average computer programmer in India, for example, only demands around $10 an hour, compared with the more than $60 per hour that the average American computer programmer can command.

What kinds of jobs do employers try to outsource? Well, currently almost any kind of job you can think of. (Or, with a bow to Winston Churchill, *every job of which you can think.*) As long as it doesn't involve touch, or require geographic proximity.

Massage therapists seem safe. So do doctors and nurses. And local delivery trucks. And waiters or waitresses. And garbage disposal jobs.

When jobs do move overseas, it's all about salaries.

---

1. As any fan of horror movies knows, this is a monstrous imaginary figure used in frightening children out of their wits—or moviegoers out of their wallets.
2. As of March 2006, an estimated 12 million unauthorized migrants were in the U.S. As of May 2005, "unauthorized workers" made up approximately 4.3 percent of our labor force in the U.S. Some 57 percent of them are from Mexico, according to the Pew Report (*The Population Reference Bureau*).
3. In Europe, future outsourcing centers are predicted to include the Czech Republic, Poland, and Hungary.

Chapter Two

Scared and Depressed

In a recent online poll 49 percent of all the respondents said that offshoring had "a somewhat negative" impact on employee morale, while an additional 37 percent said the impact was "extremely negative." The reason these developments matter so greatly to job-hunting and job-hunters in this twenty-first century is precisely this issue of "morale." Outsourcing, or the threat of it, is the biggest kick-in-the-head to job-hunters' morale in a long time.

However, the U.S. is not alone in these fears. Job-hunters in other countries are also afraid of outsourcing, or any variation on that theme. In Europe, they are afraid of their jobs being taken away when less expensive workers from other nations come to their shores. French voters, for example, overwhelmingly turned down ratification of the European Union constitution on May 30, 2005, in part because of their fears about some mythical "Polish plumber"—symbol of the workers from eastern EU countries who are increasingly free to move west, as to France, and are willing to work for lower pay than French workers.

Yes, job-hunters are afraid. The $64 million question: just how realistic are these fears?

Good question! One U.S. report cautions:

> "Despite numerous efforts, both public and private sector agencies have yet to determine a clear accurate measure of how many U.S. jobs are being lost to outsourcing, or how many might be lost in the future."[4]

In the absence of concrete data, *fear* has given birth to fantastical estimates of how many U.S. jobs could potentially be lost to outsourcing in the future. Such estimates run as high as 14.1 million U.S. jobs.

The reality? Actual U.S. outsourcing-job-losses to date appear to total a mere 500,000 jobs, out of the 143,700,000 jobs that are in the U.S. workforce currently.

---

4. "Outsourcing Statistics in Perspective," from the Center for American Progress.

And experts' predictions of the actual number of U.S. jobs that *will* be lost annually in the future, hover around 220,000[5]— which works out to mean: only two-hundredths of 1 percent of the U.S. workforce stand to lose their jobs to outsourcing.

Bogeyman, indeed!

The Nature of the Job-Market:
4. Rejection Shock

Most of us don't understand the nature of the job-market until we bump our head or stub our toe on that nature. High school or college doesn't prepare us for it. Only out there amid the hard knocks of life do we begin to slowly and painstakingly piece this information together, usually completing the task by the time we're, oh, 65 or 70. Earlier than that, the way the job-market behaves may come as a stunning surprise. Our response is usually shock.

We send out 500 resumes, and don't even get a nibble. *Shock.* Rejection shock.

In addition, if we've been fired, laid-off, or "made redundant" we will also be hurt, dejected, angry, and aghast.[6]

And especially so, if we had worked at that place for quite a number of years, given them our loyalty and our best, and expected to receive their loyalty in return—but they let us go, anyway.

If this happened to you, you are suffering from "Rejection Shock." And you are suffering from it because (*among other things*) you didn't expect to be treated this way. In fact, you didn't think *The Job-Market* ever functioned this way.

But it does.

And that's because employers "call the shots." The old adage— "Follow the money, then you'll know who has the power" or, for short, "Follow the money, find the power"—applies to the job-hunting business tenfold.

---

5. "Outsourcing Statistics in Perspective," from the Center for American Progress.
6. I've been fired twice, myself, once when I was 22, and once when I was 41 years old. In the world of work today, you can get fired for "screwing up" on the job, of course, but you also get fired (or laid off) for absolutely no comprehensible reason at all—even when you're doing an excellent job.

"Job-hunting" is *a business*, like any other, of course. Lots of people make a living off it: career counselors or coaches, newspapers, websites, employment agencies, recruiters, publishers, conference and event planners, human resource experts and writers, executive search firms, etc., etc. And in most cases it is employers' money, not yours, that maintains and drives all this apparatus.

Therefore it is they who have the power, to determine the rules of the game. This simple fact explains why parts of the whole job-hunting system will drive you *nuts*. It wasn't built for you— or me. It was built by and for *them*. This results in the following six contrasts:

1. You want the job-market to be *a hiring game*. But the employer regards it as *an elimination game*—until the very last phase. They're looking at that huge stack of resumes on their desk, with a view—first of all—to finding out who they can eliminate.

2. You want the employer to be taking lots of initiative toward finding you, but the employer generally prefers that it be you who takes the initiative, toward finding *them*.

3. In being considered for a job, you want your solid past performance—shown on your resume—to be *all that gets weighed*, but the employer weighs your whole behavior as they glimpse it from their first interaction with you, to the last.

4. You want the employer to acknowledge receipt of your resume—particularly if you post it *right on their website*, but the employer generally feels too swamped with other things, to have time to do that.

5. You want to go into the interview with their being curious to know more about *you*, but the employer is much more curious about what you know about *them*. (*One IBM recruiter I know once began an interview with a graduating senior, with the question, "What does IBM stand for?" The student hadn't even done that much research on the company, so he had to mumble, "I don't know." The interview was over.*) Employers don't like blind dates.

6. And—the *major* contrast in the whole job-market—you want to hunt for a job in a certain way, but the employer actually hunts for (someone like) you in the exact opposite way.

We can illustrate this, in a nutshell, with a simple diagram:

Many If Not Most Employers Hunt for Job-Hunters in the Exact Opposite Way from How Most Job-Hunters Hunt for Them

The Way a Typical Employer Prefers to Fill a Vacancy

1 *From Within:* Promotion of a full-time employee, or promotion of a present part-time employee, or hiring a former consultant for in-house or contract work, or hiring a former "temp" full-time. Employer's thoughts: *"I want to hire someone whose work I have already seen."* (A low-risk strategy for the employer.)

Implication for Job-Hunters: See if you can get hired at an organization you have chosen—as a temp, contract worker, or consultant—aiming at a full-time position only later (or not at all).

2 *Using Proof:* Hiring an Unknown Job-Hunter who brings proof of what he or she can do, with regards to the skills needed.

Implication for Job-Hunters: If you are a programmer, bring a program you have done—with its code; if you are a photographer, bring photos; if you are a counselor, bring a case study with you; etc.

5

3 *Using a Best Friend or Business Colleague:* Hiring someone whose work a trusted friend of yours has seen (perhaps they worked for him or her).

Implications for Job-Hunters: Find someone who knows the person-who-has-the-power-to-hire at your target organization, who also knows your work and will introduce you two.

4

4 *Using an Agency They Trust:* This may be a recruiter or search firm the employer has hired; or from a private employment agency—both of which have checked you out, on behalf of the employer.

3

5 *Using an Ad They Have Placed* (online or in newspapers, etc.).

2

6 *Using a Resume:* Even if the resume was unsolicited (if the employer is desperate).

1

The Way a Typical Job-Hunter Prefers to Fill a Vacancy

If you understood this diagram, immediately, great!—since it is crucial to understanding the job-hunt, and the job-market. But just in case you didn't, let me elaborate upon it, just a little.

Let's approach it from a different angle. Instead of the triangle diagram, let's start with two lists.

1. How job-hunters (generally speaking) prefer to look for employers.

2. How employers (generally speaking) prefer to look for job-hunters.

And let's put the two lists side by side (next page).

At first, it sounds like both parties go hunting, in exactly the same way. Ah, if only it were so!

What's the problem? Well, it has to do with the nature of lists.

LISTS
By themselves, lists are pretty useless. They're mostly just a hodgepodge of information bits, in no particular order, like grains of sand on the beach. A list is only really useful when it has been prioritized in some order: let us say of importance to you, or time it takes, or money it costs, or meaning, or frequency of use, or whatever.

Here, the two lists don't mean a thing until we ask the crucial question, *"And in what order of preference?"*

So, let's reprint these two columns (page 31), but now in order of *preference*—the job-hunter's or the career-changer's preference. And then employers' preference. It all comes out looking like this:

---

7. Resumes here is a broad umbrella term, under which is included all paper or electronic forms of approaches to employers: e.g., resumes, electronic keyword or cyber resumes, cover letters, a mailed career profile, and/or a Q (for qualifications) letter, wherein you list the qualifications a company's ad said they were looking for, and in a parallel column, side by side, the matching qualification you have.

A Job-Hunter's Alternatives	An Employer's Alternatives
Resumes[7] Using a resume to get invited in, for an interview	**Resumes**[7] Reading resumes, in order to decide who to invite in, for an interview
Colleagues Asking friends about job vacancies where they work	**Colleagues** Asking colleagues about employees, past or present, where those colleagues work
Referrals Asking friends about job vacancies they may know of, at *other* workplaces	**Referrals** Asking colleagues about employees they might know of, at *other* workplaces
Ads Answering an ad in a newspaper, or a posting on the Internet	**Ads** Placing an ad in a newspaper, or posting it on the Internet
Agencies Using an agency—private *(executive search firms, college placement offices, etc.)* or public, federal, state, or local employment agencies, to find a vacancy	**Agencies** Using an agency—private *(executive search firms, college placement offices, etc.)* or public, federal, state, or local employment agencies, to list a vacancy
Contacts Using a friend or business colleague for a direct introduction to employers (specifically, the person-who-has-the-power-to-hire)	**Contacts** Using a friend or business colleague for a direct introduction to prospective employees
Drop-Ins with Proof In an interview, initiated by the job-hunter, showing proof of what that job-hunter can do	**Drop-Ins with Proof** In an interview, initiated by the job-hunter, asking for proof of what the job-hunter can do
Inside the Company Getting inside a company as a temp worker, short-term contract worker, volunteer, or whatever, and hoping you will then be "hired from within" because you are already working there	**Inside the Company** "Hiring or promoting from within"—inside their company, either a present employee or a temp worker, or short-term contract worker, or volunteer, who is already working there

A Job-Hunter's Alternatives **In order of preference** *When looking for someone*	An Employer's Alternatives **In order of preference** *When looking for someone*
1. Resumes Using a resume to get invited in, for an interview	**1. Inside the Company** "Hiring or promoting from within"—inside their company, either a present employee or a temp worker, or short-term contract worker, or volunteer, who is already working there
2. Ads Answering an ad in a newspaper, or a posting on the Internet	**2. Colleagues** Asking colleagues about employees, past or present, where those colleagues work
3. Agencies Using an agency—private *(executive search firms, college placement offices, etc.)* or public, federal, state, or local employment agencies, to find a vacancy	**3. Referrals** Asking colleagues about employees they might know of, at *other* workplaces
4. Colleagues Asking friends about job vacancies where they work	**4. Drop-Ins with Proof** In an interview, initiated by the job-hunter, asking for proof of what the job-hunter can do
5. Referrals Asking friends about job vacancies they may know of, at *other* workplaces	**5. Contacts** Using a friend or business colleague for a direct introduction to prospective employees
6. Contacts Using a friend or business colleague for a direct introduction to employers (specifically, the person-who-has-the-power-to-hire-you-for-the-job-you-want)	**6. Agencies** Using an agency—private *(executive search firms, college placement offices, etc.)* or public, federal, state, or local employment agencies, to list a vacancy
7. Drop-Ins with Proof In an interview, initiated by the job-hunter, showing proof of what that job-hunter can do	**7. Ads** Placing an ad in a newspaper, or posting it on the Internet
8. Inside the Company Getting inside a company as a temp worker, short-term contract worker, volunteer, or whatever, and hoping you will eventually be "hired from within" because you are already working there	**8. Resumes** Reading resumes, in order to decide who to invite in, for an interview

Now, what does this all add up to? Well, I can tell you first of all what it *doesn't* mean. It doesn't mean that employers are *the bad guys*, nor does it mean that you must play *victim*. It's simply *the way things are*.

What it does mean is that you can push your own job-hunt or career-change toward greater success, if you follow this simple, now obvious, rule:

> To meet up with employers, study what employers do, go where employers go, adapt your behavior to theirs.

So, what have we learned here about the job-market and the job-hunt, that school never bothered to teach us, about how to adapt our behavior to employers' behavior?

Well, if they see job-hunting as an elimination game, you must take care not to put *anything* in your resume that would give the employer pause, and cause them to eliminate you. (Under the general employers' rubric: *When in doubt, screen them out.*)

If they want you to take lots of initiative, you must not just sit at home waiting for God to prove He loves you. Yours must be a self-directed search. And you must know as much as possible about the job-hunt, from the employer's point of view.

If they are weighing your whole interaction with them, rather than just your resume, you must think through the significance of everything you do. Employers operate intuitively on the principle of *microcosm equals macrocosm*. That is, what you do in some small *universe* reveals how you will act in a larger universe. Small job-hunting *universes* are such things as: Are you late for an appointment? Do you let the interviewer talk half the time? Do you treat everyone with respect and courtesy? Do you write a thank-you note after the interview—not only to them, but to the receptionist, secretary, and whoever else you interacted with, there—by name? (It helps if you collect their business cards while you are there, and talk with them.)

If they often don't have the time to acknowledge your resume, do you at least put it right in their path, where they could almost stumble over it? For example, on their very own website, or on a niche site devoted to the kinds of jobs that you are seeking.

If they don't like blind dates, do you do an impressive amount of research on the organization *before* you go in for an interview? Do you know what the organization does, what its product or services are, its history, its challenges, or the whole industry's current or future challenges? *(One time I had lunch with an employer friend who was grousing about the job applicants he had been encountering: "I'm so tired," he said, "of job-hunters who walk in here and say, 'Uh, what do you guys do?' that the very next person who comes in here and has actually done some research about us, I'm going to hire on the spot." The next week he phoned me, and said, "Well, I did it.")* Don't ever underestimate how desperate organizations are to be loved.

If they prefer that you approach them through a mutual friend, if they want someone to vouch for you—be it someone already working there, or someone working for a friend of theirs, or an impressive friend or business colleague of yours—so they aren't dependent just on their own impressions, do you search for such persons, using your "contacts" gathered through "networking" (or as I prefer to call it, "your grapevine") rather than just sending them a resume?

And if they like to see proof of your work, do you scratch your head to come up with some ingenious way to do that? *(I knew a programmer who applied for a vacancy in San Antonio. He was one of 19 applicants but he got the job, because he was the only one who thought to bring in 20 pages of code he had written.)* This kind of proof is easy, of course, for artists; they have portfolios. So do many other job-hunters, these days. And, let us not forget, video resumes are actually starting to be popular with some employers, so if you—for example—built, created, fashioned something large, like a house, or something beautiful, like a garden, you can show it in the video.

The Nature of the Job Market:
5. Nobody's Job Is Safe Anymore

The most useful thing you can do is to adopt, ahead of time, what we might call *a philosophy of work*. That philosophy should have, at a minimum, five points:

1. The typical job these days is best viewed as a temp job. That is, *of uncertain length*. If you work for someone else, as 90 percent

of the U.S. workforce does, then how long your job lasts is up to the people you work for, and not just you. Your job can end at any time and without warning. Therefore, you must always be mentally prepared to go out job-hunting again, at the drop of a hat.

2. The typical job these days is best viewed as **a seminar.** Almost every job these days is moving and changing so fast in its content or form, that there is a lot you will have to learn on the job, not only when you begin but throughout the whole time you are there. You would be wise not to think of your job just in terms of what you can accomplish. You must look at it in terms of what you can learn, or did learn, while you are there. If you want to be a prized employee, you must not only be *ready* to learn, but *eager* to learn. And, if it is true, you must emphasize to every would-be employer how much you love to learn new stuff, new tasks and procedures, and how fast you pick up new stuff.

3. The typical job these days is best viewed as **an adventure.** If you end up working for an organization that is of any size, it is very likely that the dramas that will be played out there, daily, weekly, and monthly, will rival any soap opera on television. Power plays! Ambition! Double-dealing! Cheating! Strange alliances! Rumors! Betrayal! Revolution! Overthrow! Sudden plot twists, that no one could have predicted! Sometimes you'll love it. Sometimes you'll hate it.

4. The typical job these days is best viewed as **one where the satisfaction lies in the work itself,** and not in some hoped-for future reward. In the old days, most of us hoped we would not only find work we enjoyed, but also work where we were appreciated, saluted, singled out, and praised to the skies. In other words, we looked for love, where we worked. And a raise. And a promotion. Unfortunately, despite your best research and hopes during your job-hunt, you may end up in a job where your bosses fail to recognize or acknowledge the fine contribution that you are making to the organization, leaving you feeling unloved and unappreciated, until—finally—even after many months or years, you may be suddenly let go, and without warning, as they cite a business turndown,

merger, bankruptcy, the need they have for *new blood*, reduced costs, or the full moon.

5. You need to approach any job with the philosophy that **it can be transformed**. No job is set in stone, just as it is. Your power lies in your conviction that you can, you may, you must, transform that job by the attitude you bring with you. And by the grace of God.

The Nature of the Job-Market:
6. The Way Things Truly Are

1. Nobody owes you a job.

2. You have to fight to get a job. *("Fight" means "persevere," "use ingenuity," "compete.")*

3. You have to fight to keep a job. Loyalty, years of service, or personal friendship with the boss does not in any way guarantee you a job at that place for the rest of your life.

4. Your employers may lay you off, or fire you, anytime they want to. They may do this because they have run out of money, and can't afford you anymore. They may do this because they are forced to outsource your job. They may do this because they have to decrease the size of their business, or are going out of business. They may do this because they find your skills do not match the work that they need to have done. Or they may do this because they have a personality conflict with you.

5. You may quit anytime you want to.

6. Your employers may fire you, or lay you off, without any warning or much notice at all to you, dumping you unceremoniously out on the street.

7. You may quit without any warning or much notice at all to your employer, leaving them high and dry.

8. If you are fired, your former employer may do everything in the world to help you find other employment, or may do nothing.

9. If you quit, you may do everything you can to help your employer find a suitable replacement, or you may do nothing.

10. As you look back, you may feel that your employer treated you very well, in accordance with their stated values—or you may feel that your employers treated you very badly, in total contradiction of their stated values.

11. If *you* were the only one who was fired or let go, the other employees may promise they will fight to save your job, but you need to be prepared for the fact that when the chips are down, they may actually do nothing to help you. You may feel very angry. You may feel very alone.

12. Nonetheless, you remain a rare and unique individual, no matter how the world of work treats you. Your worth is not defined simply by your work, but by your spirit, your heart, and your compassion toward others.

The Source of Your Hope: Alternatives

You're out of work. You're job-hunting, or contemplating a change in careers. But suppose you know:

At least two alternative ways of finding out what your skills are.

At least two alternative ways of describing each skill.

At least two alternative ways of deciding which skills are most important.

At least two alternative ways in which you would enjoy using these skills.

At least two alternative ways of uncovering any vacancies that may exist.

At least two alternative ways of constructing your resume, if you decide to use one.

At least two alternative *target* organizations that you can go after.

At least two alternative ways of going after those prospective employers.

At least two alternative people you could approach within each *target* organization, to get hired.

At least two ways you can get in to see them.

At least two alternative job titles for the kind of work that you are looking for.

At least two alternative ways of conducting the interview with them.

At least two alternative ways of negotiating salary, once they make it clear they like you—and you decide that you like them.

And so forth. And so on.

The above list isn't a *Wouldn't it be nice, if . . .* list.

These alternatives do exist. If you want to survive in the twenty-first century, your job is to know them, thoroughly, so that you will have some alternative "up your sleeve" for every step of the way. That way, you will have a delicious freedom. That way you also have hope. And in the job-hunt, as in Life, hope is everything. It is the one factor that keeps you going, when all else fails. That's why this book is all essentially a Book of Hope—masquerading as a job-hunting manual.

38

The Things
School Never Taught Us
About the Job-Hunt:

How to Deal with Handicaps

Most of us think that when we go job-hunting, we have some special handicap (hidden or obvious) that is going to keep us from getting a job. We think:

I have a physical handicap *or*
I have a mental handicap *or*
I never graduated from high school *or*
I never graduated from college *or*
I am just graduating *or*
I just graduated a year ago *or*
I graduated way too long ago *or*
I am a self-made woman *or*
I am a self-made man *or*
I am too beautiful *or*
I am too handsome *or*
I am too ugly *or*
I am too fat *or*
I am too thin *or*
I am too old *or*
I am too young *or*
I have only had one employer in life *or*

I have hopped from job to job too often *or*

I am too near retirement *or*

I am too wet behind the ears *or*

I have a prison record *or*

I have a psychiatric history *or*

I have not had enough education *or*

I have too much education and am overqualified *or*

I am an Arab *or*

I am Hispanic *or*

I am Black *or*

I am Asian *or*

I speak heavily accented English *or*

I speak no English *or*

I am too much of a specialist *or*

I am too much of a generalist *or*

I am ex-clergy *or*

I am ex-military *or*

I am too assertive *or*

I am too shy *or*

I have only worked for volunteer organizations *or*

I have only worked for small organizations *or*

I have only worked for a large organization *or*

I have only worked for the government *or*

I come from a very different culture or background *or*

I come from another industry *or*

I come from another planet.

(In other words, there are only about three weeks in any of our lives, when we are employable! *Just kidding!*)

If you have a handicap that you think will keep employers from hiring you, take heart! No matter what handicap you have, or think you have, it cannot possibly keep you from getting hired. It will only keep you from getting hired *at some places*.

There is a *mantra* you should keep repeating to yourself again and again, as you go job-hunting:

> **"There is no such thing as 'employers.'**
> **There are at least two different**
> **kinds of employers** *out there*:
>
> **Those who are interested in hiring me**
> for what I *can* do;
> and
> **Those who are not.**
>
> With the latter I should thank them for their time,
> and ask if they know of any other employers
> who might be interested in someone with my skills.
>
> Then, gently take my leave.
> And write and mail them a thank-you note
> **that very night."**

You never know what may occur to them the next day, of some way in which they can help you. A thank-you note jogs their memory.

Now, the biggest handicap any of us can have is our attitude toward our handicap. So, I would like you to think through, with me, what it means to say, "I have a handicap."

First of all, it speaks to the prejudice of some employers. For example, "I'm fat" doesn't necessarily keep you from doing anything. So if an employer won't hire you because of that, it's technically not a handicap that we're talking about; it's a *prejudice*.

A real handicap means there are some things that you can't do. So, let's talk about *that*. Let's begin with however many skills there are, in the world. Nobody knows the number, so let's make one up. Let's say there are 4,341 skills in the world. How many of those 4,341 do you think the average person has? Nobody knows the answer, so let's make one up. Let's say the average person has 1,341 skills. That's a lot. That's 1,341 things the average person *can* do. Now, my question to you: is this average person handicapped?

The answer, of course, is *Yes*. 4,341 minus 1,341 leaves 3,000 things the average person *can't* do. The average person—no, make that: *everybody*—is handicapped. Everybody.

So if, when you go job-hunting, you think of yourself as *handicapped*, then I would agree. But so is everyone. So what? What's so special about your handicap, compared with others'? The answer is *Nothing.* Unless—*unless*—you are obsessed with the fact that you are handicapped, and so disheartened by what you *can't* do, that you have forgotten all the things you *can* do. Unless you're thinking of all the reasons why employers might not hire you, instead of all the reasons why employers would. Unless you're going about your job-hunt feeling like *a job beggar*, rather than as *a resource person.*[1]

Here's a useful exercise for all of us Handicapped Job-hunters or Career-Changers: take a large piece of paper and divide it into two columns, viz.,

Things I Can't Do	Things I **CAN** Do

Then, look at the (*transferable/functional*) skills list on the next page, and copy as many as you choose onto these lists, putting each skill in the proper column, depending on whether you *can* do this skill, or *cannot.* (*Or not yet, anyway.*) Use additional sheets, as needed.

---

1. This brilliant distinction was coined by Daniel Porot, *the* job expert in Europe.

A List of 246 Skills as Verbs

achieving	acting	adapting	addressing	administering
advising	analyzing	anticipating	arbitrating	arranging
ascertaining	assembling	assessing	attaining	auditing
budgeting	building	calculating	charting	checking
classifying	coaching	collecting	communicating	compiling
completing	composing	computing	conceptualizing	conducting
conserving	consolidating	constructing	controlling	coordinating
coping	counseling	creating	deciding	defining
delivering	designing	detailing	detecting	determining
developing	devising	diagnosing	digging	directing
discovering	dispensing	displaying	disproving	dissecting
distributing	diverting	dramatizing	drawing	driving
editing	eliminating	empathizing	enforcing	establishing
estimating	evaluating	examining	expanding	experimenting
explaining	expressing	extracting	filing	financing
fixing	following	formulating	founding	gathering
generating	getting	giving	guiding	handling
having responsibility	heading	helping	hypothesizing	identifying
illustrating	imagining	implementing	improving	improvising
increasing	influencing	informing	initiating	innovating
inspecting	inspiring	installing	instituting	instructing
integrating	interpreting	interviewing	intuiting	inventing
inventorying	investigating	judging	keeping	leading
learning	lecturing	lifting	listening	logging
maintaining	making	managing	manipulating	mediating
meeting	memorizing	mentoring	modeling	monitoring
motivating	navigating	negotiating	observing	obtaining
offering	operating	ordering	organizing	originating
overseeing	painting	perceiving	performing	persuading
photographing	piloting	planning	playing	predicting
preparing	prescribing	presenting	printing	problem solving
processing	producing	programming	projecting	promoting
proofreading	protecting	providing	publicizing	purchasing
questioning	raising	reading	realizing	reasoning
receiving	recommending	reconciling	recording	recruiting
reducing	referring	rehabilitating	relating	remembering
rendering	repairing	reporting	representing	researching
resolving	responding	restoring	retrieving	reviewing
risking	scheduling	selecting	selling	sensing
separating	serving	setting	setting-up	sewing
shaping	sharing	showing	singing	sketching
solving	sorting	speaking	studying	summarizing
supervising	supplying	symbolizing	synergizing	synthesizing
systematizing	taking instructions	talking	teaching	team-building
telling	tending	testing & proving	training	transcribing
translating	traveling	treating	trouble-shooting	tutoring
typing	umpiring	understanding	understudying	undertaking
unifying	uniting	upgrading	using	utilizing
verbalizing	washing	weighing	winning	working
writing				

When you are done with these two lists, pick out the five top things that you *can* do, and *love* to do; and think of some illustrations and examples of how you demonstrated that, in the past.

What about the things you *can't* do? If your particular handicap or disability has a name, look it up on the Internet. If your issue is mobility, or lack thereof, the ADA may be of help to you. See a companion book to this one: *Job-Hunting for the So-Called Handicapped, or People Who Have Disabilities*, by Dale Susan Brown, and me, which explains all this at length.

Incidentally, there is one handicap that people rarely talk about, and yet it affects, if not job-performance, the job-hunt itself. And that is, *Shyness*. So, let's close this chapter by taking a look at that handicap, and discussing how to deal with it.

A WORD TO THOSE WHO ARE SHY

The late John Crystal often had to counsel the shy. They were often *frightened* at the whole idea of going to talk to people for information, never mind for hiring. So John developed a system to help the shy. He suggested that before you even begin doing any Informational Interviewing, you first go out and talk to people about *anything* just to get good at *talking to people*. Thousands of job-hunters and career-changers have followed his advice, over the past thirty years, and found it really helps. Indeed, people who have followed John's advice in this regard have had a success rate of 86 percent in finding a job—and not just any job, but *the* job or new career that they were looking for.

Daniel Porot, Europe's premiere job-hunting expert, has taken John's system, and brought some organization to it. He observed that John was really recommending three types of interviews: this interview we are talking about, just for practice. Then Informational Interviewing. And finally, of course, the hiring-interview. Daniel decided to call these three the *"The PIE Method,"* which has now helped thousands of job-hunters and career-changers in both the U.S. and in Europe.[2]

Why is it called *"PIE"*?

---

2. Daniel has summarized his system in a book published here in the U.S. in 1996: it is called *The PIE Method for Career Success: A Unique Way to Find Your Ideal Job,* and it is available from its publisher, JIST Works, Inc., 720 North Park Avenue, Indianapolis, IN 46202-3431. Phone 317-264-3720. Fax 317-264-3709. It is a fantastic book, and I give it my highest recommendation. Daniel has a wonderful website of "career games," at www.careergames.com. Netscape is the preferred browser when using that site.

SHYNESS VS. ENTHUSIASM

Well, I said it before, but I'm going to say it again. Throughout the job-hunt and career-change, the key to informational "interviewing" is not found in memorizing a dozen questions about what you're supposed to say.

No, the key is just this one thing: now and always, be *sure* you are talking about something you feel *passionate about.*

Enthusiasm is the key—to *enjoying* "interviewing," and conducting *effective* interviews, at any level. What this exercise teaches us is that shyness always loses its power and its painful self-consciousness—*if* and *when* you are talking about something *you love.*

For example, if you love gardens you will forget all about your shyness when you're talking to someone else about gardens and flowers. *"You ever been to Butchart Gardens?"*

If you love movies, you'll forget all about your shyness when you're talking to someone else about movies. *"I just hated that scene where they . . ."*

If you love computers, then you will forget all about your shyness when you're talking to someone else about computers. *"Do you work on a Mac or a PC?"*

That's why it is important that it be your enthusiasms that you are exploring and pursuing in these conversations with others.

P is for the *warm-up* phase. John Crystal named this warm-up "The Practice Field Survey."[3] Daniel Porot calls it **P** for *pleasure.*

I is for "Informational Interviewing."

E is for the employment interview with the-person-who-has-the-power-to-hire-you.

How do you use this **P** for *practice* to get comfortable about going out and talking to people *one-on-one?*

This is achieved by choosing a topic—*any* topic, however silly or trivial—that is a pleasure for you to talk about with your friends, or family. To avoid anxiety, it should not be connected to any present or future careers that you are considering. Rather, the kinds of topics that work best, for this exercise, are:

- **a hobby** you *love,* such as skiing, bridge playing, exercise, computers, etc.

---

3. If you want further instructions about this whole process, I refer you to "The Practice Field Survey," pp. 187–196, in *Where Do I Go from Here with My Life?* by John Crystal and friend. Ten Speed Press, Box 7123, Berkeley, CA 94707.

	Pleasure	**Information**	**Employment**
Initial:	**P**	**I**	**E**
Kind of Interview	Practice Field Survey	Informational Interviewing or Researching	Employment Interview or Hiring Interview
Purpose	To Get Used to Talking with People to Enjoy It; To "Penetrate" Networks	To Find Out If You'd Like a Job, Before You Go Trying to Get It	To Get Hired for the Work You Have Decided You Would Most Like to Do
How You Go to the Interview	You Can Take Somebody with You	By Yourself or You Can Take Somebody with You	By Yourself
Who You Talk To	Anyone Who Shares Your Enthusiasm About a (for You) Non-Job-Related Subject	A Worker Who Is Doing the Actual Work You Are Thinking About Doing	An Employer Who Has the Power to Hire You for the Job You Have Decided You Would Most Like to Do
How Long a Time You Ask for	10 Minutes (and DON'T run over—asking to see them at 11:50 a.m. may help keep you honest, since most employers have lunch appoint-ments at noon)	Ditto	
What You Ask Them	Any Curiosity You Have About Your Shared Interest or Enthusiasm	Any Questions You Have About This Job or This Kind of Work	You Tell Them What It Is You Like About Their Organization and What Kind of Work You Are Looking For

	Pleasure	Information	Employment
Initial:	**P**	**I**	**E**
What You Ask Them *(continued)*	If Nothing Occurs to You, Ask: 1. How did you start, with this hobby, interest, etc.? 2. What excites or interests you the most about it? 3. What do you find is the thing you like the least about it? 4. Who else do you know of who shares this interest, hobby, or enthusiasm, or could tell me more about my curiosity? a. Can I go and see them? b. May I mention that it was you who suggested I see them? c. May I say that you recommended them? *Get their name and address*	If Nothing Occurs to You, Ask: 1. How did you get interested in this work and how did you get hired? 2. What excites or interests you the most about it? 3. What do you find is the thing you like the least about it? 4. Who else do you know of who does this kind of work, or similar work but with this difference: _____? 5. What kinds of challenges or problems do you have to deal with in this job? 6. What skills do you need in order to meet those challenges or problems? *Get their name and address*	You tell them the kinds of challenges you like to deal with. What skills you have to deal with those challenges. What experience you have had in dealing with those challenges in the past.
AFTERWARD: That Same Night	SEND A THANK-YOU NOTE	SEND A THANK-YOU NOTE	SEND A THANK-YOU NOTE

- **any leisure-time enthusiasm** of yours, such as a movie you just saw, that you liked a lot
- **a long-time curiosity,** such as how do they predict the weather, or what policemen do
- **an aspect of the town or city you live in,** such as a new shopping mall that just opened
- **an issue** you feel strongly about, such as the homeless, AIDS sufferers, ecology, peace, health, etc.

There is only one condition about choosing a topic: it should be something you *love* to talk about with other people: a subject you know nothing about, but you feel a great deal of enthusiasm for, is far preferable to something you know an awful lot about, but it puts you to sleep.

Having identified your enthusiasm, you then need to go talk to someone who is as enthusiastic about this thing, as you are. *For best results with your later job-hunt, this should be someone you don't already know.* Use the yellow pages, ask around among your friends and family, *who do you know that loves to talk about this?* It's relatively easy to find the kind of person you're looking for.

You love to talk about skiing? *Try a ski-clothes store, or a skiing instructor.* You love to talk about writing? *Try a professor on a nearby college campus, who teaches English.* You love to talk about physical exercise? *Try a trainer, or someone who teaches physical therapy.*

Once you've identified someone you think shares your enthusiasm, you then go talk with them. When you are face-to-face with your *fellow enthusiast*, the first thing you must do is relieve their understandable anxiety. *Everyone* has had someone visit them who has stayed too long, who has worn out their welcome. If your *fellow enthusiast* is worried about you staying too long, they'll be so preoccupied with this that they won't hear a word you are saying.

So, when you first meet them, ask for *ten minutes of their time, only.* Period. Stop. Exclamation point. And watch your wrist-watch *like a hawk*, to be sure you stay no longer. *Never* stay longer, unless they *beg* you to. And I mean, *beg, beg, beg.*[4]

Once they've agreed to give you ten minutes, you tell them why you're there—that you're trying to get comfortable about talking with people, for information—and you understand that you two share a mutual interest, which is . . .

Then what? Well, a topic may have its own unique set of questions. For example, I love movies, so if I met someone who shared this interest, my

---

4. A polite, "Oh, do you have to go?" should be understood for what it is: politeness. Your response should be, "Yes, I promised to only take ten minutes of your time, and I want to keep to my word." This will almost always leave a *very* favorable impression behind you.

first question would be, "What movies have you seen lately?" And so on. If it's a topic you love, and often talk about, you'll *know* what kinds of questions you begin with. But, if no such questions come to mind, no matter how hard you try, the following ones have proved to be good conversation starters for thousands of job-hunters and career-changers before you, no matter what their topic or interest.

So, look these over, memorize them *(or copy them on a little card that fits in the palm of your hand)*, and give them a try:

QUESTIONS SHY PEOPLE CAN PRACTICE WITH

Addressed to the person you're doing the Practice Interviewing with:

- How did you get involved with/become interested in this? (*"This"* is the hobby, curiosity, aspect, issue, or enthusiasm, that you are so interested in.)
- What do you like the most about it?
- What do you like the least about it?
- Who else would you suggest I go talk to who shares this interest?
- Can I use your name?
- May I tell them it was you who recommended that I talk with them?
- *Then, choosing one person from the list of several names they may have given you, you say,* "Well, I think I will begin by going to talk to this person. Would you be willing to call ahead for me, so they will know who I am, when I go over there?"

Incidentally, during *this* Practice Interviewing, it's perfectly okay for you to take someone with you—preferably someone who is more outgoing than you feel you are. And on the first few interviews, let them take the lead in the conversation, while you watch to see how they do it.

Once it is *your turn* to conduct the interview, it will by that time usually be easy for you to figure out what to talk about.

Alone or with someone, keep at this Practice Interviewing until you feel very much at ease in talking with people and asking them questions about things you are curious about.

In all of this, *fun* is the key. If you're having fun, you're doing it right. If you're not having fun, you need to keep at it, until you are. It may take seeing four people. It may take ten. Or twenty. You'll know.

How to Deal with Handicaps

"This homework is a disgrace.
I'd like a note from your computer."

The Things
School Never Taught Us
About the Job-Hunt:

How Much Help
Is the Internet?

The Illusion

In the U.S. about two-thirds of us have access to the Internet.
If you have access to the Internet, *part of* your job-hunt or
career-change should depend on the Internet.

But never *all of* your job-hunt or career-change.

The Internet is too unreliable for that.

The Internet is good at creating illusions. The chief illusion for
job-hunters is: *if you have the Internet, your job-hunt is over; we will
do it all for you.*

The Internet is, in a sense, a stew, and many many people toss
whatever they choose into that stew. Sometimes what you'll find
there, is good—often very very good. But sometimes it's bad.
And sometimes it's downright ugly.

There are essentially five things the Internet can do for the
job-hunter or career-changer. The Internet's helpfulness in these
five areas varies greatly. So, we may divide the five into *the Good,
the Bad, and the Ugly.*

1. The Good. The Internet can help the job-hunter find tests
and counseling as to what fields or places might be best for him
or her. Some of these tests are excellent. They come in many
forms and flavors—skills tests, interests tests, values tests, psychological tests, etc.—and their names form a veritable alphabet
soup: SDS, MBTI, SII, CISS, and the like.

Of course, a lot depends on *why* you're taking these tests. If
you're hoping that the tests will tell you exactly what you should
do with your life, *forgeddit*! But if you're content with maybe
some *clues*, *hints*, and *vague hunches*, then tests can be useful.

There are rules about taking tests, and you will find them
fully discussed on page 162.

In the past, if you wanted to take them, you had to get dressed
and get yourself down to a community college counseling center, or career counselor's office, or state unemployment office, or
one-stop career center, or a Johnson O'Connor Human Engineering Laboratory—where the tests and the test administrators

can be found. You can still do that. Ask around, in your community, to see where such tests can be found.

But in this Internet Age, a new wrinkle has developed. If you have Internet access, career tests can now be plucked off the Internet, and taken by you in the privacy of your own home. *Our eyes light up! Now you're talking!*

Beyond tests and counseling sites, the Internet is extremely useful in a second way: helping you with your research, of fields, jobs, places, employers, etc.

You can do this research in a very quick way, just using your favorite search engine. Or you can do very thorough research. It's up to you. There are tutorials on the Internet, about how to find information on the Internet. Here are some, beginning with the tutorial that I like best.

► Search the Internet

A guide to finding information on the Internet; very informative
```
www.lib.berkeley.edu/TeachingLib/
    Guides/Internet/FindInfo.html
```
► Searching the Internet

Good article on Internet searches; also very informative and up-to-date page on search engines
```
www.sldirectory.com/search.html
www.sldirectory.com/searchf/engines.html#
```
► University at Albany Libraries

A Primer in Boolean Logic: Boolean Searching on the Internet
```
http://library.albany.edu/internet/
    boolean.html
```
► Bright Planet Tutorial

Guide to Effective Searching of the Internet
The Complete Source for Search Engines and Databases Tutorial
```
www.brightplanet.com/deepcontent/
    tutorials/search/index.asp
```
► Kids Research Tools (Wordsmythe, Britannica.com, etc.)

Like faith, the Internet is best approached with the eyes of a child.
```
www.rcls.org/ksearch.htm
```

► Rules for Conducting Informational Interviews in Order to Find Out About Fields and Jobs, Before You Ever Commit Yourself

    `http://danenet.wicip.org/jets/`
        `jet-9407-p.html`

► Guidelines for Informational Interviews

    `www.quintcareers.com/informational_`
        `interviewing.html`

The third good use of the Internet lies in making contacts with people you know, or want to know.

MySpace has become famous (or infamous) in this regard. It has millions and millions of members. It appeals particularly to teenagers, and to musicians, and to (dare I say it?) predators. The last has caused it to come under a cloud, and many Internet users are now leery of it. But there are other networking sites. I will mention two that I recommend (from the companion book to this one, *Job-Hunting on the Internet*, by Mark Emery Bolles and me).

LinkedIn
`www.linkedin.com`

LinkedIn is nothing less than an *excellent* business network site. In form, it is similar to the others; in implementation, superior. When you sign up (registration is free), you enter your basic information—field, job title, geographic area, and so on—and indicate what kind of connections you are looking for and what kind of incoming contacts you are willing to accept. For example, if you currently own a business, you could indicate that you are open to inquiries about employment at your business, but naturally you don't want people sending you job offers for yourself.

You then go on to invite people to enter your network—you cannot draw people in unless they actively want to be included. As the people that you know join, and the people *they* know join, your network grows. At LinkedIn, your network is defined as a maximum of four levels, or degrees, out to a friend of a friend of a friend of a friend. For example, if only five people join at each level, that is still a network of 625 people. In reality, it is likely to be far more.

LinkedIn also allows you to contact people who are not in your network, if they have said they are willing to accept such contacts (and naturally, you may allow such contacts, as well). Currently, LinkedIn has more than 74,000 such people. Anecdotally, the most connected person on the site has a network of 3,677 people. More than 50,000 of LinkedIn's registrants consider themselves job-hunters, even if their current employers do not.

Tribe
www.tribe.net

Tribe is very similar to LinkedIn, but takes a larger worldview. Why limit your network contacts to just business? What about if you needed to buy a used car—would you rather buy from a stranger or from a friend of a friend? If you were looking for a roommate, would you rather run a newspaper ad or find candidates among your network? If you needed a new dentist, whose recommendation would you trust?

This is what Tribe is about. As with other networking sites, you invite people to join, you have easy access out to four degrees, and so on. But at Tribe, your network—of course, here it is called your "tribe"—can be used for many purposes. Jobhunting is, of course, included, and the site even has job postings. But you also can use your tribe for buying and selling, housing, recommendations, special interests, and so on. There are even messaging forums, for common interest discussions among registrants.

Tribe, and its many uses, does bring up an important point: this is all about *trust*. When you are inviting people to join your tribe, you should only invite the people you know well, and trust. If a friend that you invited into your tribe sells another friend a used car with a blown engine, it's going to come back on *you*. The people you invite in are counting on your recommendation that *all* of the people you have invited to join are trustworthy, and so it goes, out through all *your* degrees and into *other* people's. Don't invite your sister's no-good kid, just to pad the numbers.

In fact, this applies to *all* of the networking sites. When you invite someone into your network, you are inviting them into not just *your* network but the networks of the hundreds and thousands of people who connect to you. These people are all—*every one of them*—depending on *your* judgment about those you have invited, just as you are depending on theirs. The system collapses if the people involved are not truthful, reliable, consistent, and principled.

2. The Bad. The Internet just is not that good about hooking up job-hunters with employers. If it works for you, great! But be prepared for the fact that it may not. I'm referring specifically here to the fourth and fifth uses of the Internet, in the service of job-hunting or career-changing: job-postings by employers, and resume-postings by job-hunters, like you and me. You saw the statistics, in an earlier chapter. Of course you're gonna try it; but don't get depressed if it just doesn't work.

3. The Ugly. Just using the Internet can expose you to a lot of annoyances, and even dangers, regardless of your age:

a. Way-too-much e-mail. It can take you half a day just to try to keep up with it.

b. Spam, which aims to part you from your money, with offers you never asked for, or downright fraudulent schemes.

c. Phishing, whereby thieves contact you by e-mail, pretending to be your bank, or credit cards, or financial services vendor, asking you to verify your account information. You click on the link they give you, which takes you to a place that amazingly duplicates the real site. It's not.

d. Identity-theft, which aims to part you from your credit cards, bank account, etc.

e. Predators and stalkers, preying upon the young and naïve, or adult innocents, who reveal too much about themselves on popular social network sites such as MySpace.com, or their own site, whereupon predators such as child-molesters, or adult con-men (and women) then contact them, pretending to be someone they're not.

All in all, the Internet is a wonderful aid to your job-hunt or career-change. You just have to be able to distinguish between the Good, the Bad, and the Ugly.[1]

---

1. See my website: www.jobhuntersbible.com. See also: *Job-Hunting on the Internet* (Fourth Edition) by Mark Emery Bolles and me (Berkeley, CA: Ten Speed Press, 2007). After May 2008, look for a revised edition (the Fifth) with a new title *(Job-Hunting Online)*. Same authors, though.

The Things
School Never Taught Us
About the Job-Hunt:

Resumes & Contacts

How to Get in to See an Employer

Rejection Shock

A **resume** is very attractive to an employer, but not for the reasons you think. It offers an easy way to cut down the time employers have to spend on job-hunters. It only takes a skilled human resource person about eight seconds to scan a resume (thirty seconds, if they're really dawdling), so getting rid of fifty job-hunters, I mean fifty *resumes*, takes only half an hour or less. Whereas, interviewing those fifty job-hunters in person would take a minimum of twenty-five hours. Great time savings!

A **resume** is very attractive to a job-hunter. It seems to offer an easy way to do your job-hunt, and to approach an employer. No maddening phone tag, no taking the bus, or driving the car, or sitting in someone's outer office for a blue moon, only to be rejected after all of that. No, with a resume you just take a piece of paper, summarize your qualifications, and mail it to the organization, if you have a particular target in mind. Or post it on the Web if you have no target and you want to cast a wide net—an *Inter*Net. And voilà!—so the myth goes—with your resume "out there," you will automatically find a job. In spite of the statistic that we already saw: *less than 10 percent of all job-hunters or career-changers actually find a job, when they start with their resume.*

Who perpetuates this myth of the magic resume? Well, everyone. For example, some employers—trying to get rid of you, will say, *"Send me your resume"* instead of *"goodbye"* as their way to close out the conversation. Of course, *sometimes* they really do want to see it! And, some coaches who know you will pay them for a concrete product, more than just for handholding and advice. And some resume websites, who know that having *content* on their sites (like, "how to write your resume") will hold visitors longer than just a list of job-postings. And job-hunting authors: some of whom emphatically tell you that a resume is the way to go, because it enables them to show off how good *they* are at writing a resume. And some of them are *very* good!

Of course this is a cynical reading of various parties' perpetuating of resumes; many simply believe, honestly and sincerely, that a resume works, and works superbly, and is the best way to job-hunt. *In spite of that 90 percent failure rate statistic.*

The Most Important Thing
School Should Have Taught Us

Simply this: Resumes and Interviewing are *not* two separate subjects, but one.

The primary purpose of a resume is to get yourself invited in for an interview *(with a prospective employer, of course).*

The primary purpose of that interview is to get yourself invited back for a second interview.

If you keep these two simple truths always in front of you, as you go about your job-hunt or career-change, you will be ahead of 97 percent of all other job-hunters or career-changers.

IMPORTANT TRUTHS ABOUT RESUMES

A resume is *one way* to get yourself invited in for an interview. There are other ways, even preferred ways, if your resume fails. Know what they are. *For example: getting introduced there, by a mutual acquaintance or friend (a contact of yours, a business contact, a personal contact or friend, a family contact, or anyone you've ever met and know well enough to have their name and address or phone number).*

A resume is more akin to a business card, than to a biography. Evaluate every item you are tempted to include in your resume by this one standard: "Will this item help to get me invited in? Or will this item seem too puzzling, or off-putting, or a red flag?"

I repeat: mention nothing (in your resume) that might keep you from getting invited in. If there is something you feel you would ultimately need to explain, or expand upon, save the explanation for the interview.

A resume *on paper* (not by e-mail) first presents itself to the fingers, before it presents itself to the eyes. Picture this scenario: an employer is going through a whole stack of resumes, and on average he or she is giving each resume about eight seconds of their time (true: we checked!). Then that resume goes either into a pile we might call "Forgeddit," or a pile we might call "Bears further investigation."

Yes, the employers' first impression of each resume is how it feels to their fingers, as they first pick it up. By *the message from their fingers* they are either prejudiced in your favor before they even start reading, or prejudiced against you. Before their eyes read even one line. Usually they are not even aware of *why*.

A resume to a particular employer is best not sent solely by e-mail, these days. That route has been overused, and abused; many employers, leery of viruses, will not even open attachments any more, such as your resume. Send it by e-mail if you must, but **always** send a nicer version of it by the postal service, or UPS, or FedEx, etc.—nicely laid out or formatted, as they say, on good paper; using a decent-sized font, size 12 or even 14 (makes it faster to read), etc.

"Depending on resumes" poses three dangers to your job-hunting health:

1. Resumes may create depression in you, and vastly lower your self-esteem. This is the greatest danger, by far, of depending on resumes. Why depression? Well, if it were just a matter of trying a job-hunting method that didn't work very well, it might be okay. You pick yourself up, and go on, still keeping good self-esteem. But in fact, the danger of resumes is that if you believe in them, and they don't work for you, you start to think something is really, really wrong with *you*. And if some of your friends tell you their resume actually got them a job *(not true: it actually got them an interview)*, you may feel lower than a snake's belly. Many job-hunters never snap out of the depression and feeling of worthlessness that follows. Every

resume should carry a warning label: "Using this may be hazardous to your mental health."

2. Resumes make you feel like they're *out there*, working for you. They make you feel as though you're really doing something about your job-hunt. But in fact they may be moribund or comatose. That is, they may not be getting read, at all, even when posted on an employer's own website. As for posting on general sites, well, Pete Weddle, an expert on recruiting, once got some resume sites on the Internet to tell him how many employers actually looked at the resumes on their sites. (Sit down, while I tell you the news.) A site that had 85,000 resumes posted: only 850 employers looked at *any* of those resumes in the previous three months before the survey. Another site with 59,283 resumes posted, only 1,366 employers looked at *any*, in the previous months. Another site with 40,000 resumes, only 400 employers in months. A site with 30,000 resumes, only 15 employers looked in, during the previous three months. So, you send out your resume or post it on the Internet, confident that employers are reading them, when—in a depressing number of cases—nobody is. Some employers, in fact, *hate* resumes (I kid you not). So many lies, on so many resumes. So much exaggeration and distortion of job-hunters' actual experience and knowledge (40 percent of the time, according to studies).

3. Depending on resumes may cause you to give up your job-hunt prematurely. Resumes can be a useful *part* of anybody's job-hunt, but they should never be your entire plan. You can send out tons of resumes, or post them on every resume site on the Internet, and not get a single nibble. Fifty-one percent of all job-hunters who base their job-hunt solely on mailing out or posting their resume, get discouraged, and abandon their job-hunt by the end of the second month. "Oh well," they say, "obviously there are no jobs out there." Au contraire, there are 30,000,000+ jobs out there, as we saw earlier in this book. Resumes are just the wrong way to find all but a portion of them.

Nonetheless, a resume still has its uses. Experts have been saying, for decades, that a resume is something you should never send ahead of you, but always leave behind you, after the interview. This is, of course, an oversimplification. But, taking its spirit, a resume does has a usefulness to you in helping you organize your own thoughts about yourself, your training, your record, your experience, your usefulness to a prospective employer. And, hand in hand with that, a resume has a usefulness to an employer, which is to jog her or his memory, *after* you've been there, when they are later trying to tell the other decision-makers at that organization, why he or she particularly favors you.

For guidance as to how to write your resume, go on the Internet and type "how to write a resume" into your favorite search engine (*e.g.*, **www.google.com** or **www.metacrawler.com**). Alternatively, type in the words "tips on writing a resume" or "keywords on an electronic resume" or "examples of resumes."

This will not only turn up free resources and advice on the Internet, but also the names of books, if you want to get *very* thorough. You should look particularly for books by Yana Parker and Susan Whitcomb.

There are no *rules* about the proper form for a resume, etc. The only question is, *If you send this resume of yours, to a place where you'd like to work, will it persuade the person who has the power to hire, there, to invite you in?* If the answer is, Yes, then it matters not what form it took.

I used to have a hobby of collecting "winning" resumes—that is, resumes that had actually gotten someone a job-interview and, ultimately, a job. I'm kind of playful by nature, so I would show these without comment, to employer friends of mine, over lunch. Many of them didn't like these winning resumes at all. "That resume will never get anyone a job," they would say. Then I would reply, "Sorry, you're wrong. It already has. I think what you mean is that it wouldn't get them a job *with you*."

The resume reproduced on the next page is a good example of what I mean; you did want an example, didn't you?

Jim Dyer, who had been in the U.S. Marines for twenty years, wanted a job as a salesman for heavy construction and mining equipment, thousands of miles from where he was then living. He devised the resume you see, and had just fifteen copies made. He mailed them out, he said, "to a grand total of seven before I got the job in the place I wanted!"

E. J. DYER   Street, City, Zip   Telephone No.

I SPEAK
THE LANGUAGE
OF
MEN
MACHINERY
AND
MANAGEMENT

. . .

OBJECTIVE: Sales of Heavy Equipment

QUALIFICATIONS   * Knowledge of heavy equipment, its use and maintenance.

                    * Ability to communicate with management and with men in the field.

                    * Ability to favorably introduce change in the form of new
                      equipment or new ideas . . . the ability to sell.

EXPERIENCE   * Maintained, shipped, budgeted and set allocation priorities for
                      85 pieces of heavy equipment as head of a 500-man organization
Men and   (1975-1977).
Machinery
                    * Constructed twelve field operation support complexes, employing
                      a 100-man crew and 19 pieces of heavy equipment (1965-1967).

                    * Jack-hammer operator, heavy construction (summers 1956-1957-1958)

    Management   * Planned, negotiated and executed large scale equipment purchases
                      on a nation to nation level (1972-1974).

    Sales   · Achieved field customer acceptance of two major new computer-
                      based systems:
                      —Equipment inventory control and repair parts expedite system
                        (1968-1971)
                      —Decision makers' training system (1977-1979).
                    * Proven leader . . . repeatedly elected or appointed to senior posts

EDUCATION   * B.A. Benedictine College, 1959. (Class President; Editor
                      Yearbook; "Who's Who in American Colleges").

                    * Naval War College, 1975. (Class President; Graduated "With
                      Highest Distinction").

                    * University of Maryland, 1973-1974. (Chinese Language).

                    * Middle Level Management Training Course, 1967-1968
                      (Class Standing: 1 of 97).

PERSONAL   * Family: Sharon and our sons Jim (11), Andy (8) and Matt (5)
                      desire to locate in a Mountain State by 1982, however, in
                      the interim will consider a position elsewhere in or outside
                      the United States . . . Health: Excellent . . . Birthdate: December
                      9, 1937 . . . Completing Military Service with the rank of
                      Lieutenant Colonel, U.S. Marine Corps.

SUMMARY   A seeker of challenge . . . experienced, proven and confident of
                    closing the sales for profit.

Like the employer who hired him, I loved this resume. Yet some of the employers I showed it to (*over lunch, as I said*) criticized it for using a picture or for being too long, or for being too short, etc. In other words, had Jim sent that resume to *them*, they wouldn't have even invited him in for an interview.

Trouble is, you don't know which employer likes *what*. That's why many job-hunters, if they use resumes, pray as they mail their resume: *Please, dear God, let them be employers who like resumes in general, and may the form of my resume appeal to those employers I care the most about, in particular.*

Alternatives to a classic resume. Many experts suggest that instead of sending a resume, you send just a "cover letter" instead, summarizing all that a longer resume might have covered. If you don't know what a cover letter is, or how to write it, the Internet can rescue you handily. Just type "cover letters" into your favorite search engine. You'll be surprised at how many tips, examples, etc., you find. Look particularly for Susan Ireland's free Cover Letter Guide (it's at `http://susanireland.com/coverletterwork.htm`). Incidentally, recent surveys have revealed that many employers prefer a cover letter to a resume.

Another alternative to a classic resume is a Job- or Career-Portfolio. A portfolio may be electronic (posted on the Internet) or on paper/a notebook/or in a large display case (as, with artists), of your accomplishments, experience, training, and commendations or awards, from the past. Painters have a portfolio, with samples of their work. You knew that. But portfolios are equally apt in other fields.

Instead of "portfolio" we might just call them "Evidence of What I Can Do and Have Done," or "Proof of Performance." One programmer I know applied for a job, and decided to bring in a kind of portfolio—about twenty to thirty pages of actual programming he had done. None of the other candidates brought in any evidence of what they could do. He got the job.

For guidance on how to prepare a job-portfolio, and what to include, type "job portfolios" into Google; you'll get a wealth of tips and information. I particularly recommend Martin Kimeldorf's site (`http://www.amby.com/kimeldorf/portfolio/`). Other names to remember (longtime advocates of career portfolios) are Kate Duttro and Carmen Croonquist. (Put their names into Google.) If you want to go deeper, like, to books, I recommend *The Career Portfolio Workbook: Using the Newest Tool in Your Job-Hunting Arsenal to Impress Employers and Land a Great Job!* by Frank Satterthwaite and Gary D'Orsi. There is also: *Proof of Performance: How to Build a Career Portfolio to Land a Great New Job* by Rick Nelles. Try your local bookstore, or online at `www.amazon.com` or `www.barnesandnoble.com`.

A STARTER KIT, FOR WRITING A RESUME
(If You Must)
OR FOR ANSWERING QUESTIONS
IN A BEHAVIORAL INTERVIEW

This is adapted, with the written permission of my friend Tom O'Neil, from an original document of his, which was and is copyright protected under the New Zealand Copyright Act (1994) © cv.co.nz 2001. You may contact Tom at www.cv.co.nz.

A resume is about your past. Here is a framework for recalling your past.

If you cannot think of any achievements under the categories below, don't be concerned, as the Flower Exercise later in this book will help you greatly.

For now, think of your working and personal experiences and skills that you believe you have innately, or have learned. What ones are you proud of? What things have you done in your life or work experience that no one else has done? Take some blank sheets of paper and fill in any answers that occur to you, please.

It is important to be quantitative when you do this
(e.g., mention dates, percents, dollars, brand names, etc.).

Volunteer, Community, and Unpaid Work

1. Have you completed any voluntary or unpaid work for any organization or company? (e.g., church, synagogue, mosque, school, community service, or special needs organization)

Educational

2. Did you work while you were studying? If so, did you receive any promotions or achievements in that role?
3. Did you gain any scholarships?
4. Were you involved in any committees, etc.?
5. Did you win any awards for study?
6. Did you have any high (e.g., A or above) grades? If so, what were the subjects—and grades?

Sales or Account Management

Have you ever been in sales? If so, what were some of your achievements? For example:

7. Have you ever consistently exceeded your set budget in that role? If so, by what percent or dollar value?
8. Have you exceeded your set budget in a particular month(s)/quarter(s) in a role? If so, by what percent or dollar value?
9. What level were you, compared to other sales professionals in your company? (e.g., "Number three out of twenty on the sales team")
10. Have you ever increased market share for your company? If so, by what percent or dollar value?
11. Have you ever brought in any major clients to your company?
12. What major clients are/were you responsible for managing and selling to?
13. Did you ever manage to generate repeat business or increase current business? If so, by what percent or dollar value?
14. Have you won any internal or external sales awards?
15. Did you develop any new successful promotional or marketing ideas that increased sales?

Administration, Customer Services, and Accounts

Have you ever been in customer service or helped run a business unit? If so:

16. Did you assist in reducing customer complaints, etc.?
17. Did you set up or improve any systems and/or processes?
18. Was there a quantifiable difference in the company or business unit when you first joined the business or project and when you completed the project or left the business?
19. Did you take any old administration- or paperwork-based systems and convert them to an IT-based system?

Responsibility

20. Have you ever been responsible for the purchase of any goods or services in some job? (e.g., air travel or PC acquisition)
21. Have you ever had any budget responsibility? If so, to what level? (e.g., "Responsible for division budget of $200,000 per annum.")
22. Have you ever been responsible for any staff oversight? If so, in what capacity and/or how many staff members were you responsible for?
23. Were you responsible for any official or unofficial training? If so, what type, for whom, and how many people have you trained? (e.g., "Responsible for training twelve new staff in customer service as well as in using the in-house computer system.")
24. Were you responsible for any official or unofficial coaching or mentoring of other staff?

Events or Conference Planning or Logistical Management

25. Have you organized any events or conferences? If so, how large were they (both people attending and total budget if possible) and where and when was the event(s) held?
26. Have you been involved in any major relocation projects?
27. Have you had responsibility with regard to any major suppliers? If so, who?

Computers, PCs, and Macs

28. What systems, software, and hardware experience do you have?
29. What software have you utilized?
30. Have you developed any websites or systems software? If so, what were they, and did it positively affect the business?
31. Were you involved in any special projects outside your job description?

Mechanical

32. Other than computers, have you had experience on any kinds of machines or equipment? Please list them together with the number of years.
33. If you ever worked on transportation devices, what were the airplane, farm equipment, truck, car, machine, or bike brands that you serviced, maintained, or repaired?

Building, Construction, Electrical, and Plumbing

34. If you ever worked in those fields, were there any major projects you have worked on? How much did the project(s) cost? (e.g., "Reception refurbishment—ABC Bank [Auckland Central Head Office] $1.2m.")

General

35. How long have you spent within any industry? (e.g., "Twelve years experience within the fashion industry.")
36. Were you promoted in any of your roles? If so, in what years and to which roles?
37. Was extra authority awarded to you after a period of time within a role? (e.g., "Commenced as receptionist; then, after three months, awarded by being given further clerical responsibilities including data entry and accounts payable.") It is not necessary that these responsibilities awarded to you should have changed your job title and/or salary.
38. Have you been asked to take part in any trainee management courses or management development programs?
39. Were you asked to get involved in any special projects outside your job description? Or, did you ever volunteer for such? What was the result?

Positive Feedback

40. Have you ever received any written or verbal client, customer, or managerial commendations or letters of praise?

41. Can you think of any occasions where you gave excellent customer service? If so, how did you know the customer was satisfied? (Also: What was the outcome? How did it benefit the company?)

42. Did you receive any awards within your company or industry? (e.g., "Acknowledged for support or service of clients or staff, etc.")

Memberships

43. Have you been a representative on any committees (e.g., health and safety committee)? Any special responsibilities there?

44. Do you belong or have you belonged to any professional clubs such as Toastmasters, Lions, or Rotary?

Published or Presented Work

45. Have you had any articles, papers, or features published in any magazines, journals, or books? If so, what publications and when?

46. Have you presented any topics at any conferences or completed any public speaking? If so, what subjects have you talked about and how large was the audience? List in detail.

Looking Ahead

- What value do you think you would add to a potential employer's business? How would you be "a resource" or even "a resource-broker" for them, rather than just "a job beggar"?
- How do you think you would stand out from other applicants who have an equal background?

When Going into a Behavioral Interview

It won't be enough to say, "I'm good at this or that." The interviewer will want to know specifics—when, where, how much—that kind of thing.

To Assist in Drawing Out Your Achievements:

If you are having trouble working out your achievements, complete this EASY task below for each role, starting with your current position and working backward.

E Experiences (What experiences have I had in this role?)

A Achievements (What achievements have I had in this role?)

S Skills (What skills have I learned in this role?)

Y You link to the relevant aspects of the job you are applying for!

(You may wish to start with "skills" to help you in drawing out these achievements.)

How to Get an Interview
When Resumes Just Aren't Working

To begin with, most discussions of job-interviewing proceed from a false assumption. They *assume* you are going to be approaching a large organization—you know, the ones where you need a floor-plan of the building, and an alphabetical directory of the staff. There are admittedly *huge* problems in approaching such giants for a hiring-interview, not the least of which is that in troubled times, many do more downsizing than hiring.

But many job-hunters don't want to work for large corporations, anyway. They want to go after the so-called "small organizations"—those with fifty or fewer employees—which, in the U.S., for example, represent 80 percent of all private businesses, and one-fourth of all workers in the private sector.

The Virtues of Small Organizations

Experts have claimed for years that small organizations create up to two-thirds of all new jobs.[1] If that makes you prefer going after a small organization, I have good news: they are *much* easier to get into than large ones, believe me.

With a small organization, you don't need to wait until there's a *known* vacancy, because they rarely advertise vacancies even when there is one. You just go there and ask if they need someone.

With a small organization, there is no Personnel or Human Resources Department to screen you out.

With a small organization, there's no problem in identifying the person-who-has-the-power-to-hire-you. It's *the boss.* Everyone there knows who it is. They can point to his or her office door, easily.

With a small organization, you do not need to approach them through the mail; if you use your personal contacts, you can get in to see the boss. And if, by chance, he or she is well protected from intruders, it is relatively easy to figure out how to get around *that.* Contacts again are the answer.

With a small organization, if it is growing, there is a greater likelihood that they will be willing to create a new position for you, *if you quietly convince them that you are too good to let slip out of their grasp.*

---

1. This statistic, first popularized by David Birch of M.I.T., and widely quoted for years, was challenged during the 1990s by economists such as Nobel laureate Milton Friedman and Harvard economist James Medoff. The debate was fueled by a study conducted jointly by Steven J. Davis, a labor economist at the University of Chicago, John Haltiwanger at the University of Maryland, and Scott Schuh at the Federal Reserve. Their study, however, was of U.S. *manufacturing,* not of the economy as a whole. Anyway, what these researchers discovered at that time is that small *manufacturing* companies with fifty or fewer employees created only *one-fifth* of all new manufacturing jobs (*New York Times,* 3/25/94). Other researchers, notably Birch, claim that if you include all small companies, they create as many as two-thirds of all new jobs. Has this changed in the new millennium? Hard to tell. Certainly, the U.S. dot.com meltdown back in 2000 made many people afraid to work for small companies—in the Internet field, at least, and in the so-called "New Economy" for sure.

Chapter Five

For all of these reasons and more, small organizations must be kept in mind, as much as or more than, large organizations, when we begin talking about techniques or strategies for securing a hiring-interview. But let's take each separately, as they involve two different techniques.

Approaching Large Organizations for an Interview

In securing hiring-interviews, it's the large organizations that are the problem—the ones, as I mentioned, where you need a floor-plan of the building, and an alphabetical directory of the staff.

But you can simplify your task, if you keep certain things in mind. To begin with, you don't want to just get into the building. You want to get in to see *a particular person* in that building, and only that person: namely, the person-who-has-the-power-to-hire-you for the job you are interested in.

Most job-hunters *don't* even *try* to find out *who* that person is, before approaching a large organization. Rather, they approach each large organization in what can only be described as a haphazard, scattershot fashion.

There is a far far more effective way to approach employers—and that, as I was saying, is to identify *who* at that organization has the power to hire you for the position you have in mind, and then to discover what mutual friend the two of you might have in common, who could help you get an appointment. **The person-who-has-the-power-to-hire-you** will see you because that mutual friend got the appointment for you.

How Do I Find Out Exactly Who Has the Power to Hire Me?

In a small organization with fifty or fewer employees, this is a relatively easy problem. Calling the place and asking for the name of the boss should do it. It's what we call *The One-Minute Research Project.*

But if the place where you are dying to work is a much larger organization, then the answer is: "Through *research and* by asking every *contact* you have."

Let's say that one of the places you are interested in is an organization that we will call *Mythical Corporation*.

You know the kind of job you'd like to get there, but first you know you need to find out the name of the **person-who-has-the-power-to-hire-you** there. What do you do?

If it's a large organization, you go on the Internet or you go to your local public library, and search the directories there. Hopefully that search will yield the name of the person you want.

But if it doesn't, which will particularly be the case with smaller organizations, *then you turn to your contacts.*

The Virtue of Contacts

So now, to our task. You want to approach *Mythical Corporation* and you know that to get in there, you will need to use your contacts. So, what do you do? Well, you approach as many people from the list below as possible and you ask each of them, "Do you know anyone who works, or used to work, at *Mythical Corporation?*"

WHO OR WHAT IS A "CONTACT"?

Since this subject of *contacts* is widely misunderstood by job-hunters and career-changers, let's be very specific, here.

Every person you know, is a contact.

Every member of your family.

Every friend of yours.

Every person in your address book.

Every person on your Christmas-card list, or comparable.

Every person you met at any party you attended in the last year or two.

Every co-worker from your last five jobs.

Every person you know at your gym or athletic place.

Every person you know on any athletic team.

Every merchant or salesperson you ever deal with.

Every person who comes to your apartment or house to do any kind of repairs or maintenance work.

Every person you meet in line at the supermarket or bank.

Every checkout clerk you know.

Every gas station attendant you know.

Everyone who does personal work on you: your barber, hairdresser, manicurist, physical trainer, body worker, and the like.

The waiters, waitresses, and manager of your favorite restaurants.

All the people you meet on the Internet. All the people whose e-mail addresses you have.

Every leisure partner you have, as for walking, exercising, swimming, or whatever.

Every doctor, or medical professional you know.

Every professor, teacher, etc., you once knew and maybe still know how to get a hold of.

Every person in your church, synagogue, mosque, or religious assembly.

Everyone you know in Rotary, Kiwanis, Lions, or other service organizations.

Every person you know at any group you belong to.

Every person you are newly introduced to.

Every person you meet, stumble across, or blunder into, during your job-hunt, whose name, address, and phone number you have the grace to ask for. (*Always* have the grace to ask for it.)

Got the picture?

You ask that question again and again of *everyone* you know, or meet, until you find someone who says, "*Yes, I do.*"

Then you ask them:

"What is the name of the person you know who works, or used to work, at *Mythical Corporation*? Do you have their phone number and/or address?"

"Would you be willing to call ahead, to tell them who I am?"

You then phone them yourself and make an appointment to go see them (*"I won't need more than twenty minutes of your time."*). Once you are talking to them, after the usual polite chit-chat, you ask them the question you are dying to know. Because they are *inside* the organization that interests you, they are usually able to give you the exact answer to the question that has been puzzling you: "Who would have the power to hire me at *Mythical Corporation*, for this kind of position *(which you then describe)*?" If they answer that they do not know, ask if they know *who* might know. If it turns out that they do know, then you ask them not only for that hiring person's name, address, phone, and e-mail address, but also what they can tell you about that person's job, that person's interests, and their style of interviewing.

Then, you ask them if they could help you get an appointment with that person. You repeat this familiar refrain:

"Given my background, would you recommend I go see them?"

"Do you know them, personally? If not, could you give me the name of someone who does?"

"If you know them personally, may I tell them it was you who recommended that I talk with them?"

"If you know them personally, would you be willing to call ahead, to tell them who I am, and to help set up an appointment?"

Also, before leaving, you can ask them about the organization, in general.

Then you thank them, and leave; and you *never never* let the day end, without sitting down to write them a thank-you note. *Always* do it. *Never* forget to.

Getting In

If the contact you talked to doesn't know the **person-who-has-the-power-to-hire-you** well enough to get you an interview, then you go back to your other contacts—now armed with the name of the person you are trying to get in to see—and pose a new question. Approaching as many of your contacts as possible, you ask each of them, "Do you know Ms. or Mr. See, at *Mythical Corporation*, or do you know someone who does?"

You ask that question again and again of *everyone* you know until you find someone who says, *"Yes, I do."*

Then of course, over the phone or—better—in person, you ask that person these questions, carefully, and in this exact order:

- "What can you tell me about him—or her?"
- "Given the kind of job I am looking for *(which you here describe)*, do you think it would be worth my while to go see them?"
- "Do you have their phone number and/or address?"
- "May I tell them it was you who recommended that I talk with them?"
- "Would you be willing to call ahead, to set up an appointment for me, and tell them who I am?"

May-Day, May-Day!

Whenever a job-hunter writes me and tells me they've run into a brick wall, and just can't find out the name of the **person-who-has-the-power-to-hire-them**, the problem *always* turns out to be: they aren't making *sufficient* use of their contacts. They're making a *pass* at using their contacts, but they aren't putting their whole heart and soul into it.

My favorite (true) story in this regard, concerns a job-hunter I know, in Virginia. He decided he wanted to work for a particular health-care organization in that state, and not knowing any better, he approached them by visiting their Human Resources Department. After dutifully filling out a job application, and talking to someone there in that department, he was told there were no jobs available. Stop. Period. End of story.

Approximately three months later he learned about this technique of approaching your favorite organization by using contacts. He explored his contacts *diligently*, and succeeded in getting an interview with the person-who-had-the-power-to-hire-him for the position he was interested in. The two of them hit it off, immediately. The appointment went swimmingly. "You're hired," said the person-who-had-the-power-to-hire-him. "I'll call Human Resources and tell them you're hired, and that you'll be down to fill out the necessary stuff."

Our job-hunter never once mentioned that he had previously approached that same organization through that same Human Resources Department, and been turned down cold.

Just remember: contacts are the key. It takes about eighty pairs of eyes, and ears, to help find the career, the workplace, the job that you are looking for.

Your contacts *are* those eighty eyes and ears.

They are what will help you get the ideal job you are looking for, and they are key to finding out the name of the person-who-has-the-power-to-hire-you.

The more people you know, the more people you meet, the more people you talk to, the more people you enlist as part of your own personal job-hunting network, the better your job-finding success is likely to be. Therefore, you must try to grow your contacts wherever you go. This, of course, is called "networking." I call it "building your grapevine."

Here's how some people have gone about doing that. If they go to hear a speaker on some subject that interests them, they make it a point to join the crowd that gathers 'round the speaker

at the end of the talk, and—with notepad poised—ask such questions as: "Is there anything special that people with my expertise can do?" And here they mention their *generalized* job-title: computer scientist, health professional, chemist, writer, or whatever. Very useful information has thus been turned up. You can also go up to the speaker afterward, and ask if you can contact him or her for further information—"and at what address?"

Conventions, likewise, afford rich opportunities to make contacts. Says one college graduate: "I snuck into the Cable Advertisers Convention at the Waldorf in N.Y.C. That's how I got my job."

Another way people have cultivated contacts, is to leave a message on their telephone answering machine that tells everyone who calls, what information they are looking for. One job-hunter used the following message: "This is the recently laid-off John Smith. I'm not home right now because I'm out looking for a good job as a computer troubleshooter in the telecommunications field; if you have any leads or just want to leave a message, please leave it after the tone."

You may also cultivate contacts by studying the *things* that you like to work with, and then writing to the manufacturer of that *thing* to ask them for a list of organizations in your geographical area that use that *thing*. For example, if you like to work on a particular machine, you would write to the manufacturer of that machine, and ask for names of organizations in your geographical area that use that machine. Or if you like to work in a particular environment, think of the supplies used in that environment. For example, let's say you love darkrooms. You think of what brand of equipment or supplies is usually used in darkrooms, and then you contact the sales manager of the company that makes those supplies, to ask where his (or her) customers are. Some sales managers will not be at all responsive to such an inquiry, but others graciously will, and thus you may gain some very helpful leads.

Because your memory is going to be overloaded during your job-hunt or career-change, it is useful to set up a filing system, where you put the name of each contact of yours on a 3 x 5 card, with addresses, phone numbers, and anything about where they work or who they know that may be of use at a later date. Those of you who are extremely computer literate can, if you prefer, use a database program to do the same thing. Go back over those cards (or their electronic equivalent) frequently.

That does add up to *a lot* of file cards, just because you've got *a lot* of contacts. But that's the whole point.

You may need *every one* of them, *when push comes to shove.*

Rescuing the Employer

As you can see, getting in to see someone, even for a hiring-interview, is not as difficult as people will tell you. It just takes some *know-how,* some *determination,* some *perseverance,* some *going the extra mile.* It works because everyone has friends, including this **person-who-has-the-power-to-hire-you.** You are simply approaching them through *their* friends. And you are doing this, not *wimpishly,* as one who is coming to ask a favor. You are doing it *helpfully,* as one who is asking to help rescue them.

Rescue? Yes, rescue! I cannot tell you the number of employers I have known over the years, who can't figure out how to find the right employee. It is absolutely mind-boggling, particularly in hard times when job-hunters would seem to be gathered on every street corner.

You're having trouble finding the employer. The employer is having trouble finding you. *What a great country!*

So, if you now present yourself directly to the **person-who-has-the-power-to-hire-you,** you are not only answering your own prayers. You are hopefully answering the employer's, as well. You will be *just* what the employer is looking for, but didn't know how to find . . .

if you first figured out what your favorite and best skills are, and

if you then figured out what your favorite Fields of Fascination or *languages* are, and

if you took the trouble to figure out what places *might* need such skills and such *languages,* and

if you researched these places with the intent of finding out what their tasks, challenges, and problems are, and

if you took the trouble to figure out who there has the power to hire you.

Chapter Five

Of course, you don't for sure *know* they need you; that remains for the hiring-interview to uncover. But at least by this thorough preparation you have *increased* the chances that you are at the right place—whether they have an announced vacancy or not. And, if you are, you are not imposing on this employer. You are coming not as "job-beggar," but as "resource person." You may well be absolutely rescuing him or her, believe me!

And yourself. *"The hiring-interview! I actually got in!"*

Yes, and so, it's time for our next section.

THE TEN GREATEST MISTAKES
MADE IN JOB INTERVIEWS

Whereby Your Chances of Finding a Job Are Greatly Decreased

I. Going after large organizations only (such as the Fortune 500).

II. Hunting all by yourself for places to visit, using ads and resumes.

III. Doing no homework on an organization before going there.

IV. Allowing the Personnel Department (or Human Resources) to interview you—*their primary function is to screen you OUT.*

V. Setting no time limit when you make the appointment with an organization.

VI. Letting your resume be used as the agenda for the job interview.

VII. Talking primarily about yourself, and what benefit the job will be for you.

VIII. When answering a question of theirs, talking anywhere from two to fifteen minutes at a time.

IX. Basically approaching them as if you were a job-beggar, hoping they will offer you a job, however humble.

X. Not sending a thank-you note right after the interview.

The Things
School Never Taught Us
About the Job-Hunt:

Interviews

The Secrets of a Successful Interview

An **interview** resembles *dating*, more than it does buying a used car (*you*). An interview is two people trying to decide if they want "to go steady."

An interview is not to be thought of as *marketing* (yourself): i.e., selling yourself to a half-interested employer. Rather, an interview is part of your *research*, i.e., the *data-collecting process* that you have been engaged in, or should have been engaged in, during your whole job-hunt.

While you are sitting there, with the employer, the question you are trying to find an answer to is: "Do I want to work here, or not?" You use the interview to find out. Only when you have concluded, *Yes*, do you then turn your energy toward *selling* (yourself).

An interview is not to be thought of as a test. It's a *data-collecting process* for the employer, too. They are still trying to decide if you *fit*. They are using the interview to find out "Do I want *him or her* to work here? Do they have skills, knowledge or experience that I really need? Do they have an attitude toward work, that I am looking for? And, how will they *fit in* with my other employees?"

An interview is a chance for you to present yourself, not as *a job-beggar* but as *a resource person*. "Behavioral interviews" are very big with organizations, these days. You will very likely run into them with any organization that has 250 employees or more, and sometimes with smaller organizations as well. These are interviews where it is no longer good enough just to make vague claims, such as *"I am good at this,* or *I am good at that."* These days, employers want proof, evidence, and real-life examples from your past, that demonstrate you have the skills, performance, and achievement you claim.

Employers are most impressed with examples that have the fourfold form of *Goal, Obstacles, Solution, and Numbers.* For example, "Here was the task we were trying to accomplish, these were the obstacles in our way, this is what I did to overcome those obstacles, and these were the results, expressed in figures or numbers." Thus you demonstrate that you are *a resource person,* and not merely *a job beggar.*

This is a cinch if you do the homework described later in this book (see chapter 13). If you don't do the homework, well, then you have a problem.

An interview is best prepared for, *before* you go in, by taking these three steps:

1. Research the organization or company, before going in. To this end, when the interview is first set up, ask them right there and then if they have anything in writing about the work of the organization. If they say yes, request they give it to you or send it to you (if the interview isn't the very next day!). Go to their website if they have one, and read everything there that is "About Us." Ask your local librarian for help in finding any news clippings or other information about the place. And, finally, ask all your friends if they know anyone who ever worked there, or works there still, so you can take them to lunch or tea (or Starbucks) and find out any inside stories. All organizations love to be loved. If you've gone to all this trouble, to find out as much as possible about them, they will be flattered and impressed, believe me, because most job-hunters never go to this amount of trouble. Most just walk in the door, knowing nothing. One time, an IBM recruiter asked a college senior he was interviewing, *What does IBM stand for?* The senior didn't know, and the interview was over.

2. When setting up the interview, specify the time you need. Experts recommend you only ask for twenty minutes, and observe this commitment *religiously*. Once you're into the interview, stay aware of the time, and don't stay one minute longer than the twenty minutes, unless the employer *begs* you to—and I mean, *begs*. Always respond with, "I said I would only require twenty minutes of your time, and I like to honor my agreements." This will always make a good impression on an employer!

3. It will help if you mentally catalog, ahead of time, not your fears, but the employer's.

As you go to the interview, keep in mind that **the person-who-has-the-power-to-hire-you** is sweating, too. Why? Because, the hiring-interview is not a very reliable way to choose an employee. In a survey conducted some years ago among a dozen top United Kingdom employers,[1] it was discovered that the chances of an employer finding a good employee through the hiring-interview was only *3 percent better* than if they had picked a name out of a hat. In a further ironic finding, it was discovered that if the interview was conducted by someone who would be working directly with the candidate, the success rate dropped to *2 percent below* that of picking a name out of a hat. And if the interview was conducted by a so-called human resources expert, the success rate dropped to *10 percent below* that of picking a name out of a hat.

No, I don't know how they came up with these figures. But they sure are a hoot! And, more important, they are totally consistent with what I have learned about the world of hiring during the past thirty years. I have watched so-called personnel or human resources experts make *wretchedly* bad choices about hiring *in their own office*, and when they would morosely confess this to me some months later, over lunch, I would playfully tease them with, "If *you* don't even know how to hire well for your own office, how do you keep a straight face when you're called in as a hiring consultant by another organization?" And

---

1. Reported in the *Financial Times Career Guide 1989* for the United Kingdom.

they would ruefully reply, "We act *as though it were* a science." Well, let me tell you, dear reader, the hiring-interview is *not* a science. It is a very very hazy art, done badly by most of its employer-practitioners, in spite of their own past experience, their very best intentions, and their carloads of goodwill.

The hiring interview is not what it seems to be. It seems to be one individual (*you*) sitting there, scared to death while the other individual *(the employer)* is sitting there, blasé and confident.

But what it really is, is two individuals (*you* and *the employer*) sitting there scared to death. It's just that the employer has learned to *hide* his or her fears better than you have, because they've had more practice.

But this employer is, after all, a human being just like you. They were *never* hired to do *this*. It got thrown in with all their other duties. And they may *know* they're not very good at it. So, they're afraid.

The employer's fears include *any or all* of the following:

A. That you won't be able to do the job: that you lack the necessary skills or experience, and the hiring-interview didn't uncover this.

B. That if hired, you won't put in a full working day, regularly.

C. That if hired, you'll be frequently "out sick," or otherwise absent whole days.

D. That if hired, you'll only stay around for a few weeks or at most a few months, and then quit without advance warning.

E. That it will take you too long to master the job, and thus it will be too long before you're profitable to that organization.

F. That you won't get along with the other workers there, or that you will develop a personality conflict with the boss himself (or herself).

G. That you will do only the minimum that you can get away with, rather than the maximum that they hired you for.

Chapter Six

H. That you will always have to be told what to do next, rather than displaying initiative—always in a responding mode, rather than an initiating mode (and mood).

I. That you will have a work-disrupting character flaw, and turn out to be dishonest, or totally irresponsible, a spreader of dissension at work, lazy, an embezzler, a gossip, a sexual harasser, a drug-user or substance abuser, a drunk, a liar, incompetent, or—in a word—*bad news.*

J. *If this is a large organization, and your would-be boss is not the top person:* that you will bring discredit upon them, and upon their department/section/division, etc., for ever hiring you in the first place—making them lose face, possibly also costing them a raise or a promotion.

K. That you will cost a lot of money, if they make a mistake by hiring you. Currently, in the U.S. the cost to an employer of a bad hire can far exceed $50,000, including relocation costs, lost pay for the period for work not done or aborted, and severance pay—if *they* are the ones who decide to let you go.

No wonder the employer is *sweating.*

In the old days, the employer had help in making this decision. They could get useful information by talking to your previous employers. No more. Employers have gotten badly burned since the 1980s by job-hunters filing lawsuits alleging "unlawful discharge," or "being deprived of an ability to make a living." Most employers have consequently adopted the policy of refusing to volunteer *any* information about past employees, except name, rank, and serial number—i.e., the person's job-title and dates of employment.

So now, during the hiring interview, the employer is completely on his or her own in trying to figure out whether or not to hire you. Their fears have moved to the front burner. The hiring-interview these days has become *everything.*

And now, to the actual conduct of the Interview.

An interview is best conducted, in the following way:

During the Interview, Determine to Observe the 50-50 Rule

Studies have revealed that, in general, the people who get hired are those who mix speaking and listening fifty-fifty in the interview. That is, half the time they let the employer do the talking, half the time in the interview they do the talking. People who didn't follow that mix, were the ones who didn't get hired, according to the study.[2] My hunch as to the *reason* why this is so, is that if you talk too much about yourself, you come across as one who would ignore the needs of the organization; if you talk too little, you come across as trying to hide something about your background.

In Answering the Employer's Questions, Observe the Twenty-Second to Two-Minute Rule

---

Studies[3] have revealed that when it is your turn to speak or answer a question, you should plan ahead of time not to speak any longer than two minutes at a time, if you want to make the best impression. In fact, a good answer to an employer's question sometimes only takes twenty seconds to give. This is useful information for you to know, in conducting a successful interview—as you certainly want to do.

Determine to Be Seen as a Part of the Solution, Not as a Part of the Problem

---

2. This one was done by a researcher at Massachusetts Institute of Technology, whose name has been lost in the mists of time.

3. This one was conducted by my friend and colleague, Daniel Porot, of Geneva, Switzerland.

Chapter Six

Every organization has two main preoccupations for its day-by-day work: the problems they are facing, and what solutions to those problems people are coming up with, there. Therefore, the main thing the employer is going to be trying to figure out during the hiring-interview with you, is: will you be part of the *solution* there, or just another part of the *problem*.

In trying to answer this concern, figure out prior to the interview how a *bad* employee would "screw up," in the position you are asking for—such things as *come in late, take too much time off, follow his or her own agenda instead of the employer's, etc.* Then plan to emphasize to the employer during the interview how much you are the very opposite: your sole goal is to increase the organization's effectiveness and service and bottom line.

Be aware of the skills employers are looking for, these days, regardless of the position you are seeking. Overall, they are looking for employees: *who are punctual, arriving at work on time or early; who stay until quitting time, or even leave late; who are dependable; who have a good attitude; who have drive, energy, and enthusiasm; who want more than a paycheck; who are self-disciplined, well-organized, highly motivated, and good at managing their time; who can handle people well; who can use language effectively; who can work on a computer; who are committed to team work; who are flexible, and can respond to novel situations, or adapt when circumstances at work change; who are trainable, and love to learn; who are project-oriented, and goal-oriented; who have creativity and are good at problem solving; who have integrity; who are loyal to the organization; who are able to identify opportunities, markets, and coming trends.* They also want to hire people who can bring in more money than they are paid. *Plan on claiming all of these that you* legitimately *can, during the hiring-interview.*

Realize That the Employer Thinks the Way You Are Doing Your Job-Hunt Is the Way You Will Do the Job

Plan on illustrating by the way you conduct your job-hunt whatever it is you claim will be true of you, once hired. For example, if you plan on claiming during the interview that you are very *thorough* in all your work, be sure to be thorough in the way you have researched the organization ahead of time. For, the manner in which you do your job-hunt and the manner in which you would do the job you are seeking, are not assumed by most employers to be two unrelated subjects, but one and the same. They can tell when you are doing a slipshod, halfhearted job-hunt (*"Uh, what do you guys do here?"*), and this is taken as a clear warning that you might do a slipshod, halfhearted job, were they foolish enough to ever hire you. Employers know this simple truth: most people job-hunt the same way they live their lives, and the way they do their work.

Bring Evidence If You Can

As we saw in the previous chapter, try to think of some way to bring evidence of your skills, to the hiring-interview. For example, if you are an artist, craftsperson, or anyone who produces a product, try to bring a sample of what you have made or produced—in person, or through photos, or even videotapes.

Determine Ahead of Time Not to Bad-Mouth Your Previous Employer(s) During the Interview

During the hiring-interview, plan on never speaking badly of your previous employer(s). Employers often feel as though they are a fraternity or sorority. During the interview you want to come across as one who displays courtesy toward *all* members of that fraternity or sorority. Bad-mouthing a previous employer only makes this employer worry about what you would say about *them,* after they hire you.

I learned this in my own experience. I once spoke graciously about a previous employer, to my (then) present employer. Unbeknownst to me, my present employer already *knew* that my previous employer had badly mistreated me. He therefore thought very highly of me because I didn't drag it up. In fact, he never forgot this incident; talked about it for years afterward. Believe me, it always makes a *big* impression when you don't bad-mouth a previous employer.

Plan on saying something nice about your previous employer, or if you are afraid that the previous employer is going to give you a very bad recommendation, seize the bull by the horns. Say something simple like, "I usually get along with everybody; but for some reason, my past employer and I just didn't get along. Don't know why. It's never happened to me before. Hope it never happens again."

You Don't Have to Spend Hours Memorizing a Lot of "Good Answers" to Potential Questions from the Employer; There Are Only Five Questions That Matter

Of course, the employer is going to be asking you some questions, as a way of helping them to figure out whether or not they want to hire you. Books on *interviewing*, of which there are many, often publish lists of these questions—or at least some *typical* ones that employers often ask. They include such questions as:

- What do you know about this company?
- Tell me about yourself.
- Why are you applying for this job?
- How would you describe yourself?
- What are your major strengths?
- What is your greatest weakness?
- What type of work do you like to do best?
- What are your interests outside of work?
- What accomplishment gave you the greatest satisfaction?
- Why did you leave your last job?
- Why were you fired (if you were)?
- Where do you see yourself five years from now?
- What are your goals in life?
- How much did you make at your last job?

Well, the list goes on and on. In some books, you'll find eighty-nine questions, or more.

You are then told that you should prepare for the hiring-interview by writing out, practicing, and memorizing some devilishly clever answers to *all* these questions—answers that those books of course furnish you with.

All of this is well intentioned, and has been *the state of the art* for decades. But, dear friend, Good News! We are in the new millennium, and things are getting simpler.

Beneath the dozens and dozens of possible questions that the employer could ask you, we now know there are only *five basic questions* that you really need to pay attention to.

Five. Just five. The people-who-have-the-power-to-hire-you usually want to know the answers to these five questions, which they may ask directly or try to find out obliquely:

1. **"Why are you here?"** *They mean by this, "Why are you knocking on my door, rather than someone else's door?"*
2. **"What can you do for us?"** *They mean by this, "If I were to hire you, would you be part of the problems I already have, or would you be a part of the solution to those problems? What are your skills, and how much do you know about some subject or field that is of interest to us?"*

Chapter Six

3. **"What kind of person are you?"** *They mean by this, "Do you have the kind of personality that makes it easy for people to work with you, and do you share the values that we have at this place?"*
4. **"What distinguishes you from nineteen other people who can do the same tasks that you can?"** *They mean by this, "Do you have better work habits than the nineteen others, do you show up earlier, stay later, work more thoroughly, work faster, maintain higher standards, go the extra mile, or . . . what?"*
5. **"Can I afford you?"** *They mean by this, "If we decide we want you here, how much will it take to get you, and are we willing and able to pay that amount—governed, as we are, by our budget, and by our inability to pay you as much as the person who would be above you, on the organizational chart?"*

These are the five principal questions that most employers are dying to know the answers to. *This is the case, even if the interview begins and ends with these five questions never once being mentioned overtly by the employer.* The questions are still *floating in the air* there, beneath the surface of the conversation, beneath all the other things that are being discussed. Anything you can do, during the interview, to help the employer find the answers to these five questions, will make the interview very satisfying to the employer. Nothing for you to go memorize.

If you just do the Flower Exercise (pages 246–247) in this book, you will know the five answers. Period. End of story.

**You Need to Find Out the Answers
to the Very Same Questions That the Employer
Would Ask You**

During the hiring-interview you have the right—nay, the duty—to find out the answers to the very same five questions *as the employer's*, only in a slightly different form. Your questions will come out looking like this:

1. **"What does this job involve?"** *You want to understand exactly what tasks will be asked of you, so that you can determine if these are the kinds of tasks you would really like to do.*
2. **"What are the skills a top employee in this job would have to have?"** *You want to know if your skills match those that*

the employer thinks a top employee in this job would have to have, in order to do this job well.

3. **"Are these the kinds of people I would like to work with, or not?"** *Do not ignore your intuition if it tells you that you would not be comfortable working with these people!! You want to know if they have the kind of personality that would make it easy for you to accomplish your work, and if they share your most important values.*

4. **"If we like each other, and both want to work together, can I persuade them there is something unique about me, that makes me different from nineteen other people who can do the same tasks?"** *You need to think out, way ahead of time, what does make you different from nineteen other people who can do the same job. For example, if you are good at analyzing problems, how do you do that? Painstakingly? Intuitively, in a flash? By consulting with greater authorities in the field? You see the point. You are trying to put your finger on the "style" or "manner" in which you do your work, that is distinctive and appealing, to* this *employer.*

5. **"Can I persuade them to hire me at the salary I need or want?"** *This requires some knowledge on your part of how to conduct salary negotiation. See the next chapter.*

You will probably want to ask questions one and two out loud. You will *observe* quietly the answer to question three. You will be prepared to make the case for questions four and five, when the *appropriate* time in the interview arises (again, see the next chapter).

How do you get into these questions? You might begin by reporting to them just exactly how you've been conducting your job-hunt, and what impressed you so much about *their* organization during your research, that you decided to come in and talk to them about a job. Then you can fix your attention, during the remainder of the interview, on finding out the answers to the five questions above—in your own way.[4]

---

4. Additional questions you may want to ask, to elaborate upon those five:
   What significant changes has this company gone through in the
      last five years?
   What values are sacred to this company?
   What characterizes the most successful employees this company has?
   What future changes do you see in the work here?
   Who do you see as your allies, colleagues, or competitors in this business?

Yes, there are only *five* questions that really count in a job-interview; but how these five questions keep popping up! They pop up in a slightly different form (yet again), if you're there to talk *not* about a job that already exists but rather, one that you want them to *create* for you. In that kind of interview, or approach to an organization, these five questions get changed into five *statements*, that you make to this person-who-has-the-power-to-hire-you:

1. What you **like** about this organization.

2. What sorts of **needs** you find intriguing in this field and in this organization (unless you first hear the word *"problems"* coming out of their mouth, don't ever use the word *"problems,"* inasmuch as most employers prefer synonyms such as *"challenges"* or *"needs"*).

3. What **skills** seem to you to be needed in order to meet such needs.

4. **Evidence** from your past experience that demonstrates you have those very skills. Employers are looking for *examples* from your past performance and achievement; not just vague statements like: "I'm good at . . ." They want concrete examples, specifically of your transferable skills, your content skills, and your self-management skills, i.e., traits.

   If you read pages 65 and 66, you already know this. It's the underlying principle of *Behavioral Interviewing*, or *competency-based interviewing*.

   You may be asked, or—if you're not—you can pose the same question yourself, near the top of the interview: "What are the three most important competencies, for this job?" Then, of course, you need to prove during the interview that you *have* those three—for the job that you are interested in.

5. What is **unique** about the way *you* perform those skills. As I said before: every prospective employer wants to know *what makes you different* from nineteen other people who can do the same kind of work as you. You *have* to know what that is. And then not merely talk about it, but actually demonstrate it by the way you conduct your part of the hiring-interview. *For example, "I am very thorough in the way I would do the job for you"* translates into the imperative that you be thorough in the

way you have researched this place before you go in for the hiring interview. That's *evidence* the employer can see with their own eyes.

A Special Note to *Those Who Consider Themselves Members of the Entitlement Generation:* Don't let "what is unique about you?" go to your head, please. If you're just out of college, and your idea of a job-interview is that you just waltz right in there and tell them how wonderful you are, how lucky they are to get you, and how you're expecting top dollar right out of college, equal to what they pay employees who've been there for twenty years, I recommend you do some more thinking. Employers are searching for men and women of a humble spirit, who know their worth, but know other people's worth also. It's like the players in an orchestra.

Throughout the Interview, Keep in Mind:
Employers Don't Really Care About Your Past;
They Only Ask About It,
in Order to Try to Predict Your Future (Behavior)

In the U.S. employers may only ask you questions that are related to the requirements and expectations of the job. They cannot ask about such things as your creed, religion, race, age, sex, or marital status. Any other questions about your past are *fair game.* But don't be fooled by any employer's absorption with your past. You must realize that the only thing any employer can possibly care about is your future . . . with *them.* Since that future is impossible to uncover, they usually try to gauge what it would be by asking about your past (behavior).

Therefore, during the hiring-interview before you answer any question the employer asks you about your past, you should pause to think out what fear about the *future* lies underneath that question—and then address that fear, obliquely or directly.

In most cases, as I have been emphasizing, the person-who-has-the-power-to-hire-you is *scared.* If you think that is too strong a word, let's settle for *anxious,* or *afraid,* or *worried.* And this worry or fear lies beneath all the questions they may ask.

Here are some *examples*:

Employer's Question	The Fear Behind the Question	The Point You Try to Get Across	Phrases You Might Use to Get This Across
"Tell me about yourself."	The employer is afraid he/she isn't going to conduct a very good interview, by failing to ask the right questions. Or is afraid there is something wrong with you, and is hoping you will blurt it out.	You are a good employee, as you have proved in the past at your other jobs. (Give the briefest history of who you are, where born and raised, interests, hobbies, and kind of work you have enjoyed the most to date.) *Keep it to two minutes, max.*	In describing your work history, use any *honest* phrases you can about your work history, that are self-complimentary: "Hard worker." "Came in early, left late." "Always did more than was expected of me." Etc.
"What kind of work are you looking for?"	The employer is afraid that you are looking for a different job than that which the employer is trying to fill. E.g., he/she wants a secretary, but you want to be an office manager, etc.	You are looking for precisely the kind of work the employer is offering (but don't say that, if it isn't true). Repeat back to the employer, in your own words, what he/she has said about the job, and emphasize the skills you have to do *that.*	If the employer hasn't described the job at all, say, "I'd be happy to answer that, but first I need to understand exactly what kind of work this job involves." *Then* answer, as at left.
"Have you ever done this kind of work before?"	The employer is afraid you don't possess the necessary skills and experience to do this job.	You have skills that are transferable, from whatever you used to do; and you did it well.	"I pick up stuff very quickly." "I have quickly mastered any job I have ever done."

Employer's Question	The Fear Behind the Question	The Point You Try to Get Across	Phrases You Might Use to Get This Across
"Why did you leave your last job?" —or "How did you get along with your former boss and co-workers?"	The employer is afraid you don't get along well with people, especially bosses, and is just waiting for you to "bad-mouth" your previous boss or co-workers, as proof of that.	Say whatever positive things you possibly can about your former boss and co-workers *(without telling lies).* Emphasize you usually get along very well with people— and then let your gracious attitude toward your previous boss(es) and co-workers prove it, right before this employer's very eyes (and ears).	If you left voluntarily: "*My boss and I both felt I would be happier and more effective in a job where [here describe your strong points, such as] I would have more room to use my initiative and creativity.*" If you were fired: "Usually, I get along well with everyone, but in this particular case the boss and I just didn't get along with each other. Difficult to say why." *You don't need to say anything more than that.* If you were laid off and your job wasn't filled after you left: "My *job* was terminated."
"How is your health?" —or "How much were you absent from work during your last job?"	The employer is afraid you will be absent from work a lot, if they hire you.	You will not be absent. If you have a health prob-lem, you want to emphasize that it is one that will not keep you from being at work, daily. Your productivity, compared with other workers', is excellent.	If you were *not* absent a lot at your last job: "I believe it's an employee's job to show up every workday. Period." If you *were* absent a lot, say why, and stress that it was due to a difficulty that is now *past.*

Employer's Question	The Fear Behind the Question	The Point You Try to Get Across	Phrases You Might Use to Get This Across
"Can you explain why you've been out of work so long?"—*or* "Can you tell me why there are these gaps in your work history?" *(Usually said after studying your resume.)*	The employer is afraid that you are the kind of person who quits a job the minute he/she doesn't like something at it; in other words, that you have no "stick-to-it-iveness."	You love to work, and you regard times when things aren't going well as challenges, which you enjoy learning how to conquer.	"During the gaps in my work record, I was studying/doing volunteer work/doing some hard thinking about my mission in life/finding redirection." (Choose one.)
"Wouldn't this job represent a step down for you?"—*or* "I think this job would be way beneath your talents and experience."—*or* "Don't you think you would be underemployed if you took this job?"	The employer is afraid you could command a bigger salary, somewhere else; and will therefore leave him/her as soon as something better turns up.	You will stick with this job as long as you and the employer agree this is where you should be.	"This job isn't a step down for me. It's a step up—from welfare." "We have mutual fears; every employer is afraid a good employee will leave too soon, and every employee is afraid the employer might fire him/her, for no good reason." "I like to work, and I give my best to every job I've ever had."
And, last "Tell me, what is your greatest weakness?"	The employer is afraid you have some character flaw, and hopes you will now rashly blurt it out, or confess it.	You have limitations just like anyone else, but you work constantly to improve yourself and be a more and more effective worker.	Mention a weakness and then stress its positive aspect, e.g., "I don't like to be oversupervised, because I have a great deal of initiative, and I like to anticipate problems before they even arise."

As the Interview Proceeds, You Want to Quietly Notice the Time-Frame of the Questions the Employer Is Asking

---

When the interview is going favorably for you, the time-frame of the employer's questions will often move—*however slowly*—through the following stages.

1. Distant past: *e.g., "Where did you attend high school?"*
2. Immediate past: *e.g., "Tell me about your most recent job."*
3. Present: *e.g., "What kind of a job are you looking for?"*
4. Immediate future: *e.g., "Would you be able to come back for another interview next week?"*
5. Distant future: *e.g., "Where would you like to be five years from now?"*

The more the time-frame of the interviewer's questions moves from the past to the future, the more favorably you may assume the interview is going for you. On the other hand, if the interviewer's questions stay firmly in the past, the outlook is not so good. *Ah well, y' can't win them all!*

When the time-frame of the interviewer's questions moves firmly into the future, *then* is the time for you to get more specific about the job in question. Experts suggest you ask, at that point, these kinds of questions:

What is the job, specifically, that I am being considered for?

If I were hired, what duties would I be performing?

What responsibilities would I have?

What would you be hiring me to accomplish?

Would I be working with a team, or group? To whom would I report?

Whose responsibility is it to see that I get the training I need, here, to get up to speed?

How would I be evaluated, how often, and by whom?

What were the strengths and weaknesses of previous people in this position?

Why did *you* yourself decide to work here?

What do you wish you had known about this company before you started here? What particular characteristics do you think have made you successful in your job here?

May I meet the persons I would be working with and for (if it isn't you)?

Remember, *the hiring process is more like choosing a mate, than it is like deciding whether or not to buy a new car.* "Choosing a mate" here is a metaphor. To elaborate upon the metaphor a little bit, it means that *the mechanisms* by which human nature decides to hire someone, are *similar to* the mechanisms by which human nature decides whether or not to marry someone. Those mechanisms, of course, are impulsive, intuitional, non-rational, unfathomable, and often made on the spur of the moment.

Interviews Are Often Lost to Mosquitoes
Rather Than to Dragons,
and Lost within the First Two Minutes

Think about this: you can have all the skills in the world, have researched this organization to death, have practiced *interviewing* until you are a master at giving "right answers," be absolutely the perfect person for this job, and yet lose the hiring-interview because . . . *your breath smells terrible.* Or some other small personal reason. It's akin to your being ready to fight dragons, and then being killed by a mosquito.

It's the reason why interviews are most often lost, when they are lost, *during the first two minutes.* Believe it or not.

Let us look at *what* interview-mosquitoes *(as it were)* can fly in, during the first thirty seconds to two minutes of your interview so that *the person-who-has-the-power-to-hire-you* starts muttering to themselves, *"I sure hope we have some other candidates besides this person"*:

1. Your appearance and personal habits: interview after interview has revealed that if you are a male, *you are much more likely to get the job if:*

- you have obviously freshly bathed, have your face freshly shaved or your hair and beard freshly trimmed, have clean fingernails, and are using a deodorant; *and*

- you have on freshly laundered clothes, pants with a sharp crease, and shoes freshly polished; *and*

- you do not have bad breath, do not dispense gallons of garlic, onion, stale tobacco, or the odor of strong drink, into the enclosed office air, but have brushed and flossed your teeth; *and*

- you are not wafting tons of aftershave cologne fifteen feet ahead of you, as you enter the room.

Remember, since the hiring process is more like choosing a mate, than deciding whether or not to buy a new car, the employer is simply trying to determine if they like you. If you "bomb" in one of these areas just listed, the person-who-has-the-power-to-hire-you may decide they really don't like you, in which case you're not going to get hired there, no matter how qualified you otherwise may be. The same thing happens on dates, incidentally.

If you are a female, interview after interview has revealed that *you are much more likely to get the job if:*

- you have obviously freshly bathed; have not got tons of makeup on your face; have had your hair newly "permed" or "coiffed"; have clean or nicely manicured fingernails, that don't stick out ten inches from your fingers; and are using a deodorant; *and*
- you wear a bra, have on freshly cleaned clothes, a suit or sophisticated-looking dress, shoes not sandals, and are not wearing clothes so daring that they call *a lot* of attention to themselves. In these days of sexual harassment lawsuits, this tends to make many employers, male and female, *very* nervous. I grant you there are some employers who might like this kind of outfit, but—trust me—in most cases you don't want to work for *them* (as with all items here, I am only reporting what can affect your chances of getting hired—not whether or not I think this employer preoccupation with just outward appearance is asinine); *and*
- you do not have bad breath; do not dispense gallons of garlic, onion, stale tobacco, or the odor of strong drink, into the enclosed office air, but have brushed and flossed your teeth; *and*
- you are not wafting tons of perfume fifteen feet ahead of you, as you enter the room.

2. Nervous mannerisms: *it is a turnoff for employers if:*
- you continually avoid eye contact with the employer (that's a *big, big* no-no), *or*
- you give a limp handshake, *or*
- you slouch in your chair, or endlessly fidget with your hands, or crack your knuckles, *or* constantly play with your hair during the interview.

3. Lack of self-confidence: *it is a turnoff for employers if:*
- you are speaking so softly you cannot be heard, or so loudly you can be heard two rooms away, *or*

- you are giving answers in an extremely hesitant fashion, *or*
- you are giving one-word answers to all the employer's questions, *or*
- you are constantly interrupting the employer, *or*
- you are downplaying your achievements or abilities, or are continuously being self-critical in comments you make about yourself during the interview.

4. The consideration you show to other people: *it is a turnoff for employers if:*

- you show a lack of courtesy to the receptionist, secretary, and (at lunch) to the waiter or waitress, *or*
- you display extreme criticalness toward your previous employers and places of work, *or*
- you drink strong stuff (Ordering a drink if and when the employer takes you to lunch is always an extremely bad idea, as it raises the question in the employer's mind, *Do they normally stop with one, or do they normally keep on going?* Don't . . . ever . . . do . . . it! Even if they do.), *or*
- you forget to thank the interviewer as you're leaving, or forget to send a thank-you note afterward. Says one human resources manager:

   "A prompt, brief, faxed business letter thanking me for my time along with a (brief!) synopsis of his/her unique qualities communicates to me that this person is an assertive, motivated, customer-service-oriented salesperson who utilizes technology and knows the rules of the 'game.' These are qualities I am looking for. . . . At the moment I receive approximately one such letter . . . for every fifteen candidates interviewed."

- Incidentally, *many* an employer watches to see if you smoke, either in the office or at lunch. *In a race between two equally qualified people, the nonsmoker will win out over the smoker 94 percent of the time, according to a study done by a professor of business at Seattle University.*

5. Your values: *it is a complete turnoff for most employers, if they see in you:*

- any sign of arrogance or excessive aggressiveness; any sign of tardiness or failure to keep appointments and commitments on time, including the hiring-interview; *or*
- any sign of laziness or lack of motivation; *or*
- any sign of constant complaining or blaming things on others; *or*
- any signs of dishonesty or lying—on your resume or in the interview; *or*
- any signs of irresponsibility or tendency to goof off; *or*
- any sign of not following instructions or obeying rules; *or*
- any sign of a lack of enthusiasm for this organization and what it is trying to do; *or*
- any sign of instability, inappropriate response, and the like; *or*
- the other ways in which you evidence your *values*, such as: what things impress you or don't impress you in the office; *or* what you are willing to sacrifice in order to get this job *and* what you are *not* willing to sacrifice in order to get this job; *or* your enthusiasm for work; *or* the carefulness with which you did or didn't research this company before you came in; and blah, blah, blah.

Well, dear reader, there you have it: the *mosquitoes* that can kill you, when you're only on the watch for dragons, during the hiring-interview.

One favor I ask of you: do not write me, telling me how picayune or asinine some of this is. Believe me, I already *know* that. I'm not reporting the world as it *should* be, and certainly not as I would like it to be. I'm only reporting what study after study has revealed about the hiring world as it *is*.

You may take all this to heart, or just ignore it. However, if you decide to ignore these points, and then—despite interview after interview—you never get hired, you might want to rethink your position on all of this. It may be *mosquitoes*, not dragons, that are killing you.

And, good news: you can *fix* all these mosquitoes. Yes, you control *every one* of these factors.

Read them all over again. There isn't a one of them that you don't have the power to determine, or the power to change. You can decide to bathe before going to the interview, you can decide to shine your shoes, you can decide not to smoke, etc., etc. All the little things which could torpedo your interview are within your control, and *you can fix* them, if they are keeping you from getting hired.

There Are Some Questions You Must Ask Before You Let the Interview Close

---

Before you let the interview end, there are six questions you should *always* ask:

#1. *"Given my skills and experience, is there work here that you would consider me for?"* This is if you haven't come after a specific job, from the beginning.

Chapter Six

#2. *"Can you offer me this job?"* **I know this seems stupid, but it is astonishing (at least to me) how many job-hunters have secured a job simply by being bold enough to ask for it, at the end of the interview, either with the words** *May I have this job,* **or something similar to it, in language they feel comfortable with.** I don't know *why* this is. I only know *that* it is. Maybe it has something to do with employers not liking to say "No," to someone who directly asks them for something. Anyway, if after hearing all about this job at this place, you decide you'd really like to have it, you must *ask for it.* The worse thing the employer can say is "No," or "We need some time to think about all the interviews we're conducting."

#3. *"Do you want me to come back for another interview, perhaps with some of the other decision-makers here?"* If you are a serious candidate in this employer's mind for this job, there usually *is* a second round of interviews. And, often, a third, and fourth. You, of course, want to make it to that second round.

#4. *"When may I expect to hear from you?"* You *never* want to leave control of the ensuing steps in this process in the hands of the employer. You want it in your own hands. If the employer says, *"We need time to think about this,"* or *"We will be calling you for a second interview,"* you don't want to leave this as an undated good intention on the employer's part. You want to nail it down.

#5. *"Might I ask what would be* the latest *I can expect to hear from you?"* The employer has probably given you their *best* guess, in answer to your previous question. Now you want to know *what is the worst-case* scenario? Incidentally, one employer, when I asked him for the *worst-case* scenario, replied, *"Never!"* I thought he had a great sense of humor. Turned out he was dead serious. I never did hear from him, despite repeated attempts at contact, on my part.

#6. *"May I contact you after that date, if for any reason you haven't gotten back to me by that time?"* Some employers resent this question. You'll know that is the case if they snap at you, *"Don't you trust me?"* But most employers appreciate your offering them what is in essence a safety-net. They know they can get busy, become overwhelmed with other things, forget their promise to you. It's reassuring, in such a case, for you to offer to rescue them.

(Optional: #7. *"Can you think of anyone else who* might *be interested in hiring me?"* This question is invoked *only* if they replied *"No,"* to your first question, above.)

Jot down any answers they give you to the questions above, then stand up, thank them sincerely for their time, give a firm handshake, and leave.

Always, Always Send a Thank-You Note the Same Night, at the Latest

---

Every expert on interviewing will tell you two things: (1) Thank-you notes *must* be sent after *every* interview, by every job-hunter; and (2) most job-hunters ignore this advice. Indeed, it is safe to say that it is the most overlooked step in the entire job-hunting process.

If you want to stand out from the others applying for the same job, send thank-you notes—to *everyone* you met there, that day.

If you need any additional encouragement *(besides the fact that it may get you the job)*, here are six reasons for sending a thank-you note, most particularly to the employer who interviewed you:

First, you were presenting yourself as one who has good skills with people. Your actions with respect to the job-interview must back this claim up. Sending a thank-you note does that. The employer can see you *are* good with people; you remember to thank them.

Second, it helps the employer to remember you.

Third, if a committee is involved in the hiring process, the one man or woman who interviewed you has something to show the rest of the committee.

Fourth, if the interview went rather well, and the employer seemed to show an interest in further talks, the thank-you letter can reiterate *your* interest in further talks.

Chapter Six

Fifth, the thank-you note gives you an opportunity to correct any wrong impression you left behind. You can add anything you forgot to tell them, that you want them to know. And from among all the things you two discussed, you can underline the main two or three points that you want to stand out in their minds.

Last, if the interview did not go well, and you lost all interest in working there, they may still hear of other openings, elsewhere, that might be of interest to you. In the thank-you note, you can mention this, and ask them to keep you in mind. Thus, from kindly interviewers, you may gain additional leads.

In the following days, rigorously keep to all that you said, and don't contact them except with that mandatory thank-you note, until after the *latest* deadline you two agreed upon, in answer to question #5, above. If you do have to contact them after that date, and if they tell you things are still up in the air, you must ask questions #3, #4, and #5, all over again. And so on, and so forth.

Incidentally, it is entirely appropriate for you to insert a thank-you note into the running stream, after *each* interview or telephone contact. Just keep it brief.

"I'll tell you why I want this job. I thrive on challenges.
I like being stretched to my full capacity. I like solving problems.
Also, my car is about to be repossessed."

When None of This Works,
and You Never Get Invited Back

There is no magic in job-hunting. No techniques that always work, and work for everyone. Anyone who tells you there is magic, is delusional. I hear regularly from job-hunters who report that they paid attention to all the matters I have mentioned in this chapter and this book, and are quite successful at getting interviews—but they still don't get hired. And they want to know what they're doing wrong.

Well, unfortunately, the answer *sometimes* is: "Maybe nothing." I don't know *how often* this happens, but I know it does happen—because more than one employer has confessed it to me, and in fact at one point in my life it actually happened to *moi*: namely, *some* employers play wicked, despicable tricks on job-hunters, whereby they invite you in for an interview despite the fact that they have already hired someone for the position in question, and they know from the beginning that they have absolutely no intention of hiring you—not in a million years!

You are cheered, of course, by the ease with which you get these interviews. But unbeknownst to you, the manager who is interviewing you (we'll say it's a *he*) has a personal friend he already agreed to give the job to. Of course, one small problem remains: the state or the federal government gives funds to this organization, and has mandated that this position be opened to all. So this manager must comply. He therefore *pretends* to choose ten candidates, including his favorite, and pretends to interview them all *as though* the job opening were still available. But, he intended, from the beginning, to reject the first nine and choose his favorite, and since you were selected for the honor of being among those nine, you automatically get rejected—even if you are a much better candidate. This tenth person is, after all, his *friend*. But you have been very helpful, even without intending to be: you have helped the manager establish his claim that he followed the mandated hiring procedures to the letter.

You will of course be baffled as to *why* you got turned down. Trouble is, you will never know if it was because you met an employer who was playing this little trick, *or* not. All you know is: you're very depressed.

If you *never* get invited back for a second interview, there is always, of course, the chance that no games are being played. You are getting rejected, at place after place, because there is something really wrong with the way you are coming across, during these hiring-interviews.

Employers will rarely ever tell you this. You will never hear them say something like, "You came across as just too cocky and arrogant during the interview." You will almost always be left completely in the dark as to *what* it is you're doing wrong.

If you've been through a whole bunch of employers, one way around this deadly silence, is to ask for *generalized* feedback from whoever was the *friendliest* employer that you saw in your whole job-hunt. You can always try phoning the friendliest one, reminding them of who you are, and then asking the following question—deliberately kept generalized, vague, unrelated to just *that* place, and above all, *future-directed*: Something like: *"You know, I've been on several interviews at several different places now, where I've gotten turned down. From what you've seen, is there something about me in an interview, that you think might be causing me not to get hired at those places? If so, I'd really appreciate your giving me some pointers so I can do better in my future hiring-interviews."*

Most of the time they'll *still* duck saying anything hurtful or helpful. First of all, they're afraid of lawsuits. Second, they don't know how you will use what they might have to say. (Said an old veteran to me once, "I used to think it was my duty to hit everyone with the truth. Now I only give it to those who can use it.")

But *occasionally* you will run into an employer who is willing to risk giving you the truth, because they think you will know how to use it wisely. If so, thank them from the bottom of your heart, no matter how painful their feedback is. Such advice, seriously heeded, can bring about just the changes in your interviewing strategy that you most need, in order to win the interview.

In the absence of any such help from employers who interviewed you, you might want to get a good business friend of yours to role-play a mock hiring-interview with you, in case they immediately see something glaringly wrong with how you're "coming across."

When all else fails, I would recommend you go to a career coach who charges by the hour, and put yourself in their tender knowledgeable hands. Role-play an interview with them, and take their advice seriously (you've just paid for it, after all).

On Planning for a Raise

I have left out the subject of salary negotiation, in this chapter. It requires a chapter of its own (next!).

Hopefully, however, with that advice plus these tips you will do well in your interviews. And if you do get hired, make one resolution to yourself right there on the spot. Plan to keep track of your accomplishments at this new job, on a weekly basis—jotting them down, every weekend, in your own private diary. Career experts recommend you do this without fail. You can then summarize these accomplishments annually on a one-page sheet, for your boss's eyes, when the question of a raise or promotion comes up.[5]

---

5. In any good-sized organization, you will often be amazed at how little attention your superiors pay to your noteworthy accomplishments, and how little they are aware at the end of the year that you really are entitled to a raise. Noteworthy your accomplishments may be, but no one is taking notes . . . unless you do. You may even need to be the one who brings up the subject of a raise or promotion. Waiting for the employer to bring this up may never happen.

THE TEN COMMANDMENTS
FOR JOB INTERVIEWS

Whereby Your Chances of Finding a Job Are Vastly Increased

I. Go after small organizations with twenty or fewer employees, since they create two-thirds of all new jobs.

II. Hunt for interviews using the aid of friends and acquaintances, because a job-hunt requires eighty pairs of eyes and ears.

III. Do thorough homework on an organization before going there, using Informational Interviews plus the library.

IV. At any organization, identify who has the power to hire you there, for the position you want, and use your friends and acquaintances' contacts, to get in to see that person.

V. Ask for just twenty minutes of their time, when asking for the appointment; and keep to your word.

VI. Go to the interview with your own agenda, your own questions and curiosities about whether or not this job fits you.

VII. Talk about yourself only if what you say offers some benefit to that organization, and their "problems."

VIII. When answering a question of theirs, talk only between twenty seconds and two minutes, at any one time.

IX. Basically approach them as if you were a resource person, able to produce better work for that organization than any predecessor.

X. Always write a thank-you note the same evening of the interview, and mail it at the latest by the next morning.

CHAPTER 7

The Things
School Never Taught Us
About the Job-Hunt:

Salary
Negotiation

Getting Paid What You're Worth

I remember once talking to a breathless college graduate, who was elated at having just landed her first job. "How much are they going to pay you?" I asked. She looked startled. "I don't know," she said, "I never asked. I just assumed they will pay me a fair wage." *Boy*! did she get a rude awakening when she received her first paycheck. It was so miserably *low*, she couldn't believe her eyes. And thus did she learn, painfully, what you must learn too: *Before accepting a job, always ask about salary*. Indeed, *ask and negotiate.*

It's the *negotiate* that throws fear into our hearts. We feel ill-prepared to do this. But, it's not all that difficult. While whole books can be (and have been) written on this subject, there are basically just six secrets to keep in mind.

Never Discuss Salary Until the End
of the Interviewing Process
When They Have Definitely Said
They Want You

"The end of the interviewing process" is difficult to define. It's the point at which the employer says, or thinks, "We've got to get this person!" That may be at the end of the first (and therefore the last) interview; or it may be at the end of a whole series of interviews, often with different people within the same company or organization. But assuming things are going favorably for you, whether after the first, or second, or third, or fourth interview, if *you* like them and *they* increasingly like you, a job offer *will* be made. Then, and only then, it is time to deal with the question that is inevitably on any employer's mind: *how much is this person going to cost me?* And the question that is on *your* mind: *how much does this job pay?*

If the employer raises the salary question earlier, in some form like "What kind of salary are you looking for?," you should have three responses at your fingertips.

Response #1: If the employer seems like a kindly man or woman, your best and most tactful reply might be: "Until you've decided you definitely want me, and I've decided I definitely could help you with your tasks here, I feel any discussion of salary is premature." That will work, in most cases.

Response #2: There are instances, however, where that doesn't work. You may be face-to-face with an employer who will not be put off so easily, and demands within the first two minutes that you're in the interview room to know what salary you are looking for. At this point, you use your second response: "I'll gladly come to that, but could you first help me to understand what this job involves?"

Response #3: That is a good response, *in most cases*. But what if it doesn't work? The employer with rising voice says, "Come, come, don't play games with me. I want to know what salary you're looking for." You have response #3 prepared for *this* very eventuality. It's an answer in terms of a *range*. For example, "I'm looking for a salary in the range of $35,000 to $45,000 a year."

If the employer still won't let it go until later, then consider what this means. Clearly, you are being interviewed by an employer who has no range in mind. Their beginning figure is their ending figure. No negotiation is possible.[1]

This happens, when it happens, because many employers are making salary their major criterion for deciding who to hire, and who not to hire, out of—say—nineteen possible candidates.

> *It's an old game, played with new determination by many employers these days, called* "among two equally qualified candidates, the one who is willing to work for the lower salary *wins*."

---

1. One job-hunter said his interviews always began with the salary question, and no matter what he answered, that ended the interview. Turned out, this job-hunter was doing all the interviewing over the phone. That was the problem. Once he went face to face, salary was no longer the first thing discussed in the interview.

If you run into this situation, and you want that job badly enough, you will have no choice but to capitulate. Ask what salary they have in mind, and make your decision. (Of course you should always say, *"I need a little time, to think about this."*)

However, all the foregoing is merely the *worst-case scenario*. Usually, things don't go this way. Not by a long shot. In most interviews, these days, the employer will be willing to save salary negotiation until they've finally decided they want you (and you've decided you want them). And at that point, salary will be negotiable.

WHEN TO DISCUSS SALARY

Not until all of the following conditions have been fulfilled —

- *Not until they've gotten to know you, at your best, so they can see how you stand out above the other applicants.*

- *Not until you've gotten to know them, as completely as you can, so you can tell when they're being firm, or when they're flexible.*

- *Not until you've found out exactly what the job entails.*

- *Not until they've had a chance to find out how well you match the job requirements.*

- *Not until you're in the final interview at that place, for that job.*

- *Not until you've decided, "I'd really like to work here."*

- *Not until they've said, "We want you."*

- *Not until they've said, "We've got to have you."*

—should you get into salary discussion with any employer.

If you'd prefer this to be put in the form of a diagram, here it is:[2]

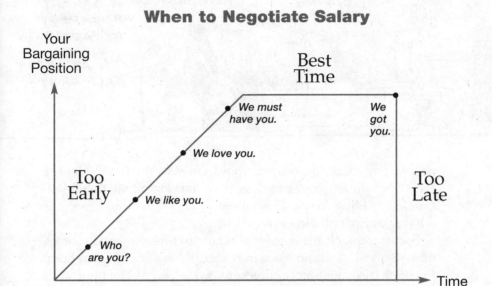

When to Negotiate Salary

Your Bargaining Position

Best Time

We must have you.

We got you.

We love you.

Too Early

Too Late

We like you.

Who are you?

Time

Why is it to your advantage to delay salary discussion? Because, if you really *shine* during the hiring-interview, they may—at the end—mention a higher salary than they originally had in mind, when the interview started—and this is particularly the case when the interview has gone so well, that they're *determined* to obtain your services.

**The Second Secret
of Salary Negotiation:**

The Purpose of Salary Negotiation Is to Uncover the Most That an Employer Is Willing to Pay to Get You

Salary negotiation would never happen if *every* employer in *every* hiring-interview were to mention, right from the start, the top figure they are willing to pay for that position. *Some* employers do, as I mentioned before. And that's the end of any salary

negotiation. But, of course, most employers don't. Hoping they'll be able to get you for less, they start *lower* than they're ultimately willing to go. This creates *a range*. And that range is what salary negotiation is all about.

For example, if the employer wants to hire somebody for no more than $12 an hour, they may start *the bidding* at $8 an hour. In which case, their *range* runs between $8 and $12 an hour. Or if they want to pay no more than $20 an hour, they may start the bidding at $16 an hour. In which case their range runs between $16 and $20 an hour.

So, why do you want to negotiate? Because, if a range *is* thus involved, you have every right to try to discover the highest salary that employer is willing to pay *within that range*.

The employer's goal, is to save money, if possible. Your goal is to bring home to your family, your partner, or your own household, the best salary that you can, for the work you will be doing. Nothing's wrong with the goals of either of you. But it does mean that, where the employer starts lower, salary negotiation is proper, and expected.

Chapter Seven

"WHILE YOU'RE WAITING FOR YOUR SHIP TO COME IN, WHY DON'T YOU DO SOME MAINTENANCE WORK ON THE PIER ?"

The Third Secret of Salary Negotiation:

During the Salary Discussion, Try Never to Be the First One to Mention a Salary Figure

Where salary negotiation has been kept *offstage* for much of the interview process, when it finally does come *onstage* you want the employer to be the first one to mention *a figure*, if you can.

Nobody knows why, but it has been observed over the years—where the goals are opposite, as in this case, you are trying to get the employer to pay the most that they can, and the employer is trying to pay the least that they can—in this back-and-forth negotiation, *whoever mentions a salary figure first, generally loses.* You can speculate from now until the cows come home, as to *why* this is; all we know is *that* it is.

Inexperienced employer/interviewers often don't know this quirky rule. But experienced ones are very aware of it; that's why they will *always* toss the ball to you, with some innocent-sounding question, such as: "What kind of salary are you

looking for?" *Well, how kind of them to ask me what I want*—you may be thinking. No, no, no. Kindness has nothing to do with it. They are hoping *you* will be the first to mention a figure, because they know this odd experiential truth: that *whoever mentions a salary figure first, generally loses salary negotiation, at the last.*

Accordingly, if they ask you to name a figure, the *counter-move* on your part should be: "Well, you created this position, so you must have some figure in mind, and I'd be interested in knowing what that figure is."

Before You Go to the Interview, Do Some Careful Research on Typical Salaries for Your Field and/or That Organization

As I said earlier, salary negotiation is possible *anytime* the employer does not open their discussion of salary by naming the top figure they have in mind, but starts instead with a lower figure.

Okay, so here is our $64,000 question: how do you tell whether the figure the employer first offers you is only their *starting bid*, or is their *final final offer*? The answer is: by doing some research on the field *and* that organization, first.

Oh, come on! I can hear you say. *Isn't this all more trouble than it's worth?* No, not if you're determined.

If you're determined, this is one step you don't want to overlook. Trust me, salary research pays off *handsomely*.

Let's say it takes you from one to three days to run down this sort of information on the three or four organizations that interest you the most. And let us say that because you've done this research, when you finally go in for the hiring-interview you are able to ask for and obtain a salary that is $4,000 a year higher in range, than you would otherwise have gotten. In just the next three years, you will be earning $12,000 extra, because of your salary research. *Not bad pay, for one to three days' work!* And it can be even more. I know *many* job-hunters and career-changers to whom this has happened. Thus you can see that there is a financial penalty exacted from those who are too lazy, or in too much of a hurry, to go gather this information. In plainer language: *if you don't do this research, it'll cost ya!*

Okay then, how do you do this research? There are two ways to go: on the Internet, and off the Internet. Let's look at each, in turn:

SALARY RESEARCH ON THE INTERNET

If you have access to the Internet, and you want to research salaries for particular geographical regions, positions, occupations, or industries, here are some free sites that may give you just what you're looking for:

▶ The Bureau of Labor Statistics' survey of salaries in individual occupations, *The Occupational Outlook Handbook 2006–2007.*

www.bls.gov/oco

▶ The Bureau of Labor Statistics' survey of salaries in individual industries (it's a companion piece to *The Occupational Outlook Handbook 2006–2007*).

http://stats.bls.gov/oco/cg/cgindex.htm

▶ "High Earning Workers Who Don't Have a Bachelor's Degree," by Matthew Mariani, appearing first in the Fall 1999 issue of the *Occupational Outlook Quarterly.* For those who want to know how to earn *a lot* without having to go to college first.

http://stats.bls.gov/opub/ooq/1999/
fall/art02.pdf

▶ The oldest of the salary-specific sites, and one of the largest and most complete lists of salary reviews on the Web; run by a genius (Mary Ellen Mort).

http://jobstar.org/tool/salary/index.cfm

▶ The most visited of all the salary-specific job-sites, with fifty online partners that use their "Salary Wizard," such as AOL and Yahoo.

www.salary.com

▶ When you need a salary expert, it makes sense to go to the Salary Expert. Lots of stuff on the subject here, including a free "Salary Report" for hundreds of job titles, varying by area, skill level, and experience. Also has one of the salary calculators mentioned earlier.

www.salaryexpert.com

Incidentally, if these free sites don't give you what you want, you can always *pay* for the info, and hopefully get more-up-to-date surveys. Salary Source (`www.salarysource.com`) offers up-to-date salary information services starting at $19.95.

If you "strike out" on all the above sites, then you're going to have to get a little more clever, and work a little harder, and pound the pavement, as I describe below.

SALARY RESEARCH OFF THE INTERNET

Off the Internet, how do you go about doing salary research? Well, there's a simple rule: generally speaking, abandon books, and go talk to people. Use books and libraries only as a *second*, or *last*, resort. (Their information is often just way too outdated.)

You can get much more complete and up-to-date information from people who are in the same job *at another company or organization*. Or, people at the nearby university or college who *train* such people, whatever that department may be. Teachers and professors will usually know what their graduates are making.

Now, exactly how do you go about getting this information, by talking to people? Let's look at some concrete examples:

First Example: Working at your first entry-level job, say at a fast-food place.

You may not need to do any salary research. They pay what they pay. You can walk in, ask for a job application, and interview with the manager. He or she will usually tell you the pay, outright. It's usually *inflexible*. But at least you'll find that it's easy to discover what the pay is. (Incidentally, filling out an application, or having an interview there, doesn't commit you to taking the job—but you probably already know that. You can always decline an offer from *any place*. That's what makes this approach harmless.)

Second Example: Working at a place where you can't discover what the pay is, say *at a construction company.*

If that construction company where you would *hope* to get a job is difficult to research, go visit a *different* construction company in the same town—one that isn't of much interest to you—and ask what they make *there*. Or, if you don't know who to talk to there, fill out one of their applications, and talk to the hiring person about what kinds of jobs they have (or might have in the future), at which time prospective wages is a legitimate subject of discussion. Then, having done this research on a place you don't care about, go back to the place that *really* interests you, and apply. You still don't know *exactly* what they pay, but you do know what their competitor pays—which will usually be *close*.

> *Third Example:* Working in a one-person office, say *as a secretary*.

Here you can often find useful salary information by perusing the *Help Wanted* ads in the local paper for a week or two. Most of the ads probably won't mention a salary figure, but a few *may*. Among those that do, note what the lowest salary offering is, and what the highest is, and see if the ad reveals some reasons for the difference. It's interesting how much you can learn about salaries, with this approach. I know, because I was a secretary myself, once upon a time (dinosaurs were still roaming the earth).

Chapter Seven

Another way to do salary research is to find a *Temporary Work Agency* that places secretaries, and let yourself be farmed out to various offices: the more, the merrier. It's relatively easy to do salary research when you're *inside* the place. (Study what that place pays *the agency*, not what the agency then pays you.) If it's an office where the other workers *like* you, you'll be able to ask questions about a lot of things, including salary. It's like *summertime*, where the research is easy.

The Fifth Secret
of Salary Negotiation:

Define a Range That the Employer Has in Mind, and Then Define an Interrelated Range for Yourself

THE EMPLOYER'S RANGE

Before you finish your research, before you go into that organization for your final interview, you want more than just *one* figure. You want *a range*: what's the *least* the employer may be willing to offer you, and what's the *most* the employer may be willing to offer you. In any organization that has more than five employees, that range is relatively easy to figure out. It will be less than what the person *who would be above you* makes, and more than what the person *who would be below you* makes.

If the Person Who Would Be Below You Makes	And the Person Who Would Be Above You Makes	The Range for Your Job Would Be
$45,000	$55,000	$47,000–$53,000
$30,000	$35,500	$31,500–$33,500
$15,240	$18,000	$16,500–$17,200

One teensy-tiny little problem: *how* do you find out the salary of those who would be above and below you? Well, first you have to find out their *names* or the names of their *positions*. If it is a small organization you are going after—one with twenty or fewer employees—finding out this information should be *duck soup*. Any employee who works there is likely to know the answer, and you can usually get in touch with one of those employees, or even an ex-employee, through your own personal contacts. Since up to two-thirds of all new jobs are created by companies that size, that's the size organization you are likely to be researching, anyway.

If you are going after a larger organization, then you fall back on our familiar life preserver, namely, every contact you have (family, friend, relative, business, or church acquaintance) who might know the company, and therefore, the information you seek. In other words, you are looking for Someone Who Knows Someone who either is working, or has worked, at the particular place or places that interest you, and who therefore has or can get this information for you.

Chapter Seven

If you absolutely run into a blank wall on a particular organization (everyone who works there is pledged to secrecy, and they have shipped all their ex-employees to Siberia), then seek out information on their nearest *competitor* in the same geographic area. *For example,* let us say you were researching Bank X, and they were proving to be inscrutable about what they pay their managers. You would then try Bank Y as your research base, to see if the information were easier to come by, there. And if it were, you would then assume the two were similar in their pay scales, and that what you learned about Bank Y was applicable also to Bank X.

Also experts say that in researching salaries, you should take note of the fact that most governmental agencies have civil service positions matching those in private industry, and their job descriptions and pay ranges are available to the public. Go to the nearest city, county, regional, state, or federal civil service office, find the job description nearest what you are seeking in private industry, and then ask for the starting salary.

YOUR OWN RANGE

Once you've made a guess at what the employer's range might be, for the job you have in mind, you then define your own range *accordingly*. Let me give an example. Suppose you guess that the employer's range is one of those stated in the chart on page 127, $16,500 to $17,200. Accordingly, you now *invent* an "asking" range for yourself, where your *minimum* "hooks in" just below that employer's *maximum*.

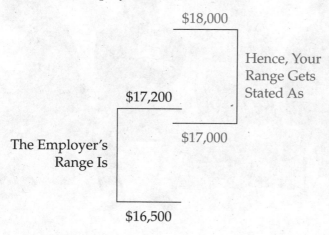

$18,000

Hence, Your
Range Gets
Stated As

$17,200

$17,000

The Employer's
Range Is

$16,500

And so, when the employer has stated a figure (probably around his or her *lowest*—i.e., $16,500), you will be ready to respond with something like: "I understand of course the constraints under which all organizations are operating, considering the present economy, but I believe my productivity is such that it would *justify* a salary"—*and here you mention a range whose bottom hooks in just below the top of their range, and goes up from there, accordingly, as shown on the diagram above*—"in the range of $17,000 to $18,000."

It will help a lot if during this discussion, you are prepared to show in what ways you will *make money* or in what ways you will *save money* for that organization, such as will justify the higher salary you are seeking. Hopefully, this will succeed in getting you the salary you want.

Daniel Porot, the job-expert in Europe, suggests that if you and an employer really hit it off, and you're *dying* to work there, but they cannot afford the salary you need, consider offering them part of your time. If you need, and believe you deserve, say $25,000, but they can only afford $15,000, you might consider offering them three days a week of your time for that $15,000 (15/25 = 3/5). This leaves you free to take work elsewhere during those other two days. You will *of course* produce so much work during those three days per week, that they will be ecstatic that they got you for even those three days.

Chapter Seven

Know How to Bring the
Salary Negotiation to a Close;
Don't Leave It "Just Hanging"

Your salary negotiation with this particular employer is not finished until you've addressed the issue of so-called fringe benefits. "Fringes" such as life insurance, health benefits or health plans, vacation or holiday plans, and retirement programs typically add anywhere from 15 to 28 percent to many workers' salaries. That is to say, if an employee receives $3000 salary per month, the fringe benefits are worth another $450 to $840 per month.

If your job is *at a high level*, benefits may include but not be limited to: health, life, dental, disability, malpractice insurance; insurance for dependents; sick leave; vacation; personal leave/ personal days; educational leave; educational cost reimbursement for coursework related to the job; maternity and/or parental leave; health leave to care for dependents; bonus system or profit sharing; stock options; expense accounts for entertaining clients; dues to professional associations; travel reimbursement; fee-sharing arrangements for clients that the employee generates; organizational memberships; parking; automobile allowance; relocation costs; sabbaticals; professional conference costs; time for community service; flextime work schedules; and fitness center memberships.

You should therefore, before you walk into the interview, know what benefits are particularly important to you, then at the end of salary negotiation remember to ask what benefits are offered—and negotiate if necessary for the benefits you particularly care about. Thinking this out ahead of time, of course, makes your negotiating easier, by far.

You also want to achieve some understanding about what their policy is about future raises. You can prepare the ground at the end of salary negotiation, by saying: *"If I accomplish this job to your satisfaction, as I fully expect to—and more—when could I expect to be in line for a raise?"*

Finally, you want to get *all of this* summarized, in writing. Always request a letter of agreement—or employment contract—that they give to you. If you can't get it in writing, now's a good time to start wondering *why*. The Road to Hell is paved with oral promises that went unwritten, and—later—unfulfilled.

Many executives unfortunately "forget" what they told you during the hiring-interview, or even deny they ever said such a thing.

Also, many executives leave the company for another position and place, and their successor or the top boss may disown any *unwritten* promises: *"I don't know what caused them to say that to you, but they clearly exceeded their authority, and of course we can't be held to that."*

Chapter Seven

Conclusion:
The Greatest Secret

All of this, of course, presumes that your interview, and salary negotiation, goes well. There are times, however, when it looks like it's going well, and then all of a sudden and without warning it comes totally unraveled. You're hired, told to report next Monday, and then get a phone call on Friday telling you that all hiring has been put, mysteriously, "on hold." You're therefore back out "on the pavement." Having seen this happen so many times, over the years, I remind you of the truth throughout this book: *successful* job-hunters and career-changers *always have alternatives.*

Alternative ideas of what they could do with their life.

Alternative ways of describing what they want to do right now.

Alternative ways of going about the job-hunt (not just the Internet, not just resumes, agencies, and ads).

Alternative job prospects.

Alternative "target" organizations that they go after.

Alternative ways of approaching employers.

And so on, and so forth.

What all this means for you, the seeker of secrets, is: make sure you are pursuing more than just one employer, right up until after you start your new job. That organization, that office, that group, that church, that factory, that government agency, that volunteer organization that you've targeted may be *the ideal place* where you would like to work. But no matter how appetizing this *first choice* looks to you, no matter how much it makes your mouth water at the thought of working there, *you are committing job-hunting suicide* if you don't have some alternative places in mind. Sure, maybe you'll get that dream-come-true. But—*big question*—what are your plans if you don't? You've *got* to have other plans **now**—not when that first target runs out of gas three months from now. You must go after more than one organization. I recommend five "targets," at least.

TARGET SMALL ORGANIZATIONS

Were I myself looking for a job tomorrow, this is what I would do. After I had figured out, using pages 239 to 279, what my ideal job looked like, and after I had collected a list of those workplaces that have such jobs, in my chosen geographical area, I would then circle the names and addresses of those that are *small* organizations (personally I would restrict my *first draft* to those with twenty-five or fewer employees)—and then go after them, in the manner I have described in previous chapters. However, as the dot-com *downturn* taught us, small organizations can sometimes be fraught with danger *(a nova-like birth, a sudden black hole death)*, I would look particularly for small organizations that are *established* or *growing*. And if "*organizations with twenty-five or fewer employees*" eventually didn't turn up enough *leads* for me, then I would broaden my search to "*organizations with fifty or fewer employees*," and finally—if that turned up nothing—to "*organizations with 100 or fewer employees*." But I would start small. Very small.

Remember, job-hunting always involves luck, to some degree. But with a little bit of luck, and a lot of hard work, plus determination, these instructions about how to get hired should work for you, as they have worked for so many hundreds of thousands before you.

Take heart from those who have gone before you, such as this determined job-hunter, who wrote me this heartfelt letter, with which I close:

"Before I read this book, I was depressed and lost in the futile job-hunt using Want Ads Only. I did not receive even one phone call from any ad I answered, over a total of four months. I felt that I was the most useless person on earth. I am female, with a two-and-a-half-year-old daughter, a former professor in China, with no working experience at all in the U.S. We came here seven months ago because my husband had a job offer here.

Chapter Seven

"Then, on June 11th of last year, I saw your book in a local book-store. Subsequently, I spent three weeks, ten hours a day except Sunday, reading every single word of your book and doing all of the flower petals in the Flower Exercise. After getting to know myself much better, I felt I was ready to try the job-hunt again. I used Parachute *throughout as my guide, from the very beginning to the very end, namely, salary negotiation.*

"In just two weeks I secured (you guessed it) two job offers, one of which I am taking, as it is an excellent job, with very good pay. It is (you guessed it again) a small company, with twenty or so employees. It is also a career-change: I was a professor of English; now I am to be a controller!

"I am so glad I believed your advice: there are jobs out there, and there are two types of employers out there, and truly there are!

"I hope you will be happy to hear my story."

When The
Unexpected Happens:

How to
Deal with
Change

On
This Restless, Unpredictable, Ever-Changing Earth:

How to Pick a New Place to Live

We live upon a restless Earth, among restless peoples, tribes, and nations, each of us dealing with it all from within an ever more vulnerable body, driven by a restless, ever-seeking heart.

Whew!

All of this means that Change is inevitable, in our life: it is something we know that we are going to have to deal with, somewhere, sometime. The only question is *when*, and *what?*

The fact that we live upon a restless Earth has been very much in the headlines, lately. It is like a world that's waiting to be born, going through its pangs of labor.

Think: tsunami, volcano, earthquake, hurricane, fire, flood, famine, and disease.

Remember: recent headlines about Indonesia, Montserrat, Peru, Afghanistan, Katrina, New Orleans, Oklahoma, Texas, Missouri, Georgia, Florida, Venice, Darfur, Somalia, and bird-flu pandemic.

They are not merely headlines. They are people. We hear their news and then we think: *Thank God that wasn't us!* But in our heart of hearts we know that we too can be displaced, at any time, and without warning, from our comfortable home, from our comfortable life, that we had been thinking would just go on and on forever, as it was.

Life can be a very *moving experience*, so they say; and this is quite literally true. In the U.S. alone, some *fourteen million* of us move each year, lock, stock, and barrel. This is the first evidence of change most of us encounter. We change our living place.

Incidentally, when we move, *why* do we move? Well, the reasons are various and manifold; I count *fourteen*, just for starters.

1. Catastrophes that come out of the blue, and are of Biblical proportions. Currently, over twenty-five million people worldwide have lost their homes, either temporarily or permanently, according to the United Nations. The tsunami, Katrina, tribal warfare in Darfur and Chad, famine in Somalia and elsewhere in Africa, earthquakes in Afghanistan, tornadoes and fires throughout the U.S. are only some of the causes. This sort of thing can herald a devastating change in our whole life's direction. Or it can signal the beginning of a transformational time in our lives. Curse, or blessing. Half depends on circumstance. Half depends on us.

These catastrophes are *moves* that are thrust upon us. We have no say about them. We have no power over them. But, other times we *move* for internal reasons, because of things going on *in* us, where *we* decide the timing and the direction of the move.

Such reasons include:

2. A safe haven. We sometimes move in order to escape harsh, often intolerable circumstances. The most urgent of these is domestic violence.[1] We find ourselves facing long-standing, hurtful hitting, beatings, or sexual molestation—and no one will come to rescue us. We have to rescue ourselves. Often this means running, far far away. In case that is your case, do know that there is aid and help in doing this. If you live in the States, see www.help guide.org. *("Domestic violence" is listed in the right-hand column; click on it. There you will find a link to State Coalition agencies, which can help you move.)* There are similar sites elsewhere in the world: for example in the UK there is www.bbc.co.uk/crime/support/ domesticviolence.shtml.

---

1. For details (statistics and so on) see: www.rainbowsendpress.com/sp/ domvio.html

3. New life, new place. Release from the military, finishing college, death of a loved one, release from prison, divorce, a new marriage, etc.—you are starting a new chapter in your life, and you decide you want to start it in a new place, away from the memories of the past.

4. Medical attention. Maybe you need more medical expertise than is offered in the place where you are; you need to go to the kind of country, place, or hospital, where you or your family can get the medical attention that you need. Don't know where to start? Type *best hospitals best doctors* into your favorite search engine on the Internet.

5. Education. Maybe you live where there is only a two-year college, and you want four years of college. Or where there's only four years, and you want a place where you can get a graduate degree. Or maybe there's a far better school in some other country, that has exactly the professors you'd most like to study with, for your field. Type *best universities best professors* into your favorite search engine, to find the best in the U.S., Europe, Asia, Australia, etc.

6. Geography as career guidance. I once met a waitress who moved from one city to another, never staying more than five months in any one place; she was a keen observer of the local scene, wherever she was, and was hoping to get from her observations some new ideas of what else she could do with her life, besides waitressing. I was quite taken with her approach. I thought to myself, "Ah, geography as a career search tool. Never thought of that!" But someone did. I later found out that someone has turned this into a business. His name is Brian

---

2. www.vocationvacations.com. A bit superficial, perhaps (one to three days). A bit pricey, perhaps ($400–$1500). But, who knows? You just might find out what you want to do, next, with your life.

Kurth. His business is called Vocation Vacations.[2] Very popular! So, geography is not a bad way to explore future kinds of jobs. Plus, careers aside, maybe you'll meet Prince Charming in your travels. Or a female rock star. Or the new Donald Trump. *"One never know, do one?" (Fats Waller).*

7. Jobs. Of course, *of course.* Just within the good ol' U.S. of A., for example, there are varying job opportunities, as you move from city to city, and from state to state. Your local federal/state employment office can usually give you the current unemployment statistics about all fifty states. The figures are also on the Internet.[3] You want to look, of course, for the states with the lowest overall unemployment rate, where finding jobs is the easiest.

As of my latest figures, released May 18, 2007, the five states with the lowest jobless rates (those rates stated as a percentage of that state's workforce), where it's therefore easiest to find a job (in theory) are:

1. Montana (2.2 percent unemployment rate)
2. Hawaii (2.4 percent unemployment rate)
3. Utah (2.5 percent unemployment rate)
4. Idaho (2.8 percent unemployment rate)
5. Nebraska (2.8 percent unemployment rate)

On the other hand, the five states with the highest jobless rates (stated as a percentage of that state's workforce) where it's therefore hardest to find a job (in theory) are:

1. Michigan (7.1 percent unemployment rate)
2. Mississippi (6.8 percent unemployment rate)
3. South Carolina (5.8 percent unemployment rate)
4. Alaska (5.8 percent unemployment rate)
5. Ohio and the District of Columbia
   (5.7 percent unemployment rate)

Louisiana's unemployment rate, in case you are wondering, (*rebuilding painfully slowly after Katrina*), is 4.3 percent.

If you want to move, in order to pursue the jobs, pick one of the first five states, say the one that appeals to you the most, get your hands on a map of that state, pick one or more areas in that

---

3. For the states see: www.bls.gov/web/laumstrk.htm. For metropolitan areas in the U.S. see: www.bls.gov/web/laummtrk.htm.

state—metropolitan or rural—and write to their chamber of commerce. You can ask *Information* for their phone number, or if you prefer you can of course look it up online, at: `www.chamberof`
`commerce.com/forms/search_state_chambers.htm`. Then you ask those chambers for all the information they have in writing, about businesses that deal with your trade or specialty, assuming you know your trade or specialty.

8. Money. Minimum hourly wages in some civilized places around the world run $1.75 or less. Sometimes much, much less. (*Try: fifty cents a day.*) Some people, when their families can manage it financially, go to places that pay better for the work they do best and most enjoy doing; they then send the money back home. Alternatively, you may just move back in with your family for a while if you have no wages, and just can't find a job to save your life.

9. "Going rural." Maybe you're looking for a simpler life, away from urban centers, out where the buffalo roam, and the deer and the antelope play, where seldom is heard a discouraging word, and the skies are not cloudy all day, etc. Good for you! Further details about this, in the body of this chapter.

10. "Going urban." You may want more choices in life, than are available to you where you are. So you move from a remote place to a more crowded one.

11. Wanderlust. You just want to be moving around. Period. You've got itchy feet. You're bored, and it feels better to be in motion, than it does to be stuck still in the same old same old. You're like a gifted dancer, looking for a new ballroom.

12. Curiosity and love of adventure. There's some place, city, country, continent you've heard about, and you always wanted to see it with your own eyes, just out of curiosity, or for the love of adventure, or maybe even to find out if you want to live there—*maybe*. One woman I know, newly single, has made a list of twelve countries she wants to visit and work in, before she retires or dies. If you're starting fresh, and need some ideas, there's a great book to help you; it's called *1000 Places to See Before You Die*.[4]

---

4. By Patricia Schultz, Workman Publishing Company, May 22, 2003. Very popular book, as I write. (*NY Times* best-seller list; also among the top 250 best-selling titles on Amazon.com, etc.)

13. Love of beauty. You want to visit or move to a more beautiful place, which fills your soul with serenity and takes your breath away. It can be the gardens of England, the music of Aspen, Colorado, Yosemite National Park in California, the mountains of Switzerland, some South Sea Island, Hawaii, Guilin in China, Ha Long Bay in Vietnam, the Tetons in Wyoming, etc. Need ideas? If you have access to the Internet, enter at the same time the words *photos* and *most beautiful places on earth* into your favorite search engine (say, www.google.com or www.a9.com). Or enter your favorite kind of scenery or environment: *music, art, museums, mountains, lakes, gardens, ocean, universities, tropical, buildings,* etc., together with the word *photos,* into that search engine. See what you find. Try also the Discovery Channel on your TV.

14. Compassion for family or for mankind. As families age, become injured, or fall ill, you may move home or at least closer to home, in order to be their caregivers during their dying or other life crisis. Or, if we define *family* more broadly, you may want to fight AIDS/HIV, or malaria, or poverty, or bird flu, or any other of the scourges of mankind, in some near or far-off place.

Katrina

So much for the geographical possibilities. Summing up: in some cases you *want* to move; in other cases, as with Katrina and similar catastrophes, you *have* to move. Immediately. With only a garbage bag of your lifelong possessions, under your arm. You *have* to move, for now. Even if, maybe—*maybe*—some day you'll be back.

The question for now is: how do you go about choosing a new place, when you haven't got even a clue where to go?

The *diaspora,* or dispersion, that occurred in Katrina's wake, found hundreds of thousands of people fleeing New Orleans, and other low-lying Gulf Coast cities, searching—most immediately— for a safe place, above all else. A higher ground, where the flood-waters could not reach them, and a place where lawlessness did not reign. They found what they were looking for, temporarily, in a nearby *parish,* or in a city or state far away.[5]

In all of our lives, there may come such a time when without any warning *Survival* will be our issue and our first consideration in defining *a new place*.

Most Immediately, Choose Any Place Where You Feel Safe

I have argued elsewhere[6] that each time we find ourselves in a new situation, there are four issues we must solve, in turn—and in this order: 1. **What's Happening?** What exactly is the situation I am facing? 2. **Survival.** What do I have to do, to survive, physically, economically, mentally, and spiritually, in the midst of all that's happening? 3. **Meaning or Mission.** How can I then find some meaning to all of this, and some meaning or mission for my future life and work? 4. **Effectiveness.** And, how can I measure how well I am achieving my goals?

The point? The point is that when *Survival* is your issue, you usually have to solve *that* first, before you can go on to deal with any other issues you may face. Hence, you must find, first of all, a place where you feel safe.

---

5. Events move swiftly, but for months if not years to come, help will be desperately needed for this largest displacement of people in the U.S. since the Civil War in the 1860s. If your heart is moved to help them (*"There, but for the grace of God, go I."*) there is a central website you can turn to, to donate online to any of a tremendously wide variety of helpers. It is called Network for Good, located at: www.networkforgood.org/topics/animal_environ/hurricanes/.

6. In my book, *The Three Boxes of Life, and How to Get Out of Them: An Introduction to Life Work Planning* (Berkeley, CA: Ten Speed Press, 1981).

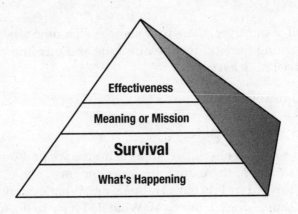

Next, Choose a Place
Where You Formerly Lived,
and Have, Still,
Family or Friends There

That place, whatever its name, has the virtue of familiarity. We've been there before. We know, basically, how to make our way around. When we feel lost and bewildered, *familiar surroundings* count for a lot.

That place has also the virtue of support. If our family is there, they offer a haven, a place of refuge and recovery, when we have nowhere else to turn. If there once was love for us there, love waits there for us still. Family will take care of us, for a time, when no one else will. Ditto for friends—*true* friends as defined by Jesus' standard: *"I was hungry and you gave me something to eat, I was thirsty and you gave me something to drink, I was a stranger and you invited me in, I needed clothes, and you clothed me, I was sick and you looked after me. . . ."*[7]

To such friends, or to a loving family, we instinctively turn when we are broke and out of money, and have no job to mention. That's true of the thousands if not millions of victims of Katrina. That's true even in lesser circumstances, as when you are an unemployed college graduate, who has to move temporarily back in with your parents, when you just can't find a job. A chance for you to exercise the good old-fashioned virtue of gratitude. Think it. Say it. Out loud. Thank you.

---

7. In *The Gospel* according to Matthew, chapter 25, verses 34–40.

Beyond Survival:
Picture a Place
Where You'd Most Like to Live

If *survival* is not your issue, but rather your issue is that of *meaning and mission*, i.e., choosing a more appropriate place where your work and your spirit can flourish, then where do you begin?

Well, begin simply. Ask yourself, *if I could live anywhere in the country (or the world), what place would it be?*

Got a name? Good!

Got some doubts? Well yes, of course, you do. That proves you're human. You've got doubts that you will ever be able to figure out a way to get there, and live there.

Well, let's be honest. It *could* all stay a daydream. But, ah! maybe it won't. You'll never know 'til you try. And try hard. So, don't set yourself up for failure, with your thinking. Picture your dream coming true. Picture yourself in that place. Keep that vision strongly in your head.

Places are like jobs.
The stronger a picture
you can see in your mind
of what you want,
the more enthusiasm you will feel,
and the more time you will put in,
toward achieving that dream.

My own motto for many many years now, is: *Pray as though everything depended on God; then work, as though everything depended on you.*

Here's how you begin, as though everything depended on you:

1. You start by interviewing all your friends and acquaintances, to ask them what places *they* have loved the most, in the U.S. or in whatever country you live. And *why*. This task can be a lot of fun, and a great conversation-starter with all your friends. But be sure and write their suggestions down—don't just nod thoughtfully! And when you have a lengthy list, choose the two or three places that intrigue you the most, and do further investigation.

2. Too shy to interview your friends and family? Well, then, you can turn to books or to the Internet. Books used to be the way to go. In the U.S., there were quite a number of them that rated various cities and towns according to *factors* that might be important to you, such as *weather, crime, educational system, recreational opportunities,* etc.

Now, they easily get out of date. Not surprisingly, considering the baby boomers are turning 50+, some of the books that are most up to date, these days, are being marketed as *retirement* books. But if you're in your twenties and thirties, and you need or want to move, ignore the fact that the title has the word *retirement* in it. These are immensely helpful to any age:

David Savageau's *Retirement Places Rated: What You Need to Know to Plan the Retirement You Deserve.* 7th edition, Sept. 2007. Completely Revised and Updated.

Bert Sperling and Peter Sander's *Cities Ranked & Rated: More than 400 Metropolitan Areas Evaluated in the U.S. and Canada (Cities Ranked and Rated).* 2nd edition, May 2007.

Bert Sperling's *Best Places to Raise Your Family.* 1st edition, May 2006.

So much for books. Websites for exploring places where you might love to live include Bert Sperling's BestPlaces site (`www.bestplaces.net`) and also Find Your Spot (`www.FindYourSpot.com`). I love this site!

It has an interesting article called *The Best Place to Live—and Other Fairy Tales.* And, then there is also CNN/Money's site: `money.cnn.com/best/bplive/`.

When You Want to "Go Rural"

Outdoors. Away from civilization. Wilderness. Do these words strike a chord with you? It may be, as you think about moving someday, that your idea of *paradise* turns out to be "going rural"—and moving, at last, to *the country.*

Sometimes the root of this lies in the desire for a simpler life; sometimes, the root lies in the desire for a less expensive way of living. Whatever the reasons, if this is your vision, take that vision seriously. Remember: you only have one life to live, on this earth at least.

Begin by interviewing anyone you know who has moved from urban to the rural life, and ask them what they liked the most about that move, and what they missed the most about their former locale. Then weigh what you learn.

Next, if you have a particular place in mind, investigate that place *thoroughly.* "Look before you leap" is always a splendid caution, and it means—in this particular case—that if there's a place that sounds *just great* to you, do your best to go visit it before you up and move there. This applies not only to rural places, but to urban, suburban, and every other kind of place, as well.

I repeat, if you can scrape together the necessary funds, *go there*, and talk to *everyone.* Through some persistent questioning on your part, search for both the good side and the bad. The dream you save may be your own.

When You Want to Just Wander

So much for finding a *place.* If you don't want to settle down, but you are thinking of leasing/buying an RV (recreational vehicle) in which to roam the U.S., you will doubtless be interested in getting your hands on, and reading, *Workamper News* (for "work camper"): `www.workamper.com/WorkamperNews/WNIndex.cfm`—a tabloid that, since 1987, has helped more than 70,000 people find jobs while roaming the West.

How to Pick a New Place to Live

Incidentally, the champion work camper in the U.S. is a man named Chuck Woodbury who started his quarterly tabloid *Out West* as a hobby back in 1987. His story is an inspiring one for anyone considering a career change. His idea was to roam the West in a motor home rigged up as a newsroom, and to write about what he found along the way. He said, "I figured if I earned enough in subscriptions to cover my gasoline I'd be happy." But the media soon got wind of his unusual "on-the-road" newspaper, and the number of subscriptions shot up to 10,000. Since then, in his 13 years on the road, Woodbury logged more than 200,000 miles, wrote a million or so words, and snapped about 15,000 pictures. His paper, *Out West*, complete with a picture of him, is on the Internet at: `www.outwestnewspaper.com/home.html`. Chuck is no longer the editor, but now edits and publishes RV Travel, available only on the Web at `www.RVtravel.com`.

Alternative scenario: you love being outdoors but you've got no RV. And you wouldn't mind putting down roots for a spell? Then you might be interested in *caretaking* jobs. These are house-sitting or ranch-sitting contracts. A man named Gary Dunn says that for those who are spiritually connected with the earth, but don't own land, *caretaking* is an ideal career. Opportunities are listed in Gary Dunn's *Caretaker Gazette*, which he e-mails to subscribers (*there are 12,000 of them*) bimonthly (*that means once every two months—okay so you knew that, but I always forget*). Cost? $29.95 a year. Details can be found on the Internet at `www.caretaker.org` or you can order it directly from Gary, at *The Caretaker Gazette*, Gary C. Dunn, Publisher, PO Box 4005-M, Bergheim, TX 78004, or call him at (830) 336-3939, or e-mail him at `caretaker@caretaker.org`. Approximately 150 caretaker/house-sitting opportunities are in each issue. Over 1,000 new assignments are available each year, and these opportunities are worldwide!

When You Want to Work Overseas

Speaking of "worldwide," 3.2 million Americans currently live abroad (not including the military stationed in Iraq, Afghanistan, and elsewhere). If you've always wanted to live and work overseas, then that is a dream you should explore. I am talking about job-hunters in the U.S. who want to move to Europe, Africa, Asia, South America, or even next door, to Canada.[8]

There is a site on the Internet that should prove immensely helpful. It is: `www.escapeartist.com/expatriate/resources.htm`. But there are some cautions that need to be voiced about living overseas. These are from Will Cantrell, former editor of *International Employment Hotline,* now merged with *International Career Employment Weekly.*

First of all, make sure you're not going overseas in order to find Utopia. Utopia rarely lives up to expectations. Even if (big *if*) you do not find the same things that irritate you about the country where you presently live, I guarantee you that you will find some brand new things to irritate you.

Regarding the mechanics of going overseas: many people assume you find an overseas job by packing a bag, buying a ticket, and passing out resumes once you reach your foreign destination. No, no, no. Work-permit requirements and high unemployment make finding jobs at foreign destinations often difficult, and sometimes impossible.

For example, if you were to study employment classifieds in, say, a newspaper from London, England, you would at first sight think you had found some grand opportunities for yourself. *Unfortunately,* these are in most cases job opportunities open only to British nationals or citizens of EU nations ("European Union"). What is true in England is true elsewhere. Your U.S. citizenship will actually preclude you from working in a foreign country—even Canada—unless your employer can prove that a local national is unavailable to take the job, and thus secure a work permit for *you.*

Your wisest approach to overseas employment is to conduct your job-hunt for an overseas job while you are still here in the U.S. How do you go about it?

Well, first of all, research the country or countries that interest you, as to living conditions, conditions of employment, etc. Talk

---

8. However, there are readers of this book who live in those places and want to move to the U.S. Much of what I have to say here will apply, as general principles, to them.

to everyone you possibly can who has in fact been overseas, most especially to those country or countries. A nearby large university will probably have such faculty or students (*ask*). Companies in your city that have overseas branches (*your library should be able to tell you which they are*) should be able to lead you to people also—possibly to the names and addresses of personnel who are still "over there" to whom you can write for the information you are seeking.

Alternatively, try asking every single person you meet for the next week (at the supermarket checkout, at your work, at home, at church or synagogue, etc.) if they know someone who used to live overseas and now lives here in your city or town. You may be amazed at how many normal-looking people are actually world travelers. By doing research with such people, you will learn a great deal. Find out what they liked and didn't like, about the country that interests you. Find out what they know about the conditions for working over there.

Next, you need to research what kinds of job possibilities exist in that country. Every *successful* overseas search starts with *some* sources of information on "who's hiring now." *Which* sources you access, and how you make use of them, will greatly affect your chances of landing an overseas assignment.

What do I mean? Well, for openers, beware of such sources as employment agencies that promise to find you an overseas job for an advance fee. Ninety-eight percent of their clients *do not* find an overseas job. This fleecing industry has flourished for years, with a few individuals often running scores of companies under an assortment of names. Such companies regularly go out of business or file for bankruptcy *once they've fleeced enough suckers*. On the Internet, see the Rip-Off Report at `http://bad businessbureau.com/default.asp`.

Beware also of directories, advertised on the Internet, or in newspapers, etc., as listing *overseas employers*. Many, though not all, of these job listings are out of date and tend to report on "who *was* hiring" rather than "who is hiring *now*."

You can still make effective use of any such directory by taking care that *if* you contact an organization listed therein, you include a cover letter that requests that your resume be kept on file "for further consideration *if there are no current openings*." As I have emphasized elsewhere in this book, pure dumb luck—which means having your name in the "right place at the right time"—plays a crucial role in finding most jobs. Since you can't get *over there*, at the moment, you will have to rely more heavily on resumes here than I would normally advise, to keep your name in the right place. In the case of overseas employment, the more employers who have your resume, the better.

Also, in your job-search do not forget that the U.S. government is a heavy overseas employer.

If you run into an absolute stonewall in your search for an overseas job, there are two backup strategies for you to consider. The first is to seek an international internship. To find lists of these, just type "international internships" into your favorite Web browser, like Google (www.google.com).

The second strategy begins with the fact that many companies operating in this country, both domestic and foreign-owned, *have branches overseas.* Thus, *sometimes* your ticket to getting overseas may be to start working here in the U.S. for such a company, hoping they will eventually send you overseas. It *does* happen. And if it happens, they will likely take care of the visa and work permit red tape, pick up your travel bill, and provide other helpful benefits. Unfortunately, however, you can't *count* on their ever sending you overseas. In other words, it's a big fat gamble. *You* have to decide whether you're willing to take it, or not.

If you decide to do either of the above strategies, you'll find the names of organizations by going to your local library and asking the reference librarian to help you find such directories as these: *Principal International Businesses*, published by Dun's Marketing Service; *International Directory of Corporate Affiliations*, published by Corporate Affiliations Information Services, of the National Register Publishing Company; and *International Organizations, revised annually*, published by Gale Research, Inc.

Last, contact every friend you have who already lives overseas—even if it's not in the country that is your target. Ask for their counsel, advice, help, and prayers. They went before you; hopefully they can now be your guide, and door-opener.

No such friends? Then try a book. If you're not easily scared, there is a fascinating book called *The World's Most Dangerous*

Places, by Robert Young Pelton. The fifth edition was published in 2003, and you can get it from bookstores or online.

One final word about hunting for an overseas job: above all, be patient. The search for an overseas job takes *more* time than looking for a job in this country. Don't expect to be in an exotic foreign capital within ninety days. Perseverance is the key.

How to Research Your New Town or City

And now, whether your choice is overseas or here in your own country, whether your choice is urban or rural, there is the $64,000 question: how do you go about finding out about *jobs* in your chosen target city or town?

If your finances are tight, it may not be possible for you to go to visit your new chosen destination, at least in the immediate future. In which case, you want to research the place, as best you can, from a distance.

How do you do this, while still remaining in your present location? More specifically, how do you find out about *jobs*, at a distance?

There are *ways*.

• If your chosen city or town has a local newspaper, *subscribe*, even while you are still living *here*. Read the whole paper, when it comes, however long delayed. Look particularly for: news of companies that are *expanding*, news of *promotions* or *transfers* (that creates vacancies *down below* in "the company store"), and the like.

Chapter Eight

- You first want to discover some organizations that, at a distance, look interesting to you.

- Then you want to research them, at a distance, as much as you can.

- It will help if you can regard the city or town where you presently are as a kind of *parallel city* to the town or city you are interested in. In which case, some of your research can be done where you are, and then its *learnings* transferred. For example, suppose you wanted to use your interests in psychiatry, plants, and carpentry, in your future career. In the city where you presently are, you would try to learn how to combine these three. You might learn, right where you are, that there is a branch of psychiatry that uses plants in the treatment of deeply withdrawn patients, and these plants have to be put, of course, in wooden planters. Now, having learned *that* where you presently are, you would then explore your chosen city or town to see what psychiatric facilities they have there, and which ones—if any—use plants in their healing program. Thus you can conduct your research where you are, and then transfer its *learnings* to the place where you want to be.

- In doing your research of organizations that interest you, it is perfectly permissible for you to write to the library in your target city, asking for information that may be only there. If the librarian is too busy to answer, then use one of your contacts there to find out. "Bill (or Billie), I need some information that I'm afraid only the library in your town has. Specifically, I need to know about company x." Or whatever.

- Develop contacts, even at a distance, as much as you can.

- Ask your friends where you currently live, if they know of anyone who lives in that city or town. The best contacts are those who know your target employer really well.[9]

---

9. Unless—the job-hunter's nightmare—your mutual "friend"/contact has *misrepresented* how close he or she is to your target employer, and as a matter of fact said employer can't stand the sight of this "mutual friend." *It has happened.* It is to die. Asking a question beforehand, of the "mutual friend," like "How *well* do you know him—or her?" may help avoid this.

- If you went to college, find out if any graduates of that college live in this chosen city or town of yours. (Contact the alumni office of your college, and ask.)

- Also any church, synagogue, or national organization you belong to, that has a presence in that city or town, may yield true helpfulness to you, *if you know what it is you want to know.* Write or phone them, and tell them that you're one of their own and you need some information. *"I need to know who can tell me what nonprofit organizations there are in that city, that deal with x." "I need to know how I can find out what corporations in town have departments of mental hygiene."* Or, whatever.

- If you decide to approach the places that interest you, first of all by mail, you will want to research each organization so that you know *who* to address the letter to, *by name.* Get the name spelled absolutely accurately, and double-check. Nothing turns off a prospective employer like your misspelling her or his name.

- Your letter will carry a lot more weight if you can mention, in it, the name of any contacts you may know there.

- As for whether or not you should enclose a resume with your initial contact letter, experts' opinions vary widely. *Everything* depends on the nature of the resume, and the nature of the person you are sending it to. With some employers I know, the sight of a resume is *death* to any future rapport between you and this person. It will *ensure* that your letter is carelessly tossed aside. Other employers *like* to see resumes. It's a big fat gamble, unless you know someone who knows them, and their preferences.

- Personally, I think a well-composed letter, summarizing all you would say in a resume, may be your best bet, with a closing paragraph indicating that your resume is available, should they wish it.

- Once you've turned up some promising job prospects you will need to set up interviews; this means you will have to go there, to that town or city, in almost all cases.

- If you have trouble setting up interviews with a particular person at a particular place, see if that town or city has any church, synagogue, or national organization that you belong to here. If so, write and tell them of your local affiliation, and ask for their help in finding the person you're trying to connect with.

- When to go? Well if you are dirt-poor you might not be able to get there right away; you might have to wait until there's a professional convention, or business meeting nearby there, that your present boss could send you to. Or you might want to reschedule your next summer's vacation so that it is *there*.

- If this is your first-ever visit to the place, try to go there a week or so ahead of whatever interviews you have set up, so you can look the whole place over, and decide: *Do I really want to move here?* It's a little late to do on-site explorations, experts will tell you; but, hey, better late than never!

- *Needless to say,* if you have a spouse or partner who is going to be moving there with you, they should be doing this same kind of research of that place, and setting up the same kinds of interviews, as you are planning.

How Hard Should I Work at This?

We kept score with one man's job-hunt. While still at a distance he turned up—by means of diligent research—107 places that seemed interesting to him. Over a period of some time, he sent a total of 297 letters to them. He also made a total of 126 phone calls to that city. When he was finally able to go there in person, he had narrowed the original 107 that looked interesting, down to just 45. He visited all 45, while there. Having done his homework on himself thoroughly and well—and having obviously conducted *this* part of his search in an extremely professional manner, he received 35 job offers. When he had finished his survey, he went back to the one job he most wanted— and accepted it.

No one can argue that you should be dealing with numbers of this magnitude. But this may at least give you some idea of *how hard you may need to work* at this. Certainly, we're not just talking about five letters and two phone calls. We're talking about rolling up your sleeves, and being *very thorough*.

Conclusion

There is a great joy in moving to a new place, particularly if it is to a place that you love. One job-hunter described this joy to me, in words that many other job-hunters could echo:

"[Not long ago,] my wife and I took a trip out to the Southwest from our home in Annapolis, Maryland, to see the Grand Canyon and sights like that. We both fell in love with the Southwest, and said, 'Wouldn't it be great if I could get a job out here as a highway engineer, and maybe we could work with the Native Americans.' Back in Annapolis, I purchased Parachute and read it with extreme interest. So I started some network planning, and scheduled another upcoming trip to Arizona in February of the following year, planning to visit various engineering offices and check out living conditions.

"Meanwhile, I visited the U.S.G.S. Headquarters in Reston, Virginia. On the way out, I noticed an ad on the bulletin board for 'Highway Engineer—Bureau of Indian Affairs, Gallup, New Mexico.' Naturally, I applied for the job but received notice that the position had been cancelled. Disappointed, my wife and I decided to each spend a day in prayer. On the following day I received a call from that office in Gallup informing me there was another position for Highway Planner now open; was I still interested? Still interested?!

"Using your advice [to go after the person-who-has-the-power-to-hire-me] I called the Bureau in Gallup and got the names of the bosses of the various divisions or sections that would impinge upon my application. I sent in the application to the person by name who was the chief decision-maker. In February of the following year we carried out the trip I had been planning, now including a visit to Gallup. We visited headquarters there, though they weren't yet ready to formally interview, since not all applicants had yet been screened. However, it was a useful visit, and on returning, I wrote thank-you notes to all the people I had met, and hoped for the best.

"In March I received another phone call, asking for further information; I used this to invite myself out for an actual interview, at my expense. My offer was accepted, I was out there in two days, the interview went well, and I received official notice to report for work in May. We were ecstatic! And we found a house in Gallup, through a friend in Annapolis who had a friend in Gallup, who knew of a co-worker who was moving out.

"In short, ours is a wonderful story. Who would think a sixty-six-year-old man could leave one job and move into another full-time job, at a salary almost equal to his present one, in a place 2,600 miles away, that he and his wife truly love! What a blessing! And what you said has stuck with me all this time: I've remembered to write my thank-you notes."

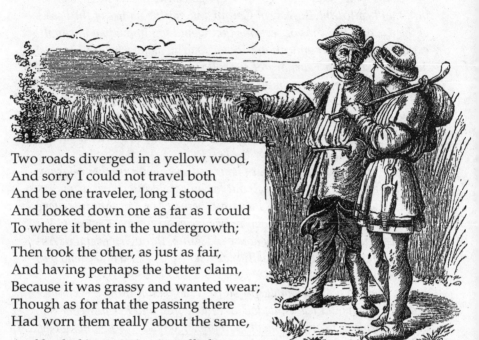

Two roads diverged in a yellow wood,
And sorry I could not travel both
And be one traveler, long I stood
And looked down one as far as I could
To where it bent in the undergrowth;

Then took the other, as just as fair,
And having perhaps the better claim,
Because it was grassy and wanted wear;
Though as for that the passing there
Had worn them really about the same,

And both that morning equally lay
In leaves no step had trodden black.
Oh, I kept the first for another day!
Yet knowing how way leads on to way,
I doubted if I should ever come back.

I shall be telling this with a sigh
Somewhere ages and ages hence:
Two roads diverged in a wood, and I—
I took the one less traveled by,
And that has made all the difference.

Robert Frost (1874–1963)[1]

---

1. The title of this poem is "The Road Not Taken," from *The Poetry of Robert Frost* edited by Edward Connery Lathem. Copyright 1916, 1969 by Holt, Rinehart & Winston. Used with permission. Incidentally, the late M. Scott Peck's classic, *The Road Less Traveled*, took its title from this poem. (*The Road Less Traveled, 25th Anniversary Edition: A New Psychology of Love, Traditional Values and Spiritual Growth*, by M. Scott Peck, M.D., Touchstone, 2003.)

In
This Restless, Unpredictable,
Ever-Changing
Job-Market:

How to Choose
a New Career

How Much Help Are Vocational Tests?

You've got to choose a new career.

Or, maybe, if you're just starting out, you've got to choose your very first career/field/industry/job.

So, what do you do? Left to our own instinct, most of us will opt for taking a test, of one kind or another.

Easy enough to do.

In the U.S. about two-thirds of all job-hunters or career-changers have access to the Internet. And tests are everywhere on the Internet.[2]

"Tests" are not really "tests." "Instruments" or "assessments" would be a more accurate description. Nonetheless, everyone loves to call them "tests." "Vocational tests." "Psychological tests." Whatever. You can take them by yourself.

Or, if you don't want to tackle this all by yourself, you can pay a career counselor to give them to you (*listings in the back, beginning on page 397*). Some career counselors make *testing* the cornerstone of everything they do with a client. *Voilà!* The tests will tell you what you should do, or what you should become. *Or will they?*

---

2. A more complete listing of what's on the Internet can be found at:
www.jobhuntersbible.com/counseling/.

Six Rules About Testing

1. You are absolutely unique. There is no person in the world like you. It follows from this that no test can measure YOU; it can only describe the family to which you belong.

Tests tend to divide the population into what we might call groups, tribes, or families—made up of all those people who answered the test the same way. After you've taken any test, don't ever say to yourself, "This must be who I am." (No, no, this must be who your family am.)[3]

I grew up in the Bolles family (surprise!), and they were all very "left-brained." I was a maverick in that family. I was right-brained. Fortunately, my father was an immensely loving man, who found this endearing. When I told him the convoluted way by which I went about figuring out something, he would respond with a hearty affectionate laugh, and a big hug, as he said: "Dick, I will never understand you." So, back to testing. Tests are about families, not individuals. The results of any test are descriptors—not of you, but of your family—i.e., all those who answered the test the same way you did. The SAI family. Or the blue family. Or the INTJ family. Or whatever. The results are an accurate description of that tribe, that family of people, in general; but are they descriptors also of you? Depends on whether or not you are a maverick in that family, the same way I was in mine. These family characteristics may or may not be true in every respect of you. You may be exactly like that group, or you may be different in important ways. And that's your call.

2. Don't predetermine how you want the test to come out. Stay loose and open to new ideas.

It's easy to have an emotional investment that the test should come out a certain way. I remember a job-hunting workshop where I asked everyone to list the factors they liked about any place where they had ever lived; and then prioritize those factors, to get the name of a new place to live. We had this immensely lovable black woman from Texas, in the workshop, and when we all got back together after a "break" I asked her how she was doing. With a glint in her eye she said, "I'm

---

3. Yes, I know that is bad grammar. But, pressing on: if you want to explore testing in any more depth, there is an excellent course online, from S. Mark Pancer, at Wilfred Laurier University in Waterloo, Ontario, Canada, at www.wlu .ca/page.php?grp_id=265&p=2941. Pay especial attention to Lectures 1 and 19.

prioritizing, and I'm gonna keep on prioritizin', until it comes out: Texas!" That was amusing, as she intended it to be; it's not so amusing when you play with test results, to try to make them come out a certain way. If you're gonna take tests, you need to be open—to new ideas. If you find yourself always trying to outguess the test, so it will confirm you on a path you've already decided upon, then testing is not for you.

3. In taking a test, you should just be looking for clues, hunches, or suggestions, rather than for a definitive picture that tells you exactly what you should do with your life.

And bear in mind that an online test isn't likely to be as insightful as one administered by an insightful psychologist or counselor, who may see things that you don't. But keep saying that mantra to yourself, as he or she is talking: Clues. Clues, I'm only looking for clues. If they prescribe exactly what you should do with your life, run for the door. (I know one career counselor who told every single female job-hunter who came to him, "You should be a nurse." Every single one!)

4. Take several tests and not just one. One may easily send you down the wrong path.

People who do their masters or doctorate program in "Testing and Measurement" know full well that tests are notoriously flawed, unscientific, and inaccurate. Sometimes they're more like parlor games than anything else. Fine for clues, hunches, and new ideas. But basing your future on tests' outcomes is like putting your trust in the man behind the curtain in The Wizard of Oz.

5. You're trying, in the first instance with tests, to broaden your horizons, and only later narrow your options down; you are *not* trying to narrow them down from the outset. Bad career planning looks like this:

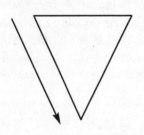

Most computerized tests embody the idea of starting with a wide range of options; and narrowing them down. So, each time you answer a question, you narrow down the number of options. E.g., If you say, "I don't like to work out of doors," immediately all outdoor jobs are eliminated from your consideration, etc., etc.

A model of good career planning looks like this, instead:

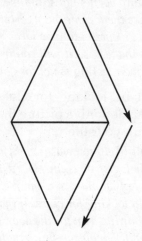

Good career-choice or career planning postpones the "narrowing down," until it has first broadened your horizons, and expanded the number of options you are thinking about. E.g., You're in the newspaper business; but have you ever thought of teaching, or drawing, or doing fashion? You first expand your mental horizons, to see all the possibilities; and only then, do you start to narrow them down to the particular two or three that interest you the most.

So, what's a good test? *All together now*: a test that shows you more possibilities for your life.

And, what's a bad test? *Again, together*: a test that narrows the possibilities for your life. Often this is the result of a counselor's interpretation of a test, or rather misinterpretation.

I'll give you an example: I met a man who, many years before, had taken the Strong Inventory.[4] He was told, by his counselor, that this inventory measured that man's native gifts or aptitudes. And, in his particular case, the counselor said, the inventory revealed he had no mechanical aptitude whatsoever. For years thereafter, this man told me, "I was afraid to even pick up a hammer, for fear of maiming myself. But there finally came a time in my life when my house needed aluminum siding, desperately, and I was too poor to hire anyone else to do it for me. So I decided I had to do it myself, regardless of what the test said. I climbed the ladder, and expected to fail. Instead, it was a glorious experience! I had never enjoyed myself so much in my whole life. I later found out that the counselor was wrong. The inventory didn't measure aptitudes; it only measured current interests. Now, today, if I could find that counselor, I would wring his neck with my own bare hands, as I think of how much of my life he ruined with his misinterpretation of that test."

---

4. See www.personalitydesk.com and similar Internet sites.

6. Testing will always have "mixed reviews." On the one hand, you can run into successful men and women who will tell you they took this or that test twenty years ago, and it made all the difference in their career direction and ultimate success.

Other men and women, however, will tell you a horror story about their encounter with testing, like that above.

If you like tests, help yourself. Counselors can give them to you, if you shop around. There are also lots of them on the Internet.

If you want to know where to start, you might try these, which are the tests that I personally like best:

▶ The Princeton Review's Career Quiz
  `www.princetonreview.com/cte/quiz/default.asp`
    `?menuID=0&careers=6`

▶ Carolyn Kalil's True Colors Test
  `www.truecolorscareer.com/quiz.asp`

▶ Dr. John Holland's Self-Directed Search
  `www.self-directed-search.com`

▶ Supplemented by the University of Missouri's Career Interests Game
  `www.career.missouri.edu/students/explore/`
    `thecareerinterestsgame.php`

▶ If you want further suggestions, you can go to my website
  `www.jobhuntersbible.com/counseling/`

If you don't like tests, what can you do? Well, there's a nice process for determining what to do with your life, later in this book. It's called the Flower Exercise (pages 246–247). It is in a test-free zone.

Seven Rules for Choosing or Changing Careers

Now, when you have to choose, or change, a career, here are seven rules to keep in mind:

Rule #1 about choosing or changing a career: go for any career that seems interesting or even fascinating to you. But *first* talk to people who are already doing that work, to find out if the career or job is as great as it seems at first impression. Ask them: *what do you like best about this work? What do you like least about this work?* And, *how did you get into this work?* This last question, which sounds like mere cheeky curiosity, actually can give you important job-hunting clues about how you get into this line of work or career.

Rule #2 about choosing or changing a career: the key to doing this successfully is to make sure that you preserve both constancy and change, in your life. In other words, don't change *everything*. Remember the words of Archimedes with his long lever,[5] loosely paraphrased as: *Give me a fulcrum and a place to stand, and with a lever I will move the Earth.* You need a place to stand, when you move your life around, and that place is provided by the things that stay constant about you: your transferable skills, your values, your faith.

We can illustrate this principle with a simple diagram of creative career change, page 167. Let us say you are an accountant, in the television industry, and you want to become a reporter, covering medicine. You can, of course, try to change everything in one big leap (labeled *the difficult path* in this diagram), but it's easier if you first change just your job title and only later your field. Or first change just your field, and only later your job title (*two steps*). This two-step plan for career change preserves *some* constancy at every turn, some continuity with the past—and allows you to always claim some past experience and expertise, each time you make a move.

Rule #3 about choosing or changing a career: you do better to start with yourself and what *you* want, rather than with the job-market, and what's "hot."

Rule #4 about choosing or changing a career: the best *work*, the best career, for you is going to be one that uses: your *favorite* transferable skills, in your *favorite* subjects, fields, or fields of fascination, in a job that offers you your *preferred* people environments, your *preferred* working conditions, with your *preferred* salary or other rewards, working toward your *preferred* goals and values. This requires thorough self-inventory. Detailed instructions are to be found in chapter 13.

Rule #5 about choosing or changing a career: the more time you give to it, the better your choice is going to be. There is a penalty for seeking "quick and dirty" fixes.

---

5. Archimedes (ca. 235 B.C.E.), Greek inventor, mathematician, and physicist.

Rule #6 about choosing or changing a career: you don't have to get it right, the first time; it's okay to make a mistake, in your choice. You'll very likely have time to correct it, down the road, regardless of your age. Most of us have three to five careers, during our lifetime.

Rule #7 about choosing or changing a career: try to make the task as much fun as possible. The more fun you're having, the more you're doing it right.

Developing a Picture

This builds upon a little-known truth in career-counseling or job-hunting: *"The clearer your vision of what you seek, the closer you are to finding it. For, what you are seeking is also seeking you."* Sounds crazy, but I've seen it happen too many times, not to believe it. Okay, here's how it goes.

Take a large piece of white paper, with some colored pencils or pens, and draw a picture of your ideal life: where you live,

Types of Career-Change Visualized

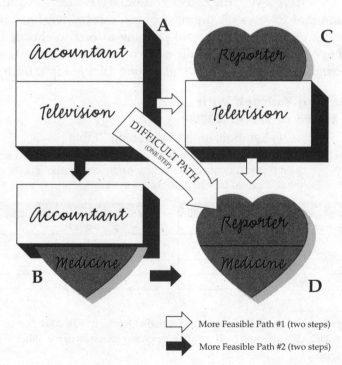

More Feasible Path #1 (two steps)

More Feasible Path #2 (two steps)

who's with you, what you do, what your dwelling looks like, what your ideal vacation looks like, etc. Don't let *reality* get in the way. Pretend a magic wand has been waved over your life, and it gives you everything you think your ideal life would be.

Now, *of course* you can't draw. Okay, then make symbols for things, or create little "doodads" or symbols, with labels—anything so that you can *see* all together on one page, your vision of your ideal life—however haltingly expressed.

The power of this exercise is sometimes amazing. Reason? By avoiding words and using pictures or symbols as much as possible, it bypasses the left side of the brain ("the safekeeping self," as George Prince calls it) and speaks directly to the right side of your brain ("the experimental self"), whose job it is to engineer change.

Oh, by the way, apropos of Rule #7, this exercise is *fun!*

Developing "A Career-Choice Vocabulary"

When asked to name some careers, most of us have no trouble coming up with *doctor, lawyer, salesperson, pilot, cab driver, writer,* and the like. But soon, we run out of gas, as it were. We just don't have a very big career vocabulary. Hence, looking over the list that follows on the next pages can be helpful, toward building up our vocabulary of possible careers to choose from. And maybe, just maybe, you'll see two or three ideas that hadn't occurred to you, but look *real interesting.* Bingo! Light bulb!

Matching Yourself with the World of Work: 2004[6]

Symbols in the "Matching" Table

The table on the following pages provides information about personal skills and job characteristics for many occupations.
Below is a guide to interpreting the symbols found there.

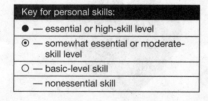

Key for personal skills:
● — essential or high-skill level
◉ — somewhat essential or moderate-skill level
○ — basic-level skill
— nonessential skill

Key for job characteristics:
● — highly probable
◉ — somewhat probable
○ — no more or less probable than improbable
— improbable

6. This list is from the Occupational Outlook Quarterly, Fall 2004; last updated March 29, 2005. Authored by Henry T. Kasper, an economist in the Office of Occu-

<table>

	Personal Skills							Job Characteristics				
	Artistic	Communication	Interpersonal	Managerial	Mathematics	Mechanical	Science	Economically sensitive	Geographically concentrated	Hazardous conditions	Outdoor work	Physically demanding
Management, business, and financial operations occupations												
Management occupations												
Administrative services managers	○	●	●	●	◉			○				
Advertising, marketing, promotions, public relations, and sales managers	●	●	●	●	●	◉						
Computer and information systems managers		●	●	●	●	●	●	●				
Construction managers	○	●	●	●	●	●	◉			◉	●	○
Education administrators		●	●	●	◉		○					
Engineering and natural sciences managers		●	●	●	●	●	●	◉				
Farmers, ranchers, and agricultural managers		●	●	●	◉	●	◉	○	●	◉	●	◉
Financial managers		●	●	●	●		○	◉				
Food service managers	◉	●	●	●	◉	◉	○	◉				○
Funeral directors	○	●	●	◉	◉	○	○					○
Human resources, training, and labor relations managers and specialists		●	●	●	○			○				
Industrial production managers		●	●	●	●	○	◉	○				○
Lodging managers	○	●	●	●	◉	○		○				
Medical and health services managers		●	●	●	◉	◉	◉					
Property, real estate, and community association managers	○	●	●	●	○	○		○			○	
Purchasing managers, buyers, and purchasing agents		●	●	●	◉		○	○				
Top executives	○	●	●	●	●			◉	○			
Business and financial operations occupations												
Accountants and auditors		○	○	◉	●			○				
Budget analysts		○	○	○	●							
Claims adjusters, appraisers, examiners, and investigators	◉	○	◉	◉	◉	○					◉	
Cost estimators		○	○	○	●	○		◉			◉	
Financial analysts and personal financial advisors		●	●	○	●		○	●				

</table>

pational Statistics and Employment Projections. In the public domain. Source: the Bureau of Labor Statistics; www.bls.gov/opub/ooq/2004/fall/contents.htm.

How to Choose a New Career

	Personal Skills							Job Characteristics				
	Artistic	Communication	Interpersonal	Managerial	Mathematics	Mechanical	Science	Economically sensitive	Geographically concentrated	Hazardous conditions	Outdoor work	Physically demanding
Insurance underwriters		○	○	○	●							
Loan counselors and officers	◉	●	○		◉			◉				
Management analysts		●	◉	○	●			○				
Tax examiners, collectors, and revenue agents		○	○	○	●							
Professional and related occupations												
Computer and mathematical occupations												
Actuaries		○	○	○	●		◉					
Computer programmers	◉	○	○	●	◉	●		○				
Computer software engineers	◉	◉	◉	●	●	●	●	○				
Computer support specialists and systems administrators	◉	◉	○	◉	●	◉		○				
Computer systems analysts, database administrators, and computer scientists	◉	○	○	●			●	○				
Mathematicians		○	○	○	●		◉					
Operations research analysts		○	○	○	●		◉	○				
Statisticians		○	○	○	●		◉					
Architects, surveyors, and cartographers												
Architects, except landscape and naval	●	◉	◉	◉	●	●	◉	◉			◉	○
Landscape architects	●	◉	◉	◉	◉	●	◉	◉			●	○
Surveyors, cartographers, photogrammetrists, and surveying technicians	◉	◉	◉	○	◉	◉	◉	◉			◉	◉
Engineers												
Aerospace engineers	○	◉	○	◉	●	●	●	◉	◉			
Agricultural engineers	○	◉	○	◉	●	●	●	○	◉			
Biomedical engineers	○	◉	○	◉	●	●	●	○				
Chemical engineers	○	◉	○	◉	●	●	●	○		○		
Civil engineers	◉	◉	○	◉	●	●	●	○			◉	
Computer hardware engineers	○	◉	○	◉	●	●	●	◉				
Electrical and electronics engineers, except computer	○	◉	○	◉	●	●	●	○				
Environmental engineers	○	◉	○	◉	●	●	●				○	

	Personal Skills							Job Characteristics				
	Artistic	Communication	Interpersonal	Managerial	Mathematics	Mechanical	Science	Economically sensitive	Geographically concentrated	Hazardous conditions	Outdoor work	Physically demanding
Industrial engineers, including health and safety	◉	◉	○	◉	●	●	●	○			○	
Materials engineers	○	◉	○	◉	●	●	●	○				
Mechanical engineers	◉	◉	○	◉	●	●	●	○		○		
Mining and geological engineers, including mining safety engineers	○	◉	○	◉	●	●	●	◉	●	◉	●	○
Nuclear engineers	○	◉	○	◉	●	●	●	○	◉	○		
Petroleum engineers	○	◉	○	◉	●	●	●	○	●	○	●	
Drafters and engineering technicians												
Drafters	●	◉	○		◉	●	○	◉				
Engineering technicians	○	◉	○		●	●	●	○		○	○	○
Life scientists												
Agricultural and food scientists		◉	○	◉	●	●	●			○	◉	○
Biological scientists		◉	○	◉	●	●	●	○		○	◉	○
Medical scientists		◉	○	◉	●	●	●	○		○		
Conservation scientists and foresters		◉	○	◉	●	●	●	○	●	○	●	◉
Physical scientists												
Atmospheric scientists		◉	○	◉	●	●	●	○			◉	
Chemists and materials scientists	○	◉	○	◉	●	●	●	◉		○		
Environmental scientists and geoscientists	○	◉	○	◉	●	●	●	○			●	○
Physicists and astronomers	○	◉	○	○	●	●	●	○	○		○	
Social scientists and related occupations												
Economists		◉	○	◉	●							
Market and survey researchers		●	●	○	●			◉				
Psychologists		●	●	○	◉		◉					
Urban and regional planners	◉	◉	◉	◉	●	○	○	○			○	
Social scientists, other		◉	◉	○	◉	○	○					
Science technicians	○	◉	○		●	●	●	◉		○	○	○

	Personal Skills							Job Characteristics				
	Artistic	Communication	Interpersonal	Managerial	Mathematics	Mechanical	Science	Economically sensitive	Geographically concentrated	Hazardous conditions	Outdoor work	Physically demanding
Community and social service occupations												
Clergy	○	●	●	●	○							○
Counselors		●	●	○	○		○					
Probation officers and correctional treatment specialists		◉	◉	○	○	○	○			●		
Social and human service assistants		◉	●				○					
Social workers		●	●	○	○		○					
Legal occupations												
Court reporters		◉	○			●						○
Judges, magistrates, and other judicial workers		●	○	○	○		○					
Lawyers		●	●	●	○		○	◉				
Paralegals and legal assistants		●	●	○	○		○	◉				
Education, training, library, and museum occupations												
Archivists, curators, and museum technicians	●	◉	○	○	◉	●	●		◉			○
Instructional coordinators	○	●	●	◉	◉	◉	◉					
Librarians	○	●	◉	●	○	◉	○					
Library technicians	○	◉	○	○	○	◉	○					○
Teacher assistants	◉	●	●	◉	○		◉					
Teachers—adult literacy and remedial and self-enrichment education	◉	●	●	●	◉		◉					
Teachers—postsecondary	◉	●	●	●	●		◉					
Teachers—preschool, kindergarten, elementary, middle, and secondary	◉	●	●	●	◉	○	◉					
Teachers—special education	◉	●	●	●	◉	○	◉					
Art and design occupations												
Artist and related workers	●	○	○	○	○	◉	○	◉			○	○
Designers	●	◉	◉	●	○	●	○	◉				
Entertainers and performers, sports and related occupations												
Actors, producers and directors	●	●	●	◉		◉	○	○	●		○	●
Athletes, coaches, umpires, and related workers	◉	◉	◉	●		○	○			○	●	●

	Personal Skills							Job Characteristics				
	Artistic	Communication	Interpersonal	Managerial	Mathematics	Mechanical	Science	Economically sensitive	Geographically concentrated	Hazardous conditions	Outdoor work	Physically demanding
Dancers and choreographers	●	◉	◉	◉			○	○	●			●
Musicians, singers, and related workers	●	◉	◉	○		○	○		○			○
Media and communication-related occupations												
Announcers	◉	●	●		○	○			○		○	
Broadcast and sound engineering technicians and radio operators		○	◉		◉	●	◉		○		○	
Interpreters and translators	●	●	○									
News analysts, reporters, and correspondents	◉	●	●	○	○	○	◉				◉	
Photographers	●	○	○	○	○	●	○	◉			◉	◉
Public relations specialists	◉	●	●	○	○				◉			
Television, video, and motion picture camera operators and editors	●	○	○	○	○	●	○		●		◉	◉
Writers and editors	●	●	●	○	○		○					
Health diagnosing and treating practitioners												
Audiologists		●	◉	●	◉	○	●					
Chiropractors		●	◉	●	◉	○	●					○
Dentists	○	●	●	●	◉	●	●			◉		○
Dietitians and nutritionists		●	●	○	◉	○	●					
Occupational therapists		●	●	◉	◉	◉	◉			◉		○
Optometrists	○	●	◉	●	◉	◉	●			◉		
Pharmacists		●	◉	◉	●	○	●					○
Physical therapists		●	●	○	◉	○	●			◉		●
Physician assistants		●	●	○	●	◉	●			◉		◉
Physicians and surgeons	◉	●	●	●	◉	●	●			◉		◉
Podiatrists	○	●	●	●	◉	◉	●					
Recreational therapists	●	●	●	○	○	○	○				●	◉
Registered nurses		●	●	◉	●	●	●			◉		◉
Respiratory therapists		●	●	○	●	●	●			◉		○
Speech-language pathologists	○	●	●	○	●	○	●					
Veterinarians	○	●	●	●	●	●	●			●	○	●

How to Choose a New Career

	Personal Skills							Job Characteristics				
	Artistic	Communication	Interpersonal	Managerial	Mathematics	Mechanical	Science	Economically sensitive	Geographically concentrated	Hazardous conditions	Outdoor work	Physically demanding
Health technologists and technicians												
Cardiovascular technologists and technicians		⊙	○	○	●	●	●					○
Clinical laboratory technologists and technicians		⊙	○	○	●	●	●			○		○
Dental hygienists		⊙	⊙	○	⊙	●	⊙			⊙		○
Diagnostic medical sonographers		⊙	○	○	●	●	●					
Emergency medical technicians and paramedics		●	●	●	○	●	●			●	●	●
Licensed practical and licensed vocational nurses		⊙	●	○	○	●	●			⊙		⊙
Medical records and health information technicians		⊙	○	○	⊙		⊙					
Nuclear medicine technologists		⊙	○	○	●	●	●			⊙		
Occupational health and safety specialists and technicians		⊙	○	⊙	⊙	⊙	⊙			⊙	○	⊙
Opticians, dispensing	⊙	⊙	⊙	⊙	⊙	⊙	○	○				○
Pharmacy technicians		⊙	⊙	○	⊙	⊙	⊙					○
Radiologic technologists and technicians		⊙	⊙	○	●	●	⊙			⊙		⊙
Surgical technologists		⊙	⊙	○	●	●	●			⊙		⊙
Veterinary technologists and technicians		⊙	⊙	⊙	⊙	●	⊙	○		●	○	●
Service occupations												
Health care support occupations												
Dental assistants		⊙	⊙	○	○	●	⊙			⊙		⊙
Medical assistants		⊙	⊙	○	⊙	●	●			⊙		⊙
Medical transcriptionists		●	○	○	○	○	●					
Nursing, psychiatric, and home health aides		⊙	⊙	○	○	⊙	○			●		●
Occupational therapist assistants and aides		⊙	●	○	○	●	⊙			⊙		⊙
Pharmacy aides		⊙	⊙	○	○		○					○
Physical therapist assistants and aides		⊙	⊙	○	⊙	⊙	⊙			⊙		●
Protective service occupations												
Correctional officers		⊙	○	○	○	○				●		⊙
Firefighting occupations		●	○	○	○	●	○			●	●	●

	Personal Skills							Job Characteristics				
	Artistic	Communication	Interpersonal	Managerial	Mathematics	Mechanical	Science	Economically sensitive	Geographically concentrated	Hazardous conditions	Outdoor work	Physically demanding
Police and detectives		●	○	◉	○	●	○			●	●	●
Private detectives and investigators		●	○	◉	○	●	○			○	◉	○
Security guards and gaming surveillance officers		○	○	○		○		○		●	◉	○
Food preparation and serving related occupations												
Chefs, cooks, and food preparation workers	●	◉	◉	●	○	◉	○	●		○		◉
Food and beverage serving and related workers	○	◉	●		○			●			○	●
Building and grounds cleaning and maintenance occupations												
Building cleaning workers	○	○			○	●		○		○		●
Grounds maintenance workers	◉	○			○	●	○	○		◉	●	●
Pest control workers		○			○	●	○		◉	●	○	●
Personal care and service occupations												
Animal care and service workers		○	○		○	◉	○	◉		●	◉	●
Barbers, cosmetologists, and other personal appearance workers	●	◉	○		○	◉	○	◉		○		○
Child care workers	○	◉	●	○	○	○					○	◉
Flight attendants		●	●	○	○	○		●	◉	○		●
Gaming services occupations	○	◉	●	●	○	○		◉	●			●
Personal and home care aides		◉	●	○	○		○			◉		●
Recreation and fitness workers	○	●	●	○	○	○	○	◉			◉	●
Sales and related occupations												
Advertising sales agents	◉	●	●		○			●				
Cashiers		○	◉		◉			◉				●
Counter and rental clerks		○	◉		◉			◉				◉
Demonstrators, product promoters, and models	●	●	●		○	○		◉				◉
Insurance sales agents		●	●		◉			◉				
Real estate brokers and sales agents	○	●	●	◉	◉			◉			○	
Retail salespersons	○	◉	●		○			◉				
Sales engineers	○	●	●		◉	○	◉	●				
Sales representatives, wholesale and manufacturing	○	●	●		◉		○	●				

	Personal Skills							Job Characteristics				
	Artistic	Communication	Interpersonal	Managerial	Mathematics	Mechanical	Science	Economically sensitive	Geographically concentrated	Hazardous conditions	Outdoor work	Physically demanding
Sales worker supervisors	○	●	●	●	◉	○	○	◉				
Securities, commodities, and financial services sales agents		●	●	●	●			●	●			
Travel agents		◉	●		○			●				
Office and administrative support occupations												
Communications equipment operators		◉	◉		◉	◉	○	◉				
Computer operators		○			○	◉	○	◉				
Customer service representatives		●	●		◉		○	○				
Data entry and information processing workers		○	○		○	◉		●				
Desktop publishers	●	○	○		○	◉	○	○				
Financial clerks		○	○		●			○				
Bill and account collectors		○	●		●			◉				
Billing and posting clerks and machine operators		○	○		○	○		○				
Bookkeeping, accounting, and auditing clerks		○	○		●			○				
Gaming cage workers		○	○		◉			◉	●			
Payroll and timekeeping clerks		○	○		◉			○				
Procurement clerks		○	○		◉			○				
Tellers		◉	●		●			○				
Information and record clerks		◉	○		◉			○				
Brokerage clerks		○	○		◉			○	●			
Credit authorizers, checkers, and clerks		◉	○	○	◉			◉				
File clerks		○	○		○							
Hotel, motel, and resort desk clerks	○	◉	●	○	○			●				◉
Human resources assistants, except payroll and timekeeping		○	○		◉			○				
Interviewers		●	◉	◉	○		○	○				
Library assistants, clerical		○	○		○	◉	○					
Order clerks		○	○		◉			◉				
Receptionists and information clerks		●	●		◉	◉		○				

	Personal Skills							Job Characteristics				
	Artistic	Communication	Interpersonal	Managerial	Mathematics	Mechanical	Science	Economically sensitive	Geographically concentrated	Hazardous conditions	Outdoor work	Physically demanding
Construction laborers	O	O	O		O	●	O	●		●	◉	●
Drywall installers, ceiling tile installers, and tapers	O	O	O		O	●	O	●		O	O	●
Electricians		O	O		◉	●	◉	●		●	O	◉
Elevator installers and repairers		O	O		O	●	O	●		●	O	●
Glaziers	◉	O	O		O	●	O	●		O	●	●
Hazardous materials removal workers		O	O		O	●	●			●	●	●
Insulation workers		O	O		O	●	O	●		O	O	●
Painters and paperhangers	◉	O	O		O	●	O	●		O	●	●
Pipelayers, plumbers, pipefitters, and steamfitters		O	O		O	●	◉	●		O	O	●
Plasterers and stucco masons	O	O	O		O	●	O	●		O	●	●
Roofers	O	O	O		O	●	O	O		●	●	●
Sheet metal workers	O	O	O		O	●	O	●		●		●
Structural and reinforcing iron and metal workers	O	O	O		O	●	O	●		●	●	●
Installation, maintenance, and repair occupations												
Electrical and electronic equipment mechanics, installers, and repairers												
Computer automated teller and office machine repairers		O	O		O	●	O				O	O
Electrical and electronics installers and repairers		O	O		◉	●	O			◉		O
Electronic home entertainment equipment installers and repairers	◉	O	O		◉	●	O	●				◉
Radio and telecommunications equipment installers and repairers		O	O		◉	●	◉	O	◉		●	◉
Vehicle and mobile equpment mechanics, installers, and repairers												
Aircraft and avionics equipment mechanics and service technicians		O	O		◉	●	◉	◉	◉	O	●	◉
Automotive body and related repairers	O	O	O		O	●	O	O		O	O	◉
Automotive service technicians and mechanics		O	O		O	●	O	◉		O	O	◉
Diesel service technicians and mechanics		O	O		O	●	◉	◉		O	O	◉

	Personal Skills							Job Characteristics				
	Artistic	Communication	Interpersonal	Managerial	Mathematics	Mechanical	Science	Economically sensitive	Geographically concentrated	Hazardous conditions	Outdoor work	Physically demanding
Heavy vehicle and mobile equipment service technicians and mechanics		○	○		○	●	◉	●		○	○	◉
Small engine mechanics		○	○		○	●	◉	◉		○	○	◉
Other installation, maintenance, and repair occupations												
Coin, vending, and amusement machine servicers and repairers		○			○	●				○	○	◉
Heating, air conditioning, and refrigeration mechanics and installers		○	○		○	●	○	◉		○	○	◉
Home appliance repairers		○	○		○	●	○			○		◉
Industrial machinery installation, repair, and maintenance workers, except millwrights		○			○	●	○	○	○	◉		◉
Line installers and repairers		○			◉	●	○	○		◉	●	◉
Maintenance and repair workers, general		○	○		○	●	○			◉	◉	◉
Millwrights		○	○		◉	●	○	●	◉	◉	○	◉
Precision instrument and equipment repairers	○	○			◉	●	○					◉
Production occupations												
Assemblers and fabricators	○	○			○	●	○				◉	
Food processing occupations		○			○	●			●		●	
Metal workers and plastics workers												
Computer control programmers and operators		○			◉	◉	○	○				
Machinists	◉	○			●	●	◉	○		◉		◉
Machine setters, operators, and tenders—metal and plastic		○			●	●	◉	○		◉		◉
Tool and die makers	○	○			●	●	◉	○		◉		◉
Welding, soldering, and brazing workers	○	○			○	●	○	○		●	◉	●
Printing occupations												
Bookbinders and bindery workers	○	○			○	●	○	○				◉
Prepress technicians and workers	◉	◉	○		◉	◉	○	○				○
Printing machine operators		○			○	●	○	○		◉		●
Textile, apparel, and furnishings occupations	◉	○			○	●		◉	◉	○		●
Woodworkers	◉	○			◉	●	○	◉		◉		○

	Personal Skills							Job Characteristics				
	Artistic	Communication	Interpersonal	Managerial	Mathematics	Mechanical	Science	Economically sensitive	Geographically concentrated	Hazardous conditions	Outdoor work	Physically demanding
Reservation and transportation ticket agents and travel clerks		○	●		◉			●				
Material recording, scheduling, dispatching, and distributing occupations		○	○		○	○		○				
Cargo and freight agents		○	○	○	◉		○	○	◉		◉	○
Couriers and messengers		○	○		○	○		◉		◉	◉	○
Dispatchers		◉	○	◉	○							
Meter readers, utilities		○			◉	○					◉	○
Production, planning, and expediting clerks		◉	○	○	◉		○	○				
Shipping, receiving, and traffic clerks		○	○		○	◉		○				
Stock clerks and order fillers		○	○		○	○		○				
Weighers, measurers, checkers, and samplers, recordkeeping		○	○		◉	◉	◉	○				○
Office and administrative support worker supervisors and managers		●	●	●	◉	○		○				
Office clerks, general		○	◉		○			◉				
Postal service workers		○	○	○	○	○					●	●
Secretaries and administrative assistants	○	●	●		○	○		○				
Farming, fishing, and forestry occupations												
Agricultural workers		○	○	○	○	●	○		◉	●	●	●
Fishers and fishing vessel operators		◉	○	○	○	●	○			●	●	●
Forest, conservation, and logging workers		○	○	○	○	●	○	○		●	●	●
Construction trades and related workers												
Boilermakers	○	○	○		○	●	○	●	◉	●		●
Brickmasons, blockmasons, and stonemasons	◉	○	○		○	●	○	●		○	◉	●
Carpenters	◉	○	○		◉	●	○	●		●	◉	●
Carpet, floor, and tile installers and finishers	◉	○	○		○	●	○	●		○	◉	●
Cement masons, concrete finishers, segmental pavers, and terrazzo workers	◉	○	○		○	●	○	●		○	◉	●
Construction and building inspectors		○	○	○	○	●	◉	○		○	◉	○
Construction equipment operators		○	○		○	●	○	●		●	●	●

	Artistic	Communication	Interpersonal	Managerial	Mathematics	Mechanical	Science	Economically sensitive	Geographically concentrated	Hazardous conditions	Outdoor work	Physically demanding
Personal Skills								**Job Characteristics**				
Plant and system operators												
Power plant operators, distributors, and dispatchers		○	◉	○	●	○	●			◉		
Stationary engineers and boiler operators		○	○	○	○	●	○			◉		
Water and liquid waste treatment plant and system operators		○	○	○	◉	●	◉			●	◉	◉
Other production occupations												
Dental laboratory technicians	◉	○			○	●	◉					○
Inspectors, testers, sorters, samplers, and weighers	○	◉	○		◉	●	◉					○
Jewelers and precious stone and metal workers	●	○	○		○	●	◉	●				○
Ophthalmic laboratory technicians	○	○	◉		○	●	◉					○
Painting and coating workers, except construction and maintenance	○	○			○	●		○		◉		◉
Photographic process workers and processing machine operators	○	○			○	●	○	○		◉		○
Semiconductor processors		○			●	◉	●	◉	●			○
Transportation and material moving occupations												
Air transportation occupations												
Aircraft pilots and flight engineers		●	●	●	●	◉	●	●	○	●	○	◉
Air traffic controllers		●	◉	◉	◉		◉		○			○
Material moving occupations		○				●		●		●	●	●
Motor vehicle operators												
Bus drivers		○	○			○				●	○	◉
Taxi drivers and chauffeurs		○	○			○			◉	●	○	◉
Truck drivers and driver / sales workers		○				○		●		●	○	●
Rail transportation occupations		◉	○	○		●	○	◉	◉	◉	◉	◉
Water transportation occupations		◉	○	●	◉	●	◉	●	●	●	◉	◉

You may, of course, find the list too short, or too long. Too short? Well, take comfort: there are at least 12,741 different careers or occupations *out there*, with 8,000 alternative titles; and a description of them all can be found in a volume known as the *Dictionary of Occupational Titles* (4th ed.). It is online, and searchable, at **www.occupationalinfo.org**. A more current edition, the fifth, bound together with its successor system, O*Net, is available, but only in book form. And it is expensive. Try your local library. O*Net itself, a database of only 950 occupations, is online, and searchable by skills (nice list!), occupations, or occupational codes at **http://online.onetcenter.org**.

Too long a list on the previous pages? Experts are continually trying to boil down the list to just the top ten hottest jobs or the top ten hottest careers.

Type the phrase "hot jobs" or "hottest careers" into your favorite Internet search engine, such as the wildly popular Google (**www.google.com**) or Yahoo (**www.yahoo.com**) or Metacrawler (**http://metacrawler.com**), and see what you get.

In my opinion, the single most useful website with regard to careers, is CNNMoney's (`http://money.cnn.com`). This site is home to *Money* magazine, *Fortune*, and *Business 2.0*. In the top bar on their home page, choose *Jobs*. Then, from the pull-down menu under it choose "Top 80 Best Jobs." It lists the top twenty jobs for each of several categories, including retirees. Fascinating stuff, and very helpful, as *Money* and *Fortune* always are.

This site also has a fascinating article, about Warren Farrell's research on salaries and careers. The easiest way to find it is to go to any search engine (my favorite, as I often report, is Webcrawler), and type in the words *"Where Women's Pay Trumps Men's."* Once you find that article you will find it is chock-full of brilliant ideas about how to make a career choice, when money is the issue. It is based on Warren's blockbuster book (in my opinion) *Why Men Earn More*. Warren is a brilliant, meticulous, highly ethical researcher, but his book is more *news* than it is just another research tome. If I had my way, I would give this book to every female career-chooser or career-changer on the planet.

You *want* to know all this! Believe me, you *want* to know! Especially if, in order to prepare for this career that interests you, it's going to take some time for you to go get some schooling, or perhaps a degree.

If you fail to ask such questions *ahead of time* you may be bitterly disappointed after you get all that training, or that degree.

Try on the Suit First

In all your search for a good career, don't believe what lists, tests, experts, or well-meaning friends try to claim is an ideal job *for you*. Just as you would when buying a suit, test it, try it on, make up your own mind. *Puh-leeze*.

Go talk to at least three people who are actually *doing* this career that you find so appealing, and ask them these questions:

How did you get into this field?

What do you like best about it?

What do you like least about it?

How do I get into this career, and how much of a demand is there for people who can do this work?

Is it easy to find a job in this career, or is it hard?

Who else would you recommend or suggest I go talk to,
*   to learn more about this career?*

Getting a Job by Degrees

Let me underline this: don't go get a degree because you think that will guarantee you a job! No, mon ami, it will not.

I wish you could see my mail, filled with bitter letters from people who believed this myth, went and got a degree in a field that looked just great, thought it would be a snap to find a job, but are still unemployed after two years. You would weep! They are bitter (often), angry (always), and disappointed in a society that they feel lied to them.

They found there was no job that went with that degree. They feel lied to, by our society and by the experts, about the value of going back to school, and getting a degree in this or that "hot" field.

Now that they have that costly worthless degree, and still can't find a job, they find a certain irony in the phrase, "*Our country believes in getting a job by degrees.*"

If you already made this costly mistake, you know what I mean.

STORE
FOR SALE

WONDERFUL
OPPORTUNITY
FOR A MAN
NAMED
AMBROSE

184

CHAPTER 10

In
The Restless, Unpredictable,
Ever-Changing
Worklife of Yours:

How to Start
Your Own Business

"All I Do the Whole Day
Through Is Dream of You . . . "

Sure, you've thought about it, a million times. Hasn't every-one? Every time you're tied up in traffic going to or from work. You've toyed with the idea of not having to go to an office or other place of business, but of running your own business, maybe even out of your own home, making your own product or selling your own services, being your own boss, and keeping all the profits for yourself. It's called *self-employment*, or being *an independent contractor*, or *freelancing* or *contracting out your services*. Great idea! *But*, nothing's ever come of all this daydreaming. Until now. Now, you're out of work, or maybe you're still work-ing but you're really fed up with your job, and—dusting off those old dreams—you're thinking to yourself: *Maybe it's now, or never. Maybe I ought to just do it.*

Home Business in General

Three hundred years ago, of course, nearly everybody did it. They worked at home or on their farm. But then the industrial revolution came, and the idea of working *away from* home became normal. In recent times, however, the idea of working at home has been finding new life, due to congestion on the highways, and the development of new technologies. If you can afford them, a telephone,[1] a fax machine, a computer with a modem, a Palm Pilot, e-mail, online services, mail-order houses, and the like, all make working for yourself feasible, as never before.

The Three Major Problems of Home Businesses

1. The first major problem of home businesses, according to experts, is that on average home-based workers *(in the U.S. at least)* only earn 70 percent of what their full-time office-based equals do. So, you must think carefully whether you could make enough money to survive—*or prosper.*

2. The second major problem of home businesses is that it's often difficult to maintain the balance between business and family time. Sometimes the *family* time gets shortchanged, while in other cases the demands of family (particularly with small children) may become so interruptive, that the *business* gets shortchanged. So, do investigate thoroughly, ahead of time, *how* you would go about doing this *well.*

3. Last, a home business puts you into a perpetual job-hunt.

Some of us who are unemployed *hate* job-hunting, and are attracted to the idea of a home business because this seems like an ideal way to cut short our job-hunt. The irony is, that a home business makes you in a very real sense a *perpetual* job-hunter—because you have to be *always* seeking new clients or customers—which is to say, new *employers.* (Well, yes, they are *employers,* because they *pay* you for the work you are doing. The only difference between this and a full-time job is that here *the contract is limited.* But if you are running your own business, you will have

---

1. This *telephone family* includes cell phones, camera cell phones, video phones, and the new ROKR combination phone from Apple and Motorola; "call-forwarding"—the technology where people call your one fixed telephone number, and then get automatically forwarded to wherever you have told the phone company you currently are—and voice/electronic mail.

to *continually* beat the bushes for new clients or customers—who are in fact *short-term employers*.)

Of course, the dream of most home business people is to become so well known, and so in demand, that clients or customers will be literally beating down your doors, and you will be able to stop this endless job-hunt. But that only happens to a relative minority, and your realistic self must know that.

The greater likelihood is that you will *always* have to beat the bushes for employers/clients. It may get easier as you get better at it, or it may get harder, if economic conditions take a severe downturn. In any event, it will probably be the one aspect of your work that you will *always* cordially dislike. If you're going to go this route, you must learn to make your peace with it— however grudgingly.

"YES, THE BUSINESS HAS BECOME BIGGER, BUT FRED STILL LIKES TO WORK AT HOME."

How to Start Your Own Business

If you can't manage that, if you avoid that task like the plague until there's literally no bread on the table, you're probably going to find *a home business* is just a glamorous synonym for *"starving."* I know *many* home business people to whom this has happened, and it happened precisely because they couldn't stomach going out to beat the bushes for clients or customers. If that's true for you, you should plan to start out by *hiring, co-opting,* or *volunteering* somebody part-time, who is willing to do this for you—one who, in fact, "eats it up"—or abandon the idea of having your own business.

When You Don't Know What Kind of Home Business to Start

Okay, so basically the *idea* of working at home intrigues the life out of you, but you can't figure out what kind of business to start. *Minor little detail!*

There are fortunately seven steps you can take to nail this down.

First, read. There are oodles of books out there that are filled with ideas for home businesses. Browse in your local bookstore. Browse Amazon.com.

The best books on home businesses are written by Paul Edwards and Sarah Edwards. Their most recent (2004), and currently most popular, one is called *Best Home Businesses for People 50+.* Earlier works include (2001) *The Best Home Businesses for the*

Chapter Ten

Twenty-First Century, and (1999) *Working from Home.* For other titles, browse Amazon's categories, or your local library, or the business shelves in your local bookstore.

Second, dream. In evaluating any ideas that you pick up, the first thing you ought to look at are your dreams. What have you always dreamed about doing? Since childhood? Since last week? Now is the time to dust off those dreams.

And please don't pay any attention, for now, to whether those dreams represent *a step up* for you in life, or not. Who cares? Your dreams are yours. You may have been dreaming of earning *more* money. But then again, you may have been dreaming of doing work that you really love, even if it means a lesser salary or income than you have not been accustomed to. Don't *judge* your dreams, and don't let anyone else judge them either.

Third, look around your own community, and ask yourself what services or products people seem to need the most. Or what service or product already offered in the community could stand a lot of *improving?* There may be something there that *grabs* you.

The underlying theme to 90 percent of the businesses that are *out there* these days is *things that save time.* It's what single parents, families where both parents work, and singles who have overcrowded lives, most want.

You might consider: offering home deliveries of local restaurants' dinners, or home delivery of grocery orders from any downtown supermarket. (Pay no attention to the fact that delivery services such as *Webvan* went "belly-up" on the Internet. Local delivery services may still be wanted.) There is also: evening delivery services of laundry, etc. Daytime or evening office cleaning services and/or home cleaning services. Home repairs, especially in the evening or on weekends, of TVs, radios, audio systems, laundries, dishwashers, etc. Lawn care. Care for the elderly in their own homes. Childcare in their own homes. Pickup and delivery of things (even personal stuff, like cleaning) at the office. Automobile care or repair services, with pickup and delivery. Offering short-term business consultancy in various fields. Other successful businesses these days deal with such arenas as leisure activities.

Fourth, consider mail order. If you find no needs within your own community, you may want to broaden your search, to ask what is needed in this country—or the world. After all, mail-order businesses can be started *small* at home, and catalogs can be sent *anywhere.* If this interests you, read up on the subject. Also, for heaven's sake, go talk to other mail-order people (for names, just look at the catalogs you're already likely receiving). There are books "out there" about mail-order businesses, but they are of very unequal value.

Fifth, consider telecommuting. Telecommuting is "working at home for others." The people who do this are called *"telecommuters"*— a term coined by Jack Nilles in 1973. To learn more about telecommuting, a good place to start is at PortaJobs, whose website is: `www.portajobs.com`.

One way to go about easing yourself into telecommuting, if you already have a job, is to talk your boss into letting you do at least *some* of your work at home. You can find plans for how you "sell" your employer on the idea, at such sites as: `www.workoptions.com/telecom.htm`.

Your boss, of course, may take the initiative here, before it has even occurred to you, and they may *ask* you to work at home, connected to the office by computer-network telephone lines.

If you are thinking about becoming a telecommuter, I advise you to investigate the idea thoroughly. In this case, the Internet is your best friend. For example, you can find more telecommuting information, including a database of work-at-home jobs, at: `www.careersfromhome.com`.

And another, similar, site with job listings is at `www.tjobs.com`, and you can find **an association for telecommuters**, ITAC (International Telework Association and Council) with conventions and everything, at: `www.telecommute.org`.

Sixth, consider a franchise. Franchises are for people who want their own business, but don't care if it's not *in the home.* (Though some franchises can be done from your home, the majority require an outside site.)

Franchises exist because some people want to have their own business, but don't want to go through the agony of starting it up. They want to *buy in* on an already established business, and they have the money in their savings with which to do that (or

they know where they can get a bank loan). Fortunately for them, there are a lot of such franchises. In the U.S., the overall failure rate for franchises is less than 4 percent. You want to keep in mind that some *types* of franchises have a failure rate *far* greater than that. The ten *riskiest* small businesses, according to experts, are local laundries and dry cleaners, used car dealerships, gas stations, local trucking firms, restaurants, infant clothing stores, bakeries, machine shops, grocery or meat stores, and car washes—though I'm sure there will be some new nominees for this list, by the time you read this. *Risky* doesn't mean you can't make them succeed. It only means the odds for failure are greater than they would be with other small businesses.

You want to keep in mind also that some individual franchises are *terrible*—and that includes well-known names. They charge too much for you to *get on board*, and often they don't do the advertising or other commitments that they promised they would.

There isn't a franchising book that doesn't warn you eighteen times to go talk to people who have *already* bought that same franchise, before you ever decide to go with them. And I mean *several* people, not just one. Most experts also warn you to go talk to *other* franchises in the same field, not just the kind you're thinking about signing up with. Maybe there's something better, that such research will uncover.

If you are drawn to the idea of a franchise, because you are in a hurry, and you don't want to do any homework first, *'cause it's just too much trouble,* you will deserve what you get, believe me. That way lies madness.

Seventh, if you've invented something, weigh doing something with it. If you are inclined toward invention or tinkering, you might want to start by improving on an idea that's already *out there*. Start with something you like, such as bicycles. You might experiment with making—let us say—a folding bicycle.

How to Start Your Own Business   **191**

Or, if you like to go to the beach, and your skills run to sewing, you might think about making and selling beach towels with weights sewn in the corners, against windy days.

If you've already invented something, and it's been sitting in your drawer, or the garage, but you've never attempted to duplicate or manufacture it before, now might be a good time to try. Think out very carefully just how you are going to get it manufactured, advertised, and marketed, etc.

There are also promoters out there (on and off the Internet) who claim to specialize in promoting inventions *such as yours*, if *you* will pay *them* a fee. However, according to the Federal Trade Commission, in a study of 30,000 people who paid such promoters, *not a single inventor* ever made a profit after giving their invention to such promoters or firms. If you want to gamble some of your hard-earned money on such firms, consider whether you might better drop it at the tables in Las Vegas. I think the odds are *better* there.

You're much better off, *of course*, if on your own, on or off the Internet, you locate other inventors, and ask if they were successful in marketing their own invention. When you find those who were, pick their brains for everything they're worth. (Of course one of the first things they're going to tell you is to go get your invention copyrighted or trademarked or patented.)

When You Know What Kind of Home Business to Start

The seven steps are, of course, if you don't know what kind of business you'd like to start. But, it may be that you already know exactly *what* business you want to start, because you've been thinking about it for *years*, and may even have been *doing* it for years—only, in the employ of someone else.

But now, the turning point: you're about to set out on your own. You're thinking about doing this kind of work yourself, and for yourself, whether it be business services, or consultancy, or repair work, or some kind of craft, or the making of some kind of product, or teaching, or offering of home services, such as childcare or delivery by night.

Some sorts of jobs are just made for working out of one's home, as when you are already some kind of writer, artist, performer, business expert, lawyer, consultant, craftsperson, or the like. Be prepared for the fact that your present home may not be big enough for the kind of thing you're dreaming of. For example, your dream may be: *I want a horse ranch, where I can raise and sell horses.* Or *I want to run a bed-and-breakfast place.* Stuff like that.

Well, the nice thing about deciding to work out of your home is that you get to define what *home* is. Given today's technology, you could *literally* work wherever your preferred environment in the whole world is—whether that be out in nature, or at your favorite vacation spot, or at a skiing chalet, or in some other country altogether.

The only rule is, if it involves a possible move, be sure to go talk to other people who have already done that. Pick their brains for everything they're worth. No need for you to step on the same *land mines* that they did.

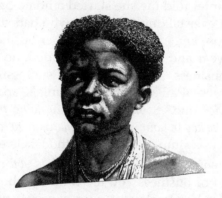

You Want to Succeed!

And that brings us to the most important part of this chapter. The key to successfully starting your own business turns out to be this one *crucial* rule: *Find out what's involved, before you hurl yourself into this new world.*

This **research** has two steps to it:

1. Finding out what skills it takes to make this kind of enterprise work. *This involves figuring out what is "A – B = C."*

2. Finding out just exactly what is involved in setting up any home-based business. *This involves going on the Internet, or reading some books.*

Step #1:
Figure Out What Is
"A – B = C"

Over the past thirty years I have found it *mindboggling* to discover how many people start their own business, at home or elsewhere, without *ever* first going to talk to anybody who started the same kind of business earlier.

One job-hunter told me she started a home-based soap business, without ever talking to anyone who had started a similar endeavor before her. Not surprisingly, her business went belly-up within a year and a half. She concluded: no one should go into such a business. Ah, but there *are* successful home-based soap businesses—Paula Gibbons' "Paula's Soap" of Seattle, Washington, for one.[2] *Someone is already doing the work you are dreaming of. The key to your success, is that you go talk to them.*

This involves a simple series of methodical steps:

1. You first write out *in as much detail as you can* just exactly what kind of business you are thinking about starting. Do you want to be a freelance writer, or a craftsperson, or a consultant, independent screenwriter, copywriter, digital artist, songwriter, photographer, illustrator, interior designer, video person, film person, counselor, therapist, plumber, electrician, agent, filmmaker, soap maker, bicycle repairer, public speaker, or *what?*

2. You identify towns or cities that are at least fifty to seventy-five miles away, and you try to get their phone books, so you can look up addresses of their chambers of commerce, etc. In some cases, the Internet will also help. An index to such help can be found at my website, **www.jobhuntersbible.com.**

---

2. **http://paulassoap.com**

3. By using the Internet or the yellow pages or the chamber of commerce, you try to identify three businesses in those towns, that are identical or similar to the business you are thinking of starting. You journey to that town or city, and talk to the founder or owner of each such business.

4. When you talk to them, you explain that you're exploring the possibility of starting your own business, similar to theirs, but seventy-five miles away. You ask them if they would mind sharing what pitfalls or obstacles they ran into when they started their own business. You ask them what skills or knowledge they think are necessary to running that kind of business successfully. Will they give you such information? Yes, most likely. Most people love to help others get started in their same business, *if* they love it, although—let's face it—occasionally you may run into owners who are of an ungenerous nature. In such a case, thank them politely for their time, and go on to the next name on your list. When you've found three people willing to help you by reminiscing about their own history, you interview each of them in turn, and make a list of the necessary skills and knowledge they all agreed were necessary. Give this list a name. Let's call it "**A**."

5. Back home you sit down and inventory your own skills and knowledge, with the information you will draw from the exercises in chapter 13, in the Flower Exercise. Give this list a name, also. Let's call it "**B**."

6. Having done this, you then subtract "**B**" from "**A**." This gives you another new list, which you should name. Let's

How to Start Your Own Business

call it "**C**." "**C**" is by definition a list of the skills or knowledge that you *don't* have, but must find—either by taking courses yourself, or by hiring someone with those skills, or by getting a friend or family member (who has those skills) to volunteer.

Why fifty to seventy-five miles away? Well, actually, that's a minimum. You want to interview businesses which, *if they were in the same geographical area as you,* would be your rivals. And if they were in the same geographical area as you, they wouldn't likely tell you how to get started. After all, they're not going to train you just so you can then take business away from them.

But, when a guy, a gal, or a business is fifty to seventy-five miles away—you're not as likely to be perceived as a rival, unless you plan a rival website, and therefore they're much more likely to tell you what you want to know about their own experience, and how *they* got started, and where the land mines are hidden.

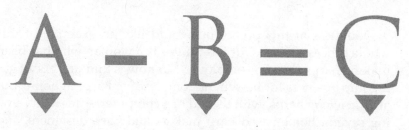

Skills and Knowledge Needed to Run This Kind of Business Successfully	Skills and Knowledge That I Have	Skills and Knowledge Needed, Which I Have to Learn or Get Someone to Volunteer, or I Will Have to Go Out and Hire
Precision-working with tools and instruments	Precision-working with tools and instruments	
Planning and directing an entire project	Planning and directing an entire project	
Programming computers, inventing programs that solve physical problems		Programming computers, inventing programs that solve physical problems
Problem solving: evaluating why a particular design or process isn't working	Problem solving: evaluating why a particular design or process isn't working	
Being self-motivated, resourceful, patient, and persevering, accurate, methodical, and thorough	Being self-motivated, resourceful, patient, and persevering, accurate, methodical, and thorough	
Thorough knowledge of: Principles of electronics	*Thorough knowledge of:*	*Thorough knowledge of:* Principles of electronics
Physics of strings	Physics of strings	
Principles of vibration	Principles of vibration	
Properties of woods	Properties of woods	
Accounting		Accounting

Doubtless at this point you would like an example of this whole process. Okay. Our job-hunter is a woman who has been making harps for some employer, but now is thinking about going into business for herself, not only *making* harps at home, but also *designing* harps, with the aid of a computer. After interviewing several home-based harp makers and harp designers, and finishing her own self-assessment, her chart of **A – B = C** came out looking like the previous page.

If she decides to try her hand at becoming an independent harp maker and harp designer, she now knows what she needs but lacks: *computer programming, knowledge of the principles of electronics, and accounting.* In other words, List **C.** These she must either go to school to acquire for herself, OR enlist from some friends of hers in those fields, on a volunteer basis, OR go out and hire, part-time. These are the essential steps for any new enterprise that you are considering: **A – B = C.**

You may also want to talk to people who have juggled two (or more) careers, at the same time. If you want to start up more than one venture, you need to interview people *in each line of work* to find out **A – B = C** for both jobs.

How Can You Do A – B = C, When No One Has Done What You Want to Do?

No matter how inventive you are, you're probably *not* going to invent a job that *no one* has ever heard of before. You're only going to invent a job that *most* people have never heard of before. But the likelihood is *great* that someone, somewhere, in this world of endless creativity, has already put together the kind of job you're dreaming about. Your task: to find them and interview them thoroughly. And then . . . well, you know the drill: **A – B = C.**

If there isn't someone doing *exactly* what you are dreaming of doing, there is at least someone who is *close.* This is how you find them.

1. Break down your projected business or new career into its parts.

2. If there are more than two parts, take any two of these parts to begin with. See what kind of job or person they describe.

3. Find out the names of such persons. You want three names, or more.

4. Go see, phone, or e-mail them. You can learn a great deal from them, and even if they are not in the same business as you are dreaming of, you will learn a great deal that is relevant to your dream.

5. They in turn may be able to give you a lead to someone whose business is even closer to what you are dreaming of. Ask for names. Go interview them.

Let's see how this works out, in practice. For our example, let's suppose your dream is—here we take a ridiculous case—to use computers to monitor the growth of plants at the South Pole. And suppose you can't find anybody who's ever done such a thing. The way to tackle this seemingly insurmountable problem, is to break the proposed business down into its parts, which—in this case—are: *computers, plants,* and *the Antarctic.*

Then you try combining any two parts, together, to define the person or persons you need to talk to. In this case, that would mean finding someone who's *used computers with plants here in the States,* or someone who's *used computers at the Antarctic,* or someone who has *worked with plants at the Antarctic,* etc. You go talk to them, and along the way you may discover there *is* someone who has used computers to monitor the growth of plants at the South Pole. Then again, you may not. In any event, you will learn most of the pitfalls that wait for you, by hearing the experience of those who are in *parallel* businesses or careers.

Thus, it is *always* possible—with a little blood, sweat, and imagination—to find out what $A - B = C$ is, for the business you're dreaming of doing.

Websites Dealing with Home-Based Business

I and my Web consultants have combed through the various home-based business *sites*, testing them (this is all very subjective, believe me) for sensible advice, ease of use, and trustworthiness *in our judgment*.

This list is excerpted from my book on Internet job-hunting.

Self-Employed and Home Business

Some people are just happier working for themselves, even if the hours are long and the pay is short. Try these sites for more on self-employment:

Business Owner's Toolkit
www.toolkit.cch.com/BOToC.asp

Yikes, there is a lot of information here for the small business owner. Everything about your business: starting, planning, financing, marketing, hiring, managing, getting government contracts, taxes . . . all that stuff.

Small Business Administration
www.sba.gov

The SBA was established to help start, manage, and grow small businesses (bear in mind that it defines "small business" as one with less than five hundred employees; it could be called the "Almost All Businesses Administration"). Lots of useful stuff here; also, check out the Starting a Business resources at **www.sba.gov/starting_business/ index.html.**

The Business Owner's Idea Café
http://businessownersideacafe.com

Great site for the small business owner.

Startup Journal
www.startupjournal.com

The *Wall Street Journal* brings its considerable resources to bear on this site for the entrepreneur. Many articles, how-tos, advice, and resources for the business owner.

Free Agent Nation
www.fastcompany.com/online/12/freeagent.html

The workplace is changing dramatically. Among these changes is the fact that for some, self-employment has become a broader concept than it was in another age. The concept (for some) now includes not only those who own their own business but also free agents: independent contractors who work for several clients; temps and contract employees who work each day through temporary agencies; limited-time-frame workers who work only for a set time, as on a project, then move on to another company; consultants; and so on. This is a fascinating article to help you decide if you want to be part of this trend, on the site of the popular magazine *Fast Company*.

Working Solo
www.workingsolo.com
www.workingsolo.com/resources/resources.html

Working Solo is a good site for the home or small business worker. The best stuff on this site is at the second URL above.

A Home-Based Business Online

`www.ahbbo.com`

`www.ahbbo.com/articles.html`

When they say "A Home-Based Business Online," they don't mean "An Online Home-Based Business," or "A Home-Based Online Business"; they mean, "Hey, we've got a lot of information on businesses you can run from your home, and we've put it all online for you."

This is a great site, with lots of information for you if you want to get information about a home-based business. There are more than a hundred articles at the second URL.

Nolo Law Center for Small Business

`www.nolo.com/lawcenter/index.cfm/catID/`
`19B45DBF-E85F-4A3D-950E3E07E32851A7`

Nolo Press publishes a lot of do-it-yourself law books; this is the part of its website that offers legal resources for the small business person. Really good.

Entrepreneur.com

`www.entrepreneurmag.com`

Entrepreneur magazine's website. It has lists of home-based businesses, startup ideas, how to raise money, shoestring start-ups, small business myths, a franchise and business opportunity site-seeing guide, and a lot more. As I write, you are allowed access to the magazine's archives, with full text of many articles, stretching back to January of 1999. (This complete, no-fee archive access is unusual for most magazines.) Many resources and articles for the self-employed, home businesses, franchises . . . cool stuff.

World Wide Web Tax

`www.wwwebtax.com/miscellaneous/`
`self_employment_tax.htm`

Wow. One of the banes of being self-employed is dealing with taxes; this site has more than 1,300 pages to help you handle all of that. Articles, resources, links, downloadable tax forms (going back ten years!) in PDF files . . . of course, the site is selling something (e-filing tax returns), but it has a lot of good, free information about what self-employed people have to do vis-à-vis taxes, in the United States, at least.

AARP
www.aarp.org

In past editions of this book, I have listed AARP's small business center . . . which is no longer there. But I didn't want to just yank this well-known organization's website out of these listings, because there is still *lots* of stuff for the small businessperson—it just isn't in one single place that I can direct you to. Best bet is to do a site search on whatever you want to know ("small business resources" works well; try others), because there are hundreds of articles and useful links on this site; they just aren't organized particularly well at the time I write this. (Remember, this is the Internet; if you don't like something, just check back tomorrow; it'll be different. Works if you *do* like something, too.)

Jobs and Moms: Work at Home
www.jobsandmoms.com/work_at_home.html

Another article on a popular women's site.

Work at Home Schemes
www.geocities.com/freehomebasedbusiness/bbb2.htm

Not everyone using the Internet is as nice as you and I; there are people in the world who might try to take advantage of a trusting nature. Here is an article to help you protect yourself.

Work at Home Schemes Now Peddled Online
www.bbb.org/alerts/article.asp?ID=205

A short article from the Better Business Bureau.

Part-Time, Contract, and Temporary Work

For the most part, I don't advocate people applying for temp jobs through the Internet; you will likely have better luck by going, in person, to your local agency such as Kelly, Manpower, and so on. To find your local agencies, use JobSeek (see below), or go to MapQuest (`www.mapquest.com`) and type "temp agency" under Business Category.

But as I said, "for the most part." It's not like a *rule*. Here are some sites and articles related to temporary, part-time, and contract work:

The Contract Employee's Handbook
`www.cehandbook.com/cehandbook/`
`htmlpages/ceh_main.html`

> This is an immensely useful handbook, covering every facet of doing temporary or contract work. The site also has a contract employee's newsletter. It's sponsored by the Professional Association of Contract Employees.

Temp Jobs
`http://jobsearch.about.com/od/tempjobs`

> From `About.com`, there are links here to articles about finding temp work, whether it's right for you, and so on.

JobSeek
`www.staffingtoday.net/jobseek/index.html`

> Best way to find a temp agency on the Internet. Indicate your area, the kind of work you want, and it kicks back a list— sometimes a very *extensive* list—of temp agencies near you.

SnagAJob
`www.snagajob.com`

> Part-time, restaurant, hourly, summer jobs . . . listings, resources, guidance, advice. Youth oriented, but not exclusively.

Net Temps
www.nettemps.com

"The Hire Power" (groan). Hey, *they* said it, not me. I'd be tempted to list this site just for its bad pun, but this is actually a pretty helpful site. Advice on resume writing and such; also a jobs database.

ContractJobHunter
www.cjhunter.com/dcsf/view
_some.html?SearchType=complete

A *huge* listing of firms that hire consultants and contract employees.

Backdoorjobs.com
www.backdoorjobs.com

This site (and the book, by Michael Landes, from which the site takes its title) is mostly aimed at young people who are looking for summer situations, temporary jobs, maybe something outdoors, maybe something overseas for a little while . . . jobs are listed, and there is a sampling of advice from Landes's excellent book, *The Back Door Guide to Short-Term Job Adventures* (published by Ten Speed Press). Basically, the author wants you to buy his book (and it's a good book), but even so, there's a lot of useful information right here, and news of opportunities online here.

Summerjobs.com
www.summerjobs.com/jobSeekers/resources/
links.html

This is the links page at SummerJobs.com. There are a number of really useful resources here, including Travel and Adventure, Immigration and Visas, and job sites for overseas and resort employment.

When You're Operating on a Shoestring

Finding clients or customers: With the Internet, came globalization. With globalization, came outsourcing off shore, as I commented earlier in this book. And this changed everything for the self-employed. You now have a much larger market at your disposal where you can sell your skills, knowledge, services, and products.

Finding employees or vendors: And in this global age if you're self-employed, but operating on a shoestring, and you need let us say to have something printed or produced as inexpensively as possible, you can search for an inexpensive printer, vendor, or manufacturer anywhere in the world. You can even solicit bids.

At `http://www.virtualecommerce.com/`, for example, you can list your talent needs or the services required, plus your budget for this task or project, the time by which you need to hire, and some insight into your style or tastes (e.g., your five favorite websites). Vendors from inside the U.S., as well as outside, can bid.

Alternatively, you can type the name of the skill-set you need, plus the word "overseas," and the word "jobs"—and see what you can find. For example, if you try "overseas cartoonist jobs" this will turn up such sites as `http://www.ifreelance.com/`.

Is hiring overseas something *you* should consider for your small business? Like everything in this world, it has its pros and cons. Some useful guidelines were in the May 1, 2006, issue of the *New York Times* (`http://www.nytimes.com/2006/05/01/business/smallbusiness/01outsource.html`).

Fall-Back Strategies When You Just Can't Get a Business Going, at First

When I first started out in this field, more than thirty-five years ago, I read every book there was on job-hunting and career-change. One thing that frustrated me was that they would offer some recommended strategies, and then act as though, *Well, of course, now you've got that job you've always wanted.*

I always wondered, as I read, *"But what if they don't?"* What if all the strategies here recommended *don't work?* So, naturally I'm concerned for my own readers who try *everything* in this chapter, and you're still out of work, and your finances are getting to the crisis stage. The advice that follows applies not only to starting your own business, but also to any kind of job target.

You know about welfare, of course. It varies from country to country, but it is a safety net that most countries have constructed.

But what if you don't want to go on welfare? Then what do you do? Well, you have several choices:

- A stop-gap job
- Temp work
- Holding down two different part-time jobs
- Job-sharing

A Stop-Gap Job

The first life-preserver is: *a stop-gap job.* This phrase, used by many experts, refers to the situation where your money is about gone, and you have exhausted all job-hunting strategies. At this point, the advice of every expert is to take *any kind of work you can get.* That fills, or stops-up, the gap between the balance in your bank account and what you need to live on—hence, it is called a *stop-gap job.*

The mark of a stop-gap job is simple: it's a short-term job that you would *hate* if it were anything but short-term. It isn't supposed to be anything you really *like* to do. Its only requirement is that it be honest work, and that it bring in some money. It will probably be less money than you are used to making, per hour. It will probably also be hard work—or boring work. *But,* who cares? Its sole purpose is to put some honest money on the table, so you can eat. And pay the rent. And that's *it.*

The way you go about finding a stop-gap job is simple. You get your local newspaper, you look at the help-wanted ads, and you circle *any* and *every* job that you could see yourself doing *for a short time,* simply for the money. Then you go and apply for those jobs.

You also go to employment agencies, and say, "I'll do *anything;* what have you got?"

Unhappily, this spirit—"I'll do anything"—is rarer than it ought to be. Many job-hunters refuse to even consider a stop-gap job; they'd rather go on welfare, first. One reason for this financially suicidal feeling is the conviction that "such jobs are *beneath me.*" You know: *"I wouldn't be caught dead washing dishes."*

I need to state the obvious here: namely, that **any honest hard work neither demeans you, nor makes you less important as a person.** The "you" who is doing that work, remains the same. Except that it is a "you" who *needs this money.* I should also add, while I'm at it, that there are many salutary lessons for the soul, to be learned from temporarily taking a stop-gap job. And this is especially true if that job is at a different level and in a different world than you have been accustomed to.[3]

Many of us delay in seeking a stop-gap job for a somewhat higher reason: namely, the conviction that we must have full-time to devote to our job-hunt. Well, that's important, of course; but so is eating. You may want to consider a part-time stop-gap job, in order to address both concerns, fairly. (Also you might want to keep a *time-log* for two weeks, to see just how much time you actually *are* spending on your job-hunt. The easiest person in the world to deceive is *ourselves.*)

A final reason many refuse to seek a stop-gap job is that they are receiving unemployment benefits, which of course would be cut off, if they took a job of any kind. But, needless to say, unemployment benefits do run out, and should they run out before you have found a job, then it is a very different story. Run, do not walk, to find a job, any job, apply for it and take it, once offered—as a stop-gap measure . . . only. Keep working on chapter 13. And *keep looking.*

For, as the birds say *(I overheard them just the other day):* "A stop-gap job is like a frail branch of a tree: a lovely place to stop and catch your breath, but a lousy place to build a permanent nest."

---

3. At one point in my life, I myself took a stop-gap job, which involved cutting grass, helping lay cement sidewalks, and building retaining walls. It was one of the most educational experiences of my life. It also brought in exactly the money that I so badly needed.

Chapter Ten

Temp Work

After stop-gap jobs, your next life-preserver is *temp work*. In these difficult times, many many employers are cutting their staff to the bone. Trouble is, as time goes on, some extra work may then come their way, work that their reduced staff can't keep up with.

At that point, employers won't usually hire back the staff they cut, but they will turn to what are called "Temporary Help" agencies, for either full- or part-time work. If you are having trouble finding a long-term full-time job, you certainly want to go register at one or more of these agencies.

In the old days, temporary agencies were solely for clerical workers and secretarial help. But the field has seen an explosion of services in recent years.

Now there are temporary agencies *(at least in the larger cities)* for many different occupations. In your city you may find temporary agencies for: accountants, industrial workers, assemblers, drivers, mechanics, construction people, engineering people, management/executives, nannies (for young and old), health care/dental/medical people, legal specialists, insurance specialists, sales/marketing people, underwriting professionals, financial services, and the like, as well as for the more obvious specialties: data processing, secretarial, and office services.

You will find the agencies listed in the yellow pages of your local phone book, under *Employment-Temporary.* Their listing or their ads will usually indicate what their specialities are.

They may find for you: a full-time job that lasts for a number of days or weeks or even months.

Or they may find for you: a part-time job that lasts for a number of days or weeks or even months.

Or they may not find anything for you. It is the case, as with all employment agencies, that there are often many more job-hunters who list themselves with such agencies, than there are employers who come there looking for help.

So, this cannot be your only strategy for finding work.

But it is certainly worth a try. You can increase the likelihood of the agency linking you up with a job, if you help them a little. For example, if you are in environmental engineering, and you know your field well, you can increase your chances of getting employment through a particular agency by compiling *for them* a list of the companies in your field, together with (if you know it) the name of the contact person there.[4] The temporary agency will do what it always does, initiate calls to those companies, soliciting their business; and if they uncover a vacancy, the odds are very great that it will be your name that is put forth for that job there.

Holding Down Two Different Part-Time Jobs

If the temporary agencies never call, and you still can't find any full-time job, your next strategy for finding work is to look for part-time work. While there are many *involuntary* part-time workers these days[5], there are also many *voluntary* part-time workers. They don't *want* to work full-time. Period. End of story. And you of course may be among them.

But suppose you do want full-time work. Often you can put a couple of part-time jobs together, so as to make the equivalent of full-time work.

In some cases, you may even prefer this to one full-time job. Perhaps you feel yourself to be multitalented and/or perhaps you have a couple of very different interests. You can sometimes find a part-time job in one of your fields of interest and a second part-time job in another one of your fields of interest, thus allowing you to use *all* your favorite skills and interests—in a way that no one full-time job might be able to do.

You can put together two part-time jobs in a variety of ways. One can be a job where you work for someone else, the other can be your own business or consultancy.

One can be a job advertised in a newspaper (or agency) or *online*, and the other can be a job that you create for yourself by approaching someone you'd really like to work with (or for), and asking what kind of help they need.

One can be a job with someone you never met before, and the other can be a job with your father, mother, brother, sister, aunt, uncle, or best friend.

---

4. I am indebted to one of our readers, Tathyana Pshevlozky, for this idea.
5. Involuntary part-time workers are those who want a full-time job, can't find one, so take a part-time job until a full-time job comes along.

One can be a job during the daytime, on weekdays, and the other can be a job you do on weekends, or on certain evenings.

How you find such jobs will depend on the nature of the job. If it's with a family member or friend, you ask them. If one of the jobs involves starting your own business, you start it. Newspaper ads also are a way of finding part-time jobs. If they want part-time workers, they will say so. Experience usually dictates that these jobs will either be at places you like, for much less money than you want, or they will be at places you hate, for a lot more money (e.g., toll-booth collectors, checkout people at supermarkets, etc.). The general rule is: the more boring the job, the higher the pay. You decide.

Job-Sharing

You're looking for part-time work. But one day, while you're looking through the ads or talking to some friends, you discover a full-time job that you are really interested in, and it's at just the kind of place where you would like to work. But they want someone full-time, and you only want to work part-time. There is a *possible* solution.

You can sometimes sell the organization on the idea of letting *two* of you fill that one job *(one of you from 8–12 noon, say, and the other from 1–5 P.M.)*. Of course in order to do this, you have to find someone else—a relative, friend, or acquaintance—who is also looking for part-time work, *and* is very competent, *and* would be willing to share that job with you. And you have to find them *first*, and talk them into it, before you approach the boss at that place that interests you. This arrangement is called *job-sharing*, and there are a number of books and places you can write to, if you need some further guidance about how to do it, and how to sell the employer on the idea.

Incidentally, don't omit larger employers, from this particular search just because they would seem to you to be too bound by their own bureaucratic rules—*some* of them are very open to the idea of job-sharing. *On the other hand, of course, a lot of them aren't.* But it never hurts to ask.

Conclusion:
New Ways to Work

It takes a lot of guts to try ANYTHING new *(to you)* in today's economy. It's easier, however, if you keep three rules in mind:

1. There is always some risk, in trying something new. Your job is not to avoid risk—there is no way to do that—but to make sure ahead of time that the risks are *manageable.*
2. You find this out before you start, by first talking to others who have already done what you are thinking of doing; then you evaluate whether or not you still want to go ahead and try it.
3. Have a Plan B, already laid out, *before you start*, as to what you will do if it doesn't work out; i.e., know where you are going to go, next. Don't wait, *puh-leaze!* Write it out, now. *This is what I'm going to do, if this doesn't work out:*_____

_____

These rules always apply, no matter where you are in your life: just starting out, already employed, unemployed, in mid-life, recovering after a crisis or accident, facing retirement, or whatever. Do take them very seriously.

If you're sharing your life with someone, sit down with that partner or spouse and ask what the implications are *for them* if you try this new thing. Will it require all your joint savings? Will they have to give up things? If so, what? Are they willing to make those sacrifices? And so on.

If you aren't out of work, you will need to debate the wisdom of quitting your job before you start up the new company, or business. And what do the experts say, here? In a word, they say, if you have a job, *don't* quit it. Better by far to move *gradually* into self-employment, doing it as a moonlighting activity first of all, while you are still holding down that regular job somewhere else. That way, you can test out your new enterprise, as you would test a floorboard in an old rundown house, stepping on it cautiously without at first putting your full weight on it, to see whether or not it will support you.

If your investigation revealed that it takes good accounting practices in order to turn a profit, and you don't know a thing about accounting, you go out and hire a part-time accountant *immediately*—or, if you absolutely have no money, you talk an accountant friend of yours into giving you some volunteer time, for a while.

It is up to you to do your research thoroughly, weigh the risks, count the cost, get counsel from those intimately involved with you, and then if you decide you want to do **it** (whatever *it* is), go ahead and try—no matter what your well-meaning but pessimistic acquaintances may say.

You only have one life here on this earth, and that life is *yours* (under God) to say how it will be spent, or not spent. Parents, well-meaning friends, etc., get no vote. Just you, and God.

"I think there has always been an obsession with youth and beauty. What's missing is the equal obsession with respect for . . . older people . . . and their wisdom and knowledge and courage."
Julie Christie, *actress*

CHAPTER 11

In
This Restless, Unpredictable,
Ever-Changing Long Life of Ours:

Entering
the World of 50+

The Last Great Change in Our Lives:[1]

The so-called "baby boomers"—the 76 million Americans born between 1945 and 1964—are beginning to enter the time of Life that is traditionally called "retirement."[2] Some people love that word. I'm not one of them. For me, it implies "being put out to pasture"—to borrow an image from a cow. It implies a kind of parole from a thing called *work*, which is assumed to be onerous, and tedious. It implies "disengagement" from both *work* and *Life*, as one patiently—or impatiently— waits to die. It thinks of Life in terms of work; I prefer instead to think of Life in terms of music. My favorite metaphor is that of a symphony. A symphony, traditionally, has four parts to it—four movements, as they're called. So does Life. There is infancy, then the time of learning, then the time of working, and finally, this time that we are talking about, often called "retirement."

---

1. This section is adapted from a new book by John E. Nelson and myself, called *What Color Is Your Parachute? For Retirement: Planning Now for the Life You Want* (Berkeley, CA: Ten Speed Press, 2007).
2. The time this disengagement begins, has gotten getting younger and younger, over the years. Fifty-plus is now the accepted start of some people's *retirement*.

But if we discourage the use of the word "retirement," then this might better be called the Fourth Movement.

The Fourth Movement, in the symphonic world, is a kind of blank slate. It was and is up to the composer to decide what to write upon it. Traditionally, the composer writes of triumph, victory, and joy—as in Beethoven's Symphony #3, *the Eroica*. But it may, alternatively, be a kind of anticlimactic, meandering piece of music—as in Tchaikovsky's Symphony #6, *the Pathetique*. There the Third Movement ends with a bombastic, stirring march. The Fourth Movement, immediately following, is subdued, meditative, meandering, and sounds almost like an afterthought.

Well, there are our choices about our own lives: shall the Fourth Movement, the final movement, of our lives be *pathetique* or *eroica*—pathetic or heroic? Your call!

I like this defining of our lives in terms of *music*, rather than in terms of *work*.

To carry the metaphor onward, in this Fourth Movement of our lives, we have instruments, which we must treat with care. They are: our **body,** our **mind,** our **spirit,** and what we poetically speak of as our **heart,** which Chinese medicine calls "the Emperor."[3] Body, mind, spirit, heart. Some of these instruments are in shiny, splendid condition, in our lives. Others are slightly dented. Or greatly dented. But these are the instruments that play the musical notes and themes of this time of our lives.

The traditional notes are: **sleep, water, eating, faith, love, loneliness, survival** (financial and spiritual), **health care, dreams** (fulfilled or unfulfilled), and **triumph**—over all adversities—and even **death.**

I will share some helpful thoughts, and websites, for each of these notes—at the end of this chapter.

Traditionally, the themes for this period of our lives also include **planning**—as in the phrase "retirement planning." But I believe planning is difficult for the Fourth Movement. It seems to me the outstanding characteristic of the Fourth Movement in our lives is the increased number of things that knock our plans into a cocked hat—the events we call *unexpected*. So I prefer to say that one of the notes we strike during the Fourth Movement

---

3. www.itmonline.org/5organs/heart.htm

in particular, is how to handle **interruptions.** Martin Luther King Jr. perhaps put it best, just before his death:

"The major problem of life is learning how to handle the costly interruptions—the door that slams shut, the plan that got sidetracked, the marriage that failed, or that lovely poem that didn't get written because someone knocked on the door."

Now, in music, interruptions are the pauses between the notes; those pauses that, in fact, keep the notes from just becoming a chaotic jumble. Just listen to the first few bars of Beethoven's Fifth. Thank God for the interruptions, the spaces between the notes.

So, where have we come thus far? Well, I suggested that it is useful to think of Life after 50 as the Fourth Movement in the symphony of our lives—the movement that comes after the first three: Infancy, then The Time of Learning, and then The Time of Working. And it is useful to think that we have instruments, which play certain themes in this movement, as we have seen. That brings us to the $64,000 question: "Toward what end?" "What is the point of all these notes, all these themes, in the Fourth Movement? What are they intended to produce?"

Ahhh, when I think of the overall impression left with me after I hear the Fourth Movement of any great symphony, such as Schubert's Ninth, one impression sticks out, above all others. And that impression is one of *energy*. I am left with an impression of great energy. And the more the better, say I. Energy is lovely to behold, and even lovelier to possess. That energy belongs in the Fourth Movement because it brings the whole symphony to triumphant resolution.

This, it seems to me, is how people evaluate the Fourth Movement of our lives, as well. Not: did we live triumphantly and die victoriously; but: do we manifest *energy*? Do we manifest enthusiasm? Do we manifest excitement, still?

Ask any employer what they are looking for, when they interview a job candidate who is 50 years or older, and they will tell you: energy. They ask themselves, "Does the candidate *(that's us)* slouch in the chair? Does the candidate look like they're just marking time in Life? Or does the candidate lean slightly forward in the chair as we talk? Does the candidate seem excited about the prospect of working here?"

Energy in people past 50 is exciting to an employer. And to those around us. It suggests the candidate will come in early, and stay late. It suggests that whatever task is given, the task will be done thoroughly and completely, and not just barely or perfunctorily.

All right, then, *energy.* Where shall we find energy, after 50? When we were young, energy resided in the *physical* side of our nature. We were "feeling our oats." We could go all day, and go all night. "My, where do you get all your energy?" our grandmother would ask us. We were a dynamo . . . of *physical* energy.

Can't say the same when we reach 50, and beyond. Oh, some of us still have it. But as we get older the rest of us start to slow down. Physical energy is often harder to come by, despite workouts and exercise and marathons. Increasingly, our energy must more and more come from *within*. It must spring not from our muscles but from our excitement about Life and about what we are doing in this Fourth and final Movement of our lives.

This brought back to me a memory I have cherished since childhood. We spent a summer in Balboa in a large cottage on the grand canal and went fishing every day and swimming in the warm southern California water. Next door to us was another cottage with an old couple who always seemed to be sitting on their front porch observing the summer activities. We made friends and the lady wanted to be called Auntie Bess. I think I was twelve and she was probably eighty and her husband the same. Auntie Bess always asked what we were going to do each day and we became friends. Each day we brought home lots of fish and she was really excited when we offered them to her. This continued through the summer and one evening she offered to take us clamming on our beach and explained how we could make a clamming probe with a coat hanger and that we should meet her at low tide around six the next morning.

We arrived at the beach in front of the cottage at the same time and I watched her slow progress and unsteady walk and very thick glasses. Her enthusiasm was boundless and she showed us the two holes in the sand that razor clams make and how to pull them out with the coat hanger wire. We probably got ten nice clams and Auntie Bess started to fade and said she would watch us from the porch. I watched her unsteady and slow progress back to her porch. I couldn't forget the energy and enthusiasm that lady had which made her actually quiver with delight in showing two little boys how to bring up clams. Never had I seen anyone burn so bright with so few resources.

Oh I hope I can be like that.

Phil Wood

This is why, past 50, we need to spend more time on the questions of our youth—*what are your favorite skills? where do you most enjoy using them? and how do you find such a place and such a job or endeavor?* These questions are entertaining when we are young, but critical when we are past 50, as they are the doorway to finding our *energy* in the Fourth and final Movement of the symphony of our lives.[4]

Energy is what impresses employers, if you still need (or want) to work, past 50. Employers often worry that older workers have lost their energy and enthusiasm for work. The best way to show that you are not the type to just coast through your remaining work-years, until you give up working, is to display some passion during the interview. Remember, *energy* is what employers are looking for, the most. Figure out what *does* get you excited.

Stay alert, *very* alert, during the whole interview. Lean forward in your chair, ever so slightly. When the employer is speaking, respond with an intelligent question (or curiosity) about what they have just said. When they have asked you a question, don't respond with a long-winded answer. Twenty seconds to two minutes at most, is best.

All in all, your age is irrelevant if you convey energy and enthusiasm—for Life, for work, for helping others. Energy. That's what every employer is looking for, when they interview someone over 50.

---

4. Detailed instructions for getting at these questions can be found in this book in chapter 13.

The nicest compliment any of us can hear people say about us, as we grow older, is: "What a passion for life she still has! Or, *he* has! It's thrilling to be around them."

Themes and Notes in the Fourth Movement of Our Lives

The Mind

By the time we reach the Fourth Movement of our lives, the life of the mind is *everything*.

Sometimes our mind has become puzzling to us in its performance: we experience more short-term memory loss, more inability to concentrate sometimes, or more difficulty retrieving words, or more difficulty than before, in recognizing faces or remembering names of neighbors, more things becoming "lost," or at least misplaced, at inopportune times, or an increasing inability to follow through on tasks, becoming instead easily distracted or diverted. Or the inability any longer to push ourselves to the limit, as we used to do.

These things can occur when we are young, but they tend to disturb us more when they come in the Fourth Movement of our lives. Oh, *aging*, we think. *Darn!*

Well, not necessarily. The causes are sometimes medicines we are taking—especially for pain or nausea; or abrupt menopause (in women, of course); or anxiety or depression; or medical treatment we have undergone in the past (particularly chemotherapy, in 15 percent of those thus treated—a condition called "chemo brain"); and the largest reason of all for these new behaviors or limits: "Idon'tknow."

Sometimes we obsess. About anything. About everything.

This is a matter of choosing what to think about.

By the Fourth Movement, we've experienced enough injustices, unfairnesses, and psychic injuries, to ourselves or to the vast and vulnerable peoples of the Earth, that we could *brood about* these things, for the rest of our lives. If we so choose.

Again, by then, we've seen enough possible, fearful, scenarios for the future of our own lives, and how we shall die, for the future of our people, and for the future of the Earth, that we can live in constant daily fear of a thousand things that will never happen, for the rest of our lives. If we so choose.

Again, by then we've seen the wondrous beauty of the world, in our garden, in the sunset, in music, in a thousand unexpected kindnesses from strangers and loved ones, and in the enchanting spirit of the best people on earth, that we could think on these things, for the rest of our lives. If we so choose.

Yes, more important than *the life that we choose*, are the thoughts that we choose, day after day after day. They determine the quality of life for us in the Fourth Movement of our lives.

I think that *The Secret*—the phenomenally popular book and DVD—has it right, at its core, even though the melodramatic story and hints of conspiracy in its *presentation* of that core, are more than a little off-putting to some.

The Will

The Will is a metaphor for *the Power of deciding*, which each of us has. We are most familiar with it when we are dieting, or making New Year's resolutions. It often feels like a battlefield, between two opposing impulses: should I eat chocolate? or, should I not eat chocolate?

But in the Fourth Movement of our lives, it is often a larger battlefield, between our diminishing power to decide, and a vast number of crooks, out there, who want to separate us from our money, by false pretense and luring promises that they will make us rich, if only we . . .

So, the Fourth Movement is a great time to relearn, or learn for the first time, *how to decide*.

I mentioned, at the beginning of this book, that this is one of the skills you would *think* school would help us to master; but, alas and alack! more often than not, it does not. So, we must pick up clues, wherever we can.

Dr. Jerome Groopman, a *hematologist*,[5] wanted to study *How Doctors Think*. In a brilliant book with that title, published in 2007, he presented his mindings. On average, he discovered, a physician will interrupt a patient describing her symptoms *within eighteen seconds*. By then, often, the doctor has decided what the diagnosis is—often correctly, but sometimes disastrously wrong.

---

5. A practitioner in a branch of medicine devoted to the study of blood.

In illuminating how doctors (and we) can make better decisions about our medical treatment, Dr. Groopman illuminates how *we* can make better decisions about *everything*. Crucial knowledge for those of us over 50.

It is a marvelous book, which I highly recommend. For our purposes, I am summarizing, here, my own learnings about the steps Dr. Groopman says a doctor (or we, the patient) should take, before making a decision (or diagnosis):

1. Take time. Hurry is the worst enemy of good decisions.

2. Question. *Cogently.* Listen. *Carefully.* Observe. *Keenly.* Think. *Differently.* Questions that will help:

Ask yourself if there is some vital piece of information that is being left out. Physician to patient: "Tell me the story again, as if I'd never heard it: what you felt, what else you remember about where and when, etc."

Ask what else we should explore to avoid premature closure. "What else could this possibly be?" Physician: Don't be influenced by how many physicians have previously examined and diagnosed this patient, or what their diagnosis is. This person has come to you because they want to hear something new, not just a reinforcement of what other doctors have said. Bring a fresh mind with the question foremost in your head: "But what if this isn't what others have said it is? What if this is something very different?"

Don't just dismiss the intuitions and feelings of patient or family. Physician to patient: "What are your worst fears, or your family's worst fears, about these symptoms?"

Recheck the initial diagnosis. "In the tests, or in the diagnosis, is there anything that doesn't fit?"

Avoid one-answer solutions to complex problems. Patient to physician: "Is it possible I have more than one problem?"

Work

If you need or want to work past 50, there are some things you need to keep in mind: you have—or should have, if you stop to think about it—lots of contacts, individuals or networks of friends. In a word, *a grapevine.* They can lead you to jobs, they can speak enthusiastically about you. And since, by your age, these contacts are likely to be of all ages, you have a rich pool to pick from. Unlike younger workers.

To find more information, see the article referenced below.[6]

To find jobs that may offer flextime, job-sharing, telecommuting to either full- or part-time workers:

▶ A List of Part-Time Jobs Available in Your Area (Zip Code) `www.snagajob.com`

▶ A List of Best Employers for Workers Over 50: `www.aarpmagazine.org/money/2006bestemployers.html`

Faith/Spirituality

Past 50, many of us think more strongly about what we believe—about the afterlife, about God, prayer, etc. There is a website that deals with news, etc., about all faiths, which you may want to look at: `www.beliefnet.com`.

A Jesuit site that leads you in a daily meditation for ten or more minutes (in more than twenty languages, with a visual, but otherwise no sound or distraction) is: `www.sacredspace.ie`.

A site that gives you a daily podcast of church bells, music, Scripture reading, and meditations or homily, with no visuals, but has sound, and an audio MP3 file that can be sent to your phone, computer, PDA, etc., is: `www.pray-as-you-go.org`.

A site dedicated to helping you keep a divine consciousness 24-7: by helping you to link up to other people of faith, through prayer circles, sharing of personal stories of faith, etc., aimed especially, but not exclusively, toward young adults. Its ultimate message: you are not alone, is: `www.24-7prayer.com/cm/articles/771`.

Lastly, a site dedicated to helping you find a spiritual counselor (or "spiritual director"), as well as retreat centers, in either the Christian, Islamic, Buddhist, Jewish, or Interfaith faiths, is: `www.sdiworld.org`.

If your spirituality isn't of the traditional kind, get out in the outdoors as much as possible. Sit. Walk. Breathe. Observe. Get excited by the simple beauty of just being alive.

---

6. For the complete article, go to `www.jobfinderssupport.com/resources.htm` and then, under "Hot Topics" click on "Secrets of Finding a Job When You're Over 50."

In
This Restless, Unpredictable,
Ever-Changing
Brain of Ours:

How to Get "Unstuck"

W henever we are faced with Change, in our life, there is always the possibility that we will unexpectedly find ourselves "stuck." Oftentimes, no one is more astonished at this development, than ourselves. *"What? Why can't I get past this barrier? Why can't I just move forward? What's blocking me?"*

This can happen at any point, but in doing the Flower Exercise, at the rear of this book, it particularly happens when we are trying to deal with the Petal called "**Fields** of Fascination."

I have seen this problem for years and years. It took us a long time to figure out how to solve it. Eventually, this is what we discovered:

1. **The problem, in a nutshell, is that something is happening, unconsciously, inside the job-hunter's or career-changer's brain,** when confronted with this task of career-change.
2. **The solution: tell the career-changer's brain just exactly what that brain is (unconsciously) doing, so that their brain—now aware of what it's doing—can change its behavior.**

How Your Brain Works

To begin with, let us consider how our brain operates. Roger Sperry, 1981 Nobel Prize winner, won that prize for research that identified that our brain has two sides to it, physically and meta-phorically. One side, normally the left side of our brain, processes information sequentially, one by one, bit by bit.

The other side of our brain, normally the right side, processes information holistically, all at once, intuitionally.[1]

So it is that each of us has one brain with two strategies at its disposal. Thus, if we try one approach to a problem in making a change in our life, and that doesn't work, our brain offers us an alternative approach—from the other side of the brain.

We can portray this in a diagram, using the spokes of a wheel. At each end of each spoke, is a pair of alternative approaches to problems, and we can fall back on one if the other doesn't work—in a particular situation, with a particular problem.

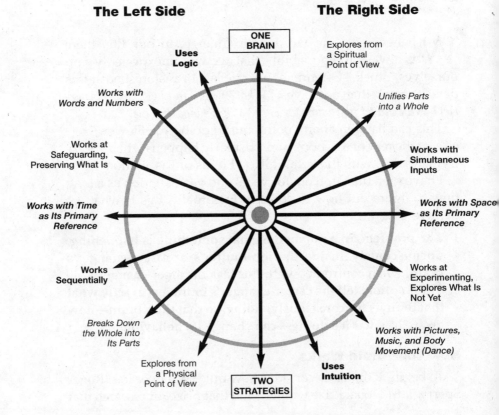

The Two Sides of the Brain and What Each Does

The Left Side   **The Right Side**

ONE BRAIN

Uses Logic

Explores from a Spiritual Point of View

Works with Words and Numbers

Unifies Parts into a Whole

Works at Safeguarding, Preserving What Is

Works with Simultaneous Inputs

Works with Time as Its Primary Reference

Works with Space as Its Primary Reference

Works Sequentially

Works at Experimenting, Explores What Is Not Yet

Breaks Down the Whole into Its Parts

Works with Pictures, Music, and Body Movement (Dance)

Explores from a Physical Point of View

Uses Intuition

TWO STRATEGIES

Chapter Twelve

Wonderful brain, God gave us! Alternatively, we can contrast the two sides of the brain in the form of two columns, and that comes out looking like this:

The Left Side of Your Brain	The Right Side of Your Brain
Excels at seeing the individual pieces.	**Excels at assembling the pieces into a coherent picture.**
Is good at perceiving details or individual elements (e.g., **text**).	Is good at seeing the broad picture, the overall **context**, integrates many inputs all at once.
Specializes in logic and analytical reasoning or thinking.	Specializes in intuition and holistic perception or thinking.
Specializes in verbal and mathematical functions.	Specializes in spatial and relational functions.
Specializes in memory and recognition of words and numbers.	Specializes in memory and recognition of objects, persons, faces, music, and pitch.
Specializes in anything related to **time,** such as history, planning.	Specializes in things related to **space,** such as body movement.
Is connected to the right side of the body, and the right side of each eye's vision.	Is connected to the left side of the body, and the left side of each eye's vision.

1. Brain scanning, in more recent years, has illuminated the fact that it is not quite so simple as was at first thought. While certain brain functions are predominantly in one side of the brain or the other, a secondary role is often played by functions in the opposite side of the brain. Still, as a metaphor, even if it is an oversimplification, it is very useful to speak of the two sides of the brain. If you wish to explore this subject of the two sides of the brain further, Bob Ornstein was (and is) a pioneer in this whole field of the two sides of the brain. His original work was *The Psychology of Consciousness* (The Viking Press, Inc., 1973), which he then updated in significant ways in a 1997 book, called *The Right Mind: Making Sense of the Hemispheres* (Harcourt Brace & Company, 1997).

"Your Safekeeping Self" vs. "Your Experimental Self"

Now, we come to the heart of the matter of *why we get stuck*, when we're trying to make changes in our life.

George Prince, of the Mind-Free Group, Inc., proposed, a number of years ago, that there is a sense in which these two sides of the brain behave almost *as though they were persons*.

They function almost like two very different personalities, two very different Selves, within each of us. George named them "the Safekeeping Self" and "the Experimental Self."

The Safekeeping Self: George suggested that the left side of the brain (in most people) functions as though its mission in life were to safeguard the person by keeping them where they are, in familiar, safe, nonthreatening territory. It is the policeman (policeperson) in us all.

The Experimental Self: George suggested that the right side of the brain (in most people) functions as though its mission in life were to lead the person into new adventures and exploration of uncharted territory. It is the explorer in us all.

You could depict the contrast between them in this way:

"The ideal is to have two selves that cooperate fully," Prince writes. And then he came to his key point, so far as those of us who are stuck, are concerned: "We know . . . that . . . to the degree Safekeeping dominates, it tends to shut down my Experimental Self."[2]

Bingo! There is the root of our "stuck-ness," when it appears.

Specializing in One Side or the Other

But let us spell all of this out, in more detail.

It becomes apparent, if you study the brain, that while each of us is in theory "whole-brained," we tend to gravitate over time toward one side of the brain or the other for our "primary processing of information." We emphasize. We specialize.

And so it is legitimate to say that some of us are *primarily* left-brained and that some of us are *primarily* right-brained. *"He is very left-brained."* Or *"She is very right-brained."*

---

2. George Prince, "Creativity and Learning as Skills, Not Talents," Phillips Exeter Bulletin, June-July and September-October, 1980, pp. 8–10.

Chapter Twelve

The Left Side of the Brain Functioning as **The Safekeeping Self**	The Right Side of the Brain Functioning as **The Experimental Self**

Guides	Is in touch with the unconscious
Evaluates	Can "touch" total experience
Analyzes	Uses seeming irrelevance
Loves words	Imagines
Reassures and supports	Is intuitive
Is realistic	Speculates
Looks at consequences	Recognizes patterns
Is logical	Makes connections
Is serious, cautious, and suspicious	Is impetuous
Is alert to danger	Does not mind being confused
Avoids surprises	Does not mind being wrong
Avoids risks	Makes impossible wishes
Avoids wrongness	Is open to anything
Makes rules, follows rules	Likes surprises
Is fearful	Breaks rules
Punishes itself for: mistakes, wrongness, and any deviations from perfection	Takes risks
	Sees the fun in things
	Feels
	Guesses
	Is curious

How to Get "Unstuck"

In some people, for example, the Experimental Self is clearly transcendent most of their lives. They are always rushing off to climb Mt. Everest, or white water rafting, or ballooning around the world.

In other people, the Safekeeping Self is transcendent most of their lives. They live lives of caution, with everything planned as carefully as may be, and risk-taking held to a minimum.

But—and this is the point—most of us switch back and forth, *choosing the appropriate Self for the activity at hand*: preferring to let our Experimental Self be in the lead—for example—while we are on vacation, but preferring to let our Safekeeping Self be in the lead, at, say, income tax time.

Why Does the Safekeeping Self Go into Panic?

The question here is: *what is the appropriate self for the activity at hand:* Making a Change in Our Lives?

Inasmuch as a career-change and its kin is a definite launching out into the deep (so to speak), it is clear that the appropriate Self should be, indeed must be, *the Experimental Self.*

The problem is, we often see the Safekeeping Self going into a panic at that point, and insisting it can handle the situation. *It's lying!*

And as George Prince said, "We know . . . that . . . to the degree Safekeeping dominates, it tends to shut down my Experimental Self." Why, we ask ourselves, does the Safekeeping Self not only leap to the fore but maintain an iron grip on us, when we are attempting to change careers? What went wrong?

We who are career counselors may teach them everything we know about new and creative and more effective ways of going about their job-hunt, only to watch in horror as—when push comes to shove—our clients fall back on the most archaic and least effective ways of job-hunting, just because they are familiar. Clearly, the Safekeeping Self has them in a death grip. What went wrong?

It often begins when life or some internal time-clock introduces a jarring note into our lives, as when we are fired, or divorced, or have to go about the job-hunt. Whammo! Our Safekeeping Self suddenly comes to full alert, hits the panic button, and starts careening off walls.

Naturally, our Experimental Self "hangs," and we don't know why. In this sense, it is just like a computer "hanging." If you have such a computer, could you possibly explain why it hung the last three times that it did? Not likely! No more does a job-hunter or career-changer know why their brain suddenly "hangs."

But we now know why—that is, if we understand all that I have been explaining about the brain. And we know what our task is: it is to come up with some strategies that will calm down the overreactive Safekeeping Self in us, and help restore the proper balance between the Safekeeping Self and the Experimental Self.

Three Strategies for Taming the Safekeeping Self And Thus Coming "Unstuck"

There are three strategies that we have found, over the years, work rather well:

First Strategy: Describe to your brain, particularly when you feel most stuck, just what the Safekeeping Self is doing, and how it is behaving. Study the information above. When the brain's unconscious behavior is illuminated to your brain, the brain goes "Aha!," and then begins to work to change the brain's behavior, in most cases. It's a loftier kind of biofeedback.

Second Strategy: Gather as much information as possible about the new world you will be moving into, or are contemplating moving into. The more information gathered, the less the new land will seem intimidating and unfamiliar. Information-gathering is not an optional exercise for job-hunters. It is crucial, if the Safekeeping Self is to stop panicking.

Third Strategy: Put a lot of music in your life, particularly when you're working on your career-change or job-hunt. Words "feed" the left side of the brain. Music "feeds" the right side of the brain, activates it, calls it more into active participation throughout each day. Classical music seems to be particularly effective in doing this.

The Sound of the Safekeeping Self
During the Job-Hunt

1. *You know your Safekeeping Self is too much in control when:*

You find yourself talking much more than you usually do—particularly about all the reasons why you shouldn't do this, when you are contemplating making a change in your life. Words, words, words are the way in which the Safekeeping Self manages to keep control and have dominion over the Experimental Self within you. Remedy: Practice silence, and meditation. Hum a lot.

2. *You know your Safekeeping Self is too much in control when:*

You are using particular words that are the "fingerprints" of the Safekeeping Self. These words are:

"I can't"

"I shouldn't"

"I'm not sufficiently *[fill in the blank: bright, talented, outgoing, etc., etc.]*"

"Yes, but . . ."

"It feels wrong to just do what I want"

"I think I may lose more than I will gain"

"What would people think?"

"This isn't realistic"

"I've never done this before"

"What if I do this wrong?"

"But, I've always done it this way"

"This will never work"

"This is just a waste of time"

"Oh, I've tried this before"

"Convince me"

"This is too hard"

"See, I knew it wouldn't work (after one try)"

"My present job's not so bad, after all"

Remedy: Make a list of the opposite of these phrases, and paste that list of affirmations on the mirror in your bathroom, and on your refrigerator. Memorize them. Repeat often, to yourself. Use them as alternatives whenever you find the above phrases creeping into your daily conversation.

3. *You know your Safekeeping Self is too much in control when:*

You are feeling very confused about each step along the way toward change, no matter how carefully and how well these steps are explained to you. Confusion is of course normal when the road ahead has a fork in it. But confusion normally starts to dissipate after a time. If your confusion not only persists, but— if anything—grows stronger, you're almost certainly listening to the sound of the Safekeeping Self. Confusion is one of its favorite weapons, much like the octopus who throws out a cloud of ink when under attack, to obscure and dumbfound and immobilize its enemies.

Remedy: Focus on what you do know, rather than on what you don't know; focus on what you are sure of, rather than on what you aren't sure of. It is easier to deal with uncertain ground, when your feet are firmly planted on certain ground. If you are a person of faith, reaffirm for yourself the certainties about "Underneath are the Everlasting Arms," etc., and ask God to lead you through all confusion.

4. *You know your Safekeeping Self is too much in control when:*

You find yourself being even more obsessive than usual about your little daily rituals and routines. In group job-hunting workshops this is manifested by: always sitting in the same place, always talking to the same few people, etc. This is the sound of the Safekeeping Self: it likes to cling to the familiar routine, as a way of metaphorically "planting a flag" that says: "I am a creature of habit, not one who goes off on flings into new adventures." In other words, this is the Safekeeping Self saying, "Hell, no, I won't go."

Remedy: Practice doing one "altered-behavior" (for you) each day. Practice thus taking one new risk a day, even if it's a little one, like speaking to a neighbor you usually never speak to, or whatever.

5. *You know your Safekeeping Self is too much in control when:*

You find yourself engaging in digressions and diversions, when you should be working on your job-hunt or career-change. This is the old magician's trick of "keep them busy watching the left hand, so they won't notice what's going on with the right hand." Digressions are of various kinds. Leaving your job-hunting and career-changing activities until all your other tasks are done, is one digression. Feeling an inordinate need to sleep is another. Devoting more and more time to going out and helping others, rather than giving yourself the time your job-hunting, career-changing exercises need, is another. Physical maladies, such as headaches, tiredness, colds, and the like, are yet another. Essentially, by means of procrastination, the Safekeeping Self is trying to cling to the status quo by getting you to "put off until tomorrow, the things you could do today." Except, it is praying tomorrow never comes. Know these tricks for what they are: the Safekeeping Self trying to play Procrastinating Magician, in order to preserve the status quo.

Remedy: Get more physical exercise. That way, you are practicing defining yourself more and more as a person of immediate action, rather than as a person who meets a challenge by taking Flight. No, no, Fight. Not Flight.

Restoring Balance to the Brain, and Getting Unstuck

In my teaching, we've used these techniques, successfully, for years, now, when a career-changer or job-hunter feels stuck. It's worked for countless others; it can work for you, when you want to make a change, but feel really stuck.

When your brain is given this information about The Sound of the Safekeeping Self, it can move surprisingly quickly to restore the equilibrium and balance between the Safekeeping Self and the Experimental Self that is its natural state. You are freed from immobility, and are able to get on with the changes in your life that you desire.

Why does the Safekeeping Self alter its behavior just because you shine light upon its ways? Who knows? I don't. I only know that it *does* work, when faithfully followed—often to an incredible degree.

Once any one of us *realizes* that the cause of our "stuck-ness" lies in the Safekeeping Self overreacting, and the Safekeeping Self's readiness to play tricks in order to stay in charge, and prevent change, you're already more than halfway home.

Where

What

How

YOUR DREAM JOB
A Visit to
The Isle of You

Resuming
The Search
To Find
Your Dream

here is a time, when we are young, when we lie out in a meadow, our hands clasped behind our head, and as we stare up at the sky, we dream of what our life might be. The possibilities seem endless, and we are enchanted at this vision. It beckons us toward Life, and Joy.

But then, as things work out, and we grow older, Reality sets in. We decide we have to *settle*. Settle for a life that's less than what we dreamed. A different life. Maybe an Okay life. But definitely a lesser life. And, at times, a boring life.

But sometime later, in our life, something awakens within us. Call it *yearning*. Call it *hope*. We come to realize the dream we dreamed has never died. And we go back to get it. We decide to resume our search . . . for the life we know within our heart that we were meant to live.

The Three Secrets
to Finding
That Dream Job
of Yours

What Did You Come into the World to Do?

It may be that as you read this, *your* whole being has wanted for some time, a new, better, more satisfying, more fulfilling life.

And now—due to your being laid off or made redundant, or due to some internal time clock ticking *within*, or some life-changing event occurring *without* (such as a death or divorce)—you find yourself at a crossroads; and the moment to actually seek that new life and new work has arrived.

There is a name for this moment in your life; in fact, there are several names.

We call it "at last going after your dreams."
We call it "finding more purpose and meaning for your life."
We call it "making a career-change."
We call it "deciding to try something new."
We call it "setting out in a different direction in your life."
We call it "getting out of the rat race."
We call it "going after your dream job."
We call it "finding your mission in life, at last."

But what you call it doesn't really matter. It is instantly recognizable as that moment when you decide that *this time* you're not going to do just a traditional job-hunt; you're going to do a life-changing job-hunt or career-change: one that begins with **you** and what it is that *you* want out of life.

This time it's all about: *Your* agenda. *Your* wishes. *Your* dreams. *Your* mission in life, given you by the Great God, our Creator.

This is a life-changing moment, and we should celebrate its arrival, in any life.

Not a Selfish Activity

You may think that this is a selfish activity—because this deals with You, you, you. But it is not. It is related to what *the world* most needs from you. That world currently is *filled* with workers whose weeklong question is, *When is the weekend going to be here?* And, then, *Thank God It's Friday!* Their work puts bread on the table *but . . .* they are bored out of their minds. Some of them are bored because even though they know what they'd rather be doing, they can't get out of their dead-end jobs, for one reason or another. But too many others, unfortunately, are bored simply because they have *never* given this sufficient priority in their life. They've kept busy with work and their social life, and partying, and vacation; and never taken the time to *think*—to think out what they uniquely can do, and what they uniquely have to offer to the world. They've flopped from one job to another, letting *accident, circumstance, coincidence,* and *whim* carry them wheresoever it would.

What the world most needs *from you* is not to add to their number, but to figure out, and then contribute to the world, what you came into this world to do.

Let's face it, dear reader, neither one of us is getting any younger. If you don't go after your dreams *now*, when will you?

Now is the time to fulfill your dreams and the vision that you once had of what your life could be. Even if it can't be done in a night and a day. Even if it takes patience. Even if it means hard work. Even if it means changing careers. Even if it means going out into the unknown, and taking risks. (*Manageable risks, please!*)

Where Do You Start?

In our search for our dream job, our instinct is to start with some survey of the job-market out there, to find out what's "hot" and what's not. The job-market! Ai-yi-yi, that could take you years. No, this is a *journey* you're embarking on, not (yet) a destination.

So, it's useful to recall what travel experts teach about *taking a journey*: before you go, they say, lay out on your bed, two piles. In one pile, put all the clothes, toiletries, and stuff that you think you'll need to take. In the other pile, put all the money you think you'll need to take.

Then, they say, pack only half the clothes, but twice the money.

By coincidence, the same kind of ratio occurs in this other journey, This Journey Toward Your Dream Job.

That is: for this journey, you will need only half the information you thought you would need about *the job-market*, but twice the amount of information you thought you would need about *yourself*.

The Road to a Dream Job
Is a Road That Passes
First of All Through You

Let your worries about the job-market *go*, for a while. Your dream job is *out there*.

But first of all you must discover the blueprint,
And that blueprint, or model, is *inside you*.

We may paraphrase Alexander Pope, here:

> *Know then thyself,*
> *Do not the Market scan*
> *Until you've surveyed all You are,*
> *Then you will have your plan.*

So, mark this, and mark it well:

> Most job-hunters who fail to find their dream job, fail not because they lack information about the job-market, but because they lack information about themselves.

Of course, being human, our first instinct is to protest that we already know loads of information about ourselves. After all, we've lived with ourselves all these years. We *surely* know who we are, by now.

Well, let's test that premise.

1. Take ten sheets of blank paper. Write, at the top of each one, the words: **Who Am I?**

2. Then write, on each sheet in turn, one answer to that question. And only one.

3. When you're done, go back over all ten sheets and expand now upon what you have written on each sheet. Looking at each answer, write below it, *why* you said that, and *what turns you on* about that answer.

4. When finished with all ten sheets, go back over them and arrange them in order of priority. That is, which identity is the most important to you? That page goes on top. Then, which is next? That goes immediately underneath the top one. Continue arranging the rest of the sheets in order, until the least important identity is at the bottom of the pile.

5. Finally, go back over the ten sheets, in order, and look particularly at your answer, on each sheet, to *What Turns Me On About This?* See if there are any common denominators, or themes, among the ten answers you gave. If so, jot them down on a separate piece of paper. Voilà! You have begun to put your finger on some things that your dream job or career, vocation, mission, or whatever, needs to give you if you are to feel truly excited, fulfilled, useful, effective, and operating at the height of your powers.

Here, incidentally, is an example, of how one man did this exercise:

Who am I?

1. A man
2. An urban dweller (and lover)
3. A loving person
4. A creator
5. A writer
6. A lover of good movies and music
7. A skilled counselor and teacher
8. An independent
9. An executive
10. An enabler

What turns me on about each of these?

1. Taking initiative, having inner strength; being open, growing, playful

2. Excitement, variety of choices available, crowds, faces

3. Feelings, empathizing, playfulness, sex, adoration given, happiness

4. Transforming things, making old things new, familiar, wondrous

5. Beauty of words, variety of images, new perspectives, new relationships of ideas, words, understandings

6. Watching people up close, merging of color, photography, music

7. Using intuition; helping; seeing totalities of people; problem solving; long-term, close, helpful relationships

8. Making own decisions, carrying out own plans

9. Taking responsibility, wise risks, using mind, seeing totalities of problems overall

10. Helping people to become freed-up, to be what they want to be

Any common denominators? Variety, totalities, rearranging of constellations, dealing with a number of different things and showing relationships between them all in a new way, helping others.

What must my career use (and include) for me to be truly happy, useful, and effective? A variety of different things that have to be dealt with, with people, where seeing totalities, rearranging their relationships, and interpreting them to people in a new way are at the heart of the career.

Now, if this exercise was easy, then you do indeed know a lot about yourself. *But* if it was harder than you thought it would be, then you see there is work still to be done. It is urgent for you to know more about who you are, individually and uniquely, in either case.

That knowledge is your secret weapon, to keep from being overwhelmed and overcome, as you search for your dream job.

This is true if you're just having trouble with the common, everyday, garden-variety job-hunt.

But it is especially true if you are not just job-hunting, but are in the process of either choosing or changing careers, as you search for that dream job.

The Three Secrets
to Finding Your Dream Job

The late Barbara B. Brown, who was the first to bring *biofeedback* to the public's awareness back in 1974, with her then groundbreaking book, *New Mind, New Body*, once gave a public lecture on what *brain scientists* had discovered—on the way to biofeedback—about **how best to gather information about yourself, so that you can make better decisions about your life.**

Her findings were of great interest to me because of my own finding that the road to your dream job is a road that passes first of all *through You*.

Barbara Brown said *brain scientists* had discovered there were three things you can do, that greatly facilitate such decision making.

Their first one was: **Put everything you know about yourself, on one piece of paper.** Jot down anything and everything that occurs to you about yourself. This doesn't mean you can only *ever* use just one piece of paper. *That* would require you to learn how to write the Declaration of Independence on the head of a pin. No, the "one piece of paper" is merely the final destination of your collecting information about your Self. Let's call it something obvious, like: "That One Piece of Paper."

On your way to that final destination, you can of course use as many different pieces of paper as you want to—give them whatever name you will. I call those other pieces of paper simply "Scribble sheets."

Brain scientists' second finding, according to Barbara, was: **Use some kind of graphic** on that piece of paper, in order to organize the information *about yourself.* A graphic—any graphic—keeps "That One Piece of Paper" interesting, and not just a mess of words and space.

Their third, and last, finding was: **Prioritize** all this information, when you have finished gathering it. Put it in its order of importance, to you. On "That One Piece of Paper." That way, when you finally go looking for a dream job or career that matches *you,* if it is not a *perfect* overlap, at least you will know what you should make sure *is* included in the overlap.

I have followed this prescription for the past twenty-five years, as I have taught millions of job-hunters and career-changers how to find their dream job. With great results.

We have called "That One Piece of Paper" by various names over the years: *The Beginning Job-Hunting Map, The Quick Job-Hunting Map, The What Color Is Your Parachute Workbook, The Flower Exercise,* etc.

And, over the years we have tried out various graphics on "That One Piece of Paper": a parachutist and his/her parachute, a Grecian temple, a clown holding a bunch of round balloons, a tree with several branches, etc., etc. The common denominator has been that each graphic has had seven or eight parts, inasmuch as any dream job has seven or eight parts. Ultimately we settled on a diagram of a Flower, with seven or eight petals,[1] because readers preferred it above all other graphics. Something about it being a living entity, beautiful and growing, I guess, and therefore a reflection of them at their best.

Here's what it came out looking like.

---

1. Seven vs. eight depends on whether you put Goals and Values on one petal, or two.

The Flower

"That One Piece of Paper"

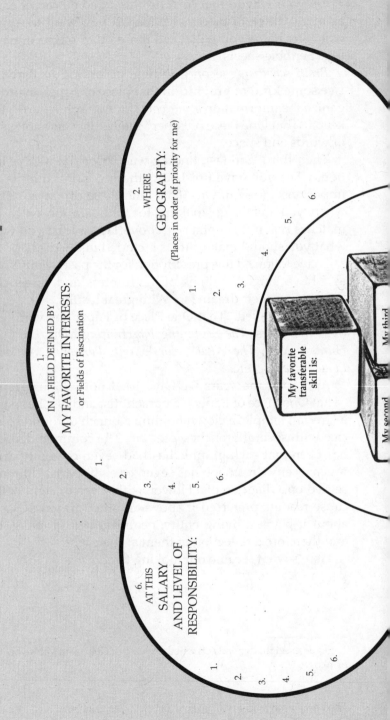

1.
IN A FIELD DEFINED BY
MY FAVORITE INTERESTS:
or Fields of Fascination

1.
2.
3.
4.
5.
6.

2.
WHERE
GEOGRAPHY:
(Places in order of priority for me)

1.
2.
3.
4.
5.
6.

6.
AT THIS
SALARY
AND LEVEL OF
RESPONSIBILITY:

1.
2.
3.
4.
5.
6.

My favorite
transferable
skill is:

My second

My third

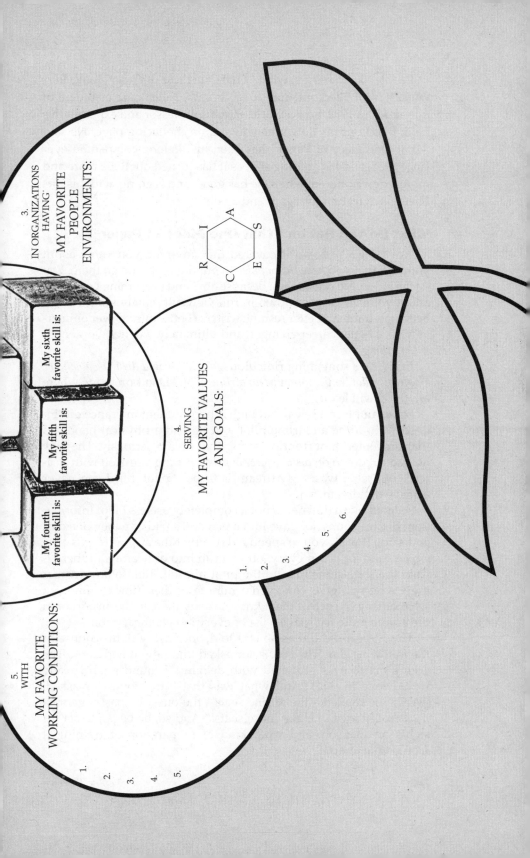

3.
IN ORGANIZATIONS HAVING:
MY FAVORITE PEOPLE ENVIRONMENTS:

4.
SERVING
MY FAVORITE VALUES AND GOALS:

1.
2.
3.
4.
5.
6.

My sixth favorite skill is:

My fifth favorite skill is:

My fourth favorite skill is:

5.
WITH
MY FAVORITE WORKING CONDITIONS:

1.
2.
3.
4.
5.

People like to see just what "That One Piece of Paper" looks like, when it is all filled out, and done. Rich W. Feller, once a student of mine back in 1982, now a world-famous professor and expert in this field, filled out his flower as you see, on the facing page. He said "That One Piece of Paper" has been his lifelong companion ever since 1982, and his guiding star, as it has turned out to be more and more a description of where he has gone, and is going, with his life. I hear such testimony, again and again.

What Do You Put on "That One Piece of Paper"?

Anything. We have discovered that anything you know about yourself, that you *have the impulse* to put there, should go there. You be the judge. No censorship. Because any- and everything you know about yourself, and jot down in full view, ultimately makes you a better job-hunter, a better resume writer, a better interviewer or interviewee, a better career-changer, and ultimately, a better worker.

Anything.

Even if it's something ridiculous, like: *"I would die to be able to be an airline pilot, but I cannot be an airline pilot."* Don't prejudge where anything will lead.

For example, a 17-year-old high school student in France did indeed want to be an airline pilot, but he had a physical handicap that prevented him from pursuing that dream seriously. The way he wrote it down on his *one piece of paper*, during a session with a career counselor, was: "My dream is to be a pilot, but I can never achieve my dream."

Seemed like a downer, if not a completely useless bit of information. But his counselor gave him a pen and a pad of paper, one day, and said, "I want you to spend a day out at the airport *(it was a big airport)* and jot down every job you run into or hear about there— from the shoe-shine man to the pilot himself. Talk to any worker there who will give you even a minute of their time, to find out what other jobs each of them knows about, there in the airport or in the airline industry. Make a list of every job you hear about."

The 17-year-old did as he was told, and met with his counselor the following day. The counselor asked him how it had gone. The young man's eyes glistened with delight: "I found a job I really would love to do." "And what was that?" the counselor asked. "Well," he replied, "the airline seats—the ones the passengers sit in? I would love to make those seats!" And so, he began to set his sights on that job, and what kind of preparation or training it would take to do it.

Salary and Level of Responsibility

1. Can determine 9/12 month contract 2. Can determine own projects 3. Considerable clout in organization's direction without administrative responsibilities 4. Able to select colleagues 5. 3 to 5 assistants 6. $35K to $50K 7. Serve on various important boards 8. Can defer clerical and budget decisions and tasks 9. Speak before large groups 10. Can run for elected office

Favorite Interests

1. Large conference planning 2. Regional geography & culture 3. Traveling on $20/day 4. Career planning seminars 5. Counseling techniques / theories 6. American policies 7. Fundamentals of sports 9. Fighting sexism 10. NASCAR auto racing 11. Interior design

Geography

1. Close to major city 2. Mild winters / low humidity 3. Change in seasons 4. Clean and green 5. 100,000 people 6. Nice shopping malls 7. Wide range of athletic options 8. Diverse economic base 9. Ample local culture 10. Sense of community (pride)

Favorite Skills

1. Observational / learning skills • continually expose self to new experiences • perceptive in identifying and assessing potential of others 2. Leadership skills • continually searches for more resonsibility • sees a problem / acts to solve it 3. Instructing / interpreting / guiding • committed to learning as a lifelong process • create atmosphere of acceptance 4. Serving / helping / human relations skills • shapes atmosphere of particular place • relates well in dealing with public 5. Detail / follow-through skills • handle great variety of tasks • resource broker 6. Influencing / persuading skills • recruiting talent / leadership • inspiring trust 7. Performing skills • getting up in front of a group (if I'm in control) • addressing small and large groups 8. Intuitional / innovative skills • continually develop / generate new ideas 9. Develop / Plan / Organize / Execute • designing projects • utilizing skills of others 10. Language / Read / Write • communicate effectively • can think quickly on my feet

Favorite People Environment

1. Strong social, perceptual skills 2. Emotionally and physically healthy 3. Enthusiastically include others 4. Heterogeneous in interests and skills 5. Social changers, innovators 6. Politically, economically astute 7. Confident enough to confront / cry and be foolish 8. Sensitive to nontraditional issues 9. I and R (see page 308) 10. Nonmaterialistic

Favorite Working Conditions

. Receive clinical supervision 2. Mentor relationship 3. Excellent secretary art of larger, highly respected organization with clear direction 5. Near rmet and health food specialty shops eterogeneous colleagues (race, x, age) 7. Flexible dress code 8. Merit system 9. Can bike / bus / walk to work 10. Private office with window

Favorite Values

1. Improve the human condition 2. Promote interdependence and futuristic principles 3. Maximize productive use of human / material resources 4. Teach people to be self-directed / self-responsible 5. Free people from self-defeating controls (thoughts, rules, barriers) 6. Promote capitalistic principles 7. Reduce exploitation 8. Promote political participation 9. Acknowledge those who give to the community 10. Give away ideas

Finding the Twenty Dollar Bills

Okay then, if our first rule is: **Put everything you know about yourself, on one piece of paper,** then we really do mean *everything*. Or *anything*. You can make it simple, or complex. I recommend *simple*.

Are some pieces of information more valuable than others? Oh, yes. And thank God, or you'd be jotting down stuff, forever. (Maybe what you know about yourself would fill an encyclopedia, a wikipedia,[2] a blog,[3] an all-day podcast,[4] a tape-recording [*an interview with yourself*], or whatever.)

But here's the deal. Let us say you are a U.S. job-hunter, and you have in your purse or wallet some $5 bills, some $1 bills, and some $20 bills. You wouldn't throw any of those bills away, would you? They are all *money*, and they are all valuable. But some of those bills are more valuable than others. A $20 bill, for example, is twenty times as valuable as a $1 bill.

So it is, with information about yourself. It's all valuable; *by analogy*, it's all money. But some of the information about yourself is comparable to $20 bills, and some of it is comparable to $1 bills, and some of it is in between.

Now, let's cut to the chase. What is $20 information about yourself?

Well, it turns out to be:

1. Any information you have about your most favorite **transferable skills,** *and specific examples of when and how you used those skills, in the past.*

2. Any information you have about those **fields** that most fascinate you, *and specific examples of when and how you had experience with those fields in the past.*

These two, together, are called *competencies*. They are your $20 information about yourself. They are valuable in a million ways, and offer the basis for Behavioral Interviews—should you run into them.

There are some $10 bits of information about yourself, of course. These are: your favorite **people-environments,** your favorite **values and goals,** your favorite **working conditions,** and your desired **salary** and **level of responsibility.**

These $20 and $10 pieces of information are all included in the Flower Diagram, as you may have already noticed.

---

2. http://en.wikipedia.org/

3. www.technorati.com/

4. www.thepodcastingebook.com/

The rest of the stuff you jot down about yourself on "That One Piece of Paper," in the margins, will likely turn out to be $1 bits of information, but you never know. Since you are jotting down *anything* and *everything*, there may be some $10 or $20 information about you, that hits you, right out of the blue. Scrutinize it all, carefully.

It is time now to begin. Here are the basic steps you must go through, in order to figure out what you want to do next, with your life, or choose a career, or change careers, or (best of all) identify your dream job.

HOW DO YOU IDENTIFY YOUR DREAM JOB, Step by Step?

1. **Favorite Transferable Skills.** You do a systematic inventory of the *transferable skills* that you already possess.
2. **Fields of Fascination.** You do a systematic inventory of the fields or *bodies of knowledge* that fascinate you the most.
3. **The Flower.** From these two inventories, you fashion a description—a picture, if you will—of what your new career *looks like*.
4. **Names of Jobs that Fit.** Then you interview people, sharing this picture, to find out *what its name is* (or names).
5. **Informational Interviewing.** Once you know your skills, and know what kind of work you want to do, you go talk to people who are doing it. Find out how they like the work, how they found their job.
6. **Research of Organizations.** Do some research, in your chosen geographical area, on organizations that interest you, to find what they do and what kinds of problems they or their industry are wrestling with.
7. **Network.** Then identify and seek out the person who actually has the power to hire you there, for the job you want.
8. **Contacts.** Use your contacts to get in to see him or her. Show this person with the power to hire you how you can help them with their problems, and how you would stand out as "one employee in a hundred."
9. **Closure.** In all of this, cut no corners, take no shortcuts.

By What Process Do You **Choose a Career**?

How Do You **Change Careers**
without Necessarily Going Back to School?

And How Do You **Find Your Dream Job**?

Now, let's say you're not looking for your dream job. Not yet, anyway. At the moment, you couldn't be less interested in finding an answer to the question, "How Do You Find Your Dream Job?"

No, you have other things on your mind. Maybe you're just entering college, and you have to choose a major, which means you are ultimately going to have to know how to choose a career. First time in your life, maybe. In which case, you're just looking for "By What Process Do You Choose a Career?"

Or, let's say you've been in the world of work for ten years or more, but you're fed up with what you've been doing, and you want to change careers. In which case, you're looking for "How Do You Change Careers, Without Necessarily Going Back to School?"

Well, good news! All three dilemmas are solved by exactly the same process. This one. So, to master one is to master all three.

Let's get on with it, then.

A creative approach to career-choice, career-change, and finding your dream job, has three main parts to it. These parts are in the form of the questions:

What, Where, and **How**

• WHAT ?

The full question here is *what are the skills you most enjoy using?*

To answer this question, you need to identify or inventory what **skills/gifts/talents** you have; and then you need to prioritize them, in their order of importance and enjoyment for you. Experts call these transferable skills, because they are transferable to any field/career that you choose, regardless of where you first picked them up, or how long you've had them.

Chapter Thirteen

• WHERE?

The full question here is *where do you most want to use those skills?*

This has to do *primarily* with knowledge of the **fields of fascination** *you have already acquired*, which you most enjoy using. But *where* also has to do with your preferred working conditions, what kinds of data or people or things you enjoy working with, etc.

• HOW?

The full question here is *how do you find such jobs, that use your favorite skills in your favorite fields of knowledge?*

To answer this question, you need to do some **interviewing of various people in order to find the information you are looking for**. You begin this interviewing with the awareness that *skills* point toward job-titles; and *Fields of Fascination* point toward a career *field*, or college major, where you would use those skills. You want also to find out the names of *organizations* in your preferred geographical area that have such jobs. *And,* the name of the person there who actually has the *power* to hire you, as well as the challenges they face. You then secure an interview with them, by using your contacts, and show them how your skills can help them with their challenges.

A Systematic Approach to
Searching for Your Dream Job, or a New Career

STEP I

What

Transferable Skills Do You Most Enjoy Using?

Steven M. Johnson

"WHAT?" Is a Matter of Skills

You are looking here for what you may think of as the basic building-blocks of your work. So, if you're going to identify your dream job, and/or attempt a thorough career-change, you should begin by first of all identifying your functional, transferable skills. And while you may think you know what your best and favorite skills are, in most cases your self-knowledge could probably use a little work.

A weekend should do it! In a weekend, you can inventory your *past* sufficiently so that you have a good picture of the *kind* of work you would love to be doing *in the future*. (*You can, of course, stretch the inventory over a number of weeks, maybe doing an hour or two one night a week, if you prefer. It's up to you as to how fast you do it.*)

254   *Chapter Thirteen*

A Crash Course on "Transferable Skills"

Many people just "freeze" when they hear the word "skills."

It begins with high school job-hunters: "I haven't really got any skills," they say.

It continues with college students: "I've spent four years in college. I haven't had time to pick up any skills."

And it lasts through the middle years, especially when a person is thinking of changing his or her career: "I'll have to go back to college, and get retrained, because otherwise I won't have any skills in my new field." Or: "Well, if I claim any skills, I'll start at a very entry kind of level."

All of this fright about the word "skills" is very common, and stems from a total misunderstanding of what the word means. A misunderstanding that is shared, we might add, by altogether too many employers, or human resources departments, and other so-called "vocational experts."

By understanding the word, you will automatically put yourself way ahead of most job-hunters. And, especially if you are weighing a change of career, you can save yourself much waste of time on the adult folly called "I must go back to school." I've said it before, and I'll say it again: *maybe* you need some further schooling, but very often it is possible to make a dramatic career-change without any retraining. It all depends. And you won't really *know* whether or not you need further schooling, until you have finished all the exercises in this section of the book.

All right, then, if transferable skills are the heart of your vision and your destiny, let's see just exactly what transferable skills *are*.

Here are the most important truths you need to keep in mind about transferable, functional skills:

1 Your transferable *(functional)* skills are the most basic unit—the atoms—of whatever career you may choose.

You can see this from this diagram:

Skills as the Basic Unit of Work

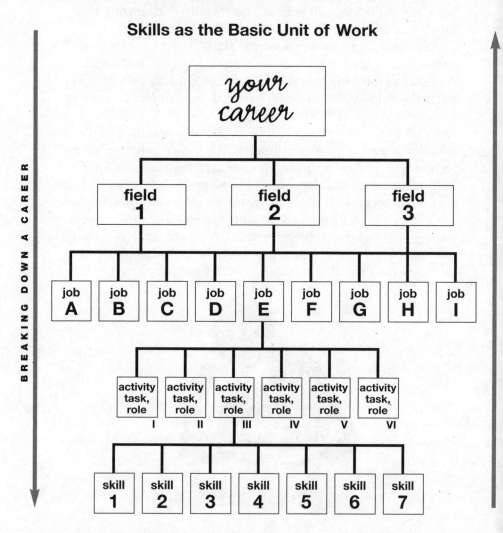

Chapter Thirteen

Now, let's look at the very bottom level of the previous diagram. It says "skill." That means "transferable skills." Here is a famous diagram of them, used by Sidney A. Fine (reprinted by special permission).

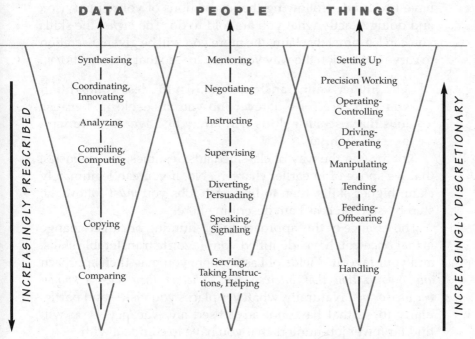

2 You should always claim the *highest* skills you legitimately can, on the basis of your past performance.

As we see in the functional/transferable skills diagram above, your transferable skills break down into three *families*, according to whether you use them with **Data/Information, People,** or **Things.** And again, as this diagram makes clear, within each family there are *simple* skills, and there are higher, or *more complex* skills, so that these all can be diagrammed as inverted pyramids, with the simpler skills at the bottom, and the more complex ones in order above it, as shown above.

Incidentally, as a general rule—to which there are exceptions—each *higher* skill requires you to be able also to do all those skills listed below it. So of course you can claim *those*, as well. But you want to especially claim the highest skill you legitimately can, on each pyramid, based on what you have already proven you can do, in the past.

3 The *higher* your transferable skills, the more freedom you will have on the job.

Simpler skills can be, and usually are, heavily *prescribed* (by the employer), so if you claim *only* the simpler skills, you will have to *"fit in"*—following the instructions of your supervisor, and doing exactly what you are told to do. The *higher* the skills you can legitimately claim, the more you will be given discretion to carve out the job the way you want to—so that it truly fits *you*.

4 The higher your transferable skills, the less competition you will face for whatever job you are seeking, because jobs that use such skills will rarely be advertised through normal channels.

Not for you the way of classified ads, resumes, and agencies, that we spoke of in earlier chapters. No, if you can legitimately claim higher skills, then to find such jobs you *must* follow the step-by-step process I am describing here.

The essence of this approach to job-hunting or career-change is that once you have identified your favorite transferable skills, and your favorite Fields of Fascination, you may then approach *any organization that interests you, whether they have a known vacancy or not.* Naturally, whatever places you visit—and particularly those that have not advertised any vacancy—you will find far fewer job-hunters that you have to compete with.

In fact, if the employers you visit happen to like you well enough, they may be willing to create for you a job that does not presently exist. *In which case, you will be competing with no one, since you will be the sole applicant for that newly created job.* While this doesn't happen all the time, it is astounding to me how many times it *does* happen. *The reason* it does is that the employers often have been *thinking* about creating a new job within their organization, for quite some time—but with this and that, they just have never gotten around to *doing* it. Until you walked in.

Then they decided they didn't want to let you get away, since *good employees are as hard to find as are good employers.* And they suddenly remember that job they have been thinking about creating for many weeks or months, now. So they dust off their *intention*, create the job on the spot, and offer it to you! And if that new job is not only what *they* need, but is exactly what *you* were looking for, then you have a dream job. Match-match. Win-win.

From our country's perspective, it is also interesting to note this: by this job-hunting initiative of yours, you have helped accelerate the creation of more jobs in your country, which is so much on everybody's mind here in the new millennium. How nice to help your country, as well as yourself!

5 **Don't confuse transferable skills with traits.**
Functional/transferable skills are often confused with **traits, temperaments,** or **type.**[5] People think transferable skills are such things as: *has lots of energy, gives attention to details, gets along well with people, shows determination, works well under pressure, is sympathetic, intuitive, persistent, dynamic, dependable,* etc. Despite popular misconceptions, these are **not** functional/transferable skills, but traits, or the *style* with which you do your transferable skills. For example, take *"gives attention to details."* If one of your *transferable skills* is *"conducting research"* then *"gives attention to details"* describes the manner or style with which you do that transferable

---

5. The Myers-Briggs Type Indicator, or "MBTI®," measures what is called *psychological type.* For further reading about this, see:

Paul D. Tieger & Barbara Barron-Tieger, *Do What You Are: Discover the Perfect Career for You Through the Secrets of Personality Type* (Revised and Updated). Fourth Edition. 2007. Little, Brown & Company, Inc., division of Time Warner Inc., 34 Beacon St., Boston MA 02108. For those who cannot obtain the MBTI®, this book includes a method for readers to identify their personality types. This is one of the most popular career books in the world. It's easy to see why. Many have found great help from the concept of Personality Type, and the Tiegers are masters in explaining this approach to career-choice. Highly recommended.

Donna Dunning, *What's Your Type of Career? Unlock the Secrets of Your Personality to Find Your Perfect Career Path.* 2001. Davies-Black Publishing, an imprint of Consulting Psychologists Press, Inc., 3803 East Bayshore Road, Palo Alto, CA 94303, 1-800-624-1765. This is a dynamite book on personality type. I found it to be the best written, most insightful, and most helpful book I have ever read about using "Type" in the workplace. Donna Dunning's knowledge of "Type" is encyclopedic!

David Keirsey and Marilyn Bates, *Please Understand Me: Character & Temperament Types.* 1978. Includes the Keirsey Temperament Sorter—again, for those who cannot obtain the MBTI® (Myers-Briggs Type Indicator)—registered trademark of Consulting Psychologists Press.

skill called *conducting research.* If you want to know what your traits are, popular tests such as the *Myers-Briggs Type Indicator* measure that sort of thing.

If you have access to the Internet, there are clues, at least, about your traits or "type":

▶ **Working Out Your Myers-Briggs Type**
    `www.teamtechnology.co.uk/mb-intro/mb-intro.htm`
An informative article about the Myers-Briggs

▶ **The 16 Personality Types**
    `www.16types.com/Request.jsp?hView`
        `=DynamicPage&Content=The16Types`
A helpful site about Myers types

▶ **What Is Your Myers-Briggs Personality Type?**
    `www.personalitypathways.com/type_inventory.html`
    `www.personalitypathways.com`
Another article about personality types; also, there's a Myers-Briggs Applications page, with links to test resources

▶ **Myers-Briggs Foundation home page**
    `www.myersbriggs.org`
The official website of the Foundation; lots of testing resources

▶ **Human Metrics Test (Jung Typology)**
    `www.humanmetrics.com/cgi-win/JTypes2.asp`
Free test, loosely based on the Myers-Briggs

▶ **Myers-Briggs Type Indicator Online**
    `www.discoveryourpersonality.com/testlist.html`
Official Myers-Briggs test, $60

▶ **The Keirsey Temperament Sorter**
    `www.keirsey.com`
Free test, similar to the Myers-Briggs

"I Wouldn't Recognize My Skills If They Came Up and Shook Hands with Me"

Now that you know what transferable skills technically *are*, the problem that awaits you now, is figuring out your own. If you are one of the few lucky people who already know what your transferable skills are, blessed are you. Write them down, and put them in the order of preference, for you, on "That One Piece of Paper," pages 246 and 247.

If, however, you don't know what your skills are (and 95 percent of all workers *don't*), then you will need some help. Fortunately there is an exercise to help. A great exercise!

It involves the following steps:

1. Write a Story (The First of Seven)

Yes, I know, I know. You can't do this exercise because you don't like to write. *Writers are a very rare breed.* That's what thousands of job-hunters have told me, over the years. And for years I kind of believed them—until "blogging" came along. ("Blog" is shorthand, of course, for "web log.") At the moment (4/8/07) there are at least 70 million people who have created their own personal blogs, on the Internet, with 1.4 million updates to those blogs each day, and 120,000 new people starting to keep a blog every 24 hours.[6] Yikes! Let's face it: we human beings are "a writing people," and we only need a topic we have a real passion for, or interest in, for the writing genie to spring forth from within each of us, pen or keyboard in hand.[7]

So, call the *Seven Stories* you're about to write your personal *offline blog*, if you prefer. But start writing. Please.

Here is a specific example:

"A number of years ago, I wanted to be able to take a summer trip with my wife and four children. I had a very limited budget, and could not afford to put my family up, in motels. I decided to rig our station wagon as a camper.

"First I went to the library to get some books on campers. I read those books. Next I designed a plan of what I had to build, so that I could outfit the inside of the station wagon, as well as topside. Then I went and purchased the necessary wood. On weekends, over a period of six weeks,

---

6. The primary site for tracking these numbers is www.technorati.com. For commentary on the "Blogosphere," see www.sifry.com. (David Sifry is the founder and CEO of Technorati.)

7. Though, with the rise of Twitter, and "twittering"—a kind of mini-blog restricted to just 140 characters or spaces—plus the more ancient IM (Instant Messaging), it could be argued that we like our writing to be brief, rather than *lengthy* (see www.msnbc.msn.com/id/17888481/site/newsweek/).

I first constructed, in my driveway, the shell for the 'second story' on my station wagon. Then I cut doors, windows, and placed a six-drawer bureau within that shell. I mounted it on top of the wagon, and pinioned it in place by driving two-by-fours under the station wagon's rack on top. I then outfitted the inside of the station wagon, back in the wheel-well, with a table and a bench on either side, that I made.

"The result was a complete homemade camper, which I put together when we were about to start our trip, and then disassembled after we got back home. When we went on our summer trip, we were able to be on the road for four weeks, yet stayed within our budget, since we didn't have to stay at motels.

"I estimate I saved $1,900 on motel bills, during that summer's vacation."

Ideally, each story you write should have the following parts, as illustrated above:

I.

Your goal: what you wanted to accomplish: *"I wanted to be able to take a summer trip with my wife and four children."*

II.

Some kind of hurdle, obstacle, or constraint that you faced (self-imposed or otherwise): *"I had a very limited budget, and could not afford to put my family up, in motels."*

III.

A description of what you did, step by step (how you set about to ultimately achieve your goal, above, in spite of this hurdle or constraint): *"I decided to rig our station wagon as a camper. First I went to the library to get some books on campers. I read those books. Next I designed a plan of what I had to build, so that I could outfit the inside of the station wagon, as well as topside. Then I went and purchased the necessary wood. On weekends, over a period of six weeks, I . . ." etc., etc.*

IV.

A description of the outcome or result: *"When we went on our summer trip, we were able to be on the road for four weeks, yet stayed within our budget, since we didn't have to stay at motels."*

V.

Any measurable/quantifiable statement of that outcome, that you can think of: *"I estimate I saved $1,900 on motel bills, during that summer's vacation."*

Now write *your* story, using the next page as a guide.

Don't pick a story where you achieved something *big*. At least to begin with, write a story about a time when you had fun!

MY LIFE STORIES

Column 1	Column 2	Column 3	Column 4	Column 5
Your Goal: What You Wanted to Accomplish	Some Kind of Obstacle (or limit, hurdle, or restraint you had to overcome before it could be accomplished)	What You Did Step-by-Step (It may help if you pretend you are telling this story to a whining 4-year-old child, who keeps asking, after each of your sentences, "An' then whadja do? An' then whadja do?")	Description of the Result (What you accomplished)	Any Measure or Quantities to Prove Your Achievement

2. Analyze the Story for Transferable Skills

Once you have written Story #1 (and before you write the other six), you will want to analyze it for the transferable skills you *used*. (You can decide later if you loved those skills or not. For now, just do an inventory.)

To do this inventory, go to the list of Skills Keys found on pages 266 to 271, which resemble a series of keyboard keys. As you see there, transferable skills divide into:

A. Physical Skills: the transferable skills you enjoy, using primarily *your hands or body*—with things, or nature;

B. Mental Skills: the transferable skills you enjoy, using primarily *your mind*—with data/information, ideas, or subjects;

C. Interpersonal Skills: the transferable skills you enjoy, involving primarily *personal relationships*—as you serve or help people or animals, and their needs or problems.[8]

Therefore you will find three sets of Skills Keys, labeled accordingly.

As you look at each key in the three sets, the question you need to ask yourself, is: "Did I use this transferable skill *in this Story* (#1)?"

That is the *only* question you ask yourself (at the moment). Then you go to the little box named #1 (under each Skill Key), and this is what you do:

If the answer is "Yes," check the little box, as shown (right):

Ignore the other little boxes there, for the time being; they belong to your other stories (all the little boxes named #2 belong to Story #2, all the little boxes named #3 belong to Story #3, etc.).

Did I Use This Skill in This Story?

Yes ✓ 1 2 3 4 5 6 7

---

8. For the curious, "animals" are placed in this category with "people," because the skills required to deal with animals are more like those used with people, than like those used with "things."

My Physical Skills

I am good at

Skills with Growing Things or Animals
→ Having a Green Thumb, causing growing things to flourish

1 2 3 4 5 6 7

Skills with Buildings or Rooms
→ Constructing or Reconstructing

1 2 3 4 5 6 7

Skills with Equipment, Machinery, or Vehicles
→ Setting Up or Assembling

1 2 3 4 5 6 7

Skills with Objects (including food, tools, instruments)
→ Washing, Cleaning, or Preparing

1 2 3 4 5 6 7

Skills with Materials (clay, wood, cloth, metals, stone, jewels)
→ Crafting, Sewing, Weaving, Hammering, etc.

1 2 3 4 5 6 7

Skills with the Body
→ Using My Hands or Fingers (including "signing," or massaging)

1 2 3 4 5 6 7

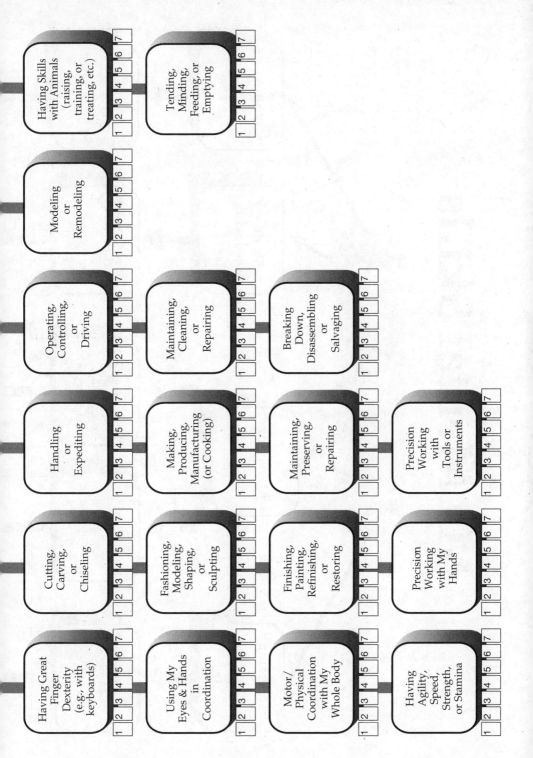

Having Skills with Animals (raising, training, or treating, etc.)
1 2 3 4 5 6 7

Tending, Minding, Feeding, or Emptying
1 2 3 4 5 6 7

Modeling or Remodeling
1 2 3 4 5 6 7

Operating, Controlling, or Driving
1 2 3 4 5 6 7

Maintaining, Cleaning, or Repairing
1 2 3 4 5 6 7

Breaking Down, Disassembling or Salvaging
1 2 3 4 5 6 7

Handling or Expediting
1 2 3 4 5 6 7

Making, Producing, Manufacturing (or Cooking)
1 2 3 4 5 6 7

Maintaining, Preserving, or Repairing
1 2 3 4 5 6 7

Precision Working with Tools or Instruments
1 2 3 4 5 6 7

Cutting, Carving, or Chiseling
1 2 3 4 5 6 7

Fashioning, Modeling, Shaping, or Sculpting
1 2 3 4 5 6 7

Finishing, Painting, Refinishing, or Restoring
1 2 3 4 5 6 7

Precision Working with My Hands
1 2 3 4 5 6 7

Having Great Finger Dexterity (e.g., with keyboards)
1 2 3 4 5 6 7

Using My Eyes & Hands in Coordination
1 2 3 4 5 6 7

Motor/ Physical Coordination with My Whole Body
1 2 3 4 5 6 7

Having Agility, Speed, Strength, or Stamina
1 2 3 4 5 6 7

267

My Mental Skills

I am good at

Gathering or Creating It
→ Compiling, Searching, or Researching
1 2 3 4 5 6 7

Managing It

STEP-BY-STEP
→ Copying and/or Comparing Similarities or Differences
1 2 3 4 5 6 7

HOLISTICALLY
→ Adapting, Translating (incl. Computer Programming), Developing, or Improving
1 2 3 4 5 6 7

Storing, Retrieving It
→ Keeping Records (incl. recording, filming, or entering on a computer)
1 2 3 4 5 6 7

Putting It to Use
→ With People
See Interpersonal Skills

268

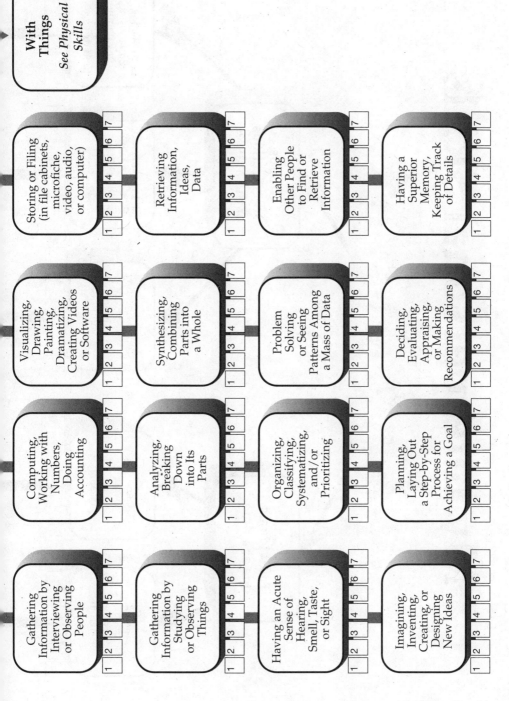

With Things

See Physical Skills

Storing or Filing (in file cabinets, microfiche, video, audio, or computer)

1 2 3 4 5 6 7

Retrieving Information, Ideas, Data

1 2 3 4 5 6 7

Enabling Other People to Find or Retrieve Information

1 2 3 4 5 6 7

Having a Superior Memory, Keeping Track of Details

1 2 3 4 5 6 7

Visualizing, Drawing, Painting, Dramatizing, Creating Videos or Software

1 2 3 4 5 6 7

Synthesizing, Combining Parts into a Whole

1 2 3 4 5 6 7

Problem Solving or Seeing Patterns Among a Mass of Data

1 2 3 4 5 6 7

Deciding, Evaluating, Appraising, or Making Recommendations

1 2 3 4 5 6 7

Computing, Working with Numbers, Doing Accounting

1 2 3 4 5 6 7

Analyzing, Breaking Down into Its Parts

1 2 3 4 5 6 7

Organizing, Classifying, Systematizing, and/or Prioritizing

1 2 3 4 5 6 7

Planning, Laying Out a Step-by-Step Process for Achieving a Goal

1 2 3 4 5 6 7

Gathering Information by Interviewing or Observing People

1 2 3 4 5 6 7

Gathering Information by Studying or Observing Things

1 2 3 4 5 6 7

Having an Acute Sense of Hearing, Smell, Taste, or Sight

1 2 3 4 5 6 7

Imagining, Inventing, Creating, or Designing New Ideas

1 2 3 4 5 6 7

269

My Interpersonal Skills

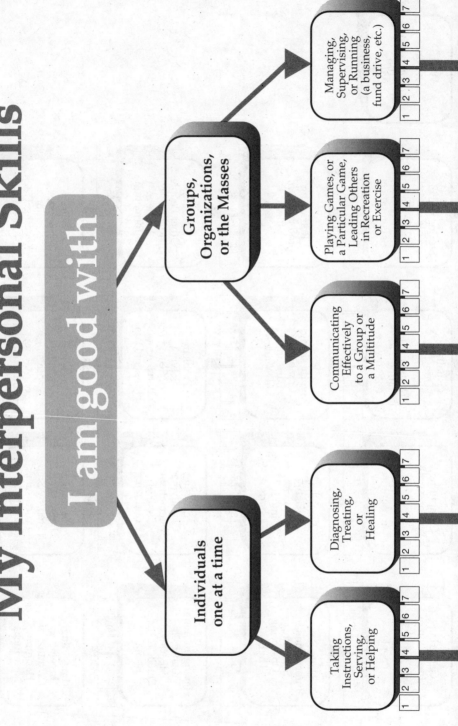

I am good with

Groups, Organizations, or the Masses

- Communicating Effectively to a Group or a Multitude
  1 2 3 4 5 6 7
- Playing Games, or a Particular Game, Leading Others in Recreation or Exercise
  1 2 3 4 5 6 7
- Managing, Supervising, or Running (a business, fund drive, etc.)
  1 2 3 4 5 6 7

Individuals one at a time

- Taking Instructions, Serving, or Helping
  1 2 3 4 5 6 7
- Diagnosing, Treating, or Healing
  1 2 3 4 5 6 7

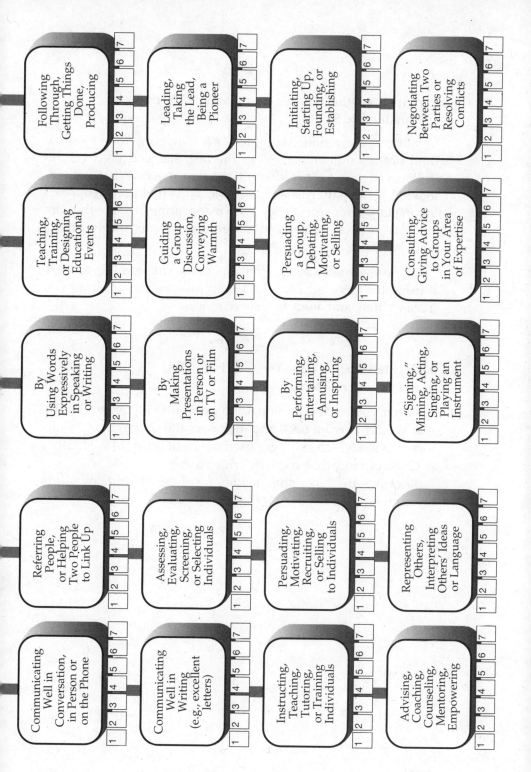

Following Through, Getting Things Done, Producing
1 2 3 4 5 6 7

Leading, Taking the Lead, Being a Pioneer
1 2 3 4 5 6 7

Initiating, Starting Up, Founding, or Establishing
1 2 3 4 5 6 7

Negotiating Between Two Parties or Resolving Conflicts
1 2 3 4 5 6 7

Teaching, Training, or Designing Educational Events
1 2 3 4 5 6 7

Guiding a Group Discussion, Conveying Warmth
1 2 3 4 5 6 7

Persuading a Group, Debating, Motivating, or Selling
1 2 3 4 5 6 7

Consulting, Giving Advice to Groups in Your Area of Expertise
1 2 3 4 5 6 7

By Using Words Expressively in Speaking or Writing
1 2 3 4 5 6 7

By Making Presentations in Person or on TV or Film
1 2 3 4 5 6 7

By Performing, Entertaining, Amusing, or Inspiring
1 2 3 4 5 6 7

"Signing," Miming, Acting, Singing, or Playing an Instrument
1 2 3 4 5 6 7

Referring People, or Helping Two People to Link Up
1 2 3 4 5 6 7

Assessing, Evaluating, Screening, or Selecting Individuals
1 2 3 4 5 6 7

Persuading, Motivating, Recruiting, or Selling to Individuals
1 2 3 4 5 6 7

Representing Others, Interpreting Others' Ideas or Language
1 2 3 4 5 6 7

Communicating Well in Conversation, in Person or on the Phone
1 2 3 4 5 6 7

Communicating Well in Writing (e.g., excellent letters)
1 2 3 4 5 6 7

Instructing, Teaching, Tutoring, or Training Individuals
1 2 3 4 5 6 7

Advising, Coaching, Counseling, Mentoring, Empowering
1 2 3 4 5 6 7

3. Write Six Other Stories, and Analyze Them for Transferable Skills

Voilà! You are done with Story #1. However, "one swallow doth not a summer make," so the fact that you used certain skills in this first Story doesn't tell you much. What you are looking for is **patterns**—transferable skills that keep reappearing in story after story. They keep reappearing because they are your favorites (assuming you chose stories where you were *really* enjoying yourself).

So, now, write Story #2, from any period in your life, analyze it using the keys, etc., etc. And keep this process up, until you have written, and analyzed, seven stories.

4. Decide Which Skills Are Your Favorites, and Prioritize Them

When you're done writing and analyzing all Seven Stories, you should now go back and look over the six pages of "Skills Keys" to see which skills got used the most often. Make a list.

Cross out any that you don't *enjoy* using.

Prioritize the remainder, using one of the Prioritizing Grids on the following pages.

The Prioritizing Grid

How to Prioritize Your Lists of Anything

Here is a method for taking (say) ten items, and figuring out which one is most important to you, which is next most important, etc.

- List the items to be prioritized, in any order, in Section A. Then compare two items at a time, circling the one you prefer—between the two—in Section B. Which one is more important to you? State the question any way you want to. In the case of geographical factors, you might ask, "If I were being offered two jobs, one in an area that had factor #1, but not factor #2, the other in an area that had factor #2, but not factor #1, all other things being equal, which job would I take?" Circle it. Then go on to the next pair, etc.

- When you are done, count up the number of times each number got circled, all told. Enter these totals on the TIMES line in Section C. Then notice the number of times each item was circled ("Times" = "Times Circled"). This determines the item's ranking. Most circled = #1, next most circled = #2, etc. Enter this ranking on the RANK line in Section C. If two items are circled the same number of times, look back in Section B to see—when those two were compared there—which one you preferred. Give that one an extra half point. List the items, now in their proper rank, in Section D.

The question to ask yourself here, as you confront each "skills pair" is: "If I were offered two jobs, and in one job I could use the first skill, but not the second, while in the other job, I could use the second skill, but not the first, which job would I choose?" When you've got your ten favorite transferable skills, in order, copy the top six onto the Flower Diagram.

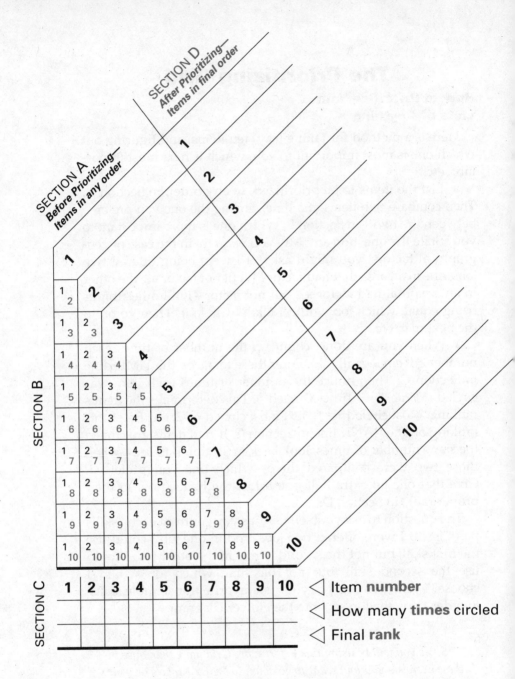

SECTION D—
After Prioritizing—
Items in final order

SECTION A—
Before Prioritizing—
Items in any order

SECTION B

SECTION C

◁ Item **number**

◁ How many **times** circled

◁ Final **rank**

Prioritizing Grid
for 10 Items

Chapter Thirteen

```
1   1   1   1   1   1   1   1   1   1   1   1   1   1   1   1   1   1   1   1   1   1   1
  2   3   4   5   6   7   8   9   10  11  12  13  14  15  16  17  18  19  20  21  22  23  24

2   2   2   2   2   2   2   2   2   2   2   2   2   2   2   2   2   2   2   2   2   2
  3   4   5   6   7   8   9   10  11  12  13  14  15  16  17  18  19  20  21  22  23  24

3   3   3   3   3   3   3   3   3   3   3   3   3   3   3   3   3   3   3   3   3
  4   5   6   7   8   9   10  11  12  13  14  15  16  17  18  19  20  21  22  23  24

4   4   4   4   4   4   4   4   4   4   4   4   4   4   4   4   4   4   4   4
  5   6   7   8   9   10  11  12  13  14  15  16  17  18  19  20  21  22  23  24

5   5   5   5   5   5   5   5   5   5   5   5   5   5   5   5   5   5   5
  6   7   8   9   10  11  12  13  14  15  16  17  18  19  20  21  22  23  24

6   6   6   6   6   6   6   6   6   6   6   6   6   6   6   6   6   6
  7   8   9   10  11  12  13  14  15  16  17  18  19  20  21  22  23  24

7   7   7   7   7   7   7   7   7   7   7   7   7   7   7   7   7
  8   9   10  11  12  13  14  15  16  17  18  19  20  21  22  23  24

8   8   8   8   8   8   8   8   8   8   8   8   8   8   8   8
  9   10  11  12  13  14  15  16  17  18  19  20  21  22  23  24

9   9   9   9   9   9   9   9   9   9   9   9   9   9   9
  10  11  12  13  14  15  16  17  18  19  20  21  22  23  24

10  10  10  10  10  10  10  10  10  10  10  10  10  10
  11  12  13  14  15  16  17  18  19  20  21  22  23  24

11  11  11  11  11  11  11  11  11  11  11  11  11
  12  13  14  15  16  17  18  19  20  21  22  23  24

12  12  12  12  12  12  12  12  12  12  12  12
  13  14  15  16  17  18  19  20  21  22  23  24

13  13  13  13  13  13  13  13  13  13  13
  14  15  16  17  18  19  20  21  22  23  24

14  14  14  14  14  14  14  14  14  14
  15  16  17  18  19  20  21  22  23  24

15  15  15  15  15  15  15  15  15
  16  17  18  19  20  21  22  23  24

16  16  16  16  16  16  16  16
  17  18  19  20  21  22  23  24

17  17  17  17  17  17  17
  18  19  20  21  22  23  24

18  18  18  18  18  18
  19  20  21  22  23  24

19  19  19  19  19
  20  21  22  23  24

20  20  20  20
  21  22  23  24

21  21  21
  22  23  24

22  22
  23  24

23
  24
```

Total times each number got circled.

1	2	3	4	5	6
7	8	9	10	11	12
13	14	15	16	17	18
19	20	21	22	23	24

Prioritizing Grid
for 24 Items

Once you've checked off your favorites, prioritize them (using another copy of the Prioritizing Grid if necessary), and then integrate your favorites into the building blocks of transferable skills below.

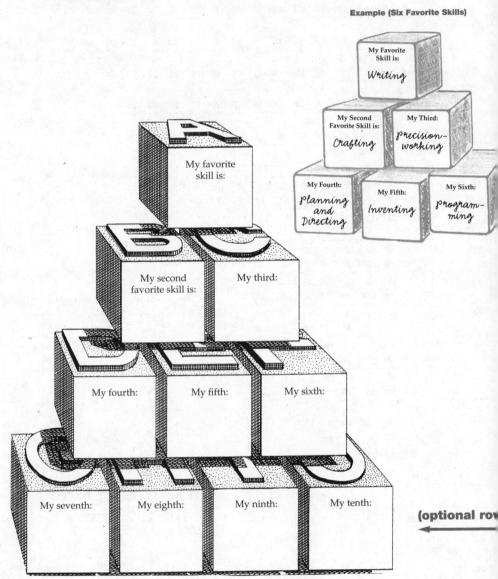

Example (Six Favorite Skills)

My Favorite Skill is: Writing

My Second Favorite Skill is: Crafting

My Third: precision-working

My Fourth: Planning and Directing

My Fifth: Inventing

My Sixth: Programming

My favorite skill is:

My second favorite skill is:

My third:

My fourth:

My fifth:

My sixth:

My seventh:

My eighth:

My ninth:

My tenth:

(optional row

5. "Flesh Out" Your Favorite Transferable Skills with Your Traits

We discussed traits earlier. In general, traits describe:
How you deal with time, and promptness.
How you deal with people and emotions.
How you deal with authority, and being told what to do at your job.
How you deal with supervision, and being told how to do your job.
How you deal with impulse vs. self-discipline, within yourself.
How you deal with initiative vs. response, within yourself.
How you deal with crises or problems.

A CHECKLIST OF MY STRONGEST TRAITS
I am very . . .

- ❏ Accurate
- ❏ Achievement-oriented
- ❏ Adaptable
- ❏ Adept
- ❏ Adept at having fun
- ❏ Adventuresome
- ❏ Alert
- ❏ Appreciative
- ❏ Assertive
- ❏ Astute
- ❏ Authoritative
- ❏ Calm
- ❏ Cautious
- ❏ Charismatic
- ❏ Competent
- ❏ Consistent
- ❏ Contagious in my enthusiasm
- ❏ Cooperative
- ❏ Courageous
- ❏ Creative
- ❏ Decisive
- ❏ Deliberate
- ❏ Dependable/have dependability
- ❏ Diligent
- ❏ Diplomatic

- ❏ Discreet
- ❏ Driving
- ❏ Dynamic
- ❏ Extremely economical
- ❏ Effective
- ❏ Energetic
- ❏ Enthusiastic
- ❏ Exceptional
- ❏ Exhaustive
- ❏ Experienced
- ❏ Expert
- ❏ Firm
- ❏ Flexible
- ❏ Humanly oriented
- ❏ Impulsive
- ❏ Independent
- ❏ Innovative
- ❏ Knowledgeable
- ❏ Loyal
- ❏ Methodical
- ❏ Objective
- ❏ Open-minded
- ❏ Outgoing
- ❏ Outstanding
- ❏ Patient
- ❏ Penetrating
- ❏ Perceptive

- ❏ Persevering
- ❏ Persistent
- ❏ Pioneering
- ❏ Practical
- ❏ Professional
- ❏ Protective
- ❏ Punctual
- ❏ Quick/work quickly
- ❏ Rational
- ❏ Realistic
- ❏ Reliable
- ❏ Resourceful
- ❏ Responsible
- ❏ Responsive
- ❏ Safeguarding
- ❏ Self-motivated
- ❏ Self-reliant
- ❏ Sensitive
- ❏ Sophisticated, very sophisticated
- ❏ Strong
- ❏ Supportive
- ❏ Tactful
- ❏ Thorough
- ❏ Unique
- ❏ Unusual
- ❏ Versatile
- ❏ Vigorous

You need to *flesh out* your skill-description for each of your ten or eight favorite skills so that you are able to describe each of your talents or skills with more than just a one-word verb or gerund, like *organizing*.

Let's take *organizing* as our example. You tell us proudly: "I'm good at *organizing*." That's a fine start at defining your skills, but unfortunately it doesn't yet tell us much. Organizing WHAT? *People*, as at a party? *Nuts and bolts*, as on a workbench? Or *lots of information*, as on a computer? These are three entirely different skills. The one word *organizing* doesn't tell us which one is *yours*.

So, please *flesh out* each of your favorite transferable skills with an object—some kind of *Data/Information*, or some kind of *People*, or some kind of *Thing*, and *then* add an adverb or adjective, too.

Why adjectives? Well, "I'm good at organizing information *painstakingly and logically*" and "I'm good at organizing information *in a flash, by intuition*," are two *entirely different* skills. The difference between them is spelled out not in the verb, nor in the object, but in the adjectival or adverbial phrase there at the end. So, expand each definition of your ten favorite skills, in the fashion I have just described.

When you are face-to-face with a person-who-has-the-power-to-hire-you, you want to be able to explain what makes you different from nineteen other people who can basically do the same thing that you can do. It is often the adjective or adverb that will save your life, during that explanation.

A Picture Is Worth a Thousand Words

When you have your top favorite skills, and *fleshed out,* it is time to put them on the central petal of the Flower Diagram. Copy this diagram on a larger piece of paper (or cardboard) if you need to.

The Flower
"That One Piece of Paper"

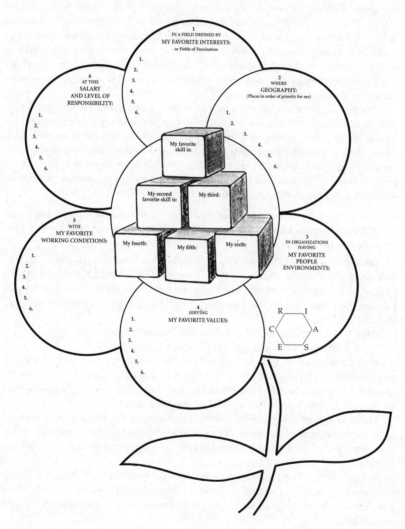

The Three Secrets to Finding That Dream Job of Yours

In trying to identify your skills, it will not be surprising if you run
into some problems. Let us look at the five most common ones
that have arisen for job-hunters in the past:

1. *"When I write my skill stories, I don't know exactly what is an achievement."*

When you're looking for a story/achievement to illustrate one of your skills,
you're *not* looking for something that only you have done, in the history of the
world. What you're looking for is a lot simpler than that. You're looking for *any* time
in your life when you did something that was, at that time of your life, a source of
pride and accomplishment *for you*. It might have been learning to ride a bike. It
might be achieving your first quota, at work. It might be a particularly significant
project that you designed, in mid-life. It doesn't matter whether or not it pleased anybody else; it only matters that it pleased you.

I like the late Bernard Haldane's definition of an achievement. He says it is: something you yourself feel you have done well, that you also enjoyed doing and felt
proud of. In other words you are looking for an accomplishment that gave
you two pleasures: enjoyment while doing it, and satisfaction from the outcome. That
doesn't mean you may not have sweated as you did it, or hated *some parts* of the
process, but it does mean that basically you enjoyed *most of* the process. The pleasure was not simply in the outcome, but along the way as well.

2. *"I don't see why I should look for skills I enjoy; it seems to me that employers
will only want to know what skills I do well. They will not care whether I enjoy using the skill or not."*

Well, sure, it is important for you to find the skills you do well, above all else.
But, generally speaking, that is hard for you to evaluate about yourself. *Do I do this
well, or not? Compared to whom?* Even aptitude tests can't resolve this dilemma for
you. So it's better to take the following circular equation, which experience has
shown to be true:

If it is a skill you do well, you will generally enjoy it.
If it is a skill you enjoy, it is generally because you do it well.

With these equations in hand, you will see that—since they are equal anyway—it
is much more useful to ask yourself, "Do I enjoy doing it?" instead of hunting for the
elusive "Do I do it well?" I repeat: listing the skills you most *enjoy* is—in most
cases—just another way of listing the skills you do *best*.

The reason why this idea—of making *enjoyment* the key—causes such feelings
of uncomfortableness in so many of us is that we have an old historical tradition in
this country that insinuates you shouldn't really enjoy yourself in life. To suffer is
virtuous.

Sample: Two girls do babysitting. One hates it. One enjoys it thoroughly. Which
is more virtuous in God's sight? According to that old tradition, the one who hates
it is more virtuous. Some of us feel this instinctively, even if more logical thought
says, Whoa!

Chapter Thirteen

We have this subconscious fear that if we are caught enjoying life, punishment looms. Thus, the story of two Scotsmen who met on the street one day: "Isn't this a beautiful day?" said one. "Aye," said the other, "but we'll pay for it."

We feel it is okay to talk about our failures, but not about our successes. To talk about our successes appears to be boasting, and that is manifestly a sin. Or so we think. We shouldn't be enjoying so much about ourselves.

But look at the birds of the air, or watch your pets at play. You will notice one distinctive fact about God's creation: when a bird or a pet does what it is meant to do, by God and nature, it manifests true joy. (Never mind "the savage beast.")

Joy is so clearly a part of God's plan for us at our best. God wants us to eat; therefore He made eating enjoyable. God wants us to sleep; therefore He made sleeping enjoyable. God wants us to procreate, love, and make love; therefore He made sex enjoyable, and love even more so.

Likewise, God gives to each of us unique combinations of skills and talents that He wants us to contribute to His general plan—to the symphony of the world, and the music of the spheres. Therefore, **when we use the talents He most wants each of us to use, He attends it with a feeling of great joy.** Everywhere in God's plan for His creation, joy rewards right action.

Bad employers will not care whether you enjoy a particular task, or not. But good employers will care greatly. They know that unless a would-be employee has **enthusiasm** for his or her work, the quality of that work will always suffer.

3. *"I have no difficulty finding stories to write up, from my life, that I consider to be enjoyable achievements; but once these are written, I have great difficulty in seeing what the skills are—even if I stare at the skills keys in the exercises for hours. I need somebody else's insight."*

You may want to consider getting two friends or two other members of your family to sit down with you, and do skill-identification through the practice of "Trio-ing," which I invented some twenty years ago to help with this very problem. This practice is fully described in my book, *Where Do I Go from Here with My Life?* But to save you the trouble of reading it there, here is—in general—how it goes:

a. Each of the three of you quietly writes up some story of an accomplishment in your and their life that was enjoyable.

b. Each of the three of you quietly analyzes just your own story to see what transferable skills you see there; you jot these down.

c. One of you then volunteers to go first. You read your story aloud. The other two jot down on a piece of paper whatever skills they hear you using. They ask you to pause if they're having trouble keeping up. You finish your story. You read aloud your own opinion about the skills *you* used in that story.

d. Then the second person tells you what's on their list: what skills *they* heard you use in your story. You copy them down, below your own list, even if you don't agree with every one of them.

e. Then the third person tells you what's on their list; what skills *they* heard you use in your story. You copy them down, below your own list, even if you don't agree with every one of them.

f. When they're both done, you ask them any questions for further elaboration that you may have. *"What did you mean by this skill? Where did you think you heard me using it?"*

g. Now it is the next person's turn, and you repeat steps "c" through "f" with them. Then it is the third person's turn, and you repeat steps "c" through "f" with them.

h. Now it is time to move on to a second story for each of you, so you begin with steps "a" through "g" all over again, except that each of you writes a new story. And so on, through seven stories.

4. **"I don't like the skill words you offer in the exercises. Can't I use my own words, the ones I'm familiar with from my past profession?"**

It's okay to invent your own words for your skills, but it is not useful to state your transferable skills in the jargon of your old profession, such as (in the case of ex-clergy), *"I am good at preaching."* If you are going to choose a new career, out there in what people call the secular world, you must not use language that locks you into the past—or suggests that you were good in one profession but maybe in one profession only. Therefore, it is important to take jargon words such as *preaching* and ask yourself what is its larger form? *"Teaching?"* Perhaps. *"Motivating people?"* Perhaps. *"Inspiring people to the depths of their being?"* Perhaps. Only you can say what is true, for you. But in one way or another be sure to get your skills out of any jargon that locks you exclusively into your past career.

5. **"Once I've listed my favorite transferable skills, I see immediately a job-title that they point to. Is that okay?"**

Nope. Once you've finished your skill-identification, steer clear of prematurely putting a job-title on the skills you see. Skills can point to *many* different jobs, which have a multitude of titles. Therefore, don't lock yourself in, prematurely. *"I'm looking for a job where I can **use** the following skills,"* is fine. But, *"I'm looking for a job where I can **be** a (job-title)"* is a no-no, at this point in your job-hunt. Always define **WHAT** you want to do with your life and **WHAT** you have to offer to the world, in terms of your favorite talents/gifts/skills—not in terms of a job-title. That way, you can hang loose in the midst of this constantly changing economy, where you never know what's going to happen next.

So much for **WHAT.** And now, on to **WHERE?**

Chapter Thirteen

STEP II

Where

Do You Want to
Use Your Skills?

PETAL #1 ON YOUR FLOWER DIAGRAM

Your Favorite Interests, or "Fields of Fascination"

Your heart has its own geography, where it prefers to be. It may be by a mountain stream. It may be in the Alps. It may be in the hustle and bustle of the streets of London or New York. It may be on an Oregon farm. It may be in a beach town. It may be in the quiet recollection of your own backyard. Your heart knows the places that it loves.

Likewise, **your mind** has its own geography, where it prefers to be. It may be among books on psychology. It may be among books on art. It may be among books on romances. It may be among books on travel. It may be among books on business trends. It may be on computers. Your mind knows the subjects that it loves.

Your body also has its own geography, where it prefers to be. It may be walking in the hills. It may be in a yoga class. It may be working out with weights. It may be in a marathon. It may be on a bicycle path. It may be in a physical therapy class. It may be in the local gym. It may be on a basketball court. It may be with massage. Your body knows the workout that it loves.

Your soul, too, has its own geography, where it prefers to be. It may be in a quiet place, it may be in a church, or synagogue, or mosque. It may be among honest folk. It may be among those who're fixed on a kind of social change. It may be almost any-where, where the values you prize—community, God, compassion, generosity, faith—are valued still by others. Your soul knows the values that it loves.

Therefore, my friend, what "a dream job" is all about (beyond skills) is identifying these favorite geographies, defining for yourself the *places* that your skills, your soul, and body, heart, and mind, most often yearn to be.

If you are to find your dream job, then, you must define these things.

There are two ways to approach this task—the *intuitional "leap-to-a-conclusion"* way, and the more labored, logical, step-by-step way. This *hurry-up* culture in which we live values most the method that is quick. Intuition is quick, and sometimes can provide just the clues you're looking for. So it is there that we begin.

Where you use your favorite skills, where you do your favorite tasks is largely a matter of what "field" you choose to use your skills in. Hence, these are the kinds of intuitions you should be searching your heart about:

Chapter Thirteen

The Intuitional Way

*Toward deciding WHERE, in a dream job,
your skills, your soul and body, heart and mind,
would most like to be.*

1 What are your favorite interests *(Computers? Gardening? Spanish? Law? Physics? Department stores? Hospitals? etc., etc.)*? If you just can't think of any favorite interest, ask yourself: "If I could talk about *something* with someone all day long, day after day, what would that subject or field of interest be?" *Or,* "If I were stuck on a desert island with a person who only had the capacity to speak on a few subjects, what would I pray those subjects were?"

If you turn out to have more than one favorite interest, take two of them at a time, and ask yourself: if you were in a conversation with someone covering two of your favorite subjects at once, toward which of the two interests would you try to steer the conversation? Repeat with another pair of favorite subjects, and keep "sifting down."

2 What are your favorite subjects—the ones you're drawn to in magazines, libraries, bookstores, trade expos, and so forth? It doesn't have to be a subject you studied in school. It can be a field that you just picked up along the way in life—say, *antiques,* or *cars,* or *interior decorating,* or *music,* or *movies,* or *psychology,* or *the kind of subjects that come up on television "game shows."*

The only important thing is that you *like* the subject a lot, and that you picked up a working knowledge of it—who cares where or how? As the late John Crystal used to say, it doesn't matter whether you learned it in college, or sitting at the end of a log.

Let's take *antiques* as an example. Suppose it's one of your favorite subjects, yet you never studied it in school. You picked up your knowledge of antiques by going around to antique stores, and asking lots of questions. And you supplemented this by reading a few books on the subject, and you subscribe to an antiques magazine. You've also bought a few antiques, yourself. That's enough for you to put *antiques* on your list of fields/interests/languages. Your degree of *mastery* of this whole field of antiques is irrelevant—*unless you want to work at a level in the field that demands and requires* mastery.

3 What are your favorite words? Every field has its own peculiar language, vocabulary, or jargon. What words or jargon do you like to use, or listen to, the most?

To illustrate this, I'll *freeze* the job-title or skills, for a moment. I'll choose "secretary." By looking then at different kinds of *secretary*, we can see how favorite *words* can give you a helpful clue about where you might like to find your dream job.

For example, if you work as a legal secretary, you have to endure a lot of talk there, all day long, about *legal procedures*. Do you like that vocabulary and *language*? If so, consider law as the field you might work in—for your next job or career.

Again, if you work as a secretary at a gardening store, there's a lot of talk there, all day long, about gardens and such. Do you like that vocabulary and *language*? If so, consider gardening as the field you might work in—for your next job or career.

If you work as a secretary at an airline, there's a lot of talk there, all day long, about airlines procedures and such. Do you like that vocabulary and *language*? If so, consider the airlines as the field you might work in—for your next job or career.

If you work as a secretary at a church, there's a lot of talk there, all day long, about church procedures and matters of faith. Do you like that vocabulary and *language*? If so, consider religion as the field you might work in—for your next job or career.

And so it continues. If you work as a secretary in a photographic laboratory, there's a lot of talk there, all day long, about photographic procedures. Do you like that vocabulary and *language*? If so, choose photography as the field you might work in—for your next job or career.

Again, if you work as a secretary at a chemical plant, there's a lot of talk there, all day long, about chemicals manufacturing. Do you like that vocabulary and *language*? If so, consider the chemical industry as the field you might work in—for your next job or career.

If you work as a secretary for the federal government, there's a lot of talk there, all day long, about government procedures.

Do you like that vocabulary and *language*? If so, consider government work as the field you might work in—for your next job or career.

And so it goes. The point is not that you should be a secretary. I just *froze* the job-title and skills for a moment, so that you could see how many different fields you might use secretarial skills in.

All of this proceeds from a simple intuition: the source of joy in your dream job derives, to a great extent, from the fact that you enjoy the *language* and vocabulary that you will be speaking or listening to all day long (provided, of course, that you also get to use your favorite skills there).

Whereas, if you don't enjoy the vocabulary or *language* that is spoken at work—you want to talk about *gardening* but you work at a place where *law* (which has a vocabulary you hate) is what you have to listen to, and work with, all day long—then you are not going to like that job or career.

4 Once you know what subjects, fields, interests, vocabulary, etc., fascinate you the most, look back at your answers to *What skills you most enjoy*, and see if you can put skills and subjects together, in terms of a particular job. For example, if you love to work with figures *(financial, that is)*, and your favorite field is hospitals, you would want to think about working in the accounting department at a hospital.

5 Once you have some idea of what jobs interest you, go visit places where those jobs are, and talk to people doing those jobs, to see if this job or career *really* interests you, or not. This is called "informational interviewing." Fancy name for *informal research*.

6 If you have decided to try a new career or go into a new field (for you), and you are dismayed at how much preparation it looks as though it would take, go talk to people doing that work. And don't look for the rules or generalizations. Look for the exceptions to the rules. For example, everyone may tell you the rule is: *"In order to do this work you have to have a master's degree and ten years' experience at it."* So what? That's a statement about the majority of people in this field. You want to find out about the exceptions. *"Yes, but do you know of anyone in the field who*

hasn't gone and gotten all those credentials? And where might I find him or her? I need to find out how they did it."

7 If you have decided to try to stay with your old career *(which you lost through downsizing or whatever)* then you need to find *"leads."* You find them by asking yourself the question: *"Who might be interested in the skills and problem-solving that I learned at my last job?"*

For example, ask yourself who you served in your last job, or came in contact with, *who might be in a position to hire someone with your talents.*

Ask yourself who supplied training or staff development in your last company or field; *do you think any of them might be interested in hiring you?* (Ask them.)

Ask yourself what machines or technology you learned, mastered, improved on, at your last job; *who is interested in those machines or technology?*

Ask yourself what raw materials *(e.g., Kodak paper in a darkroom)*, equipment, or support services you used at your last job; *would any of those suppliers know of other places where their equipment or support services are used?*

Ask yourself who were the subcontractors, outsourcing agencies, or temp agencies that were used at your last job; *would any of them be interested in hiring you?*

Ask yourself what community or service organizations were interested in your projects at your last job; *would any of them be interested in hiring you?* [9]

The Step-by-Step Way

Ways of deciding WHERE, in a dream job,
your soul and body, heart and mind, would most like to be.

Well, that's about it, for the *intuitional approach* to finding your favorite fields of fascination. Now we turn to the other approach, where we go *step-by-step*, using "That One Piece of Paper" again, with its Flower graphic.

---

9. These suggestions courtesy of Chuck Young, President, The Hadley School for the Blind; and Marty Nemko, career counselor and author.

As I said earlier, "Where?" is a matter of "Where would you most like to use your favorite skills?" In other words, we are talking about Fields, and particularly, those Fields that fascinate you.

Now, there are three basic kinds of Fields or Interests that you may have:

1. Fields That Use Your Mental Skills (the "Subjects list")

2. Fields Dealing with People's Problems or Needs (the "People list")

3. Fields Dealing with Things, Tools, or Products (the "Things list")

Here are some exercises, dealing with each of the three in turn:

1. Fields That Use Your Mental Skills

Before you begin looking at Fields, you must fight against the natural tendency to think that a Field will automatically determine what job you will do. It does not.

Think of a Field of Knowledge as, literally, *a field*—a meadow, a *large* meadow. Lots of people are standing in that meadow, or Field, no matter what Field it is. And they have many different skills, do many different things, have many different job-titles.

Let us take the Field called "Movies" as our example. Suppose you love Movies, and want to choose this Field for your next job or career. Your first instinct will be to think that this automatically means you have to be either *an actor or actress, or a screenwriter, or a director, or a movie critic.* Not so. There are many other people standing out in that Field, helping to produce Movies. Just look at the closing credits at the end of any movie, and you will see: *researchers (especially for movies set in another time), travel experts (to scout locations), interior designers (to design sets), carpenters (to build them), painters (for backdrops, etc.), artists,*

computer graphics designers (for special effects), costume design-
ers, makeup artists, hair stylists, photographers (camera opera-
tors), lighting technicians, sound mixers and sound editors,
composers (for soundtrack), conductors, musicians, singers,
stunt people, animal trainers, caterers, drivers, first-aid people,
personal assistants, secretaries, publicists, accountants, etc., etc.
My, there are a lot of people standing in that Field—some
of whom are *outstanding* in their Field!

And so it is with any Field. No matter what your skills
are, they *can* be used in *any* meadow or Field that you may
choose as your favorite.

For some people, incidentally, Majors yield *the least* helpful information about future Fields. Reason? Majors often *don't* point
to jobs. Example? Liberal Arts. But, might as well inventory
everything we've learned so far, *just in case* (using the exercise
called **The Subjects Chart**).

Okay, let's start.

Everyone has mental skills.

Your mental skills are such things as: *the ability to gather infor-*
mation, to analyze information, to organize information, to present in-
formation, and the like. The question here is: **what kinds of**
information, subjects, bodies of knowledge, ideas, or lan-
guages, do you like to use your mental skills with?

In order for you to answer this question, it is helpful to fill out
the following chart; *you may first copy it onto a larger piece of paper,*
if you wish, in order to have more room to write.

Please note that this chart is asking you what subjects you
know *anything* about, whether you *like* the subject or not. (*Later,*
you will ask yourself which of these you like or even *love*.) For
now, the task facing you is merely *inventory*. That is a task similar to inventorying what clothes you've got in your closet, before
you decide which ones to give away. Only, here, *the closet is your*

head, and you're inventorying all the stuff that's in *there*. Don't try to evaluate your degree of mastery of a particular subject. Put down something you've only read a few articles about *(if it interests you)* side by side with a subject you studied for three semesters in school.

Throwaway comes later *(though, obviously, if there's a subject you hate so much you can barely stand to write it down, then . . . don't . . . write . . . it . . . down).*

When filling this chart out, do not forget to list those things you've learned—no matter how—about *Organizations (including volunteer organizations),* and what it takes to make them work.

It is not necessary that you should have ever taken a course in management or business. Examples of things you may know something about (and should list here) are: *accounting or bookkeeping; administration; applications; credit collection of overdue bills; customer relations and service; data analysis, distribution; fiscal analysis, controls, reductions; government contracts; group dynamics or work with groups in general; hiring, human resources, or manpower; international business; management; marketing, sales; merchandising; packaging; performance specifications; planning; policy development; problem solving or other types of troubleshooting with operations or management systems; production; public speaking/ addressing people; R & D program management; recruiting; show or conference planning, organization, and management; systems analysis; travel or travel planning, especially international travel; etc.*

The Subjects Chart

SUBJECTS I KNOW SOMETHING ABOUT

Which column you decide to put a subject in, below, doesn't matter at all. The columns are only a series of pegs, to hang your memories on. Which peg is of no concern. Jot down a subject anywhere you like.

Column 1	Column 2	Column 3	Column 4	Column 5
Studied in High School or College or Graduate School	Learned on the Job	Learned from Conferences, Workshops, Training, Seminars	Learned at Home: Reading, TV, Tape Programs, Study Courses	Learned in My Leisure Time: Volunteer Work, Hobbies, etc.
Examples: Spanish, Typing, Accounting, Computer Literacy, Psychology, Geography	Examples: Publishing, Computer Graphics, How an Organization Works, How to Operate Various Machines	Examples: Welfare Rules, Job-hunting, Painting, How to Use the Internet	Examples: Art Appreciation, History, Speed Reading, a Language	Examples: Landscaping, How to Sew, Antiques, Camping, Stamps

Prioritizing
"The Subjects Chart"

When you're done, you may want to let this Chart just sit on your refrigerator door for a few days, while you see if there's anything you want to add.

But when you're sure you've listed all you want to, on the chart, it is crucial then to sort and then prioritize all these subjects. See the Prioritizing Grids on pages 274 and 275.

When you've got your ten prioritized Subjects, then go on to the next item, here.

2. Fields Dealing with People's Problems or Needs

The question here is: **if you like to help people, what problems or needs do you like to help them with?** Each of these is a field.

In order to answer this question, it is helpful to fill out either of two kinds of exercises: *a checklist,* or *"fill in the blank."* Better yet, the two together, *like this:*

---

1. Check off any kind of need you think you *might* like to help people with, and then
2. Add *which part of it,* or *what aspect of it,* you find particularly interesting or *appealing.*

The Three Secrets to Finding That Dream Job of Yours

The People List

I'd like to help people with their need for:

❏ **Clothing** (people's need to find and choose appropriate and affordable clothing); *and in my case what interests me particularly is_____.*

❏ **Food** (people's need to be fed, to be saved from starvation or poor nutrition); *and in my case what interests me particularly is_____.*

❏ **Housing and real estate** (people's need to find appropriate and affordable housing, apartment, office, or land); *and in my case what interests me particularly is_____.*

❏ **Languages** (people's need for literacy, to be able to read, or to learn a new language); *and in my case what interests me particularly is_____.*

❏ **Personal services or service occupations** (people's need to have someone do tasks they can't do, or haven't time to do, or don't want to do, for themselves—ranging from childcare to helping run a farm); *and in my case what interests me particularly is_____.*

❏ **Family and consumer economics** (people's need to have help with budgeting, taxes, financial planning, money management, etc.); *and in my case what interests me particularly is_____.*

❏ **Retail sales** (people's need for help in buying something); *and in my case what interests me particularly is_____.*

❑ **Automobile sales** (people's need for transportation); *and in my case what interests me particularly is*_____.

❑ **Legal services** (people's need for expert counseling concerning the legal implications of things they are doing, or things that have been done to them); *and in my case what interests me particularly is*_____.

❑ **Child development** (people's need for help with various problems as their children are moving from infancy through childhood, including behavioral disabilities); *and in my case what interests me particularly is*_____.

❑ **Physical fitness** (people's need to get their body in tune through physical or occupational therapy, bodywork, exercise, or diet); *and in my case what interests me particularly is*_____.

❑ **Health services** (people's need to have preventative medicine or help with ailments, allergies, and disease); *and in my case what interests me particularly is*_____.

❑ **Healing including alternative medicine and holistic health** (people's need to have various injuries, ailments, maladies, or diseases healed); *and in my case what interests me particularly is*_____.

❑ **Medicine** (people's need to have help with diagnosing and treating various diseases, or removing diseased or badly injured parts of their body, etc.); *and in my case what interests me particularly is*_____.

❏ **Mental health** (people's need for help with stress, depression, insomnia, or other forms of emotional or mental disturbance); *and in my case what interests me particularly is*_____.

❏ **Psychology or psychiatry** (people's need for help with mental illness); *and in my case what interests me particularly is*_____.

❏ **Personal counseling and guidance** (people's need for help with family relations, with dysfunctions, or with various crises in their life, including a lack of balance in their use of time); *and in my case what interests me particularly is*_____.

❏ **Career counseling, career-change, or life/work planning** (people's need for help in choosing a career or planning a holistic life); *and in my case what interests me particularly is*_____.

❏ **Job-hunting, job-placement, or vocational rehabilitation** (people's need to have help in finding the work they have chosen, particularly when handicapped, or unemployed, or enrolling for welfare under the new regulations); *and in my case what interests me particularly is*_____.

❏ **Training or learning** (people's need to learn more about something, at work or outside of work); *and in my case what interests me particularly is*_____.

❏ **Entertainment** (people's need to be entertained, by laughter, wit, intelligence, or beauty); *and in my case what interests me particularly is*_____.

❑ **Spirituality or religion** (people's need to learn as much as they can about God, character, and their own soul, including their values and principles); *and in my case what interests me particularly is*_____.

❑ **Animal or plant care** (their need for nurturing, growth, health, and other life cycles that require the kinds of sensitivities often referred to as interpersonal skills); *and in my case what interests me particularly is*_____.

❑ **Other fields** (or people's needs) not listed above, or a new field I just invented (I think): _____.

In each question where it says "*. . . and in my case what interests me particularly is . . .*" think about whether or not there are *particular age groups* you prefer to work with, *a particular gender* you prefer to work with (*or sexual orientation*), and whether you prefer to work with *individuals or groups, people of a particular background or set of beliefs, or people in a particular place (the Armed Forces, government, prison, mental institutions, etc.).* If so, write it in.

Prioritizing "The People List"

When you're done, you may want to let this List just sit on your refrigerator door for a few days, while you see if there's anything you want to add.

But when you're sure you've listed all you want to, on the List, it is crucial then to sort and then prioritize these Fields. See the Prioritizing Grids on pages 274 and 275.

3. Fields Dealing with Things, Tools, or Products

When you're done with the People list, go on to this third Fields list.

The question here is: **what things or products interest you the most?** (A product may be "a service," incidentally.)

Sampler: do you love to deal with, handle, construct, operate, market, or repair: *airplanes, antiques, bicycles, blueprints, books, bridges, clothing, computers, crops, diagrams, electricity, electronics, drugs, farms, farm machinery, fish, flowers, gardens, groceries, guidebooks, houses, kitchen appliances, lawns, machines, magazines, makeup, manuals, medicines, minerals, money, music, musical instruments, newspapers, office machines, paints, paper, plants, radios, rivers, rooms, sailboats, security systems, sewing machines, skiing equipment, soil, telephones, toiletries, tools, toys, trains, trees, valuable objects, videotapes, wine, wood—or what?*

What things or products do you *love* to deal with? In order to answer this question, you need to compile *a list*. And it is important that it is complete—that is, it's important that it list *all* the things or products that you love to deal with, in any way, shape, or form.

So, the brief *Sampler* above will not do. You need a longer list, and one that identifies what Fields those *things or products* are in. Fortunately, there is such a directory—at your very fingertips. It's called: *the yellow pages,* from your local telephone company. It has it all: things, products, fields, *and*—what you'll need later—the *location* of relevant organizations in your chosen geographical area.

If you don't plan to stay in your current community for this next job-hunt or career-change, then you will want to write to the phone company in the geographical area you are planning to move to, and secure *its* phone book. In the meantime, you can use the local phone directory for this exercise (just ignore locations).

Chapter Thirteen

The instructions for this exercise are simple. Go through the *table of contents* or *the index* of *the yellow pages* (in a phone book you don't mind marking up), and highlight any and every category or field where you think you *might* like to deal with, or handle, or construct, or operate, or market, or repair *that thing, product, or service.* It is best to work your way backward, from Z to A. Then, go back, and looking only at the items you highlighted, circle in *red* the ones that you care the most about. Jot down their names on the next page.

Prioritizing
"The Things Phone Book"

When you're done, you may want to let this Phone Book exercise just sit on your refrigerator door for a few days, while you see if there's anything you want to add.

But when you're sure you've listed all you want to, on the Phone Book exercise, it is crucial then to sort and then prioritize all these "Things" Fields. Use the Prioritizing Grids on pages 274 and 275.

Putting All Your
Favorite Fields Together

And now that you are done with all three Fields lists, it is time to put all three lists together, and make one unified list of Your Favorite Fields.

And then, choose your top five Favorite Fields, and copy them on the Favorite Interests/Fields of Fascination petal on page 246.

The Things Phone Book

_____   _____   _____   _____

_____   _____   _____   _____

_____   _____   _____   _____

_____   _____   _____   _____

_____   _____   _____   _____

_____   _____   _____   _____

_____   _____   _____   _____

_____   _____   _____   _____

_____   _____   _____   _____

_____   _____   _____   _____

_____   _____   _____   _____

_____   _____   _____   _____

_____   _____   _____   _____

_____   _____   _____   _____

_____   _____   _____   _____

_____   _____   _____   _____

Your Favorite Places to Live
(Geography)

The Point of this Petal: To answer this question: *to the degree you have a choice—now or down the line—where would you most like to live?*

Why This Is Important for You to Know: Human beings are like flowers. Our soul flourishes in some environs, but withers and dies—or at least becomes extremely unhappy—in others.

What You Want to Beware Of: Thinking that where you live is not important. Or thinking, if you have a partner, and you each want to live in different places, that one of you can get their way, but the other is going to have to give up *their* dream. Nonsense! If this were part of a course about Thinking, what would the Lesson be? The subject of the Lesson would be: how can two partners, who initially disagree, learn to agree on a place where both get what they want?

Now, of course, chapter 8, "How to Pick a New Place to Live," may have already solved this question for you. But in case it didn't, and you still haven't got a clue, there is an interesting exercise you can do. It begins with your past *(the places where you used to live)*, and extracts from it some information that is tremendously useful in plotting your future.

It is particularly useful when you have a partner, and the two of you can't seem to agree on where you want to live.

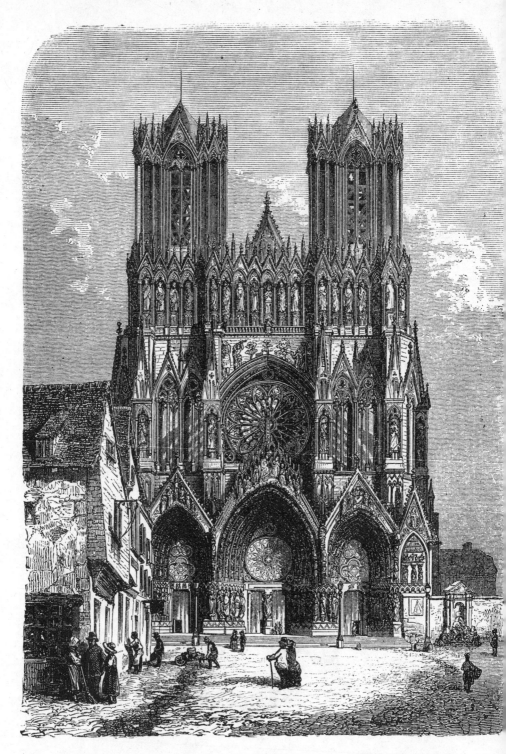

DIRECTIONS
FOR DOING THIS EXERCISE:

1. Copy the chart that is on the next two pages, onto a larger (*e.g., 24" x 36"*) piece of paper or cardboard, which you can obtain from any arts and crafts store, in your own town or city. If you are doing this exercise with a partner, make a copy for them too, so that each of you is working on a clean copy of your own, and can follow these instructions independently.

2. In *Column 1*, list all the places where you have ever lived.

3. In *Column 2*, list all the factors you disliked (and still dislike) about each place. The factors do not have to be put exactly opposite the name in *Column 1*. The names in *Column 1* exist simply to jog your memory. Once you have listed the negative factors each place reminds you of (e.g., "the sun never shone, there") you can cross out that place's name in *Column 1*.

If, as you go, you remember some good things about that place, put *those* factors at the bottom of the next column, *Column 3*.

If the same factors keep repeating, from place after place, just put a checkmark after the first listing of that factor, each time it repeats.

Keep going until you have listed the factors you hated about each and every place you named in *Column 1*. Now, in effect, throw away *Column 1*; discard it from your thoughts. The negative factors were what you were after. *Column 1* has served its purpose.

4. In *Column 3*, you look at the negative factors you listed in *Column 2*, and try to list each one's opposite. For example, "the sun never shone, there" would, in *Column 3*, be turned into "mostly sunny, all year 'round." It will not always be *the exact opposite*. For example, the negative factor "rains all the time" does not necessarily translate into the positive "sunny all the time." It might be something more like "sunny at least 200 days a year." It's your call. Keep going, until every negative factor in *Column 2* is turned into its opposite, a positive factor,

My Geographical Preferences
Decision Making for Just You

Column 1 Names of Places I Have Lived	Column 2 From the Past: Negatives	Column 3 Translating the Negatives into Positives	Column 4 Ranking of My Positives
	Factors I Disliked and Still Dislike About That Place Factors I Liked and Still Like About That Place		1. 2. 3. 4. 5. 6. 7. 8. 9. 10. 11. 12. 13. 14. 15.

Our Geographical Preferences
Decision Making for You and a Partner

Column 5 Places That Fit These Criteria	*Column 6* Ranking of His/Her Preferences	*Column 7* Combining Our Two Lists (Columns 4 & 6)	*Column 8* Places That Fit These Criteria
	a.	a. 1.	
	b.	b. 2.	
	c.	c. 3.	
	d.	d. 4.	
	e.	e. 5.	
	f.	f. 6.	
	g.	g. 7.	
	h.	h. 8.	
	i.	i. 9.	
	j.	j. 10.	
	k.	k. 11.	
	l.	l. 12.	
	m.	m. 13.	
	n.	n. 14.	
	o.	o. 15.	

in *Column 3.* At the bottom, note the positive factors you already listed there, that you thought of, when you were working on *Column 2.*

5. In *Column 4,* now, list the positive factors in *Column 3,* in the order of most important (to you), down to least important (to you). For example, if you were looking at, and trying to name a new town, city, or place, where you could be happy, and flourish, what is the first thing you would look for? Would it be, say, good weather? or lack of crime? or good schools? or access to cultural opportunities, such as music, art, museums, or whatever? or would it be inexpensive housing? etc., etc. Rank all the factors in *Column 4.* Use the Prioritzing Grids (pages 274 and 275) if you need to.

6. If you are doing this by yourself, list on a *scribble sheet* the top ten factors, in order of importance to you, and show it to everyone you meet for the next ten days, with the question: "Can you think of any places that have these ten factors, or at least the first five?" Jot down their suggestions on the back of the *scribble sheet.* When the ten days are up, look at the back of your sheet and circle the three places others suggested, that look the most interesting to you. If there is only a partial overlap between your dream factors and the places your friends and acquaintances suggested, make sure the overlap is in the factors that count the most. Now you have some names that you will want to find out more about, until you are sure which is your absolute favorite place to live, and then your second, and third, as backups.

Put the names of the three places, and/or your top five factors, on **That One Piece of Paper** with the Flower Graphic, on the Geography petal.

7. If you are doing this with a partner, skip *Column 5.* Instead, when you have finished your *Column 4,* look at your partner's *Column 4,* and copy it into *Column 6.* The numbering of *your* list in *Column 4* was 1, 2, 3, 4, etc. Number your partner's list, as you copy it into *Column 6,* as a., b., c., d., etc.

8. Now, in *Column 7*, combine your *Column 4* with *Column 6* (your partner's old *Column 4*, renumbered). Both of you can work now from just one person's chart. Combine the two lists as illustrated on the chart. First your partner's top favorite geographical factor ("a."), then *your* top favorite geographical factor ("1."), then your partner's second most important favorite geographical factor ("b."), then *yours* ("2."), etc., until you have ten or fifteen favorite geographical factors *(yours and your partner's)* listed, in order, in *Column 7*.

9. List on a *scribble sheet* the top ten factors, and both of you show it to everyone you meet, for the next ten days, with the same question as above: "Can you think of any places that have these ten factors, or at least the first five?" Jot down their suggestions on the back of the *scribble sheet*. When the ten days are up, you and your partner should look at the back of your sheet and circle the three places others suggested, that look the most interesting to the two of you. If there is only a partial overlap between your dream factors and the places your friends and acquaintances suggested, make sure the overlap is in the factors that count the most to the two of you, i.e., the ones that are at the top of your list in *Column 7*. Now you have some names of places that would make you both happy, that you will want to find out more about, until you are sure which is the absolute favorite place to live for both of you, and then your second, and third, as backups.

   Put the names of the top three places, and/or your top six factors, on **That One Piece of Paper** with the Flower Graphic, on number two, the Geography petal, page 246.

Conclusion: Was all of this too much work? Then do what one family did: they put a map of the U.S. up on a cork-board, and then they each threw a dart at the map from a few feet away, and when they were done they saw where the most darts landed. It turned out to be around "Denver." So, *Denver* it was!

Your Favorite People

With the great emphasis upon the importance of the environment, in recent years, and global warming in particular, it has become increasingly realized that jobs are environments too. The most important environmental factor always turns out to be people, since every job, except possibly that of a full-fledged hermit, surrounds us with people to one degree or another.

Indeed, many a good job has been ruined by the people one is surrounded by. Many a mundane job has been made delightful, by the people one is surrounded by. Therefore, it is important to think out what kinds of people you want to be surrounded by.

Dr. John L. Holland offers the best description of people-environments. He says there are six principal ones:

1. The **Realistic** People-Environment: filled with people who prefer activities involving "the explicit, ordered, or systematic manipulation of objects, tools, machines, and animals." "Realistic," incidentally, refers to Plato's conception of "the real" as that which one can apprehend through the senses.

I summarize this as: **R** = people who like nature, or athletics, or tools and machinery.

2. The **Investigative** People-Environment: filled with people who prefer activities involving "the observation and symbolic, systematic, creative investigation of physical, biological, or cultural phenomena."

I summarize this as: **I** = people who are very curious, liking to investigate or analyze things.

3. The **Artistic** People-Environment: filled with people who prefer activities involving "ambiguous, free, unsystematized activities and competencies to create art forms or products."

I summarize this as: **A** = people who are very artistic, imaginative, and innovative.

4. The **Social** People-Environment: filled with people who prefer activities involving "the manipulation of others to inform, train, develop, cure, or enlighten."

I summarize this as: **S** = people who are bent on trying to help, teach, or serve people.

Chapter Thirteen

5. The **Enterprising** People-Environment: filled with people who prefer activities involving "the manipulation of others to attain organizational or self-interest goals."

I summarize this as: E = people who like to start up projects or organizations, and/or influence or persuade people.

6. The **Conventional** People-Environment: filled with people who prefer activities involving "the explicit, ordered, systematic manipulation of data, such as keeping records, filing materials, reproducing materials, organizing written and numerical data according to a prescribed plan, operating business and data processing machines." "Conventional," incidentally, refers to the "values" that people in this environment usually hold—representing the broad mainstream of the culture.

I summarize this as: C = people who like detailed work, and like to complete tasks or projects.

According to John's theory and findings, everyone has three preferred people-environments, from among these six. The letters for your three preferred people-environments gives you what is called your "Holland Code."

> There is, incidentally, a relationship between the people you like to be surrounded by *and* your skills *and* your values. See John Holland's book, *Making Vocational Choices* (3rd ed., 1997). You can procure it by writing to Psychological Assessment Resources, Inc., 16204 N. Florida Avenue, Lutz, FL 33549. Phone: 1-800-331-8378. *The book is $44.00 at this writing.* PAR also has John Holland's instrument, called *The Self-Directed Search* (or SDS, for short) for discovering what your Holland Code is. PAR lets you take the test online for a small fee ($9.95) at **www.self-directed-search.com**.

For those who don't have Internet access (or are in a hurry), I invented (many years ago) a quick and easy way to get an *approximation* of your "Holland Code," as it's called. I call it "The Party Exercise." Here is how the exercise goes (do it!):

On the next page is an aerial view of a room in which a two-day (!) party is taking place. At this party, people with the same or similar interests have (for some reason) all gathered in the same corner of the room.

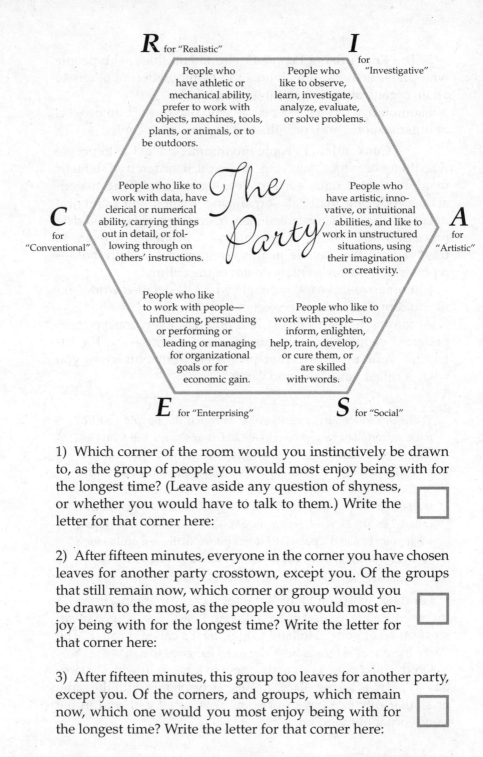

R for "Realistic"

People who have athletic or mechanical ability, prefer to work with objects, machines, tools, plants, or animals, or to be outdoors.

I for "Investigative"

People who like to observe, learn, investigate, analyze, evaluate, or solve problems.

The Party

C for "Conventional"

People who like to work with data, have clerical or numerical ability, carrying things out in detail, or following through on others' instructions.

A for "Artistic"

People who have artistic, innovative, or intuitional abilities, and like to work in unstructured situations, using their imagination or creativity.

People who like to work with people—influencing, persuading or performing or leading or managing for organizational goals or for economic gain.

People who like to work with people—to inform, enlighten, help, train, develop, or cure them, or are skilled with words.

E for "Enterprising"

S for "Social"

1) Which corner of the room would you instinctively be drawn to, as the group of people you would most enjoy being with for the longest time? (Leave aside any question of shyness, or whether you would have to talk to them.) Write the letter for that corner here:

2) After fifteen minutes, everyone in the corner you have chosen leaves for another party crosstown, except you. Of the groups that still remain now, which corner or group would you be drawn to the most, as the people you would most enjoy being with for the longest time? Write the letter for that corner here:

3) After fifteen minutes, this group too leaves for another party, except you. Of the corners, and groups, which remain now, which one would you most enjoy being with for the longest time? Write the letter for that corner here:

Chapter Thirteen

The three letters you just chose, in the three steps, are called your "Holland Code." Here is what you should now do:

1. Circle them on the People petal, on your Flower Diagram.

Put three circles around your favorite corner; two circles around your next favorite; and one circle around your third favorite.

2. Once the corners are circled, you may wish to write (for yourself and your eyes only) a temporary statement about your future job or career, using the descriptors on page 310.

If your "Code" turned out to be IAS, for example, you might write: *"I would like a job or career best if I were surrounded by people who are very curious, and like to investigate or analyze things (I); who are also very innovative (A); and who are bent on trying to help or serve people (S)."*

3. See what clues the Internet has to offer.

Back on April 11 to 14, 1977, I conducted a workshop at the University of Missouri-Columbia, introducing "The Party Exercise." Subsequently, some unknown genius there did a rhapsody on this, calling it "The Career Interests Game." It is brilliant, and can be found on that University's Career Center's website, at: `http://career.missouri.edu/students/explore/the careerinterestsgame.php`. You play the "Game" the same way, but afterward you can click on each letter of RIASEC (in color!) and find out what skills, interests, hobbies, and career possibilities go with each letter. For a complete *Holland Code*, of course, you need the *combination* of all three letters in your Code; but this at least offers a good beginning, taking one letter at a time. It is free.

Another Holland website is Lawrence Jones' *Career Key*, found at `http://careerkey.org/`. It costs $7.95 to take it, but offers suggestions as to related college majors, possible careers, etc., when you are done. Great test!

The final *Holland*-related site I want to mention is Career-Planner.com's *Career Test*, invented by Michael T. Robinson, and found at `http://www.careerplanner.com`. I recommend it; it costs you $19.95 (or more) to take this test, so you must decide if it's worth twice the cost of John L. Holland's *Self-Directed Search*. Here, you get a listing of thirty to one hundred careers related to the results of your test. As in all these sorts of test results, treat these as starting points, only, for your subsequent research and informational interviewing. Please.

PETAL #4 ON YOUR FLOWER DIAGRAM
Your Favorite Values & Goals

Goals are a matter of what problems in the world you'd like your life to help solve (if any). They may be big, big problems, but once you know what your favorite skills are, there is always some way you can plug them in, to help with the causes or problems in the world that you are passionate about helping solve. For example, suppose you are passionate about helping diminish global warming. But your favorite skill is *writing* or *creating publicity*. You can go on the Internet, type "fighting global warming" into your search engine, and come up with a site like **www.fightglobalwarming.com**. From there, contact people to find out how your skill of *writing* could be employed. So it is with any cause, and any skill.[10]

Values are the principles that guide you through every day, every task, and every encounter with another human being. Even if you are unaware of what those values are. Sometimes you can discover them by reflecting on who your heroines or heroes are. For example, my hero this year is C. C. Myers, charged with rebuilding a fire-damaged section of the freeways near the San Francisco Bay Bridge by June 27, 2007 (he did it by May 24). A newspaper article[11] described him as "gutsy," "not given to idle boasts," one who "says what he means, does what he says and will move heaven as well as Earth if he has to," one who

---

10. For encouraging examples of how individuals can employ their skills, whatever they may be, for the cause that most appeals to them, see David Bornstein's book *How to Change the World: Social Entrepreneurs and the Power of New Ideas*. Oxford University Press, 2004. See your local bookstore or any online bookstore, such as Amazon.com or BarnesandNoble.com. You can make a difference in our world, and this book gives examples of those who have.
11. In the *San Francisco Chronicle*, by Chuck Squatriglia, *Chronicle* staff writer, Sunday, May 13, 2007.

"places integrity above all and cherishes his reputation for do-ing things fast and doing things right and doing things safely," and likes to set records that may never be beaten. His chief value, he himself says, is "being proud of what you've done, the enjoyment of being able to show what you can do."

If I tell you he is a hero, to me, it's not hard for you to guess what some of *my* values are, is it? And so with you: one way to figure out what your values are, is to first figure out who your hero or heroine is. And what it is you most admire about them.

Another way to bring values to your consciousness is to imagine that shortly before the end of your life you are invited to dinner—and to your great surprise people have secretly come in from all over the country and all over the world, to attend a surprise testi-monial dinner for You.

At the dinner, to your great embarrassment, there is one testi-monial after another about the good things you did, or the good person that you were, in your lifetime. No mention of any parts of your life that you don't want to have remembered. Just the good stuff.

So, this brings us to some questions. If you get the life you re-ally want between now and then, what would you hope you would hear at that dinner, as they looked back on your life?

If you do achieve what you want with your life, what about you would you like to have remembered, after you are gone from this earth? Here is a checklist to help you:[12]

It would be a good life, if at its end here, people remembered me as one who (check as many items as are important to you):

❑ Used my skills to help fight global warming.

❑ Used my skills to help fight genocide in Darfur or other parts of the world.

❑ Used my skills to help people caught in natural disasters around the country or around the world.

---

12. I am indebted to Arthur F. Miller, of People Management, Inc., for many of these ideas.

- ❏ Used my skills to help fight malaria in Africa.
- ❏ Used my skills to help fight poverty and hunger.
- ❏ Used my skills to help fight AIDS.
- ❏ Served or helped those who were in need.
- ❏ Impressed people with my going the second mile, in meeting their needs.
- ❏ Was always a great listener.
- ❏ Was always good at carrying out orders, or bringing projects to a successful conclusion.
- ❏ Mastered some technique, or field.
- ❏ Did something that everyone said couldn't be done.
- ❏ Did something that no one had ever done before.
- ❏ Excelled and was the best at whatever it is I did.
- ❏ Pioneered or explored some new technology.
- ❏ Fixed something that was broken.
- ❏ Made something work, when everyone else had failed or given up.
- ❏ Improved something, made it better, or perfected it.
- ❏ Combatted some bad idea/philosophy/force/influence/ pervasive trend—and I persevered and/or prevailed.
- ❏ Influenced people and gained a tremendous response from them.
- ❏ Had an impact, and caused change.
- ❏ Did work that brought more information/truth into the world.
- ❏ Did work that brought more beauty into the world, through gardens, or painting, or decorating, or designing, or whatever.
- ❏ Did work that brought more justice, truth, and ethical behavior into the world.
- ❏ Brought people closer to God.
- ❏ Growing in wisdom and compassion was my great goal all my life.

❑ Had a vision of what something could be, and helped that vision to come true.

❑ Developed or built something, where there was nothing.

❑ Began a new business, or did some project from start to finish.

❑ Exploited, shaped, and influenced some situation, or market, before others saw the potential.

❑ Put together a great team, which made a huge difference in its field, industry, or community.

❑ Was a good decision-maker.

❑ Was acknowledged by everyone as a leader, and was in charge of whatever it was that I was doing.

❑ Had status in my field, industry, or community.

❑ Was in the spotlight, gained recognition, and was well-known.

❑ Made it into a higher echelon than I was, in terms of reputation, and/or prestige, and/or membership, and/or salary.

❑ Was able to acquire possessions, things, or money.

❑ Other goals that occur to me:_____

_____

When you're done checking off all the values that are important to you, go back, and pick out the ten that you care the most about, and then prioritize them in exact order of importance to you. As always, if you just can't prioritize them by guess and by gosh, then use the Prioritizing Grids on pages 274 and 275.

The question to ask yourself, there, as you confront each "pair" on the Grid is: "If I could only have this true about me, at the end of my life, but not the other, which would I prefer?" *Try not to pay attention to what others might or might not think of you, if they knew this was your heart's desire. This is just between you and God.*

Put your top six values on the Values petal, in the Flower Diagram.

Your Favorite
Working Conditions

Plants that grow beautifully at sea level, often perish if they're taken ten thousand feet up the mountain. Likewise, we do our best work under certain conditions, but not under others. Thus, the question: "What are your favorite working conditions?" actually is a question about "Under what circumstances do you do your most effective work?"

The best way to approach this is by starting with the things you *disliked* about all your previous jobs, using the following chart to list these. The chart, as you can see, has three columns, and you fill them out in the same order, and manner, that you filled out the geography chart earlier. Here, too, you may copy this chart onto a larger piece of paper if you wish, before you begin filling it out. *Column A may begin with such factors as: "too noisy," "too much supervision," "no windows in my workplace," "having to be at work by 6 A.M.," etc.*

Of course, when you get to Column B, you must rank these factors that are in Column A, in their exact order of importance, to you.

As always, if you are baffled as to how to prioritize these factors in exact order, use the Prioritizing Grid (pages 274–275).

The question to ask yourself, there, as you confront each "pair" is: "If I were offered two jobs, and in the first job I would be rid of this first distasteful working condition, but not the second, while in the second job, I would be rid of the second distasteful working condition, but not the first, which distasteful working condition would I choose to get rid of?"

Note that when you later come to Column C, the factors will already be prioritized. Your only job, there, is to think of the "positive" form of that factor that you hated so much (in Column B). (It is not always "the exact opposite." For example, *too much supervision,* listed in Column B, does not always mean *no supervision,* in Column C. It *might* mean: *a moderate amount of supervision, once or twice a day.*)

Once you've finished Column C, enter the top five factors from there on the Working Conditions petal of the Flower Diagram.

DISTASTEFUL WORKING CONDITIONS

	Column A — Distasteful Working Conditions	Column B — Distasteful Working Conditions Ranked	Column C + The Keys to My Effectiveness at Work
Places I Have Worked Thus Far in My Life	I Have Learned from the Past That My Effectiveness at Work Is Decreased When I Have to Work Under These Conditions:	Among the Factors or Qualities Listed in Column A, These Are the Ones I Dislike Absolutely the Most (in Order of Decreasing Dislike):	The Opposite of These Qualities, in Order: I Believe My Effectiveness Would Be at an Absolute Maximum, If I Could Work Under These Conditions:

The Three Secrets to Finding That Dream Job of Yours

Level & Salary

Salary is something you must think out ahead of time, when you're contemplating your ideal job or career. Level goes hand-in-hand with salary, of course.

1. The first question here is at what level would you like to work, in your ideal job?

Level is a matter of how much responsibility you want, in an organization:

❑ Boss or CEO (this may mean you'll have to form your own business)

❑ Manager or someone under the boss who carries out orders

❑ The head of a team

❑ A member of a team of equals

❑ One who works in tandem with one other partner

❑ One who works alone, either as an employee or as a consultant to an organization, or as a one-person business

Enter a two- or three-word summary of your answer, on the Salary and Level petal of your Flower Diagram.

2. The second question here is what salary would you like to be aiming for?

Here you have to think in terms of minimum or maximum. **Minimum** is what you would need to make, if you were just barely "getting by." And you need to know this *before* you go in for a job interview with anyone *(or before you form your own business, and need to know how much profit you must make, just to survive).*

Maximum could be any astronomical figure you can think of, but it is more useful here to put down the salary you realistically think you could make, with your present competency and experience, were you working for a real, *but generous*, boss. (If this maximum figure is still depressingly low, then put down the salary you would like to be making five years from now.)

Make out a detailed outline of your estimated expenses *now*, listing what you need *monthly* in the following categories:[13]

Housing

    Rent or mortgage payments . . . . $_____

    Electricity/gas . . . . $_____

    Water . . . . $_____

    Telephone . . . . $_____

    Garbage removal . . . . $_____

    Cleaning, maintenance, repairs[14] . . . . $_____

Food

    What you spend at the supermarket
    and/or meat market, etc. . . . . $_____

    Eating out . . . . $_____

Clothing

    Purchase of new or used clothing . . . . $_____

    Cleaning, dry cleaning, laundry . . . . $_____

Automobile/transportation[15]

    Car payments . . . . $_____

    Gas (who knows?). . . . . $_____

    Repairs . . . . $_____

    Public transportation (bus, train, plane) . . . . . $_____

Insurance

    Car . . . . $_____

    Medical or health care . . . . $_____

    House and personal possessions . . . . $_____

    Life . . . . $_____

Medical expenses

    Doctors' visits . . . . $_____

    Prescriptions . . . . $_____

    Fitness costs . . . . $_____

Support for other family members

    Child-care costs (if you have children) . . . . . . $_____

    Child-support (if you're paying that) . . . . $_____

    Support for your parents (if you're helping out) . . $_____

Charity giving/tithe (to help others). . . . . $_____

School/learning

    Children's costs (if you have children in school) . . $_____

    Your learning costs (adult education,
    job-hunting classes, etc.) . . . . $_____

Pet care (if you have pets) . . . . $_____

Bills and debts (usual monthly payments)

    Credit cards . . . . $_____

    Local stores. $_____

    Other obligations you pay off monthly . . . . . . $_____

Taxes
    Federal[16] (*next April's due, divided by*
    months remaining until then). . . . . $_____

    State (*likewise*) . . . . $_____

    Local/property (*next amount due, divided by*
    months remaining until then). . . . . $_____

    Tax-help (*if you ever use an accountant,*
    pay a friend to help you with taxes, etc.) . . . . $_____

Savings . . . . $_____

Retirement (Keogh, IRA, SEP, etc.) . . . . $_____

Amusement/discretionary spending
    Movies, video rentals, etc. . . . . $_____

    Other kinds of entertainment . . . . $_____

    Reading, newspapers, magazines, books . . . . . $_____

    Gifts (*birthday, Christmas, etc.*) . . . . $_____

    Vacations . . . . $_____

Total Amount You Need Each Month . . . . $_____

---

13. If this kind of financial figuring is not your cup of tea, find a buddy, friend, relative, family member, or anyone, who can help you do this. If you don't know anyone who could do this, go to your local church, synagogue, religious center, social club, gym, or wherever you hang out, and ask the leader or manager there, to help you find someone. If there's a bulletin board, put up a notice on the bulletin board.

14. If you have extra household expenses, such as a security system, be sure to include the quarterly (or whatever) expenses here, divided by three.

15. Your checkbook stubs will tell you a lot of this stuff. But you may be vague about your cash or credit card expenditures. For example, you may not know how much you spend at the supermarket, or how much you spend on gas, etc. But there is a simple way to find out. Just carry a little notepad and pen around with you for two weeks or more, and jot down *everything* you pay cash (or use credit cards) for—on the spot, right after you pay it. At the end of those two weeks, you'll be able to take that notepad and make a realistic guess of what should be put down in these categories that now puzzle you. (*Multiply the two-week figure by two, and you'll have the monthly figure.*)

16. Incidentally, for U.S. citizens, looking ahead to next April 15, be sure to check with your local IRS office or a reputable accountant to find out if you can deduct the expenses of your job-hunt on your federal (and state) income tax returns. At this writing, some job-hunters can, if—big IF—this is not your first job that you're looking for, if you haven't been unemployed too long, and if you aren't making a career-change. Do go find out what the latest "ifs" are. If the IRS says you are eligible, keep careful receipts of everything related to your job-hunt, as you go along: telephone calls, stationery, printing, postage, travel, etc.

Panel 1: HERE'S SOMETHING TO THINK ABOUT

Panel 2: LIFE IS LIKE A TEN-SPEED BICYCLE..

Panel 3: MOST OF US HAVE GEARS THAT WE NEVER USE!

Panel 4: HE'S WRONG..THAT ISN'T SOMETHING TO THINK ABOUT...

Multiply the total amount you need each month by 12, to get the yearly figure. Divide the yearly figure by 2,000, and you will be reasonably near the *minimum* hourly wage that you need. Thus, if you need $3,333 per month, multiplied by 12 that's $40,000 a year, and then divided by 2,000, that's $20 an hour.

Parenthetically, you may want to prepare two different versions of the above budget: one with the expenses you'd ideally *like* to make, and the other a minimum budget, which will give you what you are looking for, here: the floor, below which you simply cannot afford to go.

Enter the maximum, and minimum, on your Salary and Level petal on the Flower Diagram, page 246.

Optional Exercise: You may wish to put down other rewards, besides money, that you would hope for, from your next job or career. These might be:

- ❏ Adventure
- ❏ Challenge
- ❏ Respect
- ❏ Influence
- ❏ Popularity
- ❏ Fame
- ❏ Power
- ❏ Intellectual stimulation from the other workers there
- ❏ A chance to exercise leadership
- ❏ A chance to be creative
- ❏ A chance to make decisions
- ❏ A chance to use my expertise
- ❏ A chance to help others
- ❏ A chance to bring others closer to God
- ❏ Other:

If you do check off things on this list, arrange your answers in order of importance to you, and then add them to the Salary and Level petal.

Done!

Voilà! Your Flower Diagram should now be complete.
Reward yourself! Sleep for a week. Run up a mountain,
or spend a week in your partner's arms.

Then, reflect on how you might put The Flower to use.

Rich Feller, a University Distinguished Teaching Scholar and Professor at Colorado State University, whose own personal "Flower Diagram" follows, first put his personal "picture" together twenty-five years ago. Here are his comments about its usefulness since, and how "That One Piece of Paper" helped him, how he's used it, and how it's changed.

What the Parachute Flower Has Meant to Me

More than anything I've gained from an academic life, my Flower has given me hope, direction, and a lens to satisfaction. Using it to assess my life direction during crisis, career moves, and stretch assignments, it helps me define and hold to personal commitments. In many ways it's my "guiding light." Data within my Flower became and remain the core of any success and satisfaction I have achieved.

After I first filled out my own Flower diagram in a Two-Week Workshop with Dick Bolles back in 1982, I decided to teach the Flower to others. My academic position has allowed me to do this, abundantly. Having now taught The Flower to thousands of counselors, career development, and human resource specialists, I continually use it with clients, and in my own transitional retirement planning.

I'm overwhelmed with how little has changed within my Flower, over the years. My Flower is the best of what I am. Its petals are my compass, and using my "favorite skills" are the mirror to a joyful day. I trust the wisdom within "That One Piece of Paper." It has guided my work and my life, ever since 1982, and it has helped my wife and I define our hopes for our son.

The process of filling out and acting on "That One Piece of Paper" taught me a lot. Specifically, it taught me **the importance of the following ten things, often running contrary to what my studies and doctoral work had taught me previously.**

 I learned from my Flower the importance of:

1. Chasing after passions, honoring strengths, and respecting skill identification
2. Challenging societal definitions of balance and success
3. Committing to something bigger than oneself
4. Living authentically and with joy
5. Being good at what matters to oneself and its relationship to opportunity

6. Finding pleasure in all that one does
7. Staying focused on well-being and life satisfaction
8. Personal clarity and responsibility for designing "possible selves"
9. Letting the world know, humbly but clearly, what we want and
10. "Coaching" people amidst a world of abundance where individuals yearn for individual meaning and purpose more than they hunger for possessions, abject compliance with society's expectations, or simply fitting in.

This technologically enhanced, global workplace we now face in the twenty-first century, certainly challenges all we thought we knew about our life roles. Maintaining clarity, learning agility, and identifying development plans have become elevated to new and critical importance, if we are to maintain choice. As a result I've added the following four emphases to "Rich's Flower": *Have, do, learn,* and *give.* That is to say, I try to keep a running list (constantly updated) of ten things that I want to:

1. Have
2. Do
3. Learn
4. Give

Through the practice of answering the four questions listed above, I can measure change in my growth and development.

I feel so fortunate to have the opportunity to share with others how much I gained from the wisdom and hope embedded within "Rich's Flower."

I humbly offer my resume, home location and design, and family commitments on my website at `www.mycahs.colostate.edu/Rich.Feller`. I'd be honored to share my journey, and encourage others to nurture and shine light on their garden as well. I believe you'll find about 90 percent of the Flower's items influence our daily experience.

Rich Feller
Professor of Counseling and Career Development
University Distinguished Teaching Scholar
Colorado State University
Fort Collins, CO

*A Systematic Approach to
the Job-Hunt and Career-Change:*

STEP III

How

Do You Find the Person
Who Has the Power to Hire You
for the Job You Want?

Well, you begin by seeing what "That One Piece of Paper"
tells you. Let's look at Rich Feller's again.

Example
(Rich Feller's Flower)

**Favorite
Interests**

1. Large conference planning
2. Regional geography & culture
3. Traveling on $20/day 4. Career planning seminars 5. Counseling techniques / theories 6. American policies 7. Fundamentals of sports 9. Fighting sexism 10. NASCAR auto racing
11. Interior design

**Salary
and Level of
Responsibility**

1. Can determine 9/12 month contract 2. Can determine own projects
3. Considerable clout in organization's direction without administrative responsibilities 4. Able to select colleagues 5. 3 to 5 assistants 6. $35K to $50K 7. Serve on various important boards 8. Can defer clerical and budget decisions and tasks 9. Speak before large groups 10. Can run for elected office

Geography

1. Close to major city
2. Mild winters / low humidity
3. Change in seasons 4. Clean and green 5. 100,000 people 6. Nice shopping malls 7. Wide range of athletic options 8. Diverse economic base 9. Ample local culture
10. Sense of community (pride)

Favorite Skills

1. Observational / learning skills • continually expose self to new experiences • perceptive in identifying and assessing potential of others
2. Leadership skills • continually searches for more resonsibility • sees a problem / acts to solve it 3. Instructing / interpreting / guiding • committed to learning as a lifelong process • create atmosphere of acceptance 4. Serving / helping / human relations skills • shapes atmosphere of particular place • relates well in dealing with public 5. Detail / follow-through skills • handle great variety of tasks • resource broker 6. Influencing / persuading skills • recruiting talent / leadership • inspiring trust 7. Performing skills • getting up in front of a group (if I'm in control) • addressing small and large groups 8. Intuitional / innovative skills • continually develop / generate new ideas 9. Develop / Plan / Organize / Execute • designing projects • utilizing skills of others 10. Language / Read / Write • communicate effectively • can think quickly on my feet

**Favorite
People
Environment**

1. Strong social, perceptual skills
2. Emotionally and physically healthy
3. Enthusiastically include others
4. Heterogeneous in interests and skills
5. Social changers, innovators 6. Politically, economically astute 7. Confident enough to confront / cry and be foolish
8. Sensitive to nontraditional issues
9. I and R (see page 308)
10. Nonmaterialistic

**Favorite
Working
Conditions**

1. Receive clinical supervision 2. Mentor relationship 3. Excellent secretary
4. Part of larger, highly respected organization with clear direction 5. Near gourmet and health food specialty shops
6. Heterogeneous colleagues (race, sex, age) 7. Flexible dress code
8. Merit system 9. Can bike / bus / walk to work 10. Private office with window

Favorite Values

1. Improve the human condition
2. Promote interdependence and futuristic principles 3. Maximize productive use of human / material resources 4. Teach people to be self-directed / self-responsible 5. Free people from self-defeating controls (thoughts, rules, barriers)
6. Promote capitalistic principles 7. Reduce exploitation 8. Promote political participation
9. Acknowledge those who give to the community 10. Give away ideas

Put that sheet on a wall, or on the door of your refrigerator. And there you have it: a simple picture (as it were) of You.

A Light Bulb Goes On

But, it's not *just* a picture of You. Just as important, it's a picture of Your Dream Job as well. It's both of these things at once, because you're looking for a dream job or career *that matches you.* You match it. It matches you. Bingo! Mirror images.

And now that you're looking at "That One Piece of Paper," what should happen? Well, for some of you there will be a big *Aha!* as you look at your Flower Diagram. A light bulb will go on, over your head, and you will say, "My goodness, I see *exactly* what sort of career this points me to." This happens particularly with intuitive people.

If you are one of those intuitive people, I say, "Good for you!" Just two gentle warnings, if I may:

Don't prematurely close out *other* possibilities.

THE VIRTUE OF "PASSION" OR ENTHUSIASM

Whether in stages or directly, it is amazing how often people do get their dream job or career. The more you don't *cut* the dream down, because of what you *think* you know about *the real world*, the more likely you are to find what you are looking for.

Hold on to *all* of your dream. Most people don't find their heart's desire, because they decide to pursue just half their dream—and consequently they hunt for it with only *half a heart.*

If you decide to pursue your whole dream, your best dream, the one you would die to do, I guarantee you that you will hunt for it *with all your heart.* It is this *passion* that often is the difference between successful career-changers, and unsuccessful ones.

And *don't* say to yourself: "Well, I see what it is that I would die to be able to do, but I *know* there is no job in the world like that, that *I* would be able to get." Dear friend, you don't know any such thing. You haven't done your research yet. Of course, it is always possible that when you've completed all that research, and conducted your search, you still may not be able to find *all* that you want—down to the last detail. But you'd be surprised at how much of your dream you may be able to find.

Sometimes it will be found in *stages*. One retired man I know, who had been a senior executive with a publishing company, found himself bored to death in retirement, after he turned 65. He contacted a business acquaintance, who said apologetically, "We just don't have anything open that matches or requires your abilities; right now all we need is someone in our mail room." The 65-year-old executive said, "I'll take that job!" He did, and over the ensuing years steadily advanced once again, to just the job he wanted: as a senior executive in that organization, where he utilized all his prized skills, for some time. He retired as senior executive for the second time, at the age of 85. Like him, you may choose to go by stages.

Other times, it may be that you will be able to find your dream directly without having to go through stages.

Other Possibility,
You Look at Your Flower Diagram and . . .
a Light Bulb *Doesn't* Go On

In contrast to what I just said, many of you will look at your completed Flower Diagram, and you won't have *a clue* as to what job or career it points to. Soooo, we need a "fallback" strategy. Of course it involves more "step-by-step-by-step" stuff.

Here's how it goes. Take a pad of paper, with pen or pencil, or go to your computer, and keyboard in hand, make some notes:

1. First, look at your Flower Diagram, and from the center petal choose your three most *favorite* skills.
2. Then, look at your Flower Diagram and write down, from petal #2, your three *top* interests, or Fields of Fascination.
3. Now, take these notes, and show them to at least five friends, family members, or professionals whom you know.

As you will recall, skills usually point toward a **job-title** or job-level, while interests or Fields of Fascination usually point toward a **career field**. So, you want to ask them, in the case of your skills, *What job-title or jobs do these skills suggest to you?*

Then ask them, in the case of your favorite Fields of Fascination, *What career fields do these suggest to you?*

4. Jot down *everything* these five people suggest or recommend to you.
5. After you have finished talking to them, you want to go home and look at all these notes. Anything helpful or valuable here? If not, if none of it looks valuable, then set it aside, and go talk to five more of your friends, acquaintances, or people you know in the business world and nonprofit sector. Repeat, as necessary.
6. When you finally have some worthwhile suggestions, sit down, look over their combined suggestions, and ask yourself some questions.

1. Executive, Administrative, and Managerial Occupations
2. Engineers, Surveyors, and Architects
3. Natural Scientists and Mathematicians
4. Social Scientists, Social Workers, Religious Workers, and Lawyers
5. Teachers, Counselors, Librarians, and Archivists
6. Health Diagnosing and Treating Practitioners
7. Registered Nurses, Pharmacists, Dieticians, Therapists, and Physician Assistants
8. Health Technologists and Technicians
9. Technologists and Technicians in Other Fields: Computer Specialists, Programmers, Information Technicians, Information Specialists, etc.
10. Writers, Artists, Digital Artists, and Entertainers
11. Marketing and Sales Occupations
12. Administrative Support Occupations, including Clerical
13. Service Occupations
14. Agricultural, Forestry, and Fishing Occupations
15. Mechanics and Repairers
16. Construction and Extractive Occupations
17. Production Occupations
18. Transportation and Material-Moving Occupations
19. Handlers, Equipment Cleaners, Helpers, and Laborers

- First, you want to look at what these friends suggested about your skills: *what job or jobs came to their mind?* It will help you to know that most jobs can be classified under nineteen headings or families, as above. Which of these nineteen do your friends' suggestions predominantly point to? Which of these nineteen grabs you?

- Next, you want to look at what your friends suggested about your interests or *Fields of Fascination: what fields or careers came to their minds?* It will help you to know that most of the job families above can be classified under four broad headings: *Agriculture, Manufacturing, Information Industries,* and *Service*

5,708,000 POSSIBLE TARGETS (EMPLOYERS)

57,000 POSSIBLE TARGETS

5,700 POSSIBLE TARGETS

1,000 POSSIBLE TARGETS

500 POSSIBLE TARGETS

300 POSSIBLE TARGETS

60 POSSIBLE TARGETS

10 POSSIBLE TARGETS

YOUR SPIRITUAL VALUES

YOUR PREFERRED LEVEL AND SALARY

YOUR PREFERRED WORKING CONDITIONS

YOUR PREFERRED WORKING CONDITIONS

INFORMATION YOU PREFER

THINGS, KINDS OF PEOPLE, AND INFORMATION YOU PREFER

YOUR PREFERRED TASKS OR SKILLS

YOUR PREFERRED FIELD (OF KNOWLEDGE) OR CAREER FIELD

YOUR PREFERRED GEOGRAPHICAL LOCATION

Industries. Which of these four do your friends' suggestions predominantly *point to*? Which of these four grabs you?

- The next question you want to ask yourself is: both job-titles and career-fields can be broken down further, according to whether you like to work primarily with *people* **or** primarily with *information/data* **or** primarily with *things.*

Let's take agriculture as an example. Within agriculture, you could be driving tractors and other farm machinery—and thus working primarily with *things;* or you could be gathering statistics about crop growth for some state agency—and thus working primarily with *information/data;* or you could be teaching agriculture in a college classroom, and thus working primarily with *people* and *ideas.* Almost all fields as well as career families offer you these three kinds of choices, though *of course* many jobs combine two or more of the three in some intricate way.

Still, you do want to tell yourself what your *preference* is, and what you *primarily* want to be working with. Otherwise your job-hunt or career-change is going to leave you very frustrated, at the end. In this matter, it is often your favorite skill that will give you the clue. If it *doesn't*, then go back and look at your Skills Petal, on your Flower Diagram. What do you think? Are your favorite skills weighted more toward working with *people*, or toward working with *information/data*, or toward working with *things*?

And, no matter what that *petal* suggests, which do you absolutely prefer?

Giving Your Flower a Name

Once you have these *clues* from your friends, you need to go name your Flower. To do this, you need to answer four questions for yourself, in the order indicated below:

• QUESTION #1

What are the **names of jobs or careers** that would give me a chance to use my most enjoyable skills, in a field that is based on my favorite subjects?

Just make sure that you get the names of at least *two* careers, or jobs, that you think you could be happy doing. Never, ever, put all your eggs in one basket. The secret of surviving out there in the jungle is *having alternatives*.

Be careful. Be thorough. Be persistent. This is your life you're working on, and your future. Make it glorious. Whatever it takes, find out the name of your ideal career, your ideal occupation, your ideal job—*or jobs.*

• QUESTION #2

What **kinds of organizations** would and/or do employ people in these careers?

Before you think of individual places where you might like to work, it is necessary to step back a little, as it were, and think of all the *kinds* of places where one might get hired.

Let's take an example. Suppose in your new career you want to be a teacher. You must then ask yourself: *what kinds of places hire teachers?* You might answer, *"just schools"*—and finding that schools in your geographical area have no openings, you might say, *"Well, there are no jobs for people in this career."*

But that is not true. There are countless other *kinds* of organizations and agencies out there, besides schools, that employ *teachers*. For example, corporate training and educational departments, workshop sponsors, foundations, private research firms, educational consultants, teachers' associations, professional and trade societies, military bases, state and local councils on higher education, fire and police training academies, and so on and so forth.

"*Kinds* of places" also means places with different *hiring modes*, besides full-time hiring, such as:

- places that would employ you part-time (maybe you'll end up deciding to hold down two or even three part-time jobs, which altogether would add up to one full-time job, in order to give yourself more variety);
- places that take temporary workers, on assignment for one project at a time;
- places that take consultants, one project at a time;
- places that operate with volunteers, etc.;
- places that are nonprofit;
- places that are for profit;
- and, don't forget, places that you yourself would start up, should you decide to be your own boss (see chapter 10).

Don't forget that as you talk to workers about their jobs or careers (in the previous section), they will accidentally volunteer information about the *kinds* of organizations. Listen keenly, and keep notes.

• QUESTION #3

Among the kinds of organizations uncovered in the previous question, what are the names of **particular places** that I especially like?

As you interview workers about their jobs or careers, they will along the way volunteer actual names of organizations that have such jobs—including what's good or bad about the place where *they* work or used to work. This is important information for you. Jot it all down. Keep notes *as though it were part of your religion.*

Now when this name-gathering is all done, what do you have? Well, either you'll have *too few names* of places to work, or you'll end up with *too much information*—too many names of places that hire people in the career that interests you. There are ways of dealing with either of these eventualities. We'll take this last scenario, first.

Cutting Down the Territory

If you end up with the names of too many places, you will want to **cut down the territory,** so that you are left with *a manageable number* of "targets" for your job-hunt.[17]

Let's take an example. Suppose you discovered that the career that interests you the most is *welding*. You want to be a welder. Well, that's a beginning. You've cut the 16 million U.S. job-markets down to:

- I want to work in a place
  that hires welders.

But the territory is still too large. There might be thousands of places in the country, that use welders. You can't go visit them all. So, you've got to cut down the territory, further. Suppose that on your Geography Petal you said that you really want to live and work in the San Jose area of California. That's helpful: that cuts down the territory further. Now your goal is:

- I want to work in a place
  that hires welders,
  within the San Jose area.

But, the territory is still too large. There could be 100, 200, 300 organizations that fit that description. So you look at your Flower Diagram for further help, and you notice that under *preferred working conditions* you said you wanted to work for an organization with fifty or fewer employees. Good, now your goal is:

---

17. If you resist this idea of *cutting down the territory*—if you feel you could be happy anywhere just as long as you were using your favorite skills—then almost no organization in the country can be ruled out. So if you aren't willing to take some steps to cut down the territory, then you'll have to go visit them all. Good luck! We'll see you in about forty-three years.

- I want to work in a place that hires welders,
  within the San Jose area,
  and has fifty or fewer employees.

This territory may still be too large. So you look again at your Flower Diagram for further guidance, and you see that on the Things Petal you said you wanted to work for an organization that works with, or produces, *wheels*. So now your statement of what you're looking for, becomes:

- I want to work in a place that hires welders,
  within the San Jose area,
  has fifty or fewer employees,
  and makes wheels.

Using your Flower Diagram, you can thus keep cutting down the territory, until the *"targets"* of your job-hunt are no more than ten places. That's a manageable number of places for you to *start with*. You can always expand the list later, if none of these ten turns out to be very promising or interesting.

Expanding the Territory

Sometimes your problem will be just the opposite. We come here to the second scenario: if your Informational Interviewing doesn't turn up enough names of places where you could get hired in your new career, then you're going to have to expand your list. You're going to have to consult some directories.

Your salvation is going to be the yellow pages of your local phone book. Look under every heading that is of any interest to you. Also, see if the local chamber of commerce publishes a business directory; often it will list not only small companies but also local divisions of larger companies, with names of department heads; sometimes they will even include the NAICS industry codes, should you care. If you are diligent here, you won't lack for names, believe me—unless it's a very small town you live in, in which case you'll need to cast your net a little wider, to include other towns or villages that are within commuting distance.

Once you have about *ten names* of organizations or businesses that might hire you for the kind of work you are dying to do, you proceed to our fourth and last question involved in naming your Flower:

- **QUESTION #4**

Among the places that I particularly like, **what needs do they have** or what outcomes are they trying to produce, that my skills and knowledge could help with?

Talk to people, that's the key! And if shyness is a problem for you, as it is for me (believe me!!), I have some helpful things to suggest about how to deal with that, on pages 44 to 49.

But I reiterate: to gather the information you will need, you must go talk to people.

Well and good, you may say, but how do you decide *which people*? Well, that's not as hard as it may seem. Let me give you an actual example of how it's done. (We'll take an actual career-changer's story, here.)

After our job-hunter did his Flower Diagram, it turned out that his top/favorite skill was: diagnosing, treating, or healing.

His three top/favorite *languages* or Fields of Fascination were: psychiatry, plants, and carpentry.

After showing five friends this information, and mulling over what they said, he concluded:

Among the nineteen *Job Families*, he was most attracted to Health diagnosing and treating practitioners.

Among the four *broad divisions of career-fields*, he was most attracted to Service industries.

Among the *three kinds of skills*, he most wanted to use his skills with people.

So far, so good. Now, where does he go from there?

He's going to have to go talk to people. But, how does he choose whom to talk to? Easy. He takes his favorite *languages* or Fields of Fascination, above—psychiatry, plants, and carpentry—and mentally translates them into *people* with those occupations: namely, a psychiatrist, a gardener, and a carpenter.

"Same career, change of career, same career . . . change of . . ."

Then he has to go find at least one of each. That's relatively easy: the yellow pages of the telephone directory will do, or he may know some of these among the friends or acquaintances he already has. What he wants to do, now, is go visit them and ask them: *how do you combine these three fields into one occupation?* He knows it may be a career that already exists, *or* it may be he will have to create this career for himself.

And, how does he decide which of these three to go interview *first*? He asks himself which of these persons is most likely to have the *largest overview. (This is often, but not always, the same as asking: who took the longest to get their training?)* The particular answer here: the psychiatrist.

He would then go see two or three psychiatrists—say, the head of the psychiatry department at the nearest colleges or universities,[18] and ask them: *Do you have any idea how to put these*

---

18. If there were no psychiatrists at any academic institution near him, then he would do all his research with psychiatrists in private practice—getting their names from the phone book—and asking them for, and paying for, a half session. This, if there is no other way.

The Three Secrets to Finding That Dream Job of Yours

three subjects—carpentry, plants, and psychiatry—together into one job or career? And if you don't know, who do you think might? He would keep going until he found someone who had a bright idea about how you put this all together.

In this particular case (*as I said, this is an actual career-changer's experience*), he was eventually told: "Yes, it can all be put together. There is a branch of psychiatry that uses plants to help heal people. That takes care of your interest in plants and psychiatry. As for your carpentry interests, I suppose you could use that to build the planters for your plants."

Chapter Thirteen

Informational Interviewing

There is a name for this process I have just described. It is called *Informational Interviewing*—a term I invented many many years ago. But it is sometimes, incorrectly, called *by other names*. Some even call this gathering of information *Networking*, which it is not.

To avoid this confusion, I have summarized in the chart on pages 342 and 343 just exactly what *Informational Interviewing* is, and how it differs from the other ways in which *people* can help and support you, during your job-hunt or career-change— namely, *Networking, Support Groups*, and *Contacts*. I have also thrown in, at no extra charge, a *first* column in that chart, dealing with an aspect of the job-hunt that *never* gets talked about: namely, the importance before your job-hunt ever begins, of *nurturing the friendships you have let slip*—by calling them or visiting them early on in your job-hunt—just reestablishing relationships *before* you ever need anything from them, as you most certainly may, later on in your job-hunt. The first column in the chart explains this further.

Talking to Workers, "Trying on" Jobs

When you go talk to people, you are hoping they will give you ideas, as we saw, about *what careers* will use your skills and *languages* or Fields of Fascination and interest.

That's the first step.

The second step is that you want also to get some idea of *what that work feels like, from the inside*.

The Process ▼	1. Valuing Your *Community* Before the Job-Hunt	2. Networking
What Is Its Purpose?	To make sure that people whom you may someday need to do you a favor, or lend you a hand, know long beforehand that you value and prize them *for themselves*.	To gather a list of contacts now who might be able to help you with your career, or with your job-hunting, at some future date. And to go out of your way to regularly add to that lis *Networking is a term often reserved onl for the business of adding to your list; but, obviously, this presupposes you first listed everyone you already know.*
Who Is It Done With?	Those who live with you, plus your family, relatives, friends, and acquaintances, however near (geographically) or far.	People in your present field, or in a field of future interest that you yourself meet; also, people whose names are given to you by others.
When You're Doing This Right How Do You Go About It? (Typical Activities)	You make time for them in your busy schedule, long before you find yourself job-hunting. You do this by: 1. Spending "quality time" with those you live with, letting them know you really appreciate who they are, and what kind of person they are. 2. Maintaining contact (phone, lunch, a thank-you note) with those who live nearby. 3. Writing friendly notes, regularly, to those who live at a distance— *thus letting them all know that you appreciate them* for themselves.	You deliberately attend, for this purpose, meetings or conventions in your present field, or the field/ career you are thinking of switching to, someday. You talk to people at meetings and at "socials," exchanging calling cards after a brief conversation. Occasionally, someone may sugges a name to you as you are about to set off for some distant city or place recommending that while you are there, you contact them. A phone call may be your best bet, with a follow-up letter after you return home, unless *they* invite *you* to lunc during the phone call. Asking *them* to lunch sometimes "bombs." (See below.)
When You've Really Botched This Up, What Are the Signs?	You're out of work, and you find yourself having to contact people that you haven't written or phoned in ages, suddenly asking them out of the blue for their help with your job-hunt. *The message inevitably read from this is that you don't really care about them at all, except when you can use them. Further, you get perceived as one who sees others only in terms of what they can do for you, rather than in a relationship that is "a two-way street."*	It's usually when you have ap- proached a very busy individual a asked them to have lunch with you If it is an aimless lunch, with no particular agenda—they ask durin lunch what you need to talk about and you lamely say, "Well, uh, I don't know, So-and-So just though we should get to know each other' —you will not be practicing *Networking*. You will be practicing *antagonizing*. Try to restrict your *Networking* to the telephone.

Guide to Relationships with Others

3. Developing a Support Group	4. Informational Interviewing	5. Using Contacts
To enlist some of your family or close friends specifically to help you with your emotional, social, and spiritual needs, when you are going through a difficult transition period, such as a job-hunt or career-change—so that you do not have to face this time all by yourself.	To screen careers *before you* change to them. To screen jobs *before* you take them, rather than afterward. To screen places *before* you decide you want to seek employment there. To find answers to *very specific questions* that occur to you during your job-hunt.	It takes, let us say, 77 pairs of eyes and ears to find a new job or career. Here you recruit those 76 other people (don't take me literally—it can be any number you choose) to be your eyes and ears—once you know what kind of work, what kind of place, what kind of job you are looking for, *and not before.*
You try to enlist people with one or more of the following qualifications: you feel comfortable talking to them; they will take initiative in calling you, on a regular basis; they are wiser than you are; and they can be a hard taskmaster, when you need one.	Workers, workers, workers. You *only* do informational interviewing with people actually doing the work that interests you as a potential new job or career for yourself.	Anyone and everyone who is on your "networking list." (See column 2.) It includes family, friends, relatives, high school alumni, college alumni, former co-workers, church/synagogue members, places where you shop, etc.
There should be three of them, at least. They may meet with you regularly, once a week, as a group, for an hour or two, to check on how you are doing. One or more of them should also be available to you on an "as needed" basis: the Listener, when you are feeling "down," and need to talk; the Initiator, when you are tempted to hide; the Wise One, when you are puzzled as to what to do next; and the Taskmaster, when your discipline is falling apart, and you need someone to encourage you to "get at it." It helps if there is also a Cheerleader among them, whom you can tell your victories to.	You get names of workers from your co-workers, from departments at local community colleges, or career offices. Once you have names, you call them and ask for a chance to talk to them *for twenty minutes.* You make a list, ahead of time, of all the questions you want answers to. If nothing occurs to you, try these: 1. How did you get into this line of work? Into this particular job? 2. What kinds of things do you like the most about this job? 3. What kinds of things do you like the least about this job? 4. Who else, doing this same kind of work, would you recommend I go talk to?	Anytime you're stuck, you ask your contacts for help *with specific information.* For example: When you can't find workers who are doing the work that interests you. When you can't find the names of places that do that kind of work. When you have a place in mind, but can't figure out the name of "the-person-who-has-the-power-to-hire-you." When you know that name, but can't get in to see that person. At such times, you call every contact you have on your Networking list, if necessary, until someone can tell you the specific answer you need.
You've "botched it" when you have no support group, no one to turn to, no one to talk to, and you feel that you are in this, all alone. You've "botched it" when you are waiting for your friends and family to notice how miserable you are, and to prove they love you by taking the initiative in coming after you; rather than, as is necessary with a support group, *your* choosing and recruiting them—asking them for their help and aid.	You're trying to use this with people-who-have-the-power-to-hire-you, rather than with *workers.* You're claiming you want information when really you have some other hidden agenda, with this person. (*P.S. They usually can smell the hidden agenda, a mile away.*) You've botched it, whenever you're telling a lie to someone. The whole point of informational interviewing is that it is a search for Truth.	Approaching your "contacts" too early in your job-hunt, and asking them for help only in the most general and vague terms: "John, I'm out of work. If you hear of anything, please let me know." *Any what thing?* You must do all your own homework *before* you approach your contacts. They will not do your homework for you.

In the previous example, you don't just want the job-title: *psychiatrist working with plants.* You want some feel for the substance that is underneath the title. In other words, you want to find out what the day-to-day work is like.

For this purpose you must leave your *interviewees,* and talk to actual people doing the work you think you'd love to do: in the particular example we have been discussing, you would have to go talk to *psychiatrists who actually use plants, in their healing work.*

Why do you want to ask them what the work feels like, from the inside? Well, in effect, you are mentally *trying on jobs* to see if they fit you.

It is exactly analogous to your going to a clothing store and trying on different suits (or dresses) that you see in their window or on their racks. Why do you try them on? Well, the suits or dresses that look *terrific* in the window don't always look so hotsy-totsy when you see them on *you.* Lots of pins were used, on the backside of the figurine in the window. On you, without the pins, the clothes don't hang quite right, etc., etc.

Likewise, the careers that *sound* terrific in books or in your imagination don't always look so great when you see them up close and personal, in all their living glory.

You need to know that. What you're ultimately trying to find is a career that looks terrific inside and out—in the window, *and* also on you. Essentially, you are asking what *this* job *feels* like. Here are some questions that will help *(you are talking, of course, with workers who are actually doing the career you think you might like to do)*:

- How did you get into this work?
- What do you like the most about it?
- What do you like the least about it?
- And, where else could I find people who do this kind of work? *(You should always ask them for more than one name, so that if you run into a dead end at any point, you can easily go back and visit the other names they suggested.)*

If it becomes apparent to you, during the course of any of these Informational Interviews, that this career, occupation, or job you were exploring definitely *doesn't* fit you, then the last question (above) gets turned into a different kind of inquiry:

- Do you have any ideas as to who else I could talk to, about my skills and Fields of Fascination or interests—so I can find out how they all might fit together, in one job or career?

Then go visit the people they suggest.

If they can't think of *anyone*, ask them if they know who *might* know. And so on. And so forth.

"They Say I Have to Go Back to School, but I Haven't the Time or the Money"

Next step: having found the names of jobs or careers that interest you, having mentally *tried them on* to see if they fit, you next want to find out *how much training, etc., it takes, to get into that field or career*. You ask the same people you have been talking to, previously.

More times than not, you will hear *bad news*. They will tell you something like: "In order to be hired for this job, you have to have a master's degree and ten years' experience at it."

If you're willing to do that, if you have the time, and the money, fine! But what if you don't? Then you search for *the exception*:

> *"Yes, but do you know of anyone in this field who got into it without that master's degree, and ten years' experience?*
> *And where might I find him or her?*
> *And if you don't know of any such person, who might know such information?"*

Throughout this Informational Interviewing, don't assume anything ("But I just assumed that. . . ."). Question *all* assumptions, no matter how many people tell you that "this is the way things are."

The Three Secrets to Finding That Dream Job of Yours

Keep clearly in mind that there are people *out there* who will tell you something that absolutely *isn't* so, with every conviction in their being—because they *think* it's true. Sincerity they have, 100 percent. Accuracy is something else again. You will need to check and cross-check any information that people tell you or that you read in books (even this one).

No matter how many people tell you that such-and-so are the rules about getting into a particular occupation, and there are no exceptions—believe me there *are* exceptions, to almost *every* rule, except where a profession has rigid entrance examinations, as in, say, medicine or law.

Rules are rules. But what you are counting on is that somewhere in this vast country, somewhere in this vast world, *somebody* found a way to get into this career you dream of, without going through all the hoops that everyone else is telling you are *absolutely essential.*

You want to find out who these people are, and go talk to them, to find out *how they did it.*

Okay, but suppose you are determined to go into a career that takes *years* to prepare for; and you can't find *anyone* who took a shortcut? What then?

Even here, you can get *close* to the profession *without* such long preparation. Every professional speciality has one or more *shadow* professions, which require much less training. For example, instead of becoming a doctor, you can go into paramedical work; instead of becoming a lawyer, you can go into paralegal work, instead of becoming a licensed career counselor, you can become a career coach.

Have a "Plan B"

Sooner or later, as you interview one person after another, you'll begin to get some definite ideas about a career that is of interest to you. It uses your favorite skills. It employs your favorite Fields of Fascination or fields of interest. You've interviewed people *actually doing that work*, and it all sounds fine. This part of your Informational Interviewing is over.

Just make sure that you get the names of at least *two* careers, or jobs, that you think you could be happy doing. Never, ever, put all your eggs in one basket. The secret of surviving out there in the jungle is *having alternatives.*

Be careful. Be thorough. Be persistent. This is your life you're working on, and your future. Make it glorious. Whatever it takes, find out the name of your ideal career, your ideal occupation, your ideal job—*or jobs.*

Eventually, you will get the names of careers that attract you, and after that, you will find the names of particular organizations that employ "people who can do *that.*" Do you rush right over? No. You research those places, first.

Researching Places Before You Approach Them

Why should you research places, before you approach them for a hiring-interview? Well, first of all, you want to know something about the organization from the inside: what kind of work they do there. And what their needs or problems or challenges are. And what kind of goals are they trying to achieve, what obstacles are they running into, and how can your skills and knowledges help them? *(When you do at last go in for a hiring-interview, you want above all else to be able to show them that you have something to offer, that they need.)*

Second, you want to find out if you would enjoy working there. You want to take the measure of that organization or organizations. Everybody takes the measure of an organization, but the problem with most job-hunters or career-changers is they take the measure of an organization *after* they are hired there.

In the U.S., for example, a survey of the federal/state employment service once found that 57 percent of those who found jobs through that service were not working at that job just thirty days later.

They were not working at that job just thirty days later, *because* they used the first ten or twenty days *on the job* to screen out that job.

By doing this research of a place ahead of time, you are choosing a better path, by far. Essentially, you are *screening out* careers, jobs, places *before* you commit to them. How sensible! How smart!

So, what you do is try to think of every way in the world that you can find out more about those organizations *(plural, not singular)* that interest you, *before you go to see if you can get hired there.* There are several ways you can do this research ahead of time.

- **What's on the Internet.** Many job-hunters or career-changers think that every organization, company, or nonprofit, has its own website, these days. Not true. Maybe they do, and maybe they don't. It often has to do with the size of the place, its access to a good Web designer, its desperation for customers, etc. Easy way to find out: if you have access to the Internet, type the name of the place into your favorite search engine (*Google, Metacrawler, Yahoo, or whatever*) and see what it turns up. Try more than one search engine.[19] Sometimes one knows something the others don't.

- **What's in Print.** The organization itself may have stuff in print, or on its website, about its business, purpose, etc. The CEO or head of the organization may have given talks. The organization may have copies of those talks. In addition, there may be brochures, annual reports, etc., that the organization has put out, about itself. How do you get ahold of these? The person who answers the phone is the person to check with, in small organizations. In larger organizations, the publicity office, or human relations office, is the place to check. Also, if it's a decent-sized organization that you are interested in, public libraries may have files on the organization—newspaper clippings, articles, etc. You never know; and it never hurts to ask your friendly neighborhood research librarian.

- **Friends and Neighbors.** Ask *everybody* you know, if they know anyone who works at the place that interests you. And, if they do, ask them if they could arrange for you and that person to get together, for lunch, coffee, or tea. At that time, tell them why the place interests you, and indicate you'd like to know more about it. (*It helps if your mutual friend is sitting there with the two of you, so the purpose of this little chat won't be misconstrued.*) This is the vastly preferred way to find out about a place. However, obviously you need a couple of additional alternatives up your sleeve, in case you run into a dead end here.

---

19. For more names of search engines, see Danny Sullivan's *SearchEngineWatch*, at `http://searchenginewatch.com/links/`. For tips on how to search, see `http://searchenginewatch.com/facts/`.

- **People at the Organizations in Question, or at Similar Organizations.** You can also go directly to organizations and ask questions about the place, but here I must caution you about several *dangers.*

First, you must make sure you're not asking them questions that are in print somewhere, which you could easily have read for yourself instead of bothering *them.*

Second, you must make sure that you approach the people at that organization *whose business it is to give out information—* receptionists, public relations people, "the personnel office," etc.—*before* you ever approach other people higher up in that organization.

Third, you must make sure that you approach *subordinates* rather than the top person in the place, if the subordinates would know the answer to your questions. Bothering the boss there with some simple questions that someone else could have answered is committing *job-hunting suicide.*

Fourth, you must make sure you're not using this approach simply as a sneaky way to get in to see the boss, and make a pitch for them hiring you. This is supposed to be just information gathering. Keep it at that. Keep it honest.

- **Temporary Agencies.** Many job-hunters and career-changers have found that a useful way to explore organizations is to go and work at a temporary agency. Employers turn to these agencies in order to find: a) job-hunters who can work part-time for a limited number of days; and b) job-hunters who can work full-time for a limited number of days. The advantage to you of temporary work is that if there is an agency that loans out people with your particular skills and expertise, you get a chance to be sent to a number of different employers over a period of several weeks, and see each one from the inside. Maybe the temp agency won't send you to exactly the place you hoped for; but sometimes you can develop contacts in the place you love, even while you're temporarily working somewhere else—if both organizations are in the same field.

As I said earlier, some of you may balk at the idea of enrolling with a temporary agency, because you remember the old days when such agencies were solely for clerical workers and secretarial help. But the field has seen an explosion of services in the last decade, and there are temporary agencies these days *(at least in the larger cities)* for many different occupations. In your city you may find temporary agencies for: accountants, industrial workers, assemblers, drivers, mechanics, construction people, engineering people, software engineers, programmers, computer technicians, production workers, management/executives, nannies (for young and old), health care/dental/medical people, legal specialists, insurance specialists, sales/marketing people, underwriting professionals, financial services, and the like, as well as for the more obvious specialties: data processing, secretarial, and office services. See your local phone book, under "Temporary Agencies."

- **Volunteer Work.** Another useful way to research a place before you ever ask them to hire you there, is to volunteer your services at that place that interests you. Of course, some places will turn your offer down, cold. But others will be interested. If they are, it will be relatively easy for you to talk them into letting you work there for a while, because you offer your services *without pay,* and for a brief, limited period of time. In other words, from their point of view, if you turn out to be a *pain*, they won't have to endure you for long.

In this fashion, you get a chance to learn about organizations from the inside. Not so coincidentally, if you do decide you would really like to work there, and permanently, they've had a chance to see you in action, and when you are about to end your volunteer time there, *may* want to hire you permanently. I say *may.* Don't be mad if they simply say, "Thanks very much for helping us out. Goodbye. Farewell." (That's what *usually* happens.) Even so, you've learned a lot, and this will stand you in good stead, in the future—as you approach other organizations.

Send a Thank-You Note

After *anyone* has done you a favor, during this Informational Interviewing phase of your job-hunt, you must *be sure* to send them a thank-you note by the very next day, at the latest. Such

a note goes to *everyone* who helps you, or who talks with you. That means friends, people at the organization in question, temporary agency people, secretaries, receptionists, librarians, workers, or whomever.

Ask them, at the time you are face-to-face with them, for their business card (if they have one), or ask them to write out their name and work address, on a piece of paper, for you. You *don't* want to misspell their name. It is difficult to figure out how to spell people's names, these days, simply from the sound of it. What sounds like "Laura" may actually be "Lara." What sounds like "Smith" may actually be "Smythe," and so on. Get that name and address, *but get it right,* please. And let me reiterate: write or e-mail the thank-you note that same night, or the very next day at the latest. A thank-you note that arrives a week later completely misses the point.

Ideally it should be e-mailed immediately, followed by a lovely printed copy, nicely formatted, and sent through the mail. Most employers these days prefer a printed letter to a handwritten one.

It can be just two or three sentences. Something like: *"I wanted to thank you for talking with me yesterday. It was very helpful to me. I much appreciated your taking the time out of your busy schedule to do this. Best wishes to you,"* and then your signature. *Do* sign it, particularly if the thank-you note is printed. Printed letters sent through the mail without any signature seem to be multiplying like rabbits in the world of work, these days; the absence of a signature on anything other than an e-mailed thank-you note is usually perceived as making your letter *real* impersonal. You don't want to leave that impression.

What If I Get Offered a Job Along the Way, While I'm Just Gathering Information?

You probably won't. Let me remind you that during this information gathering, you are *not* talking primarily to employers. You're talking to workers.

Nonetheless, an occasional employer *may* stray across your path during all this Informational Interviewing. And that employer *may* be so impressed with the carefulness you're showing, in going about your career-change and job-search, that they want to hire you, on the spot. So, it's *possible* that you might get offered a job while you're still doing your information gathering. Not *likely*, but *possible*. And if that happens, what should you say?

Well, if you're desperate, you will of course say *yes*. I remember one wintertime when I had just gone through the knee of my last pair of pants, we were burning old pieces of furniture in our fireplace to stay warm, the legs on our bed had just broken, and we were eating spaghetti until it was coming out our ears. In such a situation, *of course* you say yes.

But if you're not *desperate*, if you have a little time to be more careful, then you respond to the job-offer in a way that will buy you some time. You tell them what you're doing: that the average job-hunter tries to screen a job *after* they take it. But you are doing what you are *sure* this employer would do if they were in your shoes: you are examining careers, fields, industries, jobs, organizations *before* you decide where you can do your best and most effective work.

And you tell them that since your Informational Interviewing isn't finished yet, it would be premature for you to accept their job offer, until you're *sure* that this is the place where you could be most effective, and do your best work.

But, you add: "Of course, I'm tickled pink that you would want me to be working here. And when I've finished my personal survey, I'll be glad to get back to you about this, as my preliminary impression is that this is the kind of place I'd like to work in, and the kind of people I'd like to work for, and the kind of people I'd like to work with."

In other words, *if you're not desperate yet*, you don't walk immediately through any opened doors; but neither do you allow them to shut.

Chapter Thirteen

CONCLUSION:

When a Dream Job Isn't Enough:

The Search for a Deeper Sense of Mission

The search for a *dream job* is, on its surface, a search for greater happiness. Most of us embark on this search because we want to be happier. We want to be happier in both our *work* and our *life*.

But some of us want even more.

We want to be happier in our *soul*.

Though others do not believe, we do. And we want our faith to be a part of our *dream*. Hence, no discussion of *work happiness* can be complete—for us—unless we also find *soul happiness*. Unless we find some sense of *mission* for our life.

That is the subject of our concluding chapter. Next.

How to Find Your Mission in Life

GOD AND ONE'S VOCATION

FOREWORD

As I started writing this chapter, I toyed at first with the idea of following what might be described as an "all-paths approach" to religion: trying to stay as general and nonspecific as I could. But, after much thought, I decided not to try that. This, because I have read many other writers who tried, and I felt the approach failed miserably. An "all-paths" approach to religion ends up being a "no-paths" approach, even as a woman or man who tries to please everyone ends up pleasing no one. It is the old story of the "universal" vs. the "particular."

Those of us who do career counseling could predict, ahead of time, that trying to stay universal is not likely to be helpful, in writing about faith. We know well from our own field that truly helpful career counseling depends upon defining the **particularity** or uniqueness of each person we try to help. No employer wants to know what you have in common with everyone else. He or she wants to know what makes you unique and individual. As I have argued throughout this book, the inventory of your uniqueness or *particularity* is crucial if you are ever to find meaningful work.

This particularity invades *everything* a person does; it is not suddenly "jettisonable" when he or she turns to matters of faith. Therefore, when I or anyone else writes about faith I believe we **must** write out of our own particularity—which *starts*, in my case, with the fact that I write, and think, and breathe as a Christian—as you might expect from the fact that I was an ordained Episcopalian minister for many years. Understandably, then, this chapter speaks from a Christian perspective. I want you to be aware of that, at the outset.

Balanced against this is the fact that I have always been acutely sensitive to the fact that this is a pluralistic society in which we live, and that I in particular owe a great deal to my readers who have religious convictions quite different from my own. It has turned out that the people who work or have worked here in my office with me, over the years, have been predominantly of other faiths. Furthermore, *Parachute*'s more than 9 million readers have not only included Christians of every variety and persuasion, Christian Scientists, Jews, members of the Baha'i faith, Hindus, Buddhists, adherents of Islam, but also believers in "new age" religions, secularists, humanists, agnostics, atheists, and many others. I have therefore tried to be very courteous toward the feelings of all my readers, *while at the same time* counting on them to translate my Christian thought forms into their own. This ability to thus translate is the indispensable *sine qua non* of anyone who wants to communicate helpfully with others in this pluralistic society of ours.

In the Judeo-Christian tradition from which I come, one of the indignant Biblical questions is, "Has God forgotten to be gracious?" The answer was a clear "No." I think it is important *for all of us* also to seek the same goal. I have therefore labored to make this chapter gracious as well as thought-provoking. ⠀⠀⠀⠀⠀⠀⠀⠀⠀⠀⠀⠀⠀⠀R.N.B

Turning Point

For many of us, the job-hunt offers a chance to make some fundamental changes in our whole life. It marks a turning point in how we live our life.

It gives us a chance to ponder and reflect, to extend our mental horizons, to go deeper into the subsoil of our soul.

It gives us a chance to wrestle with the question, "Why am I here on Earth?" We don't want to feel that we are just another grain of sand lying on the beach called humanity, unnumbered and lost in the billions of other human beings.

We want to do more than plod through life, going to work, coming home from work. We want to find that special joy, "that no one can take from us," which comes from having a sense of Mission in our life.

We want to feel we were put here on Earth for some special purpose, to do some unique work that only we can accomplish.

We want to know what our Mission is.

The Meaning of the Word "Mission"

When used with respect to our life and work *Mission* has always been a religious concept, from beginning to end. It is defined by *Webster's* as "a continuing task or responsibility that one is destined or fitted to do or specially called upon to undertake," and historically has had two major synonyms: *Calling* and *Vocation*. These, of course, are the same word in two different languages, English and Latin. Both imply God. To be given a Vocation or Calling implies *Someone who* calls. To have a Destiny implies *Someone who determined the destination for us*. Thus, the concept of Mission lands us inevitably in the lap of God, before we have hardly begun.

I emphasize this, because there is an increasing trend in our culture to try to speak about religious subjects without reference to God. This is true of "spirituality," "soul," and "Mission," in particular. More and more books talk about Mission as though it were simply "a purpose you choose for your own life, by identifying your enthusiasms."

This attempt to obliterate all reference to God from the originally religious concept of Mission, is particularly ironic because the proposed substitute word—enthusiasms—is derived from two Greek words, "en theos," and means "God in us."

In the midst of this "redefining culture" we find an oasis called the "job-hunting field." It is a field that was raised on a firm concept of "God." That's because most of its inventors, most of its leaders over the years—the late John Crystal, Arthur Miller, Ralph Mattson, Tom and Ellie Jackson, Bernard Haldane, Arthur and Marie Kirn, myself, and many others—have been people who believe firmly in God, and came into this field because we think about Him a lot, in connection with meaningful work.

Nor are we alone. Many many job-hunters also think about God a lot. In the U.S., 94 percent of us believe in God, 90 percent of us pray, 88 percent of us believe God loves us, and 33 percent of us report we have had a life-changing religious experience—and these figures have remained virtually unchanged for the past fifty years, according to opinion polls conducted by the Gallup Organization. (*The People's Religion: American Faith in the '90s*. Macmillan & Co. 1989.)

What is not so clear is whether we think about God in connection with our work. Often these two subjects—spiritual beliefs and work—live in separate mental ghettos within the same person's head.

But unemployment offers us a chance to fix all that: to marry our work and our religious beliefs together, to talk about Calling, and Vocation, and Mission in life—to think out why we are here, and what plans God has for us.

That's why a period of unemployment can absolutely change our life.

The Secret of Finding Your Mission in Life: Taking It in Stages

I will explain the steps toward finding your Mission in life that I have learned in my seventy-eight years on Earth. Just remember two things. First, I speak from a Christian perspective, and trust you to translate this into your own thought-forms.

Second, I know that these steps are not the only Way—by any means. Many people have discovered their Mission by taking other paths. And you may, too. But hopefully what I have to say may shed some light upon whatever path you take.

I have learned that if you want to figure out what your Mission in life is, it will likely take some time. It is not a *problem* to be solved in a day and a night. It is a *learning process* that has steps to it, much like the process by which we all learned to eat. As a baby we did not tackle adult food right off. As we all recall, there were three stages: first there had to be the mother's milk or bottle, then strained baby foods, and finally—after teeth and time—the stuff that grownups chew. Three stages—and the two earlier stages were not to be disparaged. It was all Eating, just different forms of Eating—appropriate to our development at the time. But each stage had to be mastered, in turn, before the next could be approached.

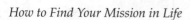

There are usually three stages also to learning what your Mission in life is, and the two earlier stages are likewise not to be disparaged. It is all "Mission"—just different forms of Mission, appropriate to your development at the time. But each stage has to be mastered, in turn, before the next can be approached.

Of course, there is a sense in which you never master any of these stages, but are always growing in understanding and mastery of them, throughout your whole life here on Earth.

As it has been impressed on me by observing many people over the years (admittedly through *Christian spectacles*), it appears that the three parts to your Mission here on Earth can be defined generally as follows:

1. *Your first Mission here on Earth* is one that you share with the rest of the human race, but it is no less your individual Mission for the fact that it is shared: and it is, **to seek to stand hour by hour in the conscious presence of God, the One from whom your Mission is derived.** *The Missioner before the Mission*, is the rule. In religious language, your Mission here is: *to know God, and enjoy Him forever, and to see His hand in all His works.*

2. Second, once you have begun doing that in an earnest way, *your second Mission here on Earth* is also one that you share with the rest of the human race, but it is no less your individual mission for the fact that it is shared: and that is, **to do what you can, moment by moment, day by day, step by step, to make this world a better place, following the leading and guidance of God's Spirit within you and around you.**

3. Third, once you have begun doing that in a serious way, *your third Mission here on Earth* is one that is uniquely yours, and that is:

a) **to exercise that Talent that you particularly came to Earth to use—your greatest gift, which you most delight to use,**

b) **in the place(s) or setting(s) that God has caused to appeal to you the most,**

c) **and for those purposes that God most needs to have done in the world.**

Chapter Fourteen

When fleshed out, and spelled out, I think you will find that there you have the definition of your Mission in life. Or, to put it another way, these are the three Missions that you have in life.

The Two Rhythms of the Dance of Mission: Unlearning, Learning, Unlearning, Learning

The distinctive characteristic of these three stages is that in each we are forced to *let go* of some fundamental assumptions that the world has *falsely* taught us, about the nature of our Mission. In other words, throughout this quest and at each stage we find ourselves engaged not merely in a process of *Learning*. We are also engaged in a process of *Un*learning. Thus, we can restate the above three Learnings, in terms of what we also need to *un*learn at each stage:

• We need in the first Stage to *un*learn the idea that our Mission is primarily to keep busy *doing* something (here on Earth), and learn instead that our Mission is first of all to keep busy *being* something (here on Earth). In Christian language (and others as well), we might say that we were sent here to learn how *to be* sons of God, and daughters of God, before anything else. *"Our Father, who art in heaven. . . ."*

• In the second stage, "Being" issues into "Doing." At this stage, we need to *un*learn the idea that everything about our Mission must be *unique* to us, and learn instead that some parts of our Mission here on Earth are *shared* by all human beings: e.g., we were all sent here to bring more gratitude, more kindness, more forgiveness, and more love, into the world. We share this Mission because the task is too large to be accomplished by just one individual.

• We need in the third stage to *un*learn the idea that the part of our Mission that is truly unique, and most truly ours, is something Our Creator just *orders* us to do, without any agreement from our spirit, mind, and heart. (On the other hand, neither is it something that each of us chooses and then merely asks God to bless.) We need to learn that God so honors our free will, that He has ordained our unique Mission be something that we have some part in choosing.

• In this third stage we need also to *un*learn the idea that our unique Mission must consist of some achievement for all the world will see—and learn instead that as the stone does not always know what ripples it has caused in the pond whose surface it impacts, so neither we nor those who watch our life will always know *what we have achieved* by our life and by our Mission. *It may be* that by the grace of God we helped bring about a profound change for the better in the lives of other souls around us, but it also may be that this takes place beyond our sight, or after we have gone on. And we may never know what we have accomplished, until we see Him face to face after this life is past.

• Most finally, we need to *un*learn the idea that what we have accomplished is our doing, and ours alone. It is God's Spirit breathing in us and through us that helps us to do whatever we do, and so the singular first person pronoun is never appropriate, but only the plural. Not "*I* accomplished this" but "*We* accomplished this, God and I, working together. . . ."

That should give you a general overview. But I would like to add some random comments on my part about each of these three Missions of ours here on Earth.

Some Random Comments About Your First Mission in Life

Your first Mission here on Earth is one that you share with the rest of the human race, but it is no less your individual Mission for the fact that it is shared: and that is, **to seek to stand hour by hour in the conscious presence of God, the One from whom your Mission is derived.** The Missioner before the Mission, is the rule. In religious language, your Mission is: to know God, and enjoy Him forever, and to see His hand in all His works.

Comment 1:
How We Might Think of God

Each of us has to go about this primary Mission according to the tenets of his or her own particular religion. But I will speak what I know out of the context of my own particular faith, and you may perhaps translate and apply it to yours. I will speak as a Christian, who believes (passionately) that Christ is the Way and the Truth and the Life. But I also believe, with St. Peter, "that God shows no partiality, but in every nation any one who fears Him and does what is right is acceptable to Him" (Acts 10:34–35).

Now, Jesus claimed many unique things about Himself and His Mission; but He also spoke of Himself as the great prototype for us all. He called Himself "the Son of Man," and He said, "I assure you that the man who believes in me will do the same things that I have done, yes, and he will do even greater things than these. . . ." (John 14:12).

Emboldened by His identification of us with His Life and His Mission, we might want to remember how He spoke about His Life here on Earth. He put it in this context: **"I came from the Father and have come into the world; again, I am leaving the world and going to the Father"** (John 16:28).

If there is a sense in which this is, in even the faintest way, true also of our lives (and I shall say in a moment in what sense I think it is true), then instead of calling our great Creator "God" or "Father" right off, we might begin our approach to the subject of religion by referring to the One Who gave us our Mission and sent us to this planet not as "God" or "Father" but—*just to help our thinking*—as: **"The One From Whom We Came and The One To Whom We Shall Return,"** when this life is done.

If our life here on Earth is to be at all like Christ's, then this is a true way to think about the One Who gave us our Mission. We are not some kind of eternal, preexistent *being*. We are **creatures,** who once did not exist, and then came into Being, and continue to have our Being, only at the will of our great Creator. But as creatures we are both body and soul; although we know our body was created in our mother's womb, our soul's origin is a great mystery. Where it came from, at what moment the Lord created it, is something we cannot know. It is not unreasonable to suppose, however, that the great God created our *soul* before it entered our body, and in that sense we did indeed stand before God before we were born; and He is indeed **"The One From Whom We Came and The One To Whom We Shall Return."**

Therefore, before we go searching for "what work was I sent here to do?" we need to establish—or in a truer sense *reestablish*—contact with this **"One From Whom We Came and The One To Whom We Shall Return."** Without this reaching out of the creature to the great Creator, without this reaching out of *the creature with a Mission* to *the One Who Gave Us That Mission*, the question *what* is my Mission in life? is void and null. The *what* is rooted in the *Who;* absent the Personal, one cannot meaningfully discuss The Thing. It is like the adult who cries, "I want to get married," without giving any consideration to *who* it is they want to marry.

Comment 2:
How We Might Think of Religion or Faith

In light of this larger view of our creatureliness, we can see that *religion* or *faith* is not a question of whether or not we choose to (*as it is so commonly put*) "have a relationship with God." Looking at our life in a larger context than just our life here on Earth, it becomes apparent that some sort of relationship with God is a given for us, about which we have absolutely no choice. God and we **were** and **are** related, during the time of our soul's existence before our birth and in the time of our soul's continued existence after our death. The only choice we have is what to do about **The Time In Between,** i.e., what we want the nature of our relationship with God to be during our time here on Earth and how that will affect the *nature* of the relationship, then, after death.

One of the corollaries of all this is that by the very act of being born into a human body, it is inevitable that we undergo a kind of *amnesia*—an amnesia that typically embraces not only our nine months in the womb, our baby years, and almost one-third of each day (sleeping), but more important any memory of our origin or our destiny. We wander on Earth as an amnesia victim. To seek after Faith, therefore, is to seek to climb back out of that amnesia. Religion or faith is **the hard reclaiming of knowledge we once knew as a certainty.**

Comment 3:
The First Obstacle to Executing This Mission

This first Mission of ours here on Earth is not the easiest of Missions, simply because it is the first. Indeed, in many ways, it is the most difficult. All can see is that our life here on Earth is a very physical life. We eat, we drink, we sleep, we long to be held, and to hold. We inherit a physical body, with very physical appetites, we walk on the physical earth, and we acquire physical possessions. It is the most alluring of temptations, *in our amnesia*, to come up with just a *Physical* interpretation of this life: to think that the Universe is merely interested in the survival of species. Given this interpretation, the story of our individual life could be simply told: we are born, grow up, procreate, and die.

But we are ever recalled to do what we came here to do: that without rejecting the joy of the Physicalness of this life, such as the love of the blue sky and the green grass, we are to reach out beyond all this to **recall** and recover a *Spiritual* interpretation of our life. *Beyond* the physical and *within* the physicalness of this life, to detect a Spirit and a Person from beyond this Earth who is with us and in us—the very real and loving and awesome Presence of the great Creator from whom we came—and the One to whom we once again shall go.

Comment 4:
The Second Obstacle to Executing This Mission

It is one of the conditions of our earthly amnesia and our creatureliness that, sadly enough, some very *human* and very *rebellious* part of us *likes* the idea of living in a world where we can be our own god—and therefore loves the purely Physical interpretation of life, and finds it *anguish* to relinquish it. Traditional Christian vocabulary calls this **"sin"** and has a lot to say about the difficulty it poses for this first part of our Mission. All who live a thoughtful life know that it is true: our greatest enemy in carrying out this first Mission of ours is indeed *our own* heart and our own rebellion.

Comment 5:
Further Thoughts About
What Makes Us Special and Unique

As I said earlier, many of us come to this issue of our Mission in life, because we want to feel that we are unique. And what we mean by that, is that we hope to discover some "specialness" intrinsic to us, which is our birthright, and which no one can take from us. What we, however, discover from a thorough exploration of this topic, is that we are indeed special—but only because God thinks us so. Our specialness and uniqueness reside in Him, and His love, rather than in anything intrinsic to our own *being*. The proper appreciation of this distinction causes our feet to carry us in the end not to the City called Pride, but to the Temple called Gratitude.

> What is religion? Religion is the service of God out of grateful love for what God has done for us. The Christian religion, more particularly, is the service of God out of grateful love for what God has done for us in Christ.
>
> Phillips Brooks, author of
> *O Little Town of Bethlehem*

Comment 6:
The Unconscious Doing
of the Work We Came to Do

You may have *already* wrestled with this first part of your Mission here on Earth. You may not have called it that. You may have called it simply "learning to believe in God." But if you ask what your Mission is in life, this one was and is the precondition of all else that you came here to do. Absent this Mission, it is folly to talk about the rest. So, if you have been seeking faith, or seeking to strengthen your faith, you have—willy-nilly—already been about *the doing of the Mission you were given*. Born into **This Time In Between,** you have found His hand again, and reclasped it. You are therefore ready to go on with His Spirit to tackle together what you came here to do—the other parts of your Mission.

Some Random Comments About Your Second Mission in Life

Your second Mission here on Earth is also one that you share with the rest of the human race, but it is no less your individual Mission for the fact that it is shared: and that is, **to do what you can moment by moment, day by day, step by step, to make this world a better place—following the leading and guidance of God's Spirit within you and around you.**

Comment 1:
The Uncomfortableness of One Step at a Time

Imagine yourself out walking in your neighborhood one night, and suddenly you find yourself surrounded by such a dense fog, that you have lost your bearings and cannot find your way. Suddenly, a friend appears out of the fog, and asks you to put your hand in theirs, and they will lead you home. And you, not being able to tell where you are going, trustingly follow them, even though you can only see one step at a time. Eventually you arrive safely home, filled with gratitude. But as you reflect upon the experience the next day, you realize how unsettling it was to have to keep walking when you could see only one step at a time, even though you had guidance you knew you could trust.

Now I have asked you to imagine all of this, because this is the essence of the second Mission to which *you* are called—and *I* am called—in this life. It is all very different than we had imagined. When the question, *"What is your Mission in life?"* is first broached, and we have put our hand in God's, as it were, we imagine that we will be taken up to *some mountaintop*, from which we can see far into the distance. And that we will hear a voice in our ear, saying, "Look, look, see that distant city? That is the goal of your Mission; that is where everything is leading, every step of your way."

But instead of the mountaintop, we find ourself in *the valley*—wandering often in a fog. And the voice in our ear says something quite different from what we thought we would hear. It says, **"Your Mission is to take one step at a time, even when you don't yet see where it all is leading, or what the Grand Plan is, or what your overall Mission in life is. Trust Me; I will lead you."**

Comment 2:
The Nature of this Step-by-Step Mission

As I said, in every situation you find yourself, you have been sent here to do whatever you can—moment by moment—that will bring more gratitude, more kindness, more forgiveness, more honesty, and more love into this world.

There are dozens of such moments every day. Moments when you stand—as it were—at a spiritual crossroads, with two ways lying before you. Such moments are typically called **"moments of decision."** It does not matter what the frame or content of each particular decision is. It all devolves, in the end, into just two roads before you, *every time.* **The one** will lead to *less* gratitude, *less* kindness, *less* forgiveness, *less* honesty, or *less* love in the world. **The other** will lead to *more* gratitude, *more* kindness, *more* forgiveness, *more* honesty, or *more* love in the world. Your Mission, each moment, is to seek to choose the latter spiritual road, rather than the former, *every time.*

Comment 3:
Some Examples of this Step-by-Step Mission

I will give a few examples, so that the nature of this part of your Mission may be unmistakably clear.

You are out on the freeway, in your car. Someone has gotten into the wrong lane, to the right of *your* lane, and needs to move over into the lane you are in. You *see* their need to cut in, ahead of you. **Decision time.** In your mind's eye you see two spiritual roads lying before you: the one leading to less kindness in the world (you speed up, to shut this driver out, and don't let them move over), the other leading to more kindness in the world (you let the driver cut in). **Since you know this is part of your Mission, part of the reason why you came to Earth, your**

calling is clear. **You know which road to take, which decision to make.**

You are hard at work at your desk, when suddenly an interruption comes. The phone rings, or someone is at the door. They
need something from you, a question of some of your time and
attention. **Decision time.** In your mind's eye you see two spiritual roads lying before you: the one leading to less love in the
world (you tell them you're just too busy to be bothered), the
other leading to more love in the world (you put aside your
work, decide that God may have sent this person to you, and
say, "Yes, what can I do to help you?"). **Since you know this is
part of your Mission, part of the reason why you came to
Earth, your calling is clear. You know which road to take,
which decision to make.**

Your mate does something that hurts your feelings. **Decision
time.** In your mind's eye you see two spiritual roads lying before
you: the one leading to less forgiveness in the world (you institute an icy silence between the two of you, and think of how you
can punish them or otherwise get even), the other leading to more
forgiveness in the world (you go over and take them in your arms,
speak the truth about your hurt feelings, and assure them of
your love). **Since you know this is part of your Mission, part
of the reason why you came to Earth, your calling is clear.
You know which road to take, which decision to make.**

You have not behaved at your most noble, recently. And now you are face to face with someone who asks you a question about what happened. **Decision time.** In your mind's eye you see two spiritual roads lying before you: the one leading to less honesty in the world (you lie about what happened, or what you were feeling, because you fear losing their respect or their love), the other leading to more honesty in the world (you tell the truth, together with how you feel about it, in retrospect). **Since you know this is part of your Mission, part of the reason why you came to Earth, your calling is clear. You know which road to take, which decision to make.**

Comment 4:
The Spectacle That Makes the Angels Laugh

It is necessary to explain this part of our Mission in some detail, because so many times you will see people wringing their hands, and saying, "*I want to know what my Mission in life is,*" all the while they are cutting people off on the highway, refusing to give time to people, punishing their mate for having hurt their feelings, and lying about what they did. And it will seem to you that the angels must laugh to see this spectacle. *For these people wringing their hands*, their Mission was right there, on the freeway, in the interruption, in the hurt, and at the confrontation.

Comment 5:
The Valley Versus the Mountaintop

At some point in your life your Mission may involve some grand *mountaintop experience*, where you say to yourself, "This, this, is why I came into the world. I know it. I know it." *But until then*, your Mission is here in *the valley*, and the fog, and the little callings moment by moment, day by day. More to the point, it is likely you cannot ever get to your mountaintop Mission unless you have first exercised your stewardship faithfully in the valley.

It is an ancient principle, to which Jesus alluded often, that if you don't use the information the Universe has already given you, you cannot expect it will give you any more. If you aren't being faithful in small things, how can you expect to be given charge over larger things? (Luke 16:10–12; 19:11–24). If you aren't trying to bring more gratitude, kindness, forgiveness, honesty, and love into the world each day, you can hardly expect that you will be entrusted with the Mission to help bring peace into the world or anything else large and important. If we do not live out our day-by-day Mission in the valley, we cannot expect we are yet ready for a larger *mountaintop* Mission.

Comment 6:
The Importance of Not Thinking of This Mission as "Just a Training Camp"

The valley is not just a kind of "training camp." There is in your imagination even now an invisible *spiritual* mountaintop to which you may go, if you wish to see where all this is leading. And what will you see there, in the imagination of your heart, but the goal toward which all this is pointed: **that Earth might be more like heaven. That human life might be more like God's.** That is the large achievement toward which all our day-by-day Missions *in the valley* are moving. This is a *large* order, but it is accomplished by faithful attention to the doing of our great Creator's **will** in little things as well as in large. It is much like the building of the pyramids in Egypt, which was accomplished by the dragging of a lot of individual pieces of stone by a lot of individual men.

The valley, the fog, the going step by step, is no mere training camp. The goal is real, however large. **"Thy Kingdom come, Thy will be done, on Earth, as it is in heaven."**

Some Random Comments About Your Third Mission in Life

Your third Mission here on Earth is one that is uniquely yours, and that is:

a) **to exercise the Talent that you particularly came to Earth to use—your greatest gift that you most delight to use,**

b) **in those place(s) or setting(s) that God has caused to appeal to you the most,**

c) **and for those purposes that God most needs to have done in the world.**

Comment 1:
Our Mission Is Already Written, "in Our Members"

It is customary in trying to identify this part of our Mission, to advise that we should ask God, in prayer, to speak to us—and **tell us** plainly what our Mission is. We look for a voice in the air, a thought in our head, a dream in the night, a sign in the events of the day, to reveal this thing that is otherwise *(it is said)* completely hidden. Sometimes, from just such answered prayer, people do indeed discover what their Mission is, beyond all doubt and uncertainty.

But having to wait for the voice of God to reveal what our Mission is, is not the truest picture of our situation. St. Paul, in Romans, speaks of a law "written in our members"—and this phrase has a telling application to the question of **how** God reveals to each of us our unique Mission in life. Read again the definition of our third Mission (above) and you will see: the clear implication of the definition is that God has **already** revealed His will to us concerning our vocation and Mission, by causing it to be "**written in our members.**" We are to begin deciphering our unique Mission by studying our talents and skills, and more particularly which ones (or One) we most rejoice to use.

God actually has written His will *twice* in our members: *first in the talents* that He lodged there, and second *in His guidance of our heart*, as to which talent gives us the greatest pleasure from its exercise **(it is usually the one that, when we use it, causes us to lose all sense of time).**

Even as the anthropologist can examine ancient inscriptions, and divine from them the daily life of a long-lost people, so we by examining **our talents** and **our heart** can *more often than we* *dream* divine the Will of the Living God. For true it is, our Mission is not something He **will** reveal; it is something He **has already** revealed. It is not to be found written in the sky; it is to be found written in our members.

Comment 2:
Career Counseling: We Need You

Arguably, our first two Missions in life could be learned from religion alone—without any reference whatsoever to career counseling, the subject of this book. Why then should career counseling claim that this question about our Mission in life is its proper concern, *in any way?*

It is when we come to this third Mission, which hinges so crucially on the question of our Talents, skills, and gifts, that we see the answer. If you've read the body of this book, before turning to this chapter, then you know without my even saying it, how much the identification of Talents, gifts, or skills is the province of career counseling. Its expertise, indeed its *raison d'être*, lies precisely in the identification, classification, and (forgive me) "prioritization" of Talents, skills, and gifts. To put the matter quite simply, career counseling knows how to do this better than any other discipline—**including** traditional religion. This is not a defect of religion, but the fulfillment of something Jesus promised: "When the Spirit of truth comes, He will guide you into all truth" (John 16:12). Career counseling is part (we may hope) of that promised late-coming truth. It can therefore be of inestimable help to the pilgrim who is trying to figure out what their greatest, and most enjoyable, Talent is, as a step toward identifying their unique Mission in life.

If career counseling needs religion as its helpmate in the first two stages of identifying our Mission in life, religion repays the compliment by clearly needing career counseling as **its** helpmate here in the third stage.

And this place where you are in your life right now—facing the job-hunt and all its anxiety—is the perfect time to seek the union within your own mind and heart of both career counseling (as in the pages of this book) and your faith in God.

Comment 3:
How Our Mission Got Chosen:
A Scenario for the Romantic

It is a mystery that we cannot fathom, in this life at least, as to why one of us has this Talent, and the other one has that; why God chose to give one gift—and Mission—to one person, and a different gift—and Mission—to another. Since we do not know, and in some degree cannot know, we are certainly left free to speculate, and imagine.

We may imagine that before we came to Earth, our souls, *our Breath, our Light*, stood before the great Creator and volunteered for this Mission. And God and we, together, chose what that Mission would be and what particular gifts would be needed, which He then agreed to give us, after our birth. Thus, our Mission was not a command given preemptorily by an unloving Creator to a reluctant slave without a vote, but was a task jointly designed by us both, in which as fast as the great Creator said, **"I wish"** our hearts responded, **"Oh, yes."** As mentioned in an earlier comment, it may be helpful to think of the condition of our becoming human as that we became amnesiac about any consciousness our soul had before birth—and therefore amnesiac about the nature or manner in which our Mission was designed.

Our searching for our Mission now is therefore a searching to recover the memory of something we ourselves had a part in designing.

I am admittedly a hopeless romantic, so of course I like this picture. If you also are a hopeless romantic, you may like it, too. There's also the chance that it just may be true. We will not know until we see Him face to face.

Comment 4:
Mission as Intersection

There are all different kinds of voices calling you to all different kinds of work, and the problem is to find out which is the voice of God rather than that of society, say, or the superego, or self-interest. By and large a good rule for finding out is this: the kind of work God usually calls you to is the kind of work a) that you need most to do and b) the world most needs to have done. If you really get a kick out of your work, you've presumably met requirement a), but if your work is writing TV deodorant commercials, the chances are you've missed requirement b). On the other hand, if your work is being a doctor in a leper colony, you have probably met b), but if most of the time you're bored and depressed by it, the chances are you haven't only bypassed a) but probably aren't helping your patients much either. Neither the hair shirt nor the soft birth will do. **The place God calls you to is the place where your deep gladness and the world's deep hunger meet.**

Fred Buechner

Wishful Thinking—A Theological ABC

Comment 5:
Examples of Mission as Intersection

Your unique and individual Mission will most likely turn out to be a mission of Love, acted out in one or all of three arenas: either in the Kingdom of the Mind, whose goal is to bring more Truth into the world; or in the Kingdom of the Heart, whose goal is to bring more Beauty into the world; or in the Kingdom of the Will, whose goal is to bring more Perfection into the world, through Service.

Here are some examples:

"My mission is, out of the rich reservoir of love that God seems to have given me, to nurture and show love to others—most particularly to those who are suffering from incurable diseases."

"My mission is to draw maps for people to show them how to get to God."

"My mission is to create the purest foods I can, to help people's bodies not get in the way of their spiritual growth."

"My mission is to make the finest harps I can so that people can hear the voice of God in the wind."

"My mission is to make people laugh, so that the travail of this earthly life doesn't seem quite so hard to them."

"My mission is to help people know the truth, in love, about what is happening out in the world, so that there will be more honesty in the world."

"My mission is to weep with those who weep, so that in my arms they may feel themselves in the arms of that Eternal Love that sent me and that created them."

"My mission is to create beautiful gardens, so that in the lilies of the field people may behold the Beauty of God and be reminded of the Beauty of Holiness."

Comment 6:
Life as Long as Your Mission Requires

Knowing that you came to Earth for a reason, and knowing what that Mission is, throws an entirely different light upon your life from now on. You are, generally speaking, delivered from any further fear about how long you have to live. You may settle it in your heart that you are here until God chooses to think that you have accomplished your Mission, or until God has a greater Mission for you in another Realm. You need to be a good steward of what He has given you, while you are here; but you do not need to be an anxious steward or stewardess.

You need to attend to your health, *but you do not need to constantly worry about it*. You need to meditate on your death, *but you do not need to be constantly preoccupied with it*. To paraphrase the glorious words of G. K. Chesterton: **"We now have a strong desire for living combined with a strange carelessness about dying. We desire life like water and yet are ready to drink death like wine."** We know that we are here to do what we came to do, and we need not worry about anything else.

Final Comment:
A Job-Hunt Done Well

If you approach your job-hunt as an opportunity to work on this issue as well as the issue of how you will keep body and soul together, then hopefully your job-hunt will end with your being able to say: "Life has deep meaning to me, now. I have discovered more than my ideal job; I have found my Mission, and the reason why I am here on Earth."

Two are better than one;
for if they fall,
the one will lift up his fellow;

but woe to him that is alone when he falleth,
and hath not another to lift him up.

Ecclesiastes 4:9–10

A Guide to Choosing a Career Coach or Counselor

If You Decide You Need One

There are a lot of people out there, anxious to help you with your job-hunt or career-change, in case this book isn't sufficient for you. They're willing to help you, for a fee in most cases. (That is how they make their living.) They go by various names: career coach, career counselor, career development specialist, you name it.

I wish I could say that *everyone* who hangs out a sign saying they are now in this business could be completely depended upon. But—alas! and alack!—they can't all be. This career-coaching or career-counseling field is largely unregulated. And even where there is some kind of certification, resulting in their being able to put a lot of degree-soundin' initials after their name, that doesn't really tell you much. It means a lot *to them* of course; in many cases, they had to sweat blood in order to be able to put those initials after their name. (Or not. Some got their initials in little more than a long weekend.)

I used to try to explain what all those initials meant. There is a veritable alphabet-soup of them, with new ones born every year. But no more; I've learned, from more than thirty-five years of experience in this field, that 99.4 percent of all job-hunters and career-changers don't care a fig about these initials. All they want to know is: *do you know how to help me find a job?* Or, more specifically, *do you know how to help me find my dream job—one that matches the gifts, skills, and experience that I have, one that makes me excited to get up in the morning, and excited to go to bed at night, knowing I helped make this Earth a little better place to be in? If so, I'll hire you. If not, I'll fire you.*

How To Lose Your Shirt (or Save It)

Okay, then, *bye-bye initials!* Let us start in a simpler place, with this basic truth:

All coaches and counselors divide basically into three groups:

a) those who are honest, compassionate, and caring, and know what they're doing;

b) those who are honest but don't know what they're doing; and

c) those who are dishonest, and merely want your money—large amounts, in a lump sum, and up front.

In other words, you've got compassionate, caring people in the same field with crooks. And your job, if you want help, is to discern the one from the other.

It would help, of course, if someone could just give you a list of those who are firmly in the first category—honest and know what they're doing. But unfortunately, no one *(including me)* has such a list. You've got to do your own homework, or research here, and your own interviewing, in your own geographical area. And if you're too lazy to take the time and trouble to do this research, you will deserve what you get.

Why is it that *you* and only *you* can do this particular research? Well, let's say a friend tells you to go see so-and-so. He's a wonderful coach or counselor, but unhappily he reminds you of your Uncle Harry, whom you detest. Bummer! But, no one except you knows that you've always disliked your Uncle Harry. That's why no one else can do this research for you— because the real question is not "Who is best?" but "Who is best for you?" Those last two words demand that it be you who "makes the call."

Job-hunters and career-changers try to avoid this research, of course. One way to do that, is through overconfidence in your own intuition: *"Well, I'll just call up one place in my area, and if I like the sound of them, I'll sign up. I'm a pretty good judge of character."* Yeah, right! I've heard this refrain from so many job-hunters who called me only after they'd lost loads of money in a bad "pay-me-first" contract, because they had been *taken*, by slicker salespeople than they had ever run into before. *"But they seemed so sincere, and charming."*

They cry. I express, of course, my sympathy and empathy (I once got taken myself, the same way), but then I add a sobering note of caution, *"I'm terribly sorry to hear that you had such a heartbreaking experience, but—as the Scots would say—'Ya dinna do your homework.' Often you could easily have discovered whether a particular coach or counselor was any good, before you ever gave them any of your money, simply by doing the preliminary research that I urge upon everybody."*

The bottom line, for you: Intuition isn't enough.

Another way people try to avoid this research is by saying, "Well, I'll just see who Bolles recommends." That's pretty futile, because I never have recommended anyone. Some try to claim I do, including, in past years, some of the coaches or counselors listed in the *Sampler* at the end of this appendix, who claim that their very listing here constitutes a recommendation from me. Oh, come on! *This Sampler is more akin to the yellow pages, than it is to* Consumer Reports.

Let me repeat this, as I have for more than thirty years, and repeat it very firmly:

The listing of a firm or coach in this book does NOT constitute an endorsement or recommendation by me. Never has meant that. Never will. *(Anyone listed here who claims that it does—in their ads, brochures, or publicity—gets permanently removed from this Sampler the following year after I find out about it.)* This is not "a hall of fame"; it is just a *sampler* of names of those *who have asked to be listed, and have answered some reasonable questions.*

Consider them just a starting point for your search. With them, as with all others, you must check them out. You must do your own homework. You must do your own research.

A Guide to Choosing a Good Career Coach

So, how do you go about finding a good career coach or counselor, if you decide you need help? Well, you start by collecting three names of career coaches or counselors in your geographical area.

How do you find those names? Several ways:

First, you can get names from your friends: ask if any of them have ever used a career coach or counselor. And if so, did they like 'em? And if so, what is that coach's or counselor's name?

Second, you can get names from the Sampler at the end of this appendix (that begins on page 394). See if there are any career coaches or counselors who are near you. They may know how you can find still other names in your community. But I repeat what I said above: just because they're listed in the Sampler *doesn't* mean I recommend them. It only means they asked to be listed, and professed familiarity with the contents of this book (current edition, not way back—say, in 2001). You've still got to research these people.

Need more names? Try your telephone book's yellow pages, under such headings as: *Aptitude and Employment Testing, Career and Vocational Counseling, Personnel Consultants,* and (if you are a woman) *Women's Organizations and Services.*

Once you have three names, you need to go do some comparison shopping. You want to talk with all three of them and decide which of the three (if any) you want to hook up with.

What will this initial interview cost you, with each of the three? The answer to that is easy: when first setting up an appointment, *ask.* You do have the right to inquire ahead of time how much they are going to have to charge you for the exploratory interview.

Some, a few, will charge you nothing for the initial interview. One of the brightest counselors I know says this: *I don't like to charge for the first interview because I want to be free to tell them I can't help them, if for some reason we just don't hit it off.*

However, do not expect that most individual coaches or counselors can afford to give you this exploratory interview for nothing! If they did that, and got a lot of requests like yours, they would never be able to make a living.

If this is not an individual counselor, but *a firm* trying to sell you a "pay-me-first" package *up front,* I guarantee they will give you the initial interview for free. They plan to use that "intake" interview (as they call it) to sell you a much more expensive program.

The Questions to Ask

When you are face to face with the individual coach or counselor (or firm), you ask each of them the same questions, listed on the form below. (Keep a little pad or notebook with you, or PDA, so you can write down their answers.)

After visiting the three places you chose for your comparison shopping, you can go home, sit down, put your feet up, look over your notes, and compare those places.

MY SEARCH FOR A GOOD CAREER COUNSELOR

Questions Will Ask Them	Answer from counselor #1	Answer from counselor #2	Answer from counselor #3
What is your program?			
Who will be counseling? And how long has this person been counseling?			
What is your success rate?			
What is the cost of your services?			
Is there a contract up front? If so, may I see it please, and take it home with me?			

You need to decide a) whether you want none of the three, or b) one of the three (and if so, which one). Remember, you don't have to choose *any* of the three coaches, if you didn't really care for any of them.

If that is the case, then go choose three new counselors out of the yellow pages or wherever, dust off the notebook, and go out again. It may take a few more hours to find what you want. But **the wallet, the purse, the job-hunt, the life, you save will be your own.**

As you look over your notes, you will soon realize there is no definitive way for you to determine a career coach's intentions. It's something you'll have to *smell out*, as you go along. But here are some clues.

These are primarily clues about large *firms*, most particularly *executive counseling firms*, and **rarely apply to individual coaches or counselors**, but read these anyway, for your own education.

Bad Vibes, on Up to *Real Bad* Vibes

If they give you the feeling that everything will be done for you, by them *(including interpretation of tests, and decision making about what this means you should do, or where you should do it)*— rather than asserting that you are going to have to do almost all the work, with their basically being your coach,

(Give them **15 bad points**)

You want to learn how to do this for yourself; you're going to be job-hunting again, you know.

If they say they are not the person who will be doing the program with you, but deny you any chance to meet the coach or counselor you would be working with,

(Give them **75 bad points**)

You're talking to a salesperson. My advice after talking to job-hunters for more than thirty years, is: avoid any firm that has a salesperson.

If you do get a chance to meet the counselor, but you don't like the counselor, period!,

(Give them **150 bad points**)

I don't care what their expertise is, if you don't like them, you're going to have a rough time getting what you want. I guarantee it. Rapport is everything.

If you ask how long the counselor has been doing this, and they get huffy or give a double-barreled answer, such as: "I've had eighteen years' experience in the business and career counseling world,"

(Give them **20 bad points**)

What that may mean is: seventeen and a half years as a fertilizer salesman, and one half year doing career counseling. Persist. "How long have you been with this firm, and how long have you been doing formal career coaching or counseling, as you are here?" You might be interested to know that some executive or career counseling firms hire yesterday's clients as today's new staff. Such new staff are sometimes given training only after they're "on-the-job." They are practicing . . . on you.

If they try to answer the question of their experience by pointing to their degrees or credentials,

(Give them **3 bad points**)

Degrees or credentials tell you they've passed certain tests of their qualifications, but often these tests bear more on their expertise at career assessment, than on their knowledge of creative job-hunting techniques.

If, when you ask about that firm's success rate, they say they have never had a client who failed to find a job, no matter what,

(Give them **500 bad points**)

They're lying. I have studied career counseling programs for more than thirty years, have attended many, have studied records at state and federal offices, and have hardly ever seen a program that placed more than 86 percent of their clients, tops, in their best years. And it goes downhill from there. A prominent executive counseling firm was reported by the Attorney General's Office of New York State to have placed only 38 out of 550 clients (a 93 percent failure rate). On the other hand, if they make it clear that they have had a good success rate, but if you fail to work hard at the whole process, then there is no guarantee you are going to find a job, give them three stars.

If a firm shows you letters from ecstatically happy former clients, but when you ask to talk to some of those clients, you get stonewalled,

(Give them **200 bad points**)

Man, these guys can be slick! No, no, not honest career coaches; I'm referring to *the crooks* in this field. Here is a job-hunter's letter about his experience with one of those firms:

"I asked to speak to a former client or clients. You would have thought I asked to speak to Elvis. The counselor stammered and stuttered and gave me a million excuses why I couldn't talk to some of these 'satisfied' former clients. None of the excuses sounded legitimate to me. We went back and forth for about thirty minutes. Finally, he excused himself and went to speak to his boss, the owner. The next thing I knew I was called into the owner's office for a more 'personal' sales pitch. We spoke for about forty-five minutes as he tried to convince me to use his service. When I told him I was not ready to sign up, he became angry and asked my counselor why I had been put before 'the committee' if I wasn't ready to commit? The counselor claimed I had given a verbal commitment at our last meeting. The owner then turned to me and said I seemed to have a problem making a decision and that he did not want to do business with me. I was shocked. They had turned the whole story around to make it look like it was my fault. I felt humiliated. In retrospect, the whole process felt like dealing with a used car salesman. They used pressure tactics and intimidation to try to get what they wanted. As you have probably gathered, more than anything else this experience made me angry."

If you ask the firm what is the cost of their services, and they reply that it is a lump sum that must all be paid "up front" before you start or shortly after you start, all at once or in rapid installments,

(Give them **1000 bad points**)

We're talking about firms here, not the average individual counselor or coach. The basic problem is that both "the good guys" and "the crooks" do this. The good guys operate on the theory that if you give them a large sum up front, you will then be really committed to the program. The crooks operate on the theory that if you give them a large sum up front, they don't have to give you anything back, except endless excuses and subterfuge, after a certain date (quickly reached). And the trouble is that, going in, there is absolutely no way for you to distinguish crook from good guy; they only reveal their true nature after they've got all your money. And by that time, you have no legal way to get it back, no matter what they verbally promised.[1]

You may think I am exaggerating: I mean, can there possibly be such mean men and women, who would prey on job-hunters, especially executive job-hunters, when they're down and out. Yes, ma'am, and yes, sir, there are. That's why you have to do your preliminary research so thoroughly.

Trust me on this. There is no way to distinguish the good guys from the crooks. I have tried for years to think of some way around this dilemma, but there just is none. So now I say, if it were me, anytime I ran into a coach, counselor, or executive counseling firm that charges a lump sum up front, I would say to myself, "You guys may be the most honest people in the world; but also you may not be; and I just can't afford to gamble that much money on the answer." (We're talking $1,000 up through $10,000 here.)

---

1. Sometimes the written contract—there is *always* a written contract, when you are dealing with the bad guys, and they will probably ask your partner to sign it, too—will claim to provide for an almost complete refund, at any time, until you reach a cutoff date in the program, which the contract specifies. Unfortunately, crafty fraudulent firms bend over backward to be extra nice, extra available, and extra helpful to you, from the time you first walk in, until that cutoff point is reached. Therefore, when the cutoff point for getting a refund has been reached, you let it pass because you are very satisfied with their past services, and believe there will be many more weeks of the same. Only, there aren't. At fraudulent firms, once the cutoff point is passed, the career counselor suddenly becomes virtually impossible for you to get ahold of. Call after call will not be returned. You will say to yourself, "What happened?" Well, what happened, my friend, is that you paid up in full, they have all the money they're ever going to get out of you, and now, they want to move on.

*So take my advice. . . . If someone offers to help you find a great job
as long as you'll pay several thousand dollars in advance, do as follows:*

A. Find door.

B. Walk out same.

C. Do not return.

Don't give anyone money you can't afford to lose; assume
that every sum you pay anyone is lost and gone forever.

If Money Is a Problem for You:
Hourly Coaching

There are career coaches or counselors who charge by the
hour. In fact, they are in the majority. With them, there is no
written contract. You sign nothing. You pay only for each hour
as you use it, according to their set rate. Each time you keep an
appointment, you pay them at the end of that hour for their
help, according to that rate. Period. Finis. You never owe them
any money (unless you made an appointment, and failed to keep
it). You can stop seeing them at any time, if you feel you are not
getting the help you wish.

What will they charge? You will find, these days, that the best
career coaches or counselors (*plus some of the worst*) will charge
you whatever a good therapist or marriage counselor charges
per hour, in your geographical area. Currently, in major metropolitan areas, that runs around $150 an hour, sometimes more.
In suburbia or rural areas, it may be much less—$40 an hour,
or so.

That fee is for *individual time* with the career coach or counselor. If you can't afford that fee, ask whether they also run
groups. If they do, the fee will be much less. And, in one of those
delightful ironies of life, since you get a chance to listen to problems that other job-hunters in your group are having, the group
will often give you more help than an individual session with a
counselor would have. Not always; but often. It's always ironic
when *cheaper* and *more helpful* go hand in hand.

If the career counselor in question does offer groups, there
should (again) never be a contract. The charge should be payable
at the end of each session, and you should be able to drop out at
any time, without further cost, if you decide you are not getting
the help you want.

There are some career counselors who run free (or almost free) job-hunting workshops through local churches, synagogues, chambers of commerce, community colleges, adult education programs, and the like, as their community service, or *pro bono* work (as it is technically called). I have had reports of workshops from a number of places in the U.S. and Canada. They exist in other parts of the world as well. If money is a problem for you, in getting help with your job-hunt, ask around your community to see if workshops exist in your community. Your chamber of commerce will know, or your church or synagogue.

You can find an incredibly useful list of all the job clubs in the U.S. compiled by my friend Susan Joyce, on her site `www.job-hunt.org` (`www.job-hunt.org/job-search-networking/job-search-networking.shtml`).

If Your Location Is a Problem for You: Distance Coaching or Telephone Counseling

The assumption, from the beginning, was that career counseling would always take place face to face. Both of you, counselor and job-hunter, together in the same room. Just like career counseling's close relatives: marriage counseling, or even AA.

Of course, a job-hunter might—on occasion—phone his or her counselor the day before an interview, to get some last-minute tips or to answer some questions that a prospective interviewer might ask, *tomorrow.*

What is different, today, is that in some cases, career counseling is being conducted exclusively over the phone from start to finish. Some counselors now report that they haven't laid eyes on over 90 percent of their clients, and wouldn't know them if they bumped into them on a street corner. I call this "distance-coaching" or "telephone-counseling."

With the invention of the Internet, with the invention of Internet *telephoning*, we are witnessing "the death of distance"—that is to say, the death of distance as an obstacle. The world, as Thomas Friedman has famously written, is in effect *flat.*

An increasing number of counselors or executive coaches are doing this *distance-counseling.* For the job-hunter, it's not all that expensive. True, counselors who offer this, charge between $80/hour and "sky-high" (usually, in that case, paid by the company).[2] But you can shop around, and ask questions to find the best price for your budget.

To their fee must be added, of course, the cost of the phone calls. *No problem*—the cost of the telephoning doesn't have to break your budget, especially if your counselor is using a technology known as Public Switched Telephone Network (PSTN) conferencing, or has an Internet phone service—technically called VoIP (Voice-over-Internet-Protocol)—which makes your phone calls free or available for a low fee.

Indeed, that's available right now. And, a program called *Skype* is especially useful. (Details, for counselor and job-hunter alike, may be found at **www.skype.com/download/**, or in the official definitive written guide by Harry Max and Taylor Ray, called—surprise!—*Skype: The Definitive Guide*.[3]) Skype requires telephones, but not necessarily computers. Or computers, but not necessarily telephones. Your options are many.

Now, this increasing availability of "distance-counseling" is good news, and bad news.

Why good news? Well, in the old days you might be a job-hunter in some remote village, with a population of only eighty-five, back in the hills somewhere, or you might be living somewhere in France or in China, miles from any career counselor or coach, and so, be totally out of luck. Now, these days you can be anywhere in the world, but as long as you have the Internet on your desk, you can still find the best distance-counseling there is.

And the bad news?

Well, just because a counselor or coach does distance-counseling or phone-counseling, doesn't mean they are really good at doing it. Some are superb; but some are not so hotsy-totsy.

So, you're still going to have to research any distance-counselor who interests you *very carefully*. It is altogether too easy for a

---

2. Two famous "distance coaches" are Joel Garfinklel in Oakland, California, **www.dreamjobcoaching.com/**; and Marshall Goldsmith of **www.marshall goldsmithlibrary.com/**, international coach to the executive elite, and author (with Mark Reiter) of the currently popular book, *What Got You Here Won't Get You There*.

3. Published by Que, 201 W. 103rd Street, Indianapolis, IN 46290.

counselor to get sloppy doing distance-counseling—for example, browsing the newspapers while you are telling some long personal story, etc., to which they are giving only the briefest attention. Since you can't see the counselor, you don't know. Because of this, I personally, were I job-hunting or changing careers, would want to sign up only for one session at a time. In case a flaw suddenly appears. *Outtahere!*

To avoid any kind of sloppiness, *you* and the counselor need discipline. Experienced distance-counselors, such as Joel Garfinkle,[4] insist on forms being used, both before and after each phone session. With his permission, I have adapted his forms, and print them here below. *And, P.S., they are equally useful for just normal, face-to-face counseling, as well.*

Client Coaching Forms
1. Before You Start

Prior to beginning the counseling, it helps if your coach or counselor asks you to fill out the following kind of form, for you to give to him or her. They are written by the counselor, addressed to you, the potential counselee. (And if they don't ask for a form like this to be filled out, you might volunteer to give them such a form on your own.)

---

4. `www.dreamjobcoaching.com/about/`

Questions to Understand You Better

(Copy this onto another sheet of paper, and leave lots of space on the form for your answer, after each question below.)

1. Why have you decided to work with me?

2. How can I have the most impact on your life in the next ninety days (three months)?

3. List three key goals you want to accomplish through our work together.

4. What stops you from achieving what you want in question #2 or #3 above?

5. Project ahead one year: As you look back, and things went well, how did you benefit from our coaching relationship?

6. What are your expectations from our work together? How can we exceed these expectations?

7. What else is helpful for me to know about you?

8. Explain your background (use the same format as the examples below).

Examples:

1. After thirty years as a commercial insurance broker, I hit a wall last May, and decided to change careers . . .

2. After twelve successful years in the high-tech industry, I found myself unfulfilled in finding a satisfying career. Over the years, I read countless books on the topic of finding one's true purpose in career pursuits, but was still missing a sense of purpose and clarity on what I wanted to do . . .

3. After working for twenty years in the investment industry I decided to start my own company . . .

4. Etc.

Client Coaching Forms
2. Before Each Coaching Session Form
3. After Each Coaching Session Form

Directions:

Please fill out these forms for each coaching session. Form #2 should be filled out and e-mailed to me twenty-four hours before the next coaching session to assist me in preparing for that session.

Immediately after each coaching session e-mail me form #3.

#2. Before Each Session, Preparation Form

(Copy this onto another sheet of paper, and leave lots of space on the form for your answer, after each question below.)

Commitments that I made to myself on the last coaching session and what I accomplished since we had the coaching session:

The challenges and opportunities I am facing now:

The one action I can take that will most affect my current goals and provide the highest payoff:

My agenda for the coaching session is:

#3. After Each Session: Reflection Form

(Copy this onto another sheet of paper, and leave lots of space on the form for your answer, after each question below.)

This week's commitment:

My greatest insights during this session were:

What you, my coach, said or asked during the session that impacted me most:

What I'd like you, as my coach, to do differently/more of/less of:

How I feel I am evolving from our work together:

What happens in a counseling session is our responsibility, not just the counselor's or coach's.

The forms, above, are one way of our taking responsibility. Another, is that when you first contact prospective coaches for distance-counseling in particular, you have a right to ask them: (1) "What training have you completed, relevant to distance-counseling, such as telephone skills, and supervised counseling?" (2) "How will our distance-counseling be organized and scheduled?" and (3) "What will the two of us do if and when interruptions occur during a session, at either end?"

You must always remember: distance-counseling, attractive as it will be for many, as necessary as it will be for some, definitely has its limits.

To the caveman, the technology that enables all this to happen in this twenty-first century, would be jaw-droppingly awesome. But, good career counseling or coaching *is not just about technology*. What is really truly awesome, in the end, is simply our power to help each other on this Earth. And how much that power resides, not in techniques or technology, though these things are important—but in each of us just being a good human being. A *loving* human being.

A Sampler

This is exactly what its name implies: a Sampler. Were I to list all the career coaches and counselors who are out there, we would end up with an encyclopedia. Some states, in fact, have encyclopedic lists of counselors and businesses, in various books or directories, and your local bookstore or library should have these, in their Job-Hunting Section, under such titles as "How to Get a Job in . . . " or "Job-Hunting in. . . ."

I did not choose the places listed in this Sampler; rather, they are listed at their own request, and I offer their information to you simply as suggestions of where you can begin your investigation—when you're trying to find decent help.[5]

---

5. Yearly readers of this book will notice that we do remove people from this Sampler, without warning. First of all, there are accidents: we drop places we didn't mean to drop, but a typographical error was made, somehow (it happens). *Oops!* Call this to our attention; we'll put you back in next year.

Do keep in mind that many truly helpful places and coaches are not listed here. If you discover such a coach or place, which is very good at helping people *with Parachute* and creative job-hunting or career-change, do send us the pertinent information. We will ask them, as we do all the listings here, a few intelligent questions, and if they sound okay, we will add that place as a suggestion in next year's edition.

We do ask a few questions—because our readers want counselors and places that have some expertise *with Parachute,* and can help job-hunters or career-changers finish their job-hunt using this book. So, if they've never even heard of *Parachute,* we don't list them. On the other hand, we can't measure a place's expertise at this distance, no matter how many questions we ask.

So, even if listed here, they need to be thoroughly researched *by you.* You must do your own sharp questioning before you decide to go with anyone. If you don't take time to research two or three places, before choosing a counselor, you will deserve whatever you get (or, more to the point, don't get). So, please, do your research. The purse or wallet you save, will be your own.

The listings that follow are alphabetical within each state, except that counselors listed by their name are in alphabetical order according to their last name.

We deliberately remove: places that have moved, and don't bother to send us their new address. *Coaches and counselors: if you are listed here, we expect you to be a professional at communication. When you move, your first priority should be to let us know, immediately. As one exemplary counselor wrote: "You are the first person I am contacting on my updated letterhead . . . hot off the press just today!" So it should always be, if you want to continue to be listed here. A number of places get removed every year, precisely because of their poor communication skills, and their sloppiness in letting us know where they've gone to.*

Other causes for removal: Places that have disconnected their telephone, or otherwise suggest that they have gone out of business. Places that our readers lodge complaints against with us, as being unhelpful or even obnoxious. The complaints may be falsified, but we can't take that chance. Places that change their personnel, and the new person has never even heard of *Parachute,* or "creative job-search techniques." College services that we discover (belatedly) serve only "Their Own." Counseling firms that employ salespeople as the initial "intake" person that a job-hunter meets. If you discover that any of the places listed in this Sampler fall into any of the above categories, you would be doing a great service to our other readers by dropping us a line and telling us so (P.O. Box 379, Walnut Creek, CA 94597).

Some offer group career counseling, some offer testing, some offer access to job-banks, etc.

One final note: generally speaking, these places counsel anybody. A few, however, may turn out to have restrictions unknown to us ("we counsel only women," etc.). If that's the case, your time isn't wasted. They may be able to help you with a referral. So, don't be afraid to ask them, "Who else in the area can you tell me about, who helps with job-searches, and are there any (among them) that you think are particularly effective?"

Area Codes

If you call a phone number in the Sampler that is any distance away from you, and they tell you "this number cannot be completed as dialed," the most likely explanation is that the area code was changed—maybe some time ago. Throughout the U.S. now, area codes are subdividing constantly, sometimes more than once during a short time span. (We ask counselors listed here to notify us when the area code changes, but some do and some don't.) Anyway, call Information and check.

Of course, if you're calling a local counselor, you probably don't need the area code anyway (unless you live in one of the metropolitan areas in the U.S. that requires ten-digit dialing).

Throughout this Sampler, an asterisk before their name, in red, means they offer both secular and religious counseling, that is, they're not afraid to talk about God if you're looking for some help, in finding your mission in life.

ALABAMA

*Career Decisions,
638 Winwood Dr.,
Birmingham, AL 35226
Phone: 205-822-8662
Contact: Carrie Anna Pearce, MSEd,
Career Counselor and Consultant

*Career Mission,
7500 Memorial Pkwy. SW, Ste. 215-C,
Huntsville, AL 35802
Phone: 256-883-3231
Fax: 256-883-9577
www.trinitycounseling.info

Chemsak, Maureen J., NCC, LPC, MCC,
Director of Counseling,
Athens State University,
300 N. Beaty St.,
Athens, AL 35611
Phone: 256-233-8285 or 256-722-0449
E-mail: maureen.chemsak@athens.edu

Vantage Associates,
2100-A Southbridge Pkwy., Ste. 480,
Birmingham, AL 35209
Phone: 205-879-0501
Contact: Michael A. Tate

WorkMatters, Inc.,
PO Box 130756,
Birmingham, AL 35213
Phone: 205-879-8494
Contact: Gayle H. Lantz
E-mail: lantz@workmatters.com
www.workmatters.com

ALASKA

Career Transitions,
2600 Denali St., Ste. 430,
Anchorage, AK 99503
Phone: 907-274-4500
Fax: 907-274-4510
Contact: Deeta Lonergan, President
E-mail: deeta@alaska.net
www.careertransitions.biz

*Carr & Associates Consulting,
PO Box 233356,
Anchorage, AK 99523
Phone: 907-348-0277
Contact: Diane Carr, Spiritual Career
Counselor and Life Coach
E-mail: dcarr@gci.net
www.carrandassociates.com

ARIZONA

Boninger, Faith, PhD,
10965 E. Mary Katherine Dr.,
Scottsdale, AZ 85259
Phone: 480-551-7097
E-mail: faithboninger@cox.net

DavenportFolio,
2415 E. Camelback Rd., 7th Floor,
Phoenix, AZ 85016
Phone: 602-553-0808
Contact: Debra B. Davenport, PhD,
EPM™, LCC
E-mail: info@davenportfolio.com
www.debradavenport.com
*(They also have a Los Angeles office;
see the California listings.)*

Renaissance Career Solutions,
PO Box 30118,
Phoenix, AZ 85046-0118
Phone: 602-867-4202
Contact: Betty Boza, MA, LCC
E-mail: bboza@cox.net
www.rcareer-solutions.com

CALIFORNIA

Bauer, Lauralyn Larsen,
Career Counselor & Coach,
2180 Jefferson St., Ste. 201,
Napa, CA 94558
Phone: 707-363-7775
E-mail: lauralynbauer@hotmail.com

Bay Area Career Center,
Mechanics Institute Library Bldg.,
57 Post St., Ste. 804,
San Francisco, CA 94104
Phone: 415-398-4881
Fax: 415-398-4897
E-mail: info@bayareacareercenter.com
www.bayareacareercenter.com
*(Ten experienced career counselors with
master's degrees in career development or
counseling with a career.)*

Berrett & Associates,
533 E. Mariners Cir.,
Fresno, CA 93730
Phone: 559-284-3549
Contact: Dwayne Berrett, MA, RPCC
E-mail: dberrett3@fresno.com
www.berrett-associates.com

California Career Services,
6024 Wilshire Blvd.,
Los Angeles, CA 90036
Phone: 323-933-2900
Fax: 323-933-9929
Contact: Susan W. Miller, MA
E-mail: swmcareer@aol.com
www.californiacareerservices.com

Career Balance,
215 Witham Rd.,
Encinitas, CA 92024
Phone: 760-436-3994
Contact: Virginia Byrd, MEd,
Work/Life Specialist
E-mail: virginia@careerbalance.net
www.careerbalance.net

*Career Choices,
Dublin, CA
Phone: 925-833-9994
Contact: Dana E. Ogden,
MS Ed, CCDV, Career & Educational
Counselor,
Workshop Facilitator
E-mail: dana@careerchoices.us
www.careerchoices.us

**Career Counseling and
Assessment Associates,**
9229 Sunset Blvd., Ste. 502,
Los Angeles, CA 90069
Phone: 310-274-3423
Contact: Dianne Y. Sundby, PhD,
Director and Psychologist

**A Career Counseling and
Psychotherapy Practice,**
1330 Lincoln Ave., Ste. 210 A,
San Rafael, CA 94901
Phone: 415-789-9113
Contact: Suzanne Penney Lindenbaum,
MSW, LCSW, MCC
E-mail: lindenccs@aol.com
www.therapistfinder.com/therapists/
suzannelindenbaum

**Career Development Center at
John F. Kennedy University,**
100 Ellinwood Way, Rm. N367,
Pleasant Hill, CA 94523
Phone: 925-969-3542
Fax: 925-969-3541
E-mail: career@jfku.edu
www.jfku.edu/career

Career Development Life Planning,
3585 Maple St., Ste. 237,
Ventura, CA 93003
Phone: 805-656-6220
Contact: Norma Zuber, MSC; Associates
www.normazubercareers.com

Career Dimensions,
PO Box 7402,
Stockton, CA 95267
Phone: 209-484-7071
Contact: Fran Abbott
E-mail: franabott@cdimensions.org
www.cdimensions.org

**Career and Personal Development
Institute,**
582 Market St., Ste. 410,
San Francisco, CA 94104
Phone: 415-982-2636
Contact: Bob Chope
www.cpdicareercounseling.com

**Center for Career Growth and
Development,**
PO Box 283,
Los Gatos, CA 95031
Phone: 408-354-7150
Contact: Steven E. Beasley
E-mail: stevenbeasley@verizon.net

*Center for Life & Work Planning,
1133 Second St.,
Encinitas, CA 92024
Phone/Fax: 760-943-0747
Contact: Mary C. McIsaac,
Executive Director

*The Center for Ministry
(an Interdenominational Ministry
and Career Development Center),
8393 Capwell Dr., Ste. 220,
Oakland, CA 94621-2123
Phone: 510-635-4246
Contact: Robert L. Charpentier, Director
E-mail: bob@centerforministry.org
www.centerforministry.org

*Cheney-Rice, Stephen, MS,
2113 Westboro Ave.,
Alhambra, CA 91803-3720
Phone: 626-824-5244
E-mail: sccheneyrice@earthlink.net

Christen, Carol, Career Strategy &
Job Search Consultant,
Atascadero, CA
Phone: 805-462-8795
E-mail: Carol@carolchristen.com
(Career coaching by phone available.)

The Clarity Group,
2159 Union St., Ste. 5,
San Francisco, CA 94123
Phone: 415-693-9719
Contact: George Schofield, PhD
E-mail: george.schofield@clarity-group.com
or george@georgeschofield.com
www.clarity-group.com or
www.georgeschofield.com

Collaborative Solutions,
3130 W. Fox Run Way,
San Diego, CA 92111
Phone: 858-268-9340
Contact: Nancy Helgeson, MA, LMFT

Cypress College,
Career Planning Center,
9200 Valley View St.,
Cypress, CA 90630
Phone: 714-484-7120

DavenportFolio,
1334 Parkview Ave., Ste. 100,
Manhattan Beach, CA 90266
Phone: 310-402-3047
Contact: Debra B. Davenport, PhD,
EPM™, LCC
E-mail: info@davenportfolio.com
www.debradavenport.com

Dream Job Coaching,
6918 Thornhill Dr.,
Oakland, CA 94611
Phone: 510-339-3201
E-mail: joel@dreamjobcoaching.com,
www.dreamjobcoaching.com,
www.garfinkleexecutivecoaching.com,
or www.14daystoajob.com

Experience Unlimited Job Club
There are twenty-four Experience Unlimited Clubs in California, found at the Employment Development Department in the following locations: Anaheim, Canoga Park, Contra Costa, Corona, Fremont, Fresno, Irvine, Lancaster, Manteca, Monterey, Oakland, Pasadena, Sacramento (Midtown and South), Santa Barbara, Santa Cruz/Capitola, San Francisco, Santa Maria, San Rafael, Simi Valley, Sunnyvale, Torrance, and West Covina. Contact the club nearest you through your local Employment Development Department (EDD) office.

Floyd, Mary Alice, MA,
Career Life Transitions,
3233 Lucinda Ln.,
Santa Barbara, CA 93105
Phone: 805-687-5462
E-mail: maryalicefloyd@cox.net
www.careerlifetrans.com

*Frangquist, Deborah Gavrin, MS,
Careers & Workplaces for Real People,
1801 Bush St., Ste. 121,
San Francisco, CA 94109
Phone: 415-346-6121
Fax: 415-346-6118
E-mail: Deborah@DeborahFrangquist.com
www.DeborahFrangquist.com

Fritsen, Jan,
Career Counseling and Coaching,
23181 La Cadena Dr., Ste. 103,
Laguna Hills, CA 92653
Phone: 949-497-4869
E-mail: janfritsen@cox.net
www.janfritsen.com

Geary & Associates, Inc.,
1100 Coddingtown Ctr., Ste. A,
PO Box 3774,
Santa Rosa, CA 95402
Phone: 707-525-8085
Fax: 707-528-8088
Contact: Jack Geary, MA;
Edelweiss Geary, MEd, CRC
E-mail: esgeary@sbcglobal.net
(Career transition programs, outplacement, resume development, and job-seeking skill training.)

Hilliard, Larkin, MA,
Counseling Psychology,
1411 Holiday Hill Rd.,
Santa Barbara, CA 93117
Phone: 805-683-5855
E-mail: larkinhill@earthlink.net
(English, French, German, and Russian.)

HR Solutions, Human Resources Consulting,
4421-2 Alla Rd.,
Marina Del Rey, CA 90292
Phone: 310-577-0972
Contact: Nancy Mann, MBA,
President/Career Consultant
E-mail: nanmanhrs@aolcom

Jewish Vocational Service,
6505 Wilshire Blvd., Ste. 200 and Ste. 700,
Los Angeles, CA 90048
Phone: 323-761-8888

Judy Kaplan Baron Associates,
6046 Cornerstone Ct. W., Ste. 208,
San Diego, CA 92121
Phone: 858-558-7400
Contact: Judy Kaplan Baron, Director
E-mail: careerguyde@aol.com

Kerwin & Associates,
3666 Arnold Ave.,
San Diego, CA 92104
Phone: 619-295-8547
Contact: Patrick Kerwin, MBA
E-mail: patrick@kerwinandassociates.com
www.kerwinandassociates.com

Life's Work Center,
109 Bartlett St.,
San Francisco, CA 94110
Phone: 415-821-0930
Contact: Tom Finnegan, Executive Director
E-mail: tom@lifesworkcenter.org

L M & A Career Coaching,
7826 W. 79th St.,
Playa del Rey, CA 90293
Phone: 310-301-2508
Contact: Liz Mohler, MS
E-mail: careeradviceliz@LizMohler.com or lizmohler@ca.rr.com
www.LizMohler.com

*Miller, Lizbeth, MS, NCC,
3425 S Bascom Ave., Ste. 250,
Campbell, CA 95128
Phone: 408-486-6763
Fax: 408-369-4990
E-mail: lizmillercareers@yahoo.com
www.lizmillercareers.com
(Helping professionals find career fulfillment.)

Nemko, Marty, PhD,
Career and Education Strategist,
5936 Chabolyn Terr.,
Oakland, CA 94618
Phone: 510-655-2777
E-mail: mnemko@comcast.net
www.martynemko.com

Networking Grace Career Counseling,
Napa, CA 94558
Phone: 707-226-3438
Contact: Lauralyn Bauer, MS

Passport to Purpose,
333 Somerset Cir.,
Thousand Oaks, CA 91360
Phone: 805-496-5654
Contact: Cathy Severson, MS
E-mail: cathys997@verizon.net
www.passporttopurpose.com

Saraf, Dilip G., Career and Worklife Strategist,
Career Transitions Unlimited,
39159 Paseo Padre Pkwy., #221,
Fremont, CA 94538
Phone: 510-791-7005
E-mail: dilip@7keys.org
www.7keys.org

*Schoenbeck, Mary Lynne, MA, NCCC,
Career/Retirement Counselor,
Coach, Consultant,
Schoenbeck & Associates,
Los Angeles, CA
Phone: 650-964-8370
E-mail: schoenbeck@mindspring.com

*Visions into Form, Coaching,
223 San Anselmo Ave., Ste. 6,
San Anselmo, CA 94960
Phone: 415- 488-4998
Contact: Audrey Seymour, MA, PCC, CPCC
E-mail: careers@visionsintoform.com
www.visionsintoform.com

Wilson, Patti,
Career Company,
PO Box 35633,
Los Gatos, CA 95030
Phone: 408-354-1964
E-mail: patti@careercompany.com
www.pattiwilson.com

Zitron Parham Career Services,
4724 25th St., Ste. A,
San Francisco, CA 94114
Phone: 415-602-5595
Contact: Nick Parham,
Career & Executive Coach
E-mail: nick@zitronparham.com
www.zitronparhamcareerservices.com

COLORADO

**Arapahoe Community College
Career Center,**
5900 S. Santa Fe Dr.,
PO Box 9002,
Littleton, CO 80160-9002
Phone: 303-797-5805
E-mail: careers@arapahoe.edu

Arp, Rosemary, MS, GCDF,
Career Counselor,
Boulder, CO
Phone: 303-527-1874
E-mail: rsarp@comcast.net

Gary Ringler & Associates,
1747 Washington St., #203,
Denver, CO 80203
Phone: 303-863-0234
Fax: 303-863-0101
E-mail: garyringler@msn.com

Helmstaedter, Sherry,
5040 S. El Camino,
Englewood, CO 80111-1122
Phone: 303-794-5122

The McGee Group,
Three locations in Colorado:
Littleton; Colorado Springs; Fort Collins
Phone: 303-794-4749
Contact: Betsy C. McGee

*Peterson, April, MA, NCC, LPC,
Career Counselor,
Denver, CO
Phone: 720-841-8264
E-mail: april.peterson@att.net

Pivotal Choices, Inc.,
PO-Box 1098,
Durango, CO 81302
Phone: 970-385-9597
Contact: Mary Jane Ward, MEd, NCC,
NCCC
E-mail: mjw@pivotalchoices.com
www.pivatolchoices.com

Women's Resource Agency,
2220 E Bijou St., Ste. 2E,
Colorado Springs, CO 80909
Phone: 719-471-3170

YWCA of Boulder County Career Services,
2222 14th St.,
Boulder, CO 80302
Phone: 303-443-0419

CONNECTICUT

Accord Career Services, LLC,
The Exchange, Ste. 305,
270 Farmington Ave.,
Farmington, CT 06032
Phone: 800-922-1480 or 860-674-9654
Contact: Tod Gerardo, MS, Director

Career Choices/RFP Associates,
630 Nortontown Rd.,
Guilford, CT 06437
Phone: 203-453-1564
Contact: Kathleen Gaughran,
Career Consultant

Career Directions, LLC,
115 Elm St.,
Enfield, CT 06082
Phone: 860-623-9476
Fax: 860-623-9473
Contact: Louise Garver
E-mail: LouiseGarver@cox.net
www.CareerDirectionsLLC.com

Career You Love Counseling Services,
761 Valley Rd.,
Fairfield, CT 06825
Phone: 203-374-7649
Contact: Bob N. Olsen, MA MCC, LPC
www.yourpassion.com

Center for Professional Development,
50 Elizabeth St.,
Hartford, CT 06105
Phone: 860-768-5619
Contact: Eleta Jones, PhD, LPC
E-mail: ejones@hartford.edu
www.thecenterforprofessionaldevelopment
.org

Cohen, James S., PhD,
8 Barbara's Way,
Ellington, CT 06029
Phone: 860-871-7832
E-mail: vocdoc56@yahoo.com
(Provides career and vocational rehab services.)

The Offerjost-Westcott Group,
263 Main St.,
Old Saybrook, CT 06475
Phone: 860-388-6094
Contact: Russ Westcott
E-mail: russwest@snet.net

Pannone, Bob, MA,
Career Specialist,
177 Patterson Ave.,
Stratford, CT 06614
Phone: 203-386-8886
E-mail: upstartinc@yahoo.com

Preis, Roger J.,
RPE Career Dynamics,
PO Box 16722,
Stamford, CT 06905
Phone: 203-322-7225
www.rpecareers.com

Preis, Roger J.,
RPE Career Dynamics,
PO Box 115,
Shelburne, CT 05487
Phone: 802-985-3775
www.rpecareers.com

DELAWARE

The Brandywine Center, LLC,
2500 Grubb Rd., Ste. 240,
Wilmington, DE 19810
Phone: 302-475-1880,
Contact: Kris Bronson, PhD
E-mail: info@brandywinecenter.com
www.brandywinecenter.com

FLORIDA

Center for Career Decisions,
3912 S. Ocean Blvd., #1009,
Boca Raton, FL 33487
Phone: 561-276-0321
Contact: Linda Friedman, MA, NCC
www.career-decisions.com

The Centre for Women,
305 S. Hyde Park Ave.,
Tampa, FL 33606
Phone: 813-251-8437
Contact: Angel Washington,
Employment Counselor

Chabon-Berger, Toby, MEd, NCC,
4900 Boxwood Cir.,
Boynton Beach, FL 33436
Phone: 561-734-0775
E-mail: tberger@chabongroup.com
www.tobycareer.com

**The Challenge Program for Displaced
Homemakers,**
Florida Community College at Jacksonville,
601 W. State St.,
Jacksonville, FL 32202
Phone: 904-633-8316
Contact: Harriet Courtney,
Project Coordinator
E-mail: hcourtney@fccj.org

Crossroads,
Palm Beach Community College,
4200 Congress Ave.,
Lake Worth, FL 33461-4796
Phone: 561-868-3586
Contact: Bobbi Marsh, Program Manager
www.pbcc.edu

**Focus on the Future: Displaced
Homemaker Program,**
Santa Fe Community College,
3000 NW 83rd St.,
Gainesville, FL 32606
Phone: 352-395-5047
Contact: Nancy Griffin,
Program Coordinator
E-mail: focusonthefuture@sfcc.edu
(Classes are free.)

Harmon, Larry, PhD,
Career Counseling Center, Inc.,
2000 S. Dixie Hwy., Ste. 103,
Miami, FL 33133
Phone: 305-858-8557

Life Designs, Inc.,
19526 E. Lake Dr.,
Miami, FL 33015
Phone: 305-829-9008 (Sept.–May)
Contact: Dulce Muccio Weisenborn
E-mail: lifedesigns@gsrhelp.com

WINGS Program,
Broward Community College,
1000 Coconut Creek Blvd.,
Coconut Creek, FL 33066
Phone: 954-201-2398

GEORGIA

Ashkin, Janis, MEd, MCC, NCC, NCCC,
2365 Winthrope Way Dr.,
Alpharetta, GA 30004
Phone: 678-319-0297
E-mail: jashkin@bellsouth.net

Career Quest/Job Search Workshop,
St. Ann,
4905 Roswell Rd. NE,
Marietta, GA 30062-6240
Phone: 404-791-8534
Contact: Tom Chernetsky
(Focus on Internet job-hunting.)

*Crown Career Resources,
601 Broad St. SE,
Gainesville, GA 30501
Phone: 800-722-1976
Contact: Bette Noble, Director

D & B Consulting,
3355 Lenox Rd., Ste. 750,
Atlanta, GA 30326
Phone: 404-504-7079
Contact: Deborah R. Brown, MBA, MSW,
Career Consultant
E-mail: Debbie@DandBconsulting.com
www.dandbconsulting.com

Jewish Family and Career Services,
4549 Chamblee Dunwoody Rd.,
Atlanta, GA 30338
Phone: 770-677-9300

Satterfield, Mark,
720 Rio Grand Dr.,
Alpharetta, GA 30022
Phone: 770-643-8566

Waldorf, William H., MBA, LPC, MCC,
Path Unfolding Career Development,
314 Maxwell Rd., Ste. 400,
Alpharetta, GA 30004
Phone: 770-442-9447, ext. 14

HAWAII

*Hubbard Counseling Services,
94-467 Kealakaa St.,
Mililani, HI 96789
Phone: 808-625-2200
Contact: Dick Hubbard, MSCP, AACC
E-mail: hubbard@pixi.com

IDAHO

**OCM Organizational Consultants
to Management,**
1578 S. Times Square Ct.,
Boise, ID 83709
Phone: 208-338-6584
E-mail: Gregd@consulting.com

*Reed, Michael, MEd,
9882 W View Dr.,
Boise, ID 83704
Phone: 208-323-2462
Career Adviser Newsletter at
www.CareerCoaching4u.com
(Career and interview coach.)

ILLINOIS

Alumni Career Center,
University of Illinois Alumni Association,
200 S. Wacker Dr.,
Chicago, IL 60606
Phone: 312- 575-7830
Contact: Claudia M. Delestowicz, Associate
Director; Julie L. Hays, Associate Director;
Marti Beddoe, Career/Life Counselor
Phone: 312-575-7830

*Career Path,
1240 Iroquois Ave., Ste. 100,
Naperville, IL 60563
Phone: 630-369-3390
Contact: Donna Sandberg, MS, NCC, LCPC,
Owner/Counselor

Career Vision / The Ball Foundation,
800 Roosevelt Rd., E-200,
Glen Ellyn, IL 60137
Phone: 800-469-8378
Contact: Peg Hendershot, Director;
Paula Kosin, MS, LCPC
E-mail: info@careervision.org
www.careervision.org
*(Aptitude-based career planning; clients across
the U.S. and Canada.)*

Davis, Jean, MA,
Counseling Psychology, specializing in
adult career transitions,
1405 Elmwood Ave.,
Evanston, IL 60201
Phone: 847-492-1002
E-mail: jdavis@careertransitions.net
www.careertransitions.net

**Dolan Career & Rehabilitation
Consulting, Ltd.,**
307 Henry St., Ste. 407,
Alton, IL 62002
Phone: 618-474-5328
Fax: 618-462-3359
Contact: J. Stephen Dolan, MA, CRC,
Career & Rehabilitation Consultant
E-mail: dolanrehab@piasanet.com

Grimard Wilson Consulting, Inc.,
333 W. Wacker Dr., Ste. 500,
Chicago, IL 60606
Phone: 312-201-1142 or cell: 312-925-5176
Contact: Diane Wilson
E-mail: info@grimardwilson.com
www.grimardwilson.com

**Harper College Community
Career Services,**
1200 W. Algonquin Rd., Rm. A-347,
Palatine, IL 60067.
Phone: 847-925-6293
Contact: Kathleen Canfield, Director

*Heartsong Consulting,
1077 Ash St.,
Winnetka, IL 60093
Phone: 847-441-0375
Contact: Regina Lopata Logan, PhD
E-mail: gina@heartsongconsulting.com

*Lansky Career Consultants,
500 N Michigan Ave., #1940,
Chicago, IL 60611
Phone: 312-494-0022
Contact: Judith Lansky, MA, MBA,
President
E-mail: lanskycareers@yahoo.com

LeBrun, Peter,
Career/Life Coach,
Executive Career Management,
4333 N. Hazel St., Ste. 100,
Chicago, IL 60613
Phone: 773-281-7274
E-mail: peterlebrun@aol.com

LifeScopes,
427 Greenwood St., Ste. 3W,
Evanston, IL 60201
Phone: 847-733-1805
Contact: Barbara H. Hill,
Career Management Consultant
E-mail: LifeScopes@aol.com

*Midwest Ministry Development Service
(an Interdenominational Church Career
Development Center),
1840 Westchester Blvd., Ste. 204,
Westchester, IL 60154
Phone: 708-343-6268
www.midwestministry.org

**Moraine Valley Community College,
Job Placement Center,**
9000 College Pkwy.,
Palos Hills, IL 60465
Phone: 708-974-5737
www.morainevalley.edu/jpc

Quest Clinical Services,
4300 Commerce Ct., Ste. 310,
Lisle, IL 60539
Phone: 630-544-3324
Contact: Camille F. Jones, LCPC, CADC;
Donna C. Bredrup, LCPC

The Summit Group,
PO Box 3794,
Peoria, IL 61612-3794
Phone: 309-657-7156
Fax: 312-896-7411
Contact: John R. Throop, DMin President
E-mail: throop@consultsummit.com

INDIANA

KCDM Associates,
10401 N. Meridian St., Ste. 300,
Indianapolis, IN 46290
Phone: 317-581-6230
Contact: David A. Mueller, President

IOWA

Sucher, Billie Ruth, MS, CTMS,
CTSB, JCTC,
7177 Hickman Rd., Ste. 10,
Des Moines, IA 50322
Phone: 515-276-0061
E-mail: billie@billiesucher.com
www.billiesucher.com

University of Iowa, Career Center,
100 Pomerantz Center, Ste. C310,
Iowa City, IA 52242
Phone: 319-335-1023

Zilber, Suzanne, PhD,
Licensed Psychologist,
Catalyst Counseling,
600 5th St., Ste. 302,
Ames, IA 50010-6072
Phone: 515-232-5340
Fax: 515-232-2070
E-mail: szilber@catalystcounseling.com
www.catalystcounseling.com

KANSAS

Keeping the People, Inc.,
13488 W. 126th Terr.,
Overland Park, KS 66213
Phone: 913-620-4645
Contact: Leigh Branham
E-mail: LB@keepingthepeople.com
www.keepingthepeople.com

*Midwest Ministry Development Service
(an Interdenominational Church Career
Development Center),
8301 State Line Rd., Ste. 216,
Kansas City, MO 64114
Phone: 816-822-1656
Contact: Ross D. Peterson, Director
www.midwestministry.org

KENTUCKY

Career Span, Inc.,
505 Lemon Drop Ln.,
Lexington KY 40511
Phone: 859-233-7726 (233-SPAN)
Contact: Carla Ockerman-Hunter, MA,
MCC, NCC
E-mail: careerspan@aol.com
www.careerspanUSA.com

LOUISIANA

Career Center,
River Center Branch, EBR Parish Library,
120 St. Louis St.,
Baton Rouge, LA 70802
Phone: 225-381-8434
Fax: 225-389-8910
Contact: Ursula B. Carmena, Director
E-mail: ursula@careercenterbr.com
www.careercenterbr.com

MAINE

**Career Perspectives at D. Gallant
Management Associates,**
75 Pearl St., Ste. 204,
Portland, ME 04101
Phone: 207 773-4800
Contact: Deborah L. Gallant, SPHR
E-mail: dhma@dgallant.com

*Heart at Work,
261 Main St.,
Yarmouth, ME 04096
Phone: 207-846-0644
Contact: Barbara Sirois Babkirk, LCPC,
NCC; Amy Wilson Jaffe, MA
Career Counselors, Presenters, Consultants
www.heartatwork.biz

Women's Worth Career Counseling,
9 Village Ln.,
Westbrook, ME 04092
Phone: 207-856-6666
Contact: Jacqueline Murphy,
Career Counselor
Email: earthwind4@juno.com

MARYLAND

Career Development Alliance,
1001 N. Noyes Dr., Ste. B,
Silver Spring, MD 20910
Phone: 301-587-1234
Contact: David M. Reile, PhD;
Barbara H. Suddarth, PhD

**The Career Evaluation and
Coaching Center,**
21 W Rd., Ste. 150,
Baltimore, MD 21204
Phone: 410-825-0042
Fax: 410-825-0310
Contact: Ralph D. Raphael, PhD
E-mail: drraphael@ralphraphael.com
www.ralphraphael.com

College of Notre Dame of Maryland,
Continuing Education Center,
4701 N. Charles St.,
Baltimore, MD 21210
Phone: 410-532-5301

CTS Consulting, Inc.,
3126 Berkshire Rd.,
Baltimore, MD 21214-3404
Phone: 410-444-5857
Contact: Michael Bryant
www.go2ctsonline.com

Friedman, Lynn, PhD,
Clinical Psychologist &
Work-Life Consultant,
5480 Wisconsin Ave., Ste. 206,
Chevy Chase, MD 20815
Phone: 301-656-9650
E-mail: drlynnfriedman@comcast.net
www.drlynnfriedman.com or
www.corporationsonthecouch.com

*Headley, Anne S., MA,
6510 41st Ave.,
University Park, MD 20782
Phone: 301-779-1917
E-mail: asheadley@aol.com
www.anneheadley.com

Mendelson, Irene N.,
BEMW, Inc.,
Counseling and Training for the Workplace,
7984-D, Old Georgetown Rd.,
Bethesda, MD 20814-2440
Phone: 301-657-8922

Positive Passages Life/Career Transition
Counseling and Coaching,
4702 Falstone Ave.,
Chevy Chase, MD 20815
Phone: 301-907-0760
Contact: Jeanette Kreiser, EdD
E-mail: jkreiser@earthlink.net

Prince George's Community College,
Career Assessment and Planning Center,
301 Largo Rd.,
Largo, MD 20772
Phone: 301 322-0608
Contact: Stephanie Cunningham, Career
Advisor

TransitionWorks,
10964 Bloomingdale Dr.,
Rockville, MD 20852-5550
Phone: 301-770-4277
Contact: Stephanie Kay, MA, AGS,
Principal; Nancy K. Schlossberg, EdD,
Principal
E-mail: skay4@verizon.net

MASSACHUSETTS

Berke & Price Associates,
Newtown Way #6,
Chelmsford, MA 01824
Phone: 978-256-0482
Contact: Judit E. Price, MS, CDFI, IJCTC,
CCM, CPRW,
Certified Resume Writer,
Certified Brand Specialist
E-mail: jprice@careercampaign.com
www.careercampaign.com

Career Planning,
Northern Essex Community College,
Elliott St., Haverhill, MA 01830
Phone: 978-556-3722

Career Assistance Center,
Worcester YWCA,
1 Salem Square,
Worcester, MA 01608
Phone: 508-767-2505, ext 3028
Contact: Helen Rinaldi, Director

*Career Management Consultants,
108 Grove St., Ste. 19A,
Worcester, MA 01605
Phone: 508-756-9998
Contact: Patricia Stepanski Plouffe,
Founder/Consultant
E-mail: info@careermc.com

Career Source,
186 Alewife Brook Pkwy., Ste. 310,
Cambridge, MA 02138
Phone: 617-661-7867
www.yourcareersource.com
(Inherited the Radcliffe Career Services Office's
library, after that office closed permanently.
Also offers career counseling.)

*Center for Career Development
& Ministry,
30 Milton St., Ste. 107,
Dedham, MA 02026
Phone: 781-329-2100
Fax: 781-407-0955
Contact: Stephen Ott, Director
E-mail: ccdmin@aol.com

Changes, Career Counseling and
Job-Hunt Training,
2516 Massachusetts Ave.,
Cambridge, MA 02140
Phone: 781-284-2751
Contact: Carl J. Schneider

Jewish Vocational Service, Career Moves
29 Winter St., 5th Floor
Boston, MA 02108
Phone: 617-399-3131 or 617-339-3101
Contact: Judy Sacks, Director
www.career-moves.org

Jewish Vocational Service,
Mature Worker Programs,
333 Nahanton St.,
Newton, MA 02159
Phone: 617-965-7940

*Liebhaber, Gail,
40 Cottage St.,
Lexington, MA 02420
Phone: 781-861-9949
Fax: 781-863-5956
Contact: Gail Liebhaber, MEd
E-mail: gliebhaber@rcn.com
www.yourcareerdirection.com

Miller, Wynne W., Career & Executive
Coaching,
1443 Beacon St.,
Brookline, MA 02446-4707
Phone: 617-232-4848
Fax: 617-232-4846
E-mail: wynne@win-coaching.com

Neil Wilson Career Services,
PO Box 793,
Newburyport, MA 01950
Phone: 978-465-1468
E-mail: info@neilwilson.com

Operation A.B.L.E. of Greater Boston, Inc.,
131 Tremont St., Ste. 301,
Boston, MA 02111
Phone: 617-542-4180 or 888-470-2253
Contact: Joan Cirillo, Executive Director
E-mail: jcirillo@operationable.net
www.operationable.net
(*Employment, training, and career counseling resources for the mature worker.*)

Stein, Phyllis R.,
Career Counseling and Coaching,
59 Parker St.,
Cambridge, MA 02138
Phone: 617-354-7948
E-mail: p.stein@ziplink.net
(*Former director of Radcliffe Career Services.*)

The Work Place,
29 Winter St., 4th Floor
Boston, MA 02111
Phone: 617-737-0093, ext. 104
Contact: Liza-Marie DiCosimo,
Coordinator of Career Services
www.theworkplace.tripod.com
(*Free workshops, free library access, free use of twenty computer workstations, etc.; low-cost counseling, assessment, and resume services.*)

MICHIGAN
*C3 Circle,
Grand Rapids, MI 49534
Phone: 616-677-1953
Contact: Lois Dye, MA, LPC
E-mail: wordpictures@gmail.com

*Career Choices Center,
St. Paul's Episcopal Church
309 S. Jackson St.,
Jackson, MI 49201
Phone: 517-787-3370

*Career Consulting Services,
PO Box 135,
Union Lake, MI 48387
Phone: 248-363-6233
Contact: Marybeth Robb, MA Counselor
E-mail: greatresumes@sbcglobal.net

*Careers Through Faith,
3025 Boardwalk St.,
Ann Arbor, MI 48108
Phone: 734-332-8800
Contact: Cathy Synko
www.CareersThroughFaith.com

*Christian Career Center,
PO Box 362
Howell, MI 48843
Phone: 517-552-0328
Contact: Kevin Brennfleck, MA, NCCC;
Kay Marie Brennfleck, MA, NCCC
E-mail: cocareer@aol.com
www.ChristianCareerCenter.com

Jewish Vocational Service,
29699 Southfield Rd.,
Southfield, MI 48076-2063
Phone: 248-559-5000

*Keystone Coaching & Consulting, LLC,
22 Cherry St.,
Holland, MI 49423
Phone: 616-396-1517
Contact: Mark de Roo
E-mail: keystonecoaching@comcast.net
www.keystonecoach.com

*LifeSteward Group, LLC,
6670 Kalamazoo SE, Ste. E-114,
Grand Rapids, MI 49508
Phone: 616-698-3125
Contact: Ken Soper, MDiv, MA, Director
E-mail: ken@kensoper.com
www.kensoper.com

New Options: Counseling for Women in Transition,
2311 E Stadium, Ste. B-2,
Ann Arbor, MI 48104
Phone: 734-973-0003 or 734-973-8699
Contact: Phyllis Perry, MSW, MFA
E-mail: pepstar27@yahoo.com
(*Specializing in career counseling and creativity pursuits.*)

Synko Associates, LLC
3025 Boardwalk St.
Ann Arbor, MI 48108
Phone: 734-332-8800
Contact: Nick Synko
www.CareersThroughFaith.com

University of Michigan,
Center for the Education of Women,
330 E. Liberty, Ann Arbor, MI 48104
Phone: 734-764-6005
www.cew.umich.edu

MINNESOTA
Human Dynamics,
3036 Ontario Rd.,
Little Canada, MN 55117
Phone: 651-484-8299
Contact: Greg J. Cylkowski, MA, Founder
E-mail: gregjcy@yahoo.com

*North Central Ministry
Development Center
(an Interdenominational Church
Career Development Center),
516 Mission House Ln.,
New Brighton, MN 55112
Phone: 651-636-5120
Contact: Mark Sundby, MDiv, PhD, LP,
Executive Director
www.ncmdc.org

Prototype Career Service,
1071 W. 7th St.,
St. Paul, MN 55102
Phone: 800-368-3197
Contact: Amy Lindgren,
Job Search Strategist
www.prototypecareerservice.com
(*Midlife career change and resumes.*)

Sizen, Stanley J.,
Vocational Services,
PO Box 363,
Anoka, MN 55303
Phone: 763-441-8053

MISSOURI

Eigles, Lorrie, MSED, LPC
432 W. 62nd Terr.,
Kansas City, MO 64113
Phone: 816-363-4171
E-mail: coachlor@swbell.net
www.artistsregister.com

The Job Doctor,
505 S. Ewing,
St. Louis, MO 63103
Phone: 314-863-1166
Contact: M. Rose Jonas, PhD
E-mail: jobdoc@aol.com
www.jobdoctoronline.com

*Midwest Ministry Development Service
(an Interdenominational Church Career
Development Center),
8301 State Line Rd., Ste. 216,
Kansas City, MO 64114
Phone: 816-822-1656
Contact: Ross D. Peterson, Director
www.midwestministry.org

MU Career Center,
Student Success Center,
University of Missouri,
Columbia, MO 65211
Phone: 573-882-6801
Fax: 573-882-5440
Contact: Craig Benson
E-mail: career@missouri.edu

Robert J. Murney Clinic of Forest Institute,
1322 S. Campbell,
Springfield, MO 65807
Phone: 417-865-8943
Contact: Brittany Bouser, Assistant Clinic
Director

Women's Center,
University of Missouri–Kansas City,
5200 Rockhill Rd.,
Kansas City, MO 64110
Phone: 816-235-1638
Contact: Brenda Bethman, Director

MONTANA

Career Transitions,
20900 E., Frontage Rd., B-Mezz
Belgrade, MT 59714
Phone: 406-388-6701
Contact: Darla Joyner, Executive Director
www.careertransitions.com

NEBRASKA

CMS: Career Management Services,
5000 Central Park Dr., Ste. 204,
Lincoln, NE 68504
Phone: 402-466-8427
Contact: Vaughn L. Carter, President

Student Success Center,
Central Community College,
Hastings Campus,
Hastings, NE 68902
Phone: 402-461-2424

NEVADA

Price, Meg, MA, NCC, NCCC
15400 Willowbrook Dr.
Reno, NV 89511
Phone: 775-722-6685
E-mail: worklife4U@aol.com

NEW HAMPSHIRE

IES (Individual Employment Services),
1 New Hampshire Ave., Ste. 125,
Portsmith, NH 03801
Phone: 603-570-4850 or 800-724-5627
Contact: James Otis, Career Counselor;
Anita Labell, Certified Professional
Resume Writer

Tucker, Janet, MEd,
Career Counselor,
10 String Bridge,
Exeter, NH 03833
Phone: 603-772-8693
E-mail: jbtucker@rcn.com

NEW JERSEY

*BBCS Counseling Services,
6 Alberta Dr.,
Marlboro, NJ 07746
(other offices in Iselin and Princeton)
Phone: 800-300-4079
Contact: Beverly Baskin, EdS, MA, CPRW,
Executive Director
E-mail: bbcs@att.net
www.bbcscounseling.com

Behavior Dynamics Associates, Inc.,
34 Cambridge Terr.,
Springfield, NJ 07081
Phone: 973-379-4393
Contact: Roy Hirschfeld
E-mail: hrhnj@aol.com

*CareerQuest,
2165 Morris Ave., Ste. 15,
Union, NJ 07083
Phone: 908-686-8400
Fax: 908-686-8400 (on request)
Contact: Don Sutaria, MS, IE (Prof), PE,
Founder, President, and Life-Work Coach
E-mail: don@careerquestcentral.com
www.careerquestcentral.com
Blog: www.careerquestcentral.blogspot.com

Center for Life Enhancement,
1156 E. Ridgewood Ave.,
Ridgewood, NJ 07450
Phone: 201-670-8443
Contact: David R. Johnson,
Director of Career Programs

Cohen, Jerry, MA, NCC, NCCC,
PO Box 235,
Chester, NJ 07930
Phone: 908-813-1188 or 800-331-0063

Collins, Loree,
3 Beechwood Rd.,
Summit, NJ 07901
Phone: 908-273-9219

Grundfest, Sandra, EdD, Licensed
Psychologist & Certified Career Counselor,
35 Clyde Rd., Ste. 101,
Somerset, NJ 08873
Phone: 609-921-8401
Fax: 609-921-9430

Job Seekers of Montclair,
St. Luke's Episcopal Church,
73 S. Fullerton Ave.,
Montclair, NJ 07042
Phone: 973-744-6220
(Meets Wednesdays, 7:30–9:15 p.m.)

JobSeekers in Princeton NJ,
Trinity Church,
33 Mercer St.,
Princeton, NJ 08540
Phone: 609-924-2277
www.trinityprinceton.org
(Meets Tuesdays, 7:30–9:30 p.m.)

Mercer County Community College,
Career Services,
1200 Old Trenton Rd.,
Trenton, NJ 08690
Phone: 609-570-3304
Contact: Patrick Corozza

Metro Career Services,
784 Morris Turnpike, Ste. 203,
Short Hills, NJ 07078
Phone: 973-912-0106
Contact: Judy Scherer, MA
E-mail: metcareer@aol.com

Princeton Management Consultants, Inc.,
99 Moore St.,
Princeton, NJ 08540
Phone: 609-924-2411
Contact: Niels H. Nielsen, MA,
Job and Career Counselor

Sigmon, Scott B., EdD,
Career Counseling and Vocational Testing,
1945 Morris Ave.,
Union, NJ 07083
Phone: 908-686-7555

*W L. Nikel & Associates,
459 Passaic Ave., Ste. 171,
W Calswell, NJ 07006
Phone: 973-439-1850
Contact: William L. Nikel, MBA Wharton
E-mail: wnikel@verizon.net

NEW YORK

Bernstein, Alan B., CSW, PC,
122 E 82nd St.,
New York, NY 10028
Phone: 212-288-4881

Bethlehem Public Library,
Career guidance available,
451 Delaware Ave.,
Delmar, NY 12054
Phone: 518-439-9314

The Career Center,
M. Robert Lowe Hall,
140 Hofstra University,
Hempstead, NY 11549
Phone: 516-463-6060

*CareerQuest,
c/o TRS, Inc., Professional Ste.,
44 E. 32nd St.,
New York, NY 10016
Phone: 908-686-8400
Fax: 908-686-8400 (on request)
Contact: Don Sutaria, MS, IE (Prof.), PE,
Founder, President, and Life-Work Coach
E-mail: don@careerquestcentral.com
www.careerquestcentral.com
Blog: www.careerquestcentral.blogspot.com

Careers by Choice, Inc.,
205 E. Main St.,
Huntington, NY 11743
Phone: 631-673-5432
Contact: Marjorie ("MJ") Feld

Careers In Transition, LLC,
Professional Career Services and Counseling,
11 Computer Dr. W #112,
Albany, NY 12205
Phone: 518-366-8451
Contact: Thomas J. Denham, MEd,
Managing Partner and Career Counselor
E-mail: careersintransition@yahoo.com
www.careersintransitionllc.com

*Center for Creativity and Work,
19 W 34th St.,
New York, NY 10001
Phone: 212-490-9158, 845-336-8318, or
800-577-8318 (NY and CA)
Contact: Allie Roth, President
E-mail: allie@allieroth.com
www.allieroth.com
*(Offices in Manhattan, NY; Woodstock, NY;
and Berkeley, CA.)*

Greene, Kera, MEd,
19 W 34th St.,
Penthouse Floor,
New York, NY 10001
Phone: 212-947-7111, ext. 244
Cell: 917-496-1804
E-mail: kera1010@yahoo.com

*Judith Gerberg Associates,
250 W 57th St., Ste. 2315,
New York, NY 10107
Phone: 212-315-2322
E-mail: Judith@gerberg.com
www.gerberg.com

Kingsborough Community College,
Office of Career Counseling and Placement,
2001 Oriental Blvd., Rm. C102,
Brooklyn, NY 11235
Phone: 718-368-5115
Contact: Brian Mitra

New York University,
Center for Career, Education & Life Planning,
50 W. 4th St., 330 Shimkin Hall,
New York, NY 10012-1165
Phone: 212-998-7060

Onondaga County Public Library,
The Galleries of Syracuse,
447 S Salina St.,
Syracuse, NY 13202-2494
Phone: 315-435-1900
Contact: Reference Department
E-mail: reference@onlib.org

Orange County Community College,
Counseling Center,
115 S St.,
Middletown, NY 10940
Phone: 845-341-4070

Passion into Practice,
395 S End Ave.
New York, NY
Phone: 646-649-3568
Contact: Laurel Donnellan, Director
E-mail: info@passionintopractice.com
www.passionintopractice.com

Personnel Sciences Center,
40 Briarcliff Rd.,
Westbury, NY 11590
Phone: 516-338-5340
Fax: 516-338-5341
Contact: Dr. Jeffrey A. Goldberg, PhD,
President, Licensed Psychologist
E-mail: jag_psc@juno.com
(Services also provided in Manhattan.)

The Prager-Bernstein Group,
122 E. 42nd St., Ste. 2815,
New York, NY 10168
Phone: 212-697-0645
Contact: Leslie B. Prager, MA, CMP,
Senior Partner/Career Counselor
E-mail: Leslie-PBG@email.msn.com
www.prager-bernsteingroup.com
(Specializes in career transitions and job changes for mid-career professionals, recent college graduates, and pre-retirement coaching.)

Premium Career Management for Attorneys,
1776 Broadway, Ste. 1806,
New York, NY 10019
Phone: 212-397-1020
Contact: Celia Paul, President
www.celiapaulassociates.com
(Specializes in lawyers.)

Psychological Services Center,
Career Services Unit,
University at Albany, SUNY,
229 Washington Ave.,
Albany, NY 12206
Phone: 518-442-4900
Contact: George B. Litchford, PhD, Director
(Individual career counseling.)

Professional Experience and Career Planning,
Long Island University,
CW Post Campus,
Brookville, NY 11548 -9988
Phone: 516-299-2251
Contact: Jeanette Grill, Director

Science & Technology Advisory Board,
1776 Broadway, Ste. 1806,
New York, NY 10019
Phone: 212-397-1021
Contact: Dr. Stephen Rosen, Chairman
E-mail: srosen@verison.net
www.careerchangeability.com/scientists
and www.careerchangeability.com/doctors
Blog:
www.careerchangechampions.blogspot.com
(Specializes in scientists and engineers.)

NORTH CAROLINA

Allman & Co., Inc.,
Wilmington, NC 28412
Phone: 910-395-5219
Contact: Steven Allman, LPC, MCC
E-mail: sallman@ecc.rr.com

Career, Educational, Psychological Evaluations,
4425 Randolph Rd., Ste. 411,
Charlotte, NC 28211
Phone: 704-362-1942
Contact: Elizabeth Long, President

Career Focus Workshops,
8301 Brittains Field Rd.,
Oak Ridge, NC 27310
Phone: 336-643-1419
Contact: Glenn Wise, President
E-mail: gwise001@triad.rr.com

*The Career and Personal Counseling Service,
4108 Park Rd., Ste. 200,
Charlotte, NC 28209
Phone: 704-523-7751
Fax: 704-523-7752
Contact: Vickie P. McCreary, PhD,
Executive Director
E-mail: vpmccreary@careerservice.org
www.careerservice.org

Carolina Career Consulting,
1145A Executive Cir.,
Cary, NC 27511
Phone: 919-238-5050
Contact: Lisa Schwartz, MA, LPC, NCC
E-mail: careerconsulting@mindspring.com
www.careerconsulting.com

Joyce Richman & Associates, Ltd.,
2911 Shady Lawn Dr.,
Greensboro, NC 27408
Phone: 336-288-1799
E-mail: jerichman@aol.com
www.joycerichman.com

Kochendofer, Sally, PhD,
Charlotte, NC 28211
Phone: 704-362-1514
E-mail: careerconsult@earthlink.net

*The Life/Career Institute
131 Chimney Rise Dr.,
Cary, NC 27511
Phone: 919-469-5775
Contact: Mike Thomas, PhD
E-mail: mikethomas@nc.rr.com
www.LifeCareerInstitute.com

Appendix

Life Management Services, LC,
127 Chimney Rise Dr.,
Cary, NC 27511
Phone: 919-481-4707
Contact: Marilyn and Hal Shook
*(The Shooks originally trained with the late,
great John Crystal, though they went on to
develop their own program thereafter.)*

**Personal and Professional Development
Systems,**
Forest Park Ct.,
Pisgah Forest Park/Farms,
Pisgah Forest, NC 28768
Contact: William P. Henning, Counselor
E-mail: ppdsi@verizon.net

Triangle Business Coaching,
3203 Woman's Club Dr., Ste. 100,
Raleigh, NC 27612
Phone: 919-862-0301
Contact: Temple G. Porter, Director
E-mail: temple@tricoach.biz

OHIO

Community Services of Stark County, Inc.,
625 Cleveland Ave. NW,
Canton, OH 44702
Phone: 330-305-9696
Contact: Victor W. Valli, Director, Career &
Business Services
E-mail: vvalli@nci2000.net

Cuyahoga County Public Library,
The Career Center,
5225 Library Ln.,
Maple Heights, OH 44137-1291
Phone: 216-475-2225
E-mail: beaston@cuyahogalibrary.org
www.cuyahogalibrary.org

*Diversified Career Services, Inc.,
Columbus, OH 43204
Phone: 614-488-3359
Contact: Laura Armstrong,
Career Counselor & Executive Coach
E-mail: careers@DCScreatingfutures.com
www.DCScreatingfutures.com
(Services provided in person and by phone)

*Flood, Kay Reynolds,
MA Ministry degree
3600 Parkhill Cir. NW,
Canton, OH 44718
Phone: 330-493-1448

The Human Touch,
Phone: 513-683-9603
Contact: Judy R. Kroger, LPC,
Career Counselor and Coach
E-mail: judykroger@aol.com

**J&K Associates and Success Skills
Seminars,** Inc.,
607 Otterbein Ave.,
Dayton, OH 45406-4507
Phone: 937-274-3630
Fax: 937-274-4375
Contact: Pat Kenney, PhD, President

*KSM Careers & Consulting,
1655 W. Market St., Ste. 506,
Akron, OH 44313
Phone: 330-867-0242
Contact: Kathryn Musholt, President

*Midwest Development Service
(an Interdenominational Church
Career Development Center),
1520 Old Henderson Rd., Ste. 102B,
Columbus, OH 43221-3616
Phone: 614-442-8822
www.midwestministry.org

New Career,
328 Race St.,
Dover, OH 44622
Phone: 330-364-5557
Contact: Marshall Karp, MA, NCC, LPC,
Owner

***Professional Pastoral-Counseling
Institute,** Inc. (PPI),
8035 Hosbrook Rd., Ste. 300,
Cincinnati, OH 45236
Phone: 513-791-5990
Contact: Judy Kroger, LPC (voicemail 103),
Career Counselor and Coach
E-mail: judykroger@aol.com

Woods, Anne,
8225 Markhaven Ct.,
Columbus, OH 43235
Phone: 614-888-7941

OKLAHOMA

Career Development Services, Inc.,
4137 S. Harbor, Ste. A,
Tulsa, OK 74135
Phone: 918-293-0500
Fax: 918-293-0503
E-mail: bboyd@cardevser.com
www.cardevser.com

OREGON

*Exceptional Living Coach,
Lisa Anderson, MA, NCC, GCDF,
Eugene, OR
Phone: 541-484-6785
www.ExceptionalLivingCoach.com
*(Individual and group career coaching.
English and Spanish.)*

Careerful Counseling Services,
9860 SW Hall Blvd., Ste. E,
Tigard, OR 97223
Phone: 503-997-9506
Contact: Andrea King, MS, NCC,
Career Counselor
E-mail: aking@careerful.com
www.careerful.com

Verk Consultants, Inc.,
1190 Olive St.,
PO Box 11277,
Eugene, OR 97440
Phone: 541-687-9170
Contact: Larry H. Malmgren, MS, President

*Bartholomew, Uda.,
Vocational Transformations/
Vocational Liberation Workshops,
PO Box 2112,
Center City Philadelphia, PA 19103
Phone: 215-618-1572
Contact: Uda Bartholomew,
Lead Facilitator
E-mail: VocTransVocLib@comcast.net

Career by Design,
340 N. Main St.,
Telford, PA 18969
Phone: 215-723-8413
Contact: Henry D. Landes, Consultant
www.dvfambus.com

Career Development Center,
Jewish Family & Children's Service,
5743 Bartlett St.,
Pittsburgh, PA 15217
Phone: 412-422-5627
Contact: Cheryl Finlay, PhD, Director
E-mail: info@careerdevelopmentcenter.org
www.careerdevelopcenter.org

Hannafin, Christine, PhD,
Personal and Career Counseling
Bala Farm,
380 Jenissa Dr.,
West Chester, PA 19382
Phone: 610-431-0588
E-mail: chrishannafin@aol.com
www.christinehannafin.com

Haynes, Lathe, PhD,
401 Shady Ave., Ste. C107,
Pittsburgh, PA 15206
Phone: 412-361-6336

JEVS Career Strategies,
1845 Walnut St., 7th Floor,
Philadelphia, PA 19103-4707
Phone: 215-854-1874
Fax: 215-854-1880
E-mail: cs@jevs.org
www.jevs.org

Kelly, Jack, Career Counselor,
Career Pro Resume Services,
251 DeKalb Pike, Ste. E608,
King of Prussia, PA 19406
Phone: 610-337-7187
www.careerproresumes-kop.com

Kessler, Jane E., MA,
Licensed Psychologist,
252 W. Swamp Rd., Ste. 56,
Doylestown, PA 18901
Phone: 215-348-8212
Fax: 215-348-0329

Priority Two,
PO Box 425,
Warrendale, PA 15086
Phone: 724-935-0252
Contact: Don Priestly, Executive Director
www.ptwo.org

Taylor, Alan, MS, MDiv, CRC, CAC, LPC,
part-time office at:
2405 E. Swamp Rd.,
Quakertown, PA 18951
Phone: 215-847-4451
E-mail: twotaylors97_@yahoo.com

Crystal-Barkley Corp.
(formerly The John C. Crystal Center),
293 E Bay St.,
Charleston, SC 29401
Phone: 800-333-9003
Fax: 800-560-5333
Contact: Nella G. Barkley, President
E-mail: crystalbarkley@careerlife.com
www.careerlife.com
(*John Crystal, the founder of the Crystal Center,
died in 1988; Nella, his business partner for
many years, now continues his work.*)

Banks, Mary M., Career Counselor,
4536 Chickasaw Rd.,
Kingsport, TN 37664
Phone: 423-288-2646
E-mail: careers@chartertn.net

*Career Resources, Inc.,
208 Elmington Ave.,
Nashville, TN 37205
Phone: 615-292-0292
Contact: Jane C. Hardy, Principal
www.CareerResources.net

Karlson, Bill, CPC, CPS,
2000 Mallory Ln., Ste. 130-399,
Franklin, TN 37067-8231
E-mail: bill@billkarlson.com

*Slay, Patrick, MA, NCC
Career Counselor,
3200 W End Ave., Ste. 500,
Nashville, TN 37203
Phone: 615-585-7529
E-mail: patrickslay@yahoo.com

*RHM Group, Inc.,
PO Box 291822
Nashville, Tennessee 37229
Phone: 615-391-4500 or 800-956-3320
Fax: 615-882-0900
Contact: Robert H. McKown, President
E-mail: bob@rhmgroup.com
www.rhmgroup.com

Career Action Associates PC,
8350 Meadow Rd., Ste. 272,
Dallas, TX 75231
Phone: 214-378-8350
Contact: Joyce Shoop, LPC;
Rebecca Hayes, MEd, CRC, LPC
Phone: 817-926-9941;
E-mail: rhayescaa@aol.com

Appendix

Career Art Innovators,
1902 E. Common Street, Ste. 400
New Braunfels, TX 78130
Phone: 830-626-6334
Cell: 830-832-7448
Contact: Shell Herman, MS
*(Career transition counseling for individuals
and groups.)*

Career and Recovery Resources, Inc.,
2525 San Jacinto,
Houston, TX 77002
Phone: 713-754-7000
Contact: Vernal Swisher, Director

Life Transitions, Inc.,
6800 Park Ten Blvd., Ste. 298 W,
San Antonio, TX 78213
Phone: 210-737-2100
www.life-career.com

***New Life Institute,**
PO Box 4487,
Austin, TX 78765
Phone: 512-469-9447
Contact: Bob Breihan

Quereau, Jeanne, MA, LPC,
9500 Jollyville Rd., #121,
Austin, TX 78759
Phone: 512-342-9552
E-mail: jeanneq19@gmail.com

Southwest Ministry Development Service
(an Interdenominational Church Career
Development Center),
8215 Westchester Dr., Ste. 307,
Dallas, TX 75225
Phone: 214-346-9790
Contact: Ross D. Peterson, Director
www.midwestministry.org

***Sue Cullen & Associates,**
7000 Bee Caves Rd., Ste. 300,
Austin, TX 78746
Phone: 512-732-1249
Contact: Sue Cullen
E-mail: sue@suecullen.com
www.suecullen.com

***Worklife Institute Consulting,**
1900 St. James Pl., Ste. 880,
Houston, TX 77056
Phone: 713-266-2456
Contact: Diana C. Dale, Director
E-mail: info@worklifeinstitute.com
www.worklifeinstitute.com

UTAH
Lue, Keith,
PO Box 971482,
Orem, UT 84097-1482
Phone: 801-885-1389
E-mail: keithlue@keydiscovery.com

VERMONT
Career Networks,
1372 Old Stage Rd.,
Williston, VT 05495
Phone: 802-872-1533
Contact: Markey Read
www.employvt.com

VIRGINIA
Beach Counseling & Career Center,
Offices in Virginia Beach and Norfolk,
Phone: 757-306-9100
Cell: 757-560-0357
Contact: Suzan Thompson, PhD
www.my-career-counselor.com

The BrownMiller Group,
312 Granite Ave.,
Richmond, VA 23226
Phone: 804-288-2157
Contact: Bonnie Miller
www.BrownMiller.com

Conrad, Dale, EdD, NCC, NCCC,
Career Development Counselor,
New River Community College,
PO Box 1127,
Dublin, VA 24084
Phone: 540-674-3609
TTY: 540-674-3619
Fax: 540-674-3644
Floyd County: 430-745-4595;
Giles County: 540-021-4595;
Toll Free: 1-866-462-6722
E-mail: nrconrd@nr.edu

Fairfax County Office for Women,
12000 Government Center Pkwy., Ste. 318,
Fairfax, VA 22035
Phone: 703-324-5730

Hollins University, Career Center,
PO Box 9628,
Roanoke, VA 24020-1628
Phone: 540-362-6272
Contact: Tina Rolen, Director

Mary Baldwin College,
Rosemarie Sena Center for Career and Life
Planning,
Kable House,
Staunton, VA 24401
Phone: 540-887-7111

McCarthy & Company,
Career Transition Management,
4201 S 32nd Rd.,
Arlington, VA 22206
Phone: 703-671-4300
Contact: Peter McCarthy, President

Psychological Consultants, Inc.,
6724 Patterson Ave.,
Richmond, VA 23226
Phone: 804-288-4125

Virginia Commonwealth University,
University Career Center,
907 Floyd Ave., Rm.143,
Richmond, VA 23284-2007
Phone: 804-828-1645

The Women's Center,
133 Park St., NE,
Vienna, VA 22180
Phone: 703-281-2657
www.thewomenscenter.org

Bridgeway Career Development,
227 Bellevue Way NE, #257,
Bellevue, WA 98004
Phone: 1-877-250-2103
Contact: Janet Scarborough,
PhD, LMHC, MCC, Owner
E-mail: js@bridgewaycareer.com
www.bridgewaycareer.com

Career Management Institute,
8404 27th St. W.,
University Pl., WA 98466
Phone: 253-565-8818
Contact: Ruthann Reim McCraffree, MA,
NCC, LMHC, CPC
E-mail: careermi@nwrain.com
www.CareerMI.com

**Centerpoint Institute for Career and
Life Renewal,**
4000 NE 41st St., Bldg. D, Ste. 2,
Seattle, WA 98105-5428
Phone: 206-686-LIFE (5433)
E-mail: admin@centerpointonline.org
www.centerpointonline.org

Churchill, Diana,
300 W. Hawthorne,
Whitworth University, Spokane, WA 99251
Phone: 509-458-0962

The Individual Development Center, Inc.
(I.D. Center),
1020 E. John,
Seattle, WA 98102
Phone: 206-329-0600
Contact: Margaret Porter, MEd, President

MJT Consulting,
302 Park Ave.,
Yakima, WA 98902
Contact: Marilyn J. Tellez, MA
Cell: 509-307-2396
E-mail: doitnow@nwinfo.net
www.doitnowcareercoach.info

WASHINGTON, DC

**Blackwell Career Management of
Capitol Hill,**
626 A St. SE,
Washington, DC 20003
Phone: 202-546-6835
E-mail: mblackwell519@msn.com
www.blackwellcareermanagement.com

Hoppin, Prue,
Career Counselor/Coach,
2632 Woodley Pl. NW,
Washington, DC 20008
Phone: 202-986-9345
E-mail: pruehoppin@ix.netcom.com

Horizons Unlimited, Inc.,
717 D St. NW, Ste. 300,
Washington, DC 20004
17501 McDade Ct.,
Rockville, MD 20855
Phone: 301-258-9338
Contact: Marilyn Goldman,
LPC, NCCC, MCC
www.career-counseling.com

The Women's Center,
1025 Vermont Ave. NW, Ste. 310,
Washington DC, 20005
Phone: 202-293-4580
www.thewomenscenter.org

WEST VIRGINIA

Ticich, Frank, MS, CRC, CVE,
Career Consultant,
153 Tartan Dr.,
Follansbee, WV 26037
Phone: 304-748-1772
E-mail: freedom1@swave.net
(Free services available.)

WISCONSIN

Guarneri Associates,
Career Focus and Job Search
Coaching, and Personal Branding,
6670 Crystal Lake Rd.,
Three Lakes, WI 54562
Phone: 715-546-4449 or 866-881-4055
Contact: Susan Guarneri, NCCC, DCC,
CERW, CPBS
E-mail: Susan@AssessmentGoddess.com

Making Alternative Plans,
Career Education Center,
Alverno College,
3401 S. 39th St.,
PO Box 343922,
Milwaukee, WI 53234-3922
Phone: 414-382-6010

Swanson, David,
Career Seminars and Workshops,
7235 W Wells St.,
Wauwatosa, WI 53213-3607
Phone: 414-774-4755
E-mail: dswanson@wi.rr.com
*(David was on staff at my Two-Week Workshop
twenty times.)*

WYOMING

University of Wyoming,
The Center for Advising and Career Services,
PO Box 3195/Knight Hall, #222,
Laramie, WY 82071-3195
Phone: 307-766-2398
www.uwyo.edu/cacs

CANADA

British Columbia
CBD Network, Inc.,
#201-2033 Gordon Dr.,
Kelowna, BC V1Y 3J2
Phone: 250-717-1821

Curtis, Susan, MEd, RCC, CEAP,
4513 W. 13th Ave.,
Vancouver, BC V6R 2V5
Phone: 604-228-9618
E-mail: susancurtis@telus.net

Find Work You Love, Inc.,
2277 W 2nd Ave., Ste. 704,
Vancouver, BC V6K 1H8
Phone: 604-737-3955 or 888-737-3922
Fax: 604-737-3958
Contact: Marlene Haley, BA, MEd,
Career Counselor
www.findworkyoulove.com

Westcoast Vocational, Inc.,
400-1681 Chestnut St.,
Vancouver, BC V6J 4M6
Phone: 604-737-9884 (Vancouver) or
604-948-8063 (Tsawwassen)
Contact: Barbara Wilkinson, MA, RCC,
Career Counselor, Consultant & Coach
www.westvoc.com

Manitoba
Westcoast Vocational, Inc.,
400-1681 Chestnut St.,
Vancouver, BC V6J 4M6
Phone: 604-737-9884 (Vancouver) or
604-948-8063 (Tsawwassen)
Contact: Barbara Wilkinson, MA,
Career Counselor, Consultant & Coach
www.westvoc.com

Nova Scotia
People Plus,
7001 Mumford Rd.,
Halifax Shopping Centre,
Tower 1, Ste. 203,
Halifax, NS B3L 4N9
Phone: 902-453-6556
Fax: 902-453-2345
www.peopleplusconsulting.com

Ontario
After Graduation Career Counseling,
121 Richmond St. W, Ste. 302,
Toronto, ON M5H 2K1
Phone: 416-359-9212, ext. 224
Contact: Teresa Snelgrove, PhD, Director

André Filion & Associates, Inc.,
151 Slater St., Ste. 500,
Ottawa, ON K1P 5H3
Phone: 613-230-7023
Contact: Kenneth Des Roches

Career Partners International/
Hazell & Assoc.,
95 St. Clair W., Ste. 1604,
Toronto, ON M4V 1N6
Phone: 416-961-3700
E-mail: mhazell@hazell.com

*CareersPlus, Inc.,
55 Village Pl., Ste. 203,
Mississaugua, ON L4Z 1V9
Phone: 905-272-8258
Contact: Douglas H. Schmidt,
BA, MEd, EdD
www.careersplusinc.com

Career Strategy Counselling,
2 Briar Hill Pl.,
London, ON N5Y 1P7
Phone: 519-455-4609
Contact: Ruth Clarke, BA
E-mail: rclarke4609@rogers.com
www.careerstrategycounselling.com

Career Development Consultants,
Health Services Sector,
1 Belvedere Ct., Ste. 1207,
Brampton, ON L6V 4M6
Phone: 905-450-1086
Contact: Mary M. Wheeler RN, MEd, ACC
E-mail: info@donnerwheeler.com
www.donnerwheeler.com
(Offers workshops and coaching particularly
for those in the health services sector.)

Human Achievement Associates,
22 Cottonwood Crescent,
London, ON N6G 2Y8
Phone: 519-657-3000
Contact: Mr. Kerry A. Hill
E-mail: haa.no.1@rogers.com

JVS of Greater Toronto,
74 Tycos Dr.,
Toronto, ON M6B 1V9
Phone: 416-787-1151, ext. 210
Fax: 416-785-7529
Contact: Wendy Fields,
Manager of Marketing
E-mail: wfields@jvstoronto.org

Mid-Life Transitions,
252 Salem Ave.,
Toronto, ON M6H 3C7
Phone: 416-537-6269
Contact: Marilyn Melville
E-mail: thepilgrim@look.ca

Puttock, Judith, BBA, CHRP,
Career Management Consultant,
The Puttock Group,
913 Southwind Ct.,
Newmarket, ON
Phone: 905-898-0180

YMCA Career Planning & Development,
42 Charles St. E,
Toronto, ON M4Y 1T4
Phone: 416-928-9622

Quebec
Jewish Vocational Service,
Centre Juif D'Orientation et de L'Emploi,
5151, ch. de la Côte Ste-Catherine, Ste. 310,
Montreal, QC H3W 1M6
Phone: 514-345-2625
Fax: 514-345-2648
Contact: Alta Abramowitz, Director,
Employment Development Services.
(Uses both French and English versions of
Parachute. Utilise des versions Françaises et
Anglaises de Parachute.)

La Passerelle Career Transition Centre,
1255 Phillips Square, Ste. 903,
Montreal, QC H3B 3G1
Contact: Lisa Boyle
Phone: 514-866-5982
E-mail: lapasserelle@videotron.ca

Roy, Marie-Carmelle,
Career Development Consultant,
Phone: 514-992-5219
E-mail: mcroy20@sympatico.ca
(Marie-Carmelle was on my staff at the
Two-Week Workshop for seven years.)

OVERSEAS

Australia
Career Action Centre,
5 Bronte Ave.,
Burwood, Victoria 3125
Phone: 03 9808 5500
Contact: Jackie Rothberg
E-mail: jackie@careeractioncentre.com.au
www.careeractioncentre.com.au

Designing Your Life,
10 Nepean Pl.,
Macquarie, ACT 2614
Phone: 61 6 253 2231
Contact: Judith Bailey

The Growth Connection,
56 Berry St., Ste. 402, 4th Floor,
North Sydney, NSW 2060
Phone: 61 2 9954 3322
Contact: Imogen Wareing, Director

Life by Design,
PO Box 50,
Newport Beach, NSW 2106
Phone: 61 2 9979 4949
Contact: Ian Hutchinson, Lifestyle Strategist
E-mail: info@lifebydesign.com.au
www.lifebydesign.com.au

Milligan, Narelle,
Career Consultant (regional NSW)
Cell: 0411 236 124
E-mail: nmilligan2000@yahoo.com.au

Taccori, John, EdD,
Career Counsellor,
1 Marau Pl.,
Winmalee, NSW, 2777
Phone: 02 47542002

Brazil
Adigo Consultores,
Av. Doria 164,
Sao Paulo SP 04635-070
Phone: 55-11-530-0330
Contact: Alberto M. Barros, Director

Germany
Buddensieg, Marc,
Spechtweg 6,
30938 Burgwedel
Phone: +49(0)163 /624 2639
Fax: 012120 / 277 627
E-mail: buddensieg@gmx.de

Glöer, Julia,
Bahrenfelder Straße 265,
22765 Hamburg
Phone: +49(0)40 390 65 19
Cell: 0171 213 40 20
E-mail: julia.gloeer@web.de
www.life-work-planning.de

Hoff, Rüdiger,
Rönnkamp 14a,
22457 Hamburg
Phone: +49 (0)40 - 4321 38 69
E-mail: ruediger.hoff@gmx.de
www.jobolution.de

Leitner, Madeleine, Dipl. Psych.,
Ohmstrasse 8, 80802 Munchen
Phone: 089/33079444
Fax: 089/33079445
E-mail: ML@Karriere-Management.de
www.Karriere-Management.de

Webb, John Carl,
Meinenkampstr 83a,
48165 Munster-Hiltrup
Phone: +49 (0) 2501/ 92 16 96
E-mail: john@muenster.de
www.learnline.de/angebote/lwp
(*Universities offering Life/Work Planning
courses based on* Parachute *are located in
Berlin, Bochum, Bremen, Freiburg, Hannover,
Konstanz, and Münster. See website for details*).

Ireland
Brian McIvor & Associates,
Newgrange Mall, Unit 4B,
Slane, County Meath
Phone: (00) 353 41 988 4035
E-mail: bmcivor1@eircom.net
www.brianmcivor.com
(*Brian was on the staff at my international
Two-Week Workshop for five years.*)

New Zealand
DreamMakers,
12 Hollywood Ave.,
Titirangi, Auckland
Phone: 64 9 817 5189
Contact: Liz Constable
lizconstable@slingshot.co.nz

Life Work Career Counselling,
PO Box 2223,
Christchurch
Phone: 64 03 379 2781
Contact: Max Palmer

McLennan, Felicity,
4th Floor, Braemar House,
32 The Terrace,
PO Box 3058,
Wellington
Phone: (04) 385 97 90
Cell: 0275 620 097
E-mail: felicity.mclennan@xtra.co.nz

Singapore
Transformation Technologies Pte Ltd.,
122 Thomson Green,
574986 Singapore
Phone: 65 98197858
Contact: Anthony Tan, Director
E-mail: anthonyt@singnet.com.sg

South Africa
Andrew Bramley Career Consultants,
12 Ridge Way/PO Box 1311,
Proteaville, Durbanville 7550
Phone: +27 (0)21 9755573
Fax: +27 (0)88 (0)21 9755573
Contact: Andrew Bramley
E-mail: abramley@mweb.co.za
www.andrewbramley.co.za

South Korea
Byung Ju Cho,
Seocho-Ku Banpo-dong
104-16 Banpo Hyundai Villa A-402,
Seoul, 137-040,
South Korea
Phone: 011-9084-6236
(BJ is the translator of the Korean version of
Parachute.*)*

Spain
Analisi-Nic,
Via Augusta, 120,
Principal 1,
08006 Barcelona
Phone: (34) 932119503
Fax: (34) 932172128
Contact: José Arnó
E-mail: analisi@arrakis.es

Switzerland
Bamert-Widmer, Maria,
Berufs- & Lebensgestaltung,
Churerstrasse 26,
CH-8852, Altendor
Phone: 055 442 55 76
E-mail: mbamert@motivatorin.ch
www.motivatorin.ch

Baumgartner, Peter,
Lowen Pfaffikon,
Postfach 10,
8808 Pfaffikon
Phone: 055 415 66 22

Hans-U. Sauser,
Beratung und Ausbildung,
Rosenauweg 27,
CH-5430 Wettingen
Phone: 056 426 64 09
E-mail: husauser@gmx.ch

HCM Honegger Career Mgmt.,
Im Gsteig 2,
CH-8703 Erlenbach ZH
Phone: +4179 420 48 78
Contact: Urs W. Honegger
E-mail: karriere@hcm.ch
www.hcm.ch

KLB LifeDesigning,
Alpenblickstrasse 33,
CH-8645 Jona-Kempraten
Phone: + 41 (0)55 211 09 77
Fax: +41 (0)55 211 09 79
Contact: Peter Kessler, LifeDesigning Coach
Email: p.kessler@bluewin.ch
www.LifeDesigning.ch

LifeProject,
Career Coaching, Work/Life Planning,
Consulting,
Baechlerweg 29,
CH-8802, Kilchburg/Zurich
Phone: +41 (0) 44 715 15 63
Cell: +41 (0)78 626 11 58
Contact: Dr. Peter A. Vollenweider,
E-mail: peter.vollenweider@gmail.com

Porot & Partenaire
Rue de la Terrassière, 8
1207 Genève - Suisse
Phone: +41 (0) 22 700 82 10
Fax: +41 (0) 22 700 82 14
Contact: Daniel Porot, Founder
E-mail: porot@compuserve.com
www.porot.com, www.careergames.com,
www.cabinet-porot.ch,
www.porot.com/pictocv,
www.outplacement3d.com
(Daniel was co-leader with me each summer for
twenty years, at my international Two-Week
Workshops—though I have now retired from
doing these.)

United Kingdom
Bridgeway Associates Ltd.,
Career Consultants,
PO Box 16,
Chipping Campden, GL55 6ZB
London and Midlands
Phone: 01386 841840
Contact: Jane Bartlett

Career Dovetail
4 E. Hill Ct.,
Oxted, Surrey RH8 9AD
and
Hub Working Centre
5 Wormwood St.
London EC2M 1RW
Contact: Duncan Bolam Dip CG,
Director and Founder
E-mail: duncanbolam@careerdovetail.co.uk
www.careerdovetail.co.uk

Castle Consultants International,
9 Drummond Park, Crook of Devon,
Kinross, KY13 0UX
Scotland
Phone: +44-1577-840-122
Fax: +44-1577-842-168
Cell: +44-777-563-0486
Contact: Walt Hopkins,
Founder and Director
E-mail: Walt@WaltHopkins.com
www.WaltHopkins.com

Cavendish Consulting LLP
The Stable Courtyard, Leigh Ct.,
Abbots Leigh, Bristol BS8 3RA
Phone: +44 (0) 7790001360
Contact: Philip Houghton
E-mail: phil.houghton@cavendish2.com

The Chaney Partnership, Hillier House,
509 Upper Richmond Rd. W,
London SW14 7EE
Phone: 020 8878 322
Contact: Isabel Chaney, BA

Hawkins, Dr. Peter,
Mt. Pleasant,
Liverpool, L3 5TF
Phone: 0044 (0) 151 709-1760
Fax: 0044 (0) 151 709-1576
E-mail: p.Hawkins@gieu.co.uk

John Lees Associates,
37 Tatton St.,
Knutsford, Cheshire WA16 6AE
Phone: 01565 631625
Contact: John Lees
E-mail: johnlees@dsl.pipex.com
www.johnleescareers.com

Passport Coaching and Consulting
74 Blenheim Crescent,
South Croyden CR2 6BP
Phone: 020 8681 4838 or 07968 027 344
Contact: Janie Wilson
E-mail: janie@passport.co.uk
www.passport.co.uk

Sherridan Hughes,
Career Management Expert,
110 Pretoria Rd.,
London SW16 6RN
Phone: 020 8769 5737
www.sherridanhughes.com

Readers often write to ask us which of these overseas counselors are familiar with my approach to job-hunting and career-changing. The answer is: virtually all of them have attended my Two-Week Workshop, and therefore know my approach well.

Other overseas counselors not trained by me, but who may still be quite helpful to you, since they are experienced counselors, and are familiar with *Parachute*, are:

Israel
Mendel, Lori,
PO Box 148,
Caesarea, Israel 38900
Phone: 972-3-524-1068
Cell: 972-54-814-4442
E-mail: bizcom@bezeqint.net

Transitions & Resources, Ltd.,
1 Yam Hamelach, Apt. 4,
Jerusalem, Israel 93396
Phone: 02-6710673
Cell: 050 5739496;
U.S. phone line in Israel until 4 p.m. EST:
516-216-4457
Fax: 02-6721985
Contact: Judy Feierstein, CEO
E-mail: info@maavarim.biz
www.maavarim.biz

The Netherlands
Pluym Career Consultants,
Career executive coaching services,
Boshoekerweg 16,
NL/8167 LS EPE/OENE
Contact: Johan Veeninga, Director
E-mail: johan.veeninga@gmail.com or
info@careerconsultants.nl

PHONE AND INTERNET DISTANCE COUNSELING

Career Options,
Phone: 925-270-7430
Contact: Joan Schippman, MA, NCCC
E-mail: joangoforth1@comcast.net
(Successful mid-career transitions.)

McKinney, Donald, EdD, Career Counselor,
131 River Rd.,
DeQueen, AR 71832
Phone: 879-642-5628
E-mail: eaglenest131@yahoo.com

Piazzale, Steve, PhD,
Career/Life Coach,
Mountain View, CA
Phone: 650-964-4366
E-mail: Steve@BayAreaCareerCoach.com
www.BayAreaCareerCoach.com

A

AARP, 203

Accomplishments, documenting, 112

Achievements
 definition of, 280
 drawing out, 71
 extracting skills from, 281–82

Administrative support occupations, 176–77

Ads
 answering, 13
 employer's vs. job-hunter's preference for, 28, 31
 researching salaries through, 126

Affirmations, 232

Agencies. *See* Employment agencies; Governmental agencies

Aggressiveness, 105

Aging
 energy and, 217–20
 mind and, 220–21
 planning and, 216–17
 retirement and, 215–16
 spirituality and, 223
 will and, 221–22
 work and, 222–23

Alternatives
 for employers vs. job-hunters, 28, 30–31
 importance of, 18, 19, 36–37, 133, 333, 346–47

Alumni offices, 15, 156

Americans with Disabilities Act (ADA), 44

"A – B = C" method, 193–99

Answering machine messages, 79

Appearance, personal, 102–3

Area codes, 396

Arrogance, 105

Art and design occupations, 172

Attitude, 41, 103–4

B

The Back Door Guide to Short-Term Job Adventures (Landes), 205

Backdoorjobs.com, 205

Barron-Tieger, Barbara, 259
Bates, Marilyn, 259
Behavioral Interviewing, 71,
    83–84, 95
Benefits, 131–32
*Best Home Businesses for People
    50+* (Edwards and
    Edwards), 198
*Best Home Businesses for the
    Twenty-First Century*
    (Edwards and Edwards),
    198–99
BestPlaces, 148
Best Places to Raise Your Family
    (Sperling), 148
Better Business Bureau, 203
Biofeedback, 244–45
Birch, David, 72
Blocks, overcoming, 225–35
Blogging, 261
Bornstein, David, 312
Brain, left and right sides of,
    225–29
Brooks, Phillips, 366
Brown, Barbara, 244–45
Buechner, Fred, 375
Building-block diagram, 276
Bureau of Labor Statistics, 124,
    169
Business occupations, 169–70
The Business Owner's Idea
    CafÈ, 201
Business Owner's Toolkit, 200

C

Calling, 357. *See also* Mission in
    life

Cantrell, Will, 151
Career centers, 15
Career-change. *See also* Careers
    creative approach to, 252–53
    feeling "stuck" and, 225–35
    frequency of, over lifetime,
        18
    motivations for, 239–40
    paths of, vi–vii
    rules for, 165–67
    school and, 345–46
    types of, 166, 167
Career counselors/coaches
    choosing, 379–89
    contracts for, 387, 388
    degrees for, 379, 385
    fees for, 382, 386–88
    forms for, 391–94
    fraud by, 379, 380–81, 385–88
    free workshops by, 389
    groups run by, 388
    by Internet or telephone,
        389–94, 416
    Mission in life and, 373
    questions to ask, 383–88
    religious, 396
    sampler of, 381, 394–416
    success rate for, 385
Career Interests Game, 165, 311
Careerkey.org, 311
CareerPlanner.com, 311–12
Career-portfolios, 65–66
The Career Portfolio Workbook
    (Satterthwaite and D'Orsi),
    66
Careers. *See also* Career-change;
    Jobs

choosing, vi–vii, 165–67, 252–53
hot, 181
list of, with skills and job
 characteristics, 168–80
number of different, 181
Career tests, 52–53, 161–65
Caretaker Gazette, 150
Caretaking, 150
Center for American Progress,
 25, 26
Chambers of commerce, 143
Change. *See also* Career-change
 fear of, 225, 230–35
 inevitability of, 139
China, outsourcing to, 24
Churning, 22–23
Cities Ranked and Rated (Sperling
 and Sander), 148
Civil service examinations, 14
Classified ads. *See* Ads
CNN/Money, 149, 182
Communication-related occupa-
 tions, 173
Community service occupations,
 172
Companies. *See* Employers;
 Organizations
Competencies, 250
Competency-based interview-
 ing. *See* Behavioral Inter-
 viewing
Computer occupations, 170
Confusion, 233
Considerateness, importance of,
 104
Construction occupations,
 179–80

Consulting, 334
Contacts
 asking for job leads from, 14,
  15
 cultivating, 54–56, 78–79
 definition of, 74–75
 employer's vs. job-hunter's
  preference for, 28, 31
 identifying the person-who-
  has-the-power-to-hire-
  you through, 74–76, 77
 importance of, 78
 Internet and, 54–56
 keeping track of, 79–80
 for older job-hunters,
  222–23
 for salary research, 128–29
 using, 343
The Contract Employee's
 Handbook, 204
ContractJobHunter, 205
Contracts
 for career counselors/coaches,
  387, 388
 employment, 132
Conventions, 79
Counseling. *See* Career
 counselors/coaches;
 Spiritual counselors
Courtesy, 32, 91, 104
Cover letters, 65
Co-workers, preferred, 308–12
Croonquist, Carmen, 65
Crystal, John, 16, 44, 45, 285,
 358, 410
Curricula vitae (c.v.). *See*
 Resumes

D

Data, skills dealing with, 257, 268–69

Davis, Steven, 72

Decision making, tips for, 221–22, 244–45

Degrees

for career counselors, 379, 385

without job guarantees, 183

Depression, 12, 25, 61–62, 110

Design occupations, 172

Desperation, 18, 352

Dictionary of Occupational Titles, 181

Digressions, 233–34

Discrimination, 39–44

Distance-counseling, 389–94, 416

Domestic violence, 140

D'Orsi, Gary, 66

Do What You Are (Tieger and Barron-Tieger), 259

Downsizing, 23

Dreams, pursuing your, 185, 189, 239–41, 326, 353

Dunn, Gary, 150

Dunning, Donna, 259

Duttro, Kate, 65

E

Education

career-change and, 345–46

moving for, 141

occupations in, 172

reform, 5

worthless degrees, 183

Edwards, Paul and Sarah, 198

E-mail

resumes by, 61

thank-you notes by, 10, 351

Employees, good vs. bad, 89

Employers. *See also* Organizations; Person-who-has-the-power-to-hire-you

contacting interesting, 15

fears of, 85–87, 96–99

preferred methods to fill vacancies, 28–31

previous, 87, 91

questions asked by, at interviews, 91–93, 96–101

rescuing, 80–81

type of employee sought by, 89–90

Employment agencies

employer's vs. job-hunter's preference for, 28, 31

for overseas jobs, 151

success rate for, 13–14

temporary, 127, 204–5, 209–10, 334, 349–50

Employment interviews. *See* Hiring-interviews

Energy, importance of, 217–20

Engineering occupations, 170–71

Entertainment occupations, 172–73

Enthusiasm

importance of, 45, 326

lack of, 105

Entrepreneur.com, 202

Executive search firms. *See* Search firms

Exercise, 234

Expenses, estimating, 318–21

Experience Unlimited Job Club, 399

Experimental Self
functions of, 228, 229
Safekeeping Self vs., 228–31, 235

F

Faith. *See* Mission in life; Religious beliefs; Spirituality

Family
asking for job leads from, 15
home businesses and, 186, 212
identifying skills with, 281–82
moving and, 144, 146, 157
researching location through, 148
support from, 146

Farming occupations, 179

Farrell, Warren, 182

Fast Company, 201

Fear
of change, 225, 230–35
employers', 85–87, 96–99
of outsourcing, 25

Feller, Rich, 248, 249, 323–25

Fields. *See also* Interests
dealing with people's problems or needs, 293–98
dealing with things, 298–300
different jobs within, 289–90
of fascination, 253, 283–300, 328, 329
intuitional approach to, 285–88
step-by-step approach to, 288–300

using mental skills, 289–91
vocabulary and, 286–87

50-50 rule, 88

Financial operations occupations, 169–70

Find Your Spot, 148–49

Fine, Sidney, 257

Fishing occupations, 179

Flextime, 223

Flower Diagram
blank, 246–47
example of filled-in, 249, 323–25
geographical preferences (petal), 301, 303–7
interests/fields of fascination (petal), 288–300
level and salary (petal), 318–21
naming, 333–40
people-environments (petal), 308–12
transferable skills (center), 279
using, 325–29, 332
values and goals (petal), 312–15
working conditions (petal), 316–17

Food preparation and serving occupations, 175

Forestry occupations, 179

Fourth Movement, 215–23

Franchises, 190–91

Fraud, 379, 380–81, 385–88

Free Agent Nation, 201

Free-lancing. *See* Self-employment

Friedman, Milton, 72

Friends
  asking for job leads from, 15,
    28
  career counselors/coaches
    used by, 382
  identifying skills with, 281–82
Friends *(continued)*
  moving and, 146
  nurturing relationships with,
    341, 342
  researching location through,
    148
  researching organizations
    through, 84, 348
  support from, 146
Fringe benefits, 131–32
Frost, Robert, 160

G

Garfinkle, Joel, 390, 391
Geographical preferences,
    147–49, 153–54, 283–84, 301,
    303–7. *See also* Moving
Giving up, 8–9
Goals, 312
God's plan. *See* Mission in life
Goldsmith, Marshall, 390
Governmental agencies, 14,
    129
Graduates, recent, 96
Grooming, 102–3
Groopman, Jerome, 221–22

H

Haldane, Bernard, 280, 358
Haltiwanger, John, 72
Handicaps, dealing with, 39–44

Health
  employers' questions about, 98
  moving for, 141
Health care occupations, 173–74
Hellman, Paul, 120
Hiring-interviews. *See also*
    Behavioral Interviewing;
    Person-who-has-the-power-
    to-hire-you
  asking for feedback after, 111
  bad-mouthing previous
    employers during, 91
  bringing evidence of skills to,
    84, 90–91, 95
  characteristics of, 46–47
  dating metaphor for, 83, 101,
    102–3
  employers' fears during,
    85–87, 96–99
  ending, 85, 106–8
  energy and, 219
  50-50 rule, 88
  focus on employer during,
    89–90
  importance of first two minutes
    of, 102–6
  length of, 85
  length of answers at, 9, 88
  mistakes made in, 82
  obtaining, 60, 71, 73, 80–81
  personal appearance and
    conduct at, 102–6
  preparing for, 84, 90–93
  questions asked by employer
    at, 91–93, 96–101
  questions asked by job-hunter
    at, 93–94, 106–8

researching organization
    before, 84
role-playing, 112
salary negotiation and, 116–19
ten commandments of, 113
thank-you notes after, 10, 47,
    104, 108–9
as a trick, 110
Holland, John, 165, 308–9, 312
Holland Codes, 309, 311
A Home-Based Business Online,
    202
Home businesses
    "A – B = C" method, 193–99
    determining type of, 188–93
    fall-back strategies for,
        206–13
    finding clients or customers,
        206
    finding employees or vendors,
        206
    gradual approach to, 213
    key to success in, 193
    problems of, 186–88
    recent popularity of, 186
    researching, 188–89, 193–203
    on a shoestring, 206
Hope
    importance of, 19
    sources of, 36–37
How Doctors Think (Groopman),
    221–22
How to Change the World
    (Bornstein), 312
Human Metrics Test, 260
Hurricane Katrina, 142, 144, 145,
    146

I

Ideal life, visualizing, 167–68
Identity-theft, 57
Illegal immigrants, 24
Income. See Salary
India. See also Outsourcing
    outsourcing to, 24
Information
    gathering, for taming Safe-
        keeping Self, 231
    skills dealing with (mental),
        257, 268–69, 289–91
Informational Interviewing
    definition of, 287, 343
    to find out about organiza-
        tions, 348–49
    job offers during, 352
    networking vs., 341, 342–43
    PIE Method and, 44, 45, 46–47
    questions for, 343, 344–45
    steps in, 341, 344
    thank-you notes after, 47,
        350–51
    websites for, 54
Interests. See also Fields
    favorite, 283–300
    placing on Flower Diagram,
        288–300
International Directory of Corpo-
    rate Affiliations, 153
International Organizations, 153
International Telework Associa-
    tion and Council (ITAC), 200
Internet. See also Websites
    annoyances and dangers on,
        56–57
    contacts through, 54–56

Internet (*continued*)
job-hunting on, 11–12, 51–52,
56
posting resumes on, 11–12, 56,
62
researching on, 53–54, 124–25,
348
testing and counseling on,
52–53, 389–94, 416
Internships, 153
Interruptions, handling, 217
Interviews. *See* Behavioral Interviewing; Hiring-interviews;
Informational Interviewing;
Practice Interviewing
Inventions, 191–92
Ireland, Susan, 65

J

Jackson, Tom and Ellie, 358
Job beggar vs. resource person,
42
Job clubs, 16, 389, 399
Job environments, 17
JobHuntersBible.com, 57, 161, 165
Job-hunting. *See also* Career-
change
abandonment of, 8–9
as art, not science, 18
best methods for, 14–17
as a business, 27
frequency of, over lifetime, 18
fundamental truths about,
18–19
groups, 16, 389
importance of alternatives in,
18, 19, 36–37, 133, 346–47

on the Internet, 11–12, 51–52, 56
life-changing, 16–17, 357
luck and, 19
mastering, 19
methods for, 7–9, 11–17
number of targets in, 133
as a reflection of job
performance, 90
research on, 8–10
"right" vs. "wrong" ways of, 19
Safekeeping Self and, 232–35
targeting small organizations,
134
tax deductions for, 320
using multiple methods for, 9,
18
worst methods for, 11–14
*Job-Hunting for the So-Called
Handicapped* (Brown and
Bolles), 44
Job-Hunting Online (Bolles and
Bolles), 57
Job-Hunting on the Internet (Bolles
and Bolles), 54, 57
Job-interviews. *See* Hiring-
interviews
Job leads, 14, 15, 288
Job market
churning in, 22–23
contrasting views of,
employer's vs. job-
hunter's, 27–33
true nature of, 35–36
vacancies in, 22
Job offers
during Informational
Interviewing, 352

at the job-interview, 107
withdrawn, 133
in writing, 132
Job-portfolios, 65–66
Jobs. *See also* Careers; Fields
availability of, 21–22
creation of, 21–22, 72
dream, 239–41, 251, 284, 326,
353
families of, 329
moving to locations with,
142–43
outsourcing and, 24–26
part-time, 130, 204–5, 210–11,
223, 334
philosophical approaches to,
33–35
satisfaction and, 34
screening out, while on the
job, 347
stop-gap, 207–8
transforming, 35
trying on, 182–83, 341, 344–45,
347
uncertain length of, 33–34
Jobs and Moms, 203
Job security, lack of, 33–35
Job-sharing, 211–12, 223
Jobstar.org, 124
Job-titles, 181, 282, 328
Jones, Lawrence, 311
Joyce, Susan, 389

K

Kalil, Carolyn, 165
Kasper, Henry T., 168
Keirsey, David, 259

Keirsey Temperament Sorter,
259, 260
Kimeldorf, Martin, 65
Kirn, Arthur and Marie, 358
Kurth, Brian, 141–42

L

Landes, Michael, 205
Large organizations
hiring-interviews at, 71, 73
job creation at, 72
person-who-has-the-power-to-
hire-you at, 73, 74
Lathrop, Richard, 6
Legal occupations, 172
Level
desired, 318
salary and, 127
Library occupations, 172
Life skills, three essential, 3–5
LinkedIn, 54–55
Lists, nature of, 29
Luck, 19

M

Mail order, 190
Maintenance occupations, 175,
177–78
Making Vocational Choices
(Holland), 309
Management occupations, 169
Mannerisms, nervous, 103
Mariani, Matthew, 124
Mathematical occupations, 170
Mattson, Ralph, 358
Max, Harry, 390
Media occupations, 173

Meditation, 223, 232
Mexico
  outsourcing to, 24
  unauthorized migrants from,
    24
Miller, Arthur, 358
Mission in life
  first stage, 360, 361, 362–66
  second stage, 360, 361,
    367–71
  third stage, 360, 361–62,
    371–77
  career counseling and, 373
  definition of, 357–58
  as intersection, 375–76
  job-hunting and, 357–58
  secret of finding, 359–61
  unlearning and learning,
    361–62
Money. *See* Salary
Mort, Mary Ellen, 124
Moving
  frequency of, 140
  geographical preferences
    and, 147–49, 153–54, 301,
    303–7
  joys of, 158–59
  to a location with jobs, 142–43
  overseas, 150–54
  reasons for, 140–44
  research before, 154–57
  to rural locations, 143, 149
  for survival, 145–46
  to urban locations, 143
Museum occupations, 172
Music, effects of, 231
Myers, C. C., 312

Myers-Briggs Type Indicator,
  259, 260
MySpace, 54, 57

N
National Center on Education
  and the Economy, 5
Natural disasters, 139, 140,
  144–46
Nelles, Rick, 66
Nelson, John E., 215
Nemko, Marty, 286
Nervousness, 103
Net Temps, 205
Network for Good, 145
Networking, 54–56, 78, 341, 342.
  See also Contacts; Informa-
  tional Interviewing
New Mind, New Body (Brown),
  244
Newspaper ads. *See* Ads
Nilles, Jack, 200
Nolo Law Center for Small
  Business, 202

O
*The Occupational Outlook
  Handbook*, 124
Occupations. *See* Careers; Jobs
Offers. *See* Job offers
Office and administrative
  support occupations,
  176–77
Offshoring. *See* Outsourcing
Older job-hunters. *See* Aging
O'Neil, Tom, 66
O*Net, 181

1000 Places to See Before You Die (Schultz), 143

Organizations. *See also* Large organizations; Small organizations
international, 153
kinds of, 333–34
making list of, 334–38
researching, 84, 347–50
size of, 71
websites of, 348

Ornstein, Bob, 227

Outsourcing, 24–26, 206

Out West, 150

Overseas jobs, 150–54, 206, 414–16

P

Pancer, S. Mark, 162

Part-time work, 130, 204–5, 210–11, 223, 334. *See also* Temporary work

Party Exercise, 309–11

Passion, importance of, 45, 326

Pay. *See* Salary

Peck, M. Scott, 160

Pelton, Robert Young, 154

People. *See also* Contacts; Family; Friends
favorite to work with, 308–12
fields dealing with, 293–98
skills dealing with (interpersonal), 257, 270–71
as sources of job information, 338–41
as sources of salary information, 125–27

People-environments, 308–9

People List exercise, 293–98

The People's Religion: American Faith in the '90s, 358

Personal appearance, 102–3

Personal care occupations, 175

Personality types, 259–60

Person-who-has-the-power-to-hire-you. *See also* Employers
fears of, 85–87, 96–99
identifying, 73–76, 77
setting up appointment with, 76–77

Petals. *See* Flower Diagram

Philosophy of life. *See* Mission in life

Philosophy of work, 33–35

Phishing, 56

Phone Book exercise, 299–300

PIE Method, 44–49

The Pie Method for Career Success (Porot), 44

Please Understand Me (Keirsey and Bates), 259

Pleasure interviews. *See* Practice Interviewing

Porot, Daniel, 42, 44, 88, 130, 415

PortaJobs, 200

Portfolios, 33, 65–66

Practice Interviewing, 44–49

Prejudice, 41

Prince, George, 228, 230

Princeton Review, 165

Principal International Businesses, 153

Prioritizing Grid, 273–75

Procrastination, 233–34

Production occupations, 178–79
Professional occupations, 170–74
Proof of Performance (Nelles), 66
Protective service occupations,
174–75
Psychological Assessment Resources (PAR), 309
The Psychology of Consciousness
(Ornstein), 227

R
Racism. *See* Discrimination
Raises, 112, 131
Ray, Taylor, 390
Ready, Aim, You're Hired (Hellman), 120
Referrals, 28, 31
Reiter, Mark, 390
Rejection shock, 26, 59–60
Religious beliefs, 356, 358, 364,
366, 396. *See also* Mission in
life; Spirituality
Research
before hiring-interviews, 84
on home businesses, 188–89,
193–203
on the Internet, 53–54, 124–25,
348
on job-hunting, 8–10
before moving, 154–57
on organizations, 84, 347–50
on salary, 123–27
Resource person vs. job beggar,
42
Resumes
alternatives to, 65–66
contents of, 60–61

dangers of depending on,
61–62
definition of, 29
e-mailing, 61
employers' vs. job-hunters'
views of, 28, 31, 59
example of "winning," 64
first impression from, 61
format and style for, 63, 65
mailing out randomly, 12–13
posting online, 11–12, 56, 62
purpose of, 60
screening through, 59
success rate for, 12–13, 59–60
tips for writing, 63, 66–71
uses for, 62–63
Retirement, 215–16. *See also*
Fourth Movement
Retirement Places Rated (Savageau), 148
Rewards, favorite, 322
RIASEC system. *See* Holland
Codes
The Right Mind (Ornstein), 227
*The Road Less Traveled, 25th
Anniversary Edition* (Peck),
160
Robinson, Michael T., 311
Routine, clinging to, 233
Rural locations, 143, 149
RVs, 149–50

S
Safekeeping Self
change and, 230–35
Experimental Self vs., 228–31,
235

"fingerprints" of, 232
functions of, 228, 229
job-hunting and, 232–35
strategies for taming, 231
Salary
desired, 318–21
fringe benefits and, 131–32
level and, 127
of men vs. women, 182
negotiating, 115–32
raises, 112, 131
ranges, 117, 127–30
researching, 123–27
time to discuss, 116–19
Salary.com, 124
Salary Expert, 124
Salary Source, 125
Sales occupations, 175–76
Sander, Peter, 148
Satterthwaite, Frank, 66
Savageau, David, 148
School. *See* Education
Schultz, Patricia, 143
Science occupations, 171
Search engines, 53, 348
Search firms, 13–14. *See also*
    Employment agencies
The Secret, 221
Self-confidence/self-esteem,
    lack of, 12, 103–4
Self-Directed Search (SDS), 165,
    309
Self-employment
    "A – B = C" method, 193–99
    determining business type,
        188–93
    fall-back strategies for, 206–13

finding clients or customers,
    206
finding employees or vendors,
    206
gradual approach to, 213
key to success for, 193
problems of, 186–88
recent popularity of, 186
researching, 188–89, 193–203
on a shoestring, 206
Self-knowledge, importance of,
    241–44
Service occupations, 174–75
Seven Stories exercise, 261–65
Shyness, overcoming, 44–49
Sifry, David, 261
Skills
    avoiding jargon and job-titles
        to describe, 282
    dealing with data/information
        (mental), 257, 268–69,
        289–91
    dealing with people (inter-
        personal), 257, 270–71
    dealing with things (physical),
        257, 266–67
    enjoyment vs. competency,
        280–81
    essential life, 3–5
    evidence of, 84, 90–91, 95
    identifying, 42–44, 252, 254–61,
        265–72, 280–82
    levels of, 257–58
    occupations listed by, 168–80
    prioritizing, 272, 276
    traits vs., 259–60
    transferable, 17, 254–61, 265, 272

Skills *(continued)*
  as verbs, 43
  writing stories about, 261–65
Skype, 390
Small Business Administration
    (SBA), 200–201
Small organizations
  advantages of, 72–73
  job creation at, 72
  person-who-has-the-power-
      to-hire-you at, 73–74
  targeting, 134
Smoking, 104
SnagAJob, 204
Social service occupations, 172
Spam, 56
Sperling, Bert, 148
Sperry, Roger, 225
Spiritual counselors, 223
Spirituality, 223. *See also* Religious
    beliefs
Startup Journal, 201
Stop-gap jobs, 207–8
Strong Inventory, 164
"Stuck," feeling, 225–35
Style. *See* Traits
Subjects Chart exercise, 290–93.
    See also Fields; Interests
Success stories, 134–35, 158–59,
    323–24
Sullivan, Danny, 348
Summerjobs.com, 205
Support groups, 343
Survival, 145–46

T
Tardiness, 105
Tax deductions, 320

Technorati, 261
Telecommuting, 190, 223
Telephone. *See also* Yellow pages
  answering machine messages,
      79
  area codes, 396
  counseling by, 389–94, 416
  low-cost, 390
Temperaments, 259–60
Temporary work, 127, 204–5,
    209–10, 334, 349–50
Ten Commandments for Job
    Interviews, 113
Testimonial Dinner exercise,
    313–15
Tests
  career, 52–53, 161–65
  civil service, 14
  on the Internet, 52–53
  of traits, 259, 260
Thank-you notes
  after hiring-interviews, 10, 47,
      104, 108–9
  after Informational Interview-
      ing, 47, 350–51
  after Practice Interviewing, 47
"That One Piece of Paper" exer-
    cise, 244–51, 323–26. *See also*
    Flower Diagram
Things
  fields dealing with, 298–300
  Phone Book exercise, 299–300
  skills dealing with (physical),
      257, 266–67
*The Three Boxes of Life, and How
    to Get Out of Them* (Bolles),
    145
Tieger, Paul, 259

Tough Choices or Tough Times, 5
Trade journals, 13
Traits, 259–60, 277
Transportation occupations, 180
Tribe, 55–56
Trioing, 281–82
True Colors Test, 165
Turnover, 22–23, 347
Twitter, 261
Types, 259–60

U

Unemployment
  benefits, 208
  national statistics on, 21–22
  rates since 1929, 6
  by state, 142
Union hiring halls, 14
Unlearning and learning, 361–62

V

Vacancies, existence of, 22
Values
  determining your, 312–15
  importance of, 105
Vision, refining your, 167–68
Vocation, 357. *See also* Mission
    in life
Vocation Vacations, 141, 142
Volunteer work, 67, 334, 350

W

Wanderlust, 143, 149–50
Want ads. *See* Ads
Websites. *See also* Internet
  for career information, 165,
    181–82, 311–12

for home businesses, 200–203
for Informational Interview-
    ing, 54
with Internet tutorials, 53
for moving, 148–49, 150
for networking, 54–56
of organizations, 348
for part-time and temporary
    work, 204–5
on salaries, 124–25
for telecommuting, 190
*What Color Is Your Parachute?
    For Retirement* (Nelson and
    Bolles), 215
*What Got You Here Won't Get
    You There* (Goldsmith and
    Reiter), 390
What's Your Type of Career?
    (Dunning), 259
*Where Do I Go from Here with My
    Life?* (Crystal), 44
"Who Am I?" exercise, 242–44
Who's Hiring Who? (Lathrop), 6
Why Men Earn More (Farrell),
    182
*Wishful Thinking—A Theological
    ABC* (Buechner), 375
Women
  employment agencies and,
    14
  interview tips for, 103
  salaries of, 182
  self-employment and, 203
Woodbury, Chuck, 150
Workamper News, 149
Working conditions, 316–17
Working from Home (Edwards
    and Edwards), 199

Working Solo, 201
Work satisfaction, 34
Workshops, free, 389
*The World's Most Dangerous
    Places* (Pelton), 154–55
World Wide Web Tax, 202–3

Y

Yellow pages
    calling employers from, 16
    career counselors/coaches in,
        382
    using, to make list of fields,
        298–300
    using, to make list of organiza-
        tions, 337
Young, Chuck, 286

Update 2009

To: PARACHUTE
P.O. Box 379
Walnut Creek, CA 94597

I think that the information in the 2008 edition needs to be changed, in your next revision, regarding (or, the following resource should be added):

_____

_____

_____

_____

_____

_____

_____

I cannot find the following resource, listed on page _____:

_____

_____

_____

_____

_____

_____

_____

Name _____

Address _____

Please make a copy.

Submit this so as to reach us by February 1, 2008. Thank you.

Other Resources

Additional materials by Richard N. Bolles
to help you with your job-hunt:

The What Color Is Your Parachute? Workbook
This handy workbook leads the job-seeker through
the process of determining exactly what sort of job
or career they are most suited for, easily streamlining
this potentially stressful and confusing task. $9.95

*The Three Boxes of Life,
And How to Get Out of Them*
An introduction to life/work planning. $18.95

How to Find Your Mission in Life
Originally created as an appendix to *What Color
Is Your Parachute?*, this book was written to
answer one of the questions most often asked
by job-hunters. $14.95

What Color Is Your Parachute? For Teens
(with Carol Christen and Jean M. Blomquist)
Using *Parachute's* central philosophy and strategies,
this new addition to the *Parachute* library teaches
high school and college students to zero in on their
favorite skills and then to apply that knowledge
to finding their perfect college major or job. $14.95

*What Color Is Your Parachute? For Retirement
Planning Now for the Life You Want* (with John E. Nelso
Using *Parachute's* central philosophy and strategies,
this new addition to the *Parachute* library teaches
those approaching 50, or beyond, how to prepare
for the Fourth Movement of their lives. $16.95

Job-Hunting on the Internet, Fourth Edition,
revised and expanded (with Mark Bolles)
(The Fifth Edition, titled *Job-Hunting Online*,
due out in May 2008)
This handy guide has quickly established itself as
the ideal resource for anyone who's taking the
logical step of job-hunting on the Internet. $9.95

Job-Hunting for the So-Called Handicapped
(with Dale Brown)
A unique perspective on job-hunting and career
changing, addressing the experiences of the
disabled in performing these tasks. $12.95

The Career Counselor's Handbook, 2nd edition
(with Howard Figler)
A complete guide for practicing or aspiring
career counselors. $19.95

FOREIGN EDITIONS OF
What Color Is Your Parachute?

Recent Translations *(available now or forthcoming)*
  Russian (Capital Publishing House, 1997)
  Slovenian (Gnosis & Quatro, 1997)
  Bulgarian (Kibea Publishers, 1998)
  Estonian (K Publishing, 2000)
  Russian (Olympus Business, 2001)
  Japanese (Shoeisha, 2002)
  Latvian (Zvaigane ABC Publishers, 2003)
  Turkish (Elma Yayinevi, 2004)
  Slovak (Motyl Publishing, 2004)

  Spanish (Ediciones Gestion 2000, 2005)
      *¿De que color es su paracaidas?: Un manual practico para los
      que buscan trabajo o un cambio en su carrera*

  French (Les Editions Reynald Goulet, 2005)
      *De quelle couleur est votre parachute? Le best-seller pour
      les gens en recherche d'emploi et en reorientation de carrière*

  Dutch (Nieuwezijds Publishing, 2007)
      *Welke kleur heeft jouw parachute? Een praktisch handboek
      voor werkzoekers en carriereplanners*

  German (Campus Verlag, 2007)
      Durchstarten zum Traumjob Das Bewerbungshandbuch

  Complex Chinese (Faces Publications, 2005)
  Slovene (Katarina Zrinski, 2005)
  Lithuanian (Mijalba, 2005)
  Croatian (Katarina Zrinski, 2005)
  Korean (Dong Do Won Publishing Co., 2007)
  Simplified Chinese (Modern Curriculum Press, 2007)
  Vietnamese (Tinh Van Corp., 2007)
  Italian (Edizioni Sonda, 2008)

For this printing of *What Color Is your Parachute?* using 13 tons of Rolland Enviro 100 Book instead of virgin fibres paper reduces your ecological footprint of :

Tree(s)	Solid waste	Water	Suspended particles in the water	Air emissions	Natural gas
221	14.043 lb	132.548 gal	88.8 lb	30.838 lb	32.136ft³

It's the equivalent of :

Tree(s)	Water	Air emissions
4.5 american football field(s)	a shower of 27.9 day(s)	Emissions of 2.8 car(s) per year

100%